MW01281583

BLACK HUNDRED

The Rise of the Extreme Right in Russia

OTHER BOOKS BY WALTER LAQUEUR

BLACK HUNDRED

The Rise of the Extreme Right in Russia

WALTER LAQUEUR

HarperPerennial

A Division of HarperCollinsPublishers

A hardcover edition of this book was published in 1993 by HarperCollins Publishers.

BLACK HUNDRED: THE RISE OF THE EXTREME RIGHT IN RUSSIA. Copyright © 1993 by Walter Laqueur. All rights reserved. Printed in the United States of America. No part of this book may be used or reproduced in any manner whatsoever without written permission except in the case of brief quotations embodied in critical articles and reviews. For information address HarperCollins Publishers, Inc., 10 East 53rd Street, New York, NY 10022.

HarperCollins books may be purchased for educational, business, or sales promotional use. For information, please write: Special Markets Department, HarperCollins Publishers, Inc., 10 East 53rd Street, New York, NY 10022.

First HarperPerennial edition published 1994.

Designed by George J. McKeon

The Library of Congress has catalogued the hardcover edition as follows:

Laqueur, Walter, 1921–
    Black hundred: the rise of the extreme right in Russia / Walter Laqueur. — 1st ed.
        p.   cm.
    Includes bibliographical references and index.
    ISBN 0-06-018336-5
    1. Russia (Federation)—Politics and government. 2. Nationalism—Russia (Federation) 3. Radicalism—Russia (Federation) 4. Right and left (Political science) I. Title.
DK510.6.L37   1993
320.5´3´0947—dc20   92-54728

ISBN 0-06-092534-5 (pbk.)

94 95 96 97 98 CC/CW 10 9 8 7 6 5 4 3 2 1

CONTENTS

Illustrations follow page 174.

INTRODUCTION

TIME HAS NOT stood still since the first American edition of this book appeared about one year ago. Scenes of unprecedented violence took place in the streets of Moscow in October 1993 such as had not been witnessed since 1917. Two weeks earlier, a distinguished expert on Russian affairs (Professor Richard Pipes), in a review of *Black Hundred* entitled "False Alarm," argued that the political forces discussed in this book were a small minority and likely to remain uninfluential as Russia was opting for a peaceful way to democratic reform. But as the events in October were to show, and as the victory of the brown-red coalition in December 1993 confirmed, the extreme rightists in collaboration with the neo-Communists were not that weak, nor were they fervent believers in non-violence.

True, the great revival of Cossacks and monarchists predicted by their protagonists has not taken place and *Pamyat* has shrunk even further. But the Zhirinovsky movement celebrated an astonishing victory in the elections of December 1993, and the Communists and their satellites have not done badly either. At the same time, the forces of reform have become weaker and the splits among the democrats affected their prospects in a negative way. All over Eastern Europe a political backlash is taking place.

My intention in the present book was not to speculate about future events. Instead, I wanted to shed some light on the specific character of one influential strand in Russian political life, its motives and beliefs, the strange political culture (or subculture) of the extreme right. This is a world of which little is known outside Russia, and I hope that this book has broken some fresh ground.

Once again in her stormy history Russia has entered a *smuta,* an age of troubles which may last long and the outcome of which is unpredictable. One of the few certainties at this time is the reappearance of a nationalist movement firmly believing that Russia can only be saved by a strong, authoritarian government that restores law and order and pursues a conservative policy. The present book deals with the origins of this movement, its strengths, its inner contradictions, and its likely consequences for Russia and the world.

Russian politics, generally speaking, have become more "national," and this trend is bound to continue. It is the inevitable consequence of the breakup of the old Soviet Union. Many millions of Russians have found themselves outside the new Russia, and on the other hand, separatist groups inside Russia, such as the Tatars, insist on autonomy, if not full independence. If given free rein this tendency would put into question the survival of the Russian Republic. These problems could perhaps be solved or at least eased and defused if moderation and common sense prevailed. But such attitudes are always in short supply at a time of crisis, and since a strongly nationalist mood has prevailed among all the non-Russia republics and nationalities, the stage is set for a collision. The age of nationalist conflict that ended in Europe in 1945 has reopened in Eastern Europe and the former Soviet Union.

For many years students of Russia have focused their attention on the left. There seemed to be good reason to do so: The right had been decisively defeated in 1917; the dissemination of right-wing ideas after this date was limited to small sectarian groups among the Russian and even smaller circles among Soviet dissenters. Politically they did not count; ideologically they had nothing of interest to offer. Why, in the circumstances, waste attention on the manifestos of small groups of eccentrics whose future prospects seemed nil?

True, this impression was not entirely correct. Nationalism and right-wing ideas, even if submerged, were by no means entirely dead. Ever since Stalin had opted by necessity for "socialism in one country," the Soviet Union had become increasingly nationalist socialist. While communism claimed to be internationalist in inspiration, many observers realized that Russia had become as nationalist as it had been under the tsars. There had been some such prophets even in the early 1920s, mainly among the émigrés, who had predicted that the Soviet regime would become increasingly nationalist and Russian-traditionalist and that the left-wing element would gradually wither away. This was the Smena Vekh ("Change of the

Landmarks") group in Berlin and Paris; some of its leading members subsequently chose to return to Russia, where most of them perished. They had correctly diagnosed a certain trend, but their timetable was mistaken. They were prophetic in some respects—and very wrong in others. The first article I wrote on Russian history was on the Smena Vekh phenomenon, which taught me that it is relatively easy to spot a new intellectual and political trend early on. But in the real world, some of these trends never ripen, and, in any case, the ripening usually takes long, because there are always retarding factors.

It took the greatest political earthquake of our time, the collapse of communism and the Soviet Union to enable the Russian right to make a comeback. As long as the Soviet regime existed, the most that a Russian nationalist could hope for was something akin to National Bolshevism—a movement that still has many followers even now: One should not underrate the strong Communist elements in the new Russian right. Only after the disintegration of official Soviet ideology could traditionally right-wing thoughts and slogans openly be propagated. It could be argued that the difference between official anti-Zionism before the age of reform, and present-day anti-Semitism is not enormous. Everyone knew that "anti-Zionism" was a code word; its true meaning was clear to even the least sophisticated. Or, to give another example: "Russophobia" has been of late the great watchword of the Russian right; but the concept did exist before 1987, under other names such as "anti-Sovietism." There is some truth in these arguments, but it is also correct that the official ideology could not be frontally attacked before *glasnost*, and it would have been unthinkable to praise monarchism or the White armies of the civil war.

The breakdown of Soviet communism caused an ideological as well as a political void, and nature abhors a vacuum in Russia even more than elsewhere. Some saw the breakdown of the dictatorship as the great opportunity for the return of freedom to Russia, part of a worldwide trend toward democratic institutions, the realization of the dream of generations of the Russian intelligentsia. But the odds were heavily stacked against it. Democratic traditions have not been deeply rooted in Russian history. Furthermore, the breakdown of Soviet rule was bound to result in severe crises, political, social, and economic. Such periods are not conducive to the consolidation of democratic institutions. Thus, the right-wing–nationalist forces had a good chance in the struggle both for the soul of Russia and for its political future.

The present study deals with the Russian far right and the extreme nationalists. But aggressive chauvinism and xenophobia can be found in all the former Soviet republics. As a result, the prospects for democracy in most of these republics cannot be rated high, even not in the most developed of them, certainly not in the near future. The odds would have been better if a modus vivendi would have been found enabling the ex-republics to coexist and collaborate peacefully. But this was not to be, and as a result nationalist tensions have been exacerbated everywhere. If democracy should fail in Russia, the list of those responsible will be long, including both tsars and Communist rulers who failed to transform in time their empire into a commonwealth of free nations. But the list of gravediggers will also include the separatists who used their newly won freedom not for reconciliation and compromise but to turn against each other and against Russia, who almost overnight turned from oppressed to oppressors.

Let us summarize the case of the Russian nationalists. The right argues that a gradual, slower transformation of the Soviet Union would have been greatly preferable. The price to be paid for dismantling the old system—the loss of all the non-Russian republics, including the Ukraine—was too high. Three centuries of Russian history were undone in a few days in August 1991 as the result of the weakness of the center. To save the remnant, a spiritual as well as a political renaissance is needed, a return to the national and religious values of the Russian people. It is pointless to embrace Western values and to copy Western institutions. Russia had always followed a road of its own; political systems that functioned elsewhere were unsuitable for Russia. So was parliamentary democracy—for, as Solzhenitsyn has written, party rivalry distorted the national will.

In this time of troubles the country needed not only a strong leadership but a set of national and religious beliefs that would sustain it through the hard years (or decades) ahead. These beliefs existed, they had only to be disinterred from underneath the rubble and brought again to the consciousness of the people. The only alternative is nihilism, further decline, the descent to anarchy, perhaps the eventual disappearance of the Russian people.

This, in briefest outline, is the case of the "Russian party" against the "Westerners."[1] It is agreed in, at least to a certain extent, by some liberals, who agree that nowhere (except perhaps after total defeat in war and military occupation) has a society ever transformed itself from a totalitarian system to a democracy. A transition period was needed in which a strong, authoritarian central power provided leadership.

The worse the situation became, the more persuasive appeared the slogans of the Russian party. But its case suffered from some basic weak-

1. "Westerners" is the incorrect term used by their political foes. Today's Russian Westerners are not uncritical admirers of the West, nor were the *zapadniki* of the nineteenth century.

nesses and inconsistencies. The Russian nationalists always argued that the former (Communist) regime had been one of "nationalist nihilism"—which was unfair to Stalin and his heirs, whose anticosmopolitan fervor had been second to none. The Communist regime had claimed, inter alia, that all important inventions had been made by Russians. Ever since the 1930s the traditional heroes of Russian history, from Alexander Nevsky to the nineteenth-century generals, had been paid due reverence. Following the demise of communism, Dmitri Donskoi, the hero of the battle of Kulikovo (1380), and Sergei of Radonezh, the priest who had blessed Dmitri and his soldiers on the eve of the battle, also became national heroes. This was certainly a change in emphasis, but it did not amount to a spiritual revolution.

The immediate difficulties facing Russia are largely economic and social. Yet nationalism *pur sang* does not have a specific economic and social doctrine. The Russian nationalists have been vocal insofar as their anticapitalist dislikes and complaints are concerned. But they have not offered specific alternatives other than some generalities concerning national interest and national solidarity.

Nationalism can still be a powerful force for the mobilization of dissatisfied and disadvantaged elements, and of all those whose patriotic sentiments were deeply offended and who believe that radical, possibly violent action has to be taken to save the fatherland. There is the time-honored Russian tendency toward radicalism and extremism, toward pursuing an idea or ideal relentlessly, well beyond the confines of good sense. The Russians did take socialism, a political doctrine that elsewhere led to social democracy and the welfare state, and turned it into a nightmare. There is the danger that nationalism, an explosive force at the best of times, might fare similarly, fueled by hatred and selfishness and pursued at the expense of all other values, and become yet another monster.

Communism and nationalism were always my main fields of interest; in the 1960s my research into the ideological origins of Nazism led me to the Black Hundred and the *Protocols of the Elders of Zion*.[2] The fact that I grew up under a totalitarian regime at a time when nationalist passions were running high in Europe helped me, I am inclined to believe, to understand other nationalisms. But it also led me to the conclusion that historical parallels are of limited validity only. Some Western and Russian writers have stressed the similarities between Russia's present situation and the last years

2. *Russia and Germany* (New York, 1963 and New Brunswick, N.J., 1987; a Russian edition appeared in 1991).

of the Weimar Republic, with the rise of the Nazi movement. There are some striking ideological similarities (about which more below), but there is also much that is totally different. The political constellation in postcommunist Russia is altogether different from the state of affairs in Germany in 1932.

At a time of political polarization and radicalization in Russia, foreigners writing about the Russian right are bound to be charged with "Russophobia" unless they display uncritical support. This book has not been written in a polemical spirit. The presence of a right-wing extremist movement in Russia should not be a particularly shocking discovery. Such parties exist in virtually every European country as well as in America and elsewhere. It would have been a miracle if Russia alone among all nations were an exception.

I am not a Russian, and Russians' pain cannot be my pain. But I can understand their feelings in the face of the disaster and feel sympathy. I am sufficiently familiar with things Russian to know that the history of Russia is not only one of servitude, backwardness, and missed opportunities. There is much I admire in Russian culture, and much in the Russian people appeals to me. I am firmly convinced that the Russian people have deserved a better fate. There are ebbs and flows in the history of nations, and it seems more likely than not that Russia will eventually recover from its present plight.

I can well understand the resentment and humiliation felt by many Russians at this time of trial. It was probably inevitable that the old Soviet (Russian) empire should have crumbled. But the way it did unravel was a disaster, which is bound to have dire consequences for a long time to come.

To expect Russia to accept all the demands of the new republics, to give in to all separatist aspirations, oblivious of its own national interest, would involve a degree of self-abnegation without precedent in history. On these issues there cannot be radical differences of opinion between Russian patriots of the "left" and of the "right." There is no moral or historical law that commands peoples or societies to commit suicide.

But patriotism is not a monopoly of the right. In a famous article on the occasion of Konstantin Aksakov's death, Alexander Herzen wrote:

> Yes, we were their opponents, but very strange ones. We had the same love but not the same way of loving—and like Janus or the two-headed eagle, we looked in different directions, though the heart that beat within us was but one.

In that more civilized age, the conflict between Slavophiles and Westerners was an in-house quarrel among the Russian intelligentsia. To which side, in retrospect, did Peter I belong? He was the greatest Westernizer of all but he also said that "we shall need Europe for a few decades; later we must turn our backs on it." Cha'adayev wrote that he saw nothing in Russian history but barbarism and crude superstition—no enchanting memories, no edifying examples. But he was still not drummed out of the ranks of Russian patriots for arrant Russophobia. Even his critics knew that he was not motivated by hate, but by love of his country coupled with deep despair. They were even willing to understand, though not to forgive, an eccentric like Pecherin who left Russia, converted to Roman Catholicism, and wrote: "How sweet it is to hate one's native land and eagerly await its utter ruin." True, the split deepened with the second generation of Slavophiles, "men repelled by reality, escaping into historical fantasy." Pógodin discovered that Russia was totally different from Europe in every respect, beginning with climate and physiognomy, and that it embodied all human achievements in one great synthesis and brought to harmony all civilizations, reconciling heart and reason. The idea of the "putrid West" spread—but then, after the victory of the reactionary forces in 1849, not a few left-wing Westerners came to share it.

I have referred to nineteenth-century "Westerners" and Slavophiles to put into perspective the attitude of present-day rightwing nationalists toward the Russian intelligentsia. As the right sees it, the democrats (or "demofascists," as they sometimes call them) do not have the same love of their country; they are intruders who hate Russia's heritage, and their baneful influence has to be stamped out. If there is a historical paradigm, it is the attitude of the far right toward the German intellectuals in the last years of the Weimar Republic. They saw soulless materialism and spiritual decay wherever they looked. National values were openly undermined; crime and perverted sex were glorified. Rootless cosmopolitans derided all manifestations of healthy patriotism.

Such moral disintegration was no accident; it was a deliberate conspiracy by world Jewry to undermine everything that was still healthy so that the country could never recover and rise to greatness. While arguing that he represented the great majority, the intellectual of the extreme right felt himself acutely isolated. The enemy was omnipresent, he dominated the scene, he always sat in the front row and awarded knighthoods of the spirit and Europeanism. The enemy's commodity was commended, whether it was the theory of relativity or modern art, democracy or bolshevism, propaganda for abortion or against the legal system, rotten Negro music or dancing in the nude. In brief, there was never a more shameless dictatorship than that of the democratic intelligentsia.[3]

These lines were written in 1933 referring to Germany; they could have

---

3. F. Hussong, quoted in W. Laqueur, *Weimar: A Cultural History* (New York, 1974), chapter 3, passim.

appeared, without changing a word, in yesterday's *Den* or *Russkii vestnik,* expressing the views of the Russian right.

A time of deep spiritual and political crisis like the present in Russia taxes the mental equilibrium of people, and there is the danger of taking refuge in all kind of fantasies—and worse. In a quieter age some prophets announced Russia's historical mission to bring salvation to all mankind. Such a belief in the global mission of one's nation and its superiority is not particularly dangerous unless supported by force of arms, nor is it specifically Russian. A Frenchman wrote that everyone had two fatherlands, "le sien et plus la France." For decades German schoolchildren learned by heart the verse of the poet Geibel

> *und es mag am deutschen Wesen*
> *einmal noch die Welt genesen.*

Addison wrote about the fundamental beliefs common to all true Englishmen—that each one of them could beat three Frenchmen, that the River Thames was the noblest in Europe, and that there was no greater work of art than London Bridge.

In Russia the belief in an eternal mission is not now on the historical agenda. But there is another aspect of the mentality of the Russian far right that does constitute a threat, and this is its paranoid streak.

I shall deal in the present book with various manifestations of persecution mania and the belief in conspiracy theories. A relatively harmless one is the assumption that whenever a ruler died—from Ivan IV's son Dmitri, to Alexander I, to Stalin—either there had been foul play or the ruler had not died in the first place but had been spirited away.[4] The same is true, a fortiori, with regard to the death of the idols of the right. In a mild form such delusions are propagated in many countries by thriller writers, moviemakers, and also the lunatic fringe. A certain part of the public always has a weakness for stories based on plots and conspiracies; that is the lure of the detective story. In Russia this inclination has a time-honored history. One hundred years ago Vladimir Solovyov, the great Russian philosopher gave a nearly perfect description:

Let us imagine a person [he wrote] healthy in body and strong, talented and not unkind—for such is, quite justly, the general view of the Russian people. We know that this person (or people) is now in a very sorry state. If we want to help him, we have first to understand what is wrong with him. Thus we learn that he is not really

---

4. One of my ancestors was among the doctors who signed the death certificate of Alexander I in Taganrog in 1825. But a great many Russians still believed that the tsar had not died but went on to live as a hermit in the Urals.

mad, his mind is merely afflicted to a considerable extent by false ideas approaching *folie de grandeur* and a hostility toward everyone and everything. Indifferent to his real advantage, indifferent to damage likely to be caused, he imagines dangers that do not exist, and builds upon this the most absurd propositions. It seems to him that all his neighbors offend him, that they insufficiently bow to his greatness and in every way want to harm him. He accuses everyone in his family of damaging and deserting him, of crossing over to the enemy camp. He imagines that his neighbors want to undermine his house and even to launch an armed attack. Therefore he will spend enormous sums on the purchase of guns, revolvers, and iron locks. If he has any time left, he will turn against his family.

We shall not, of course, give him money, even though we are eager to help him, but will try to persuade him that his ideas are wrong and unjustified. If he will still not be convinced and if he perseveres in his mania, neither money nor drugs will help.[5]

Solovyov believed that the Russian people had the inner strength to cure themselves. But he also conceded that hallucinations had caused the ruin of nations.

This uncannily accurate description of the specific affliction of the Russian extreme right was written exactly one hundred years ago, well before the emergence of modern psychiatry. The general situation in Russia was stable at the time; the Revolution of 1905 had not yet occurred, the "Black Hundred" had not appeared on the scene, the concept of Russophobia had not yet been invented. Yet there was even then a firm belief in imaginary conspiracies. This has been an essential part of the mental makeup of the extreme right ever since. If some were willing to accept manifestly absurd ideas in a calm era, how much greater the danger of a descent into collective madness at a time of real disaster.

This point has to be stressed because it will recur time and time again in the sections that follow. It does not imply that everyone on the right of the political spectrum shares these fantasies. Liberal, moderate nationalists dismiss them with contempt.

How to draw the dividing line between the moderates and the extreme right? There is a simple rule of thumb. A basic difference exists between those who seek the cause of Russia's misfortunes entirely in the machinations and intrigues of foreign and domestic enemies—and the others, who are willing to engage in introspection, self-criticism, and, where called for, penitence.

5. Vl. Solovyov, *Sobranie sochineniya* (St. Petersburg 1902–1907), vol. 5, pp. 430–31. This essay was written in 1892. Another intriguing feature of some contemporary groups of the extreme right is the frequent preoccupation with pathological sexual practices, always attributed to their democratic enemies. While claiming to constitute the "spiritual opposition" to the present decadent regime and upholding high moral standards, they obviously seem to enjoy these topics. For an illustration, see *Russkii puls,* 5 (1992).

It has been said earlier on that political paranoia is not a disorder confined to one country. It can be found virtually everywhere, more frequently (and more intensely) in some places than in others. And it has been more prevalent in Russian history than in other countries. Why has this been the case? Even if we knew much more about group dynamics, about what stimulates suspicion and rage, about the displacement of anger and the projection of guilt, we still would not have a satisfactory reply. Xenophobic hostility is as old as the hills. It can be found among populist movements and groups of the extreme right in many countries, and it was one of the prominent features of Stalinism. But it is not quite the same as the phenomenon we have tried to describe—that of fighters with chimeras and phantoms, a collective Don Quixote fighting with windmills, seeing everywhere outrageous giants, who nurse inveterate malice against our hero, who use pernicious wiles and stratagems. This Don Quixote is neither funny nor tragic; he is without any redeeming features, motivated only by hatred, a menace to himself and others.

Psychopathology is of some help in understanding phenomena such as Hitler and Stalin and their followers. But it is not the master key; there is an element of evil outside the normal parameter of mental health and disease. The same is true with regard to the fanatics of the Russian right; their main motivation is resentment and burning hatred, a "hatred which leads to the extinction of all values."[6] To understand the depth of these passions, perhaps nothing is more instructive than the contempt with which the journals of the extreme right so frequently refer to the "human values" allegedly common to all mankind.

A few remarks about the structure of this book. The present-day "Russian idea," as interpreted by the extreme right, contains not very much that is essentially new. The mixture may be novel, not the ingredients. To trace its origins, it is necessary to go back into history. The first part of the present book deals, therefore, with prerevolutionary doctrines that provide the inspiration and the background of present-day ideologies. I have had to discuss Dostoyevsky, the Slavophiles, and the Orthodox church even though they are no more responsible for Pamyat than Fichte and Nietzsche were for Adolf Hitler. The ideological resemblance between the Black Hundred (and their émigré disciples) and present-day far-right-wing thought is much closer and it is discussed in detail. But a "Russian party" evolved not only among the emigrants; there were also precursors inside the Soviet Union after the Second World War, and they cannot be ignored

6. The phrase is Ortega y Gasset's, from *Meditations on Quixote,* 1914.

in this context. Later on I shall discuss present-day manifestations of far-right thought and practice.

One argument will almost certainly be made in criticism of this study: Why concentrate on various fringe groups, thus creating the impression that all Russian patriots are chauvinists, villains, and madmen? This is misreading my intentions. Russian patriotism is as natural and legitimate as any other. My concern has been with the extremist views and their proponents. Some of these groups are small sects, others are not. A political-literary journal circulated in hundreds of thousands of copies is not a fringe phenomenon; there are now scores of groups and publications of this kind. The influence of the extremists may not grow in the years to come; perhaps time does not work for them, as they believe. But there is a substantial reservoir of support for their ideas at a time of grave crisis. It is foolish to ignore the possibility.

The chances that a group such as Pamyat will ever come to power in Russia are nil. However, "Black Hundredism" refers not just to a specific political group but to "a matter of morals and character which has deeper roots: It is rooted in the primordial darkness of the Russian soul, its unenlightened deposits."[7] The watershed is not between left and right, but between those who believe in freedom and humanistic values, in a state ruled by law, and those who reject these values with contempt. Semyon Frank, who wrote about the moral-political watershed between the first and second revolutions of 1917, predicted that at a time of chaos, when society and government were reconstructed (he actually used the term *"perestroika"*) "Black Hundredism" could well become an important destructive force. The same is true today.

In the first section of this book I had to go, by necessity, over ground familiar to experts. There are some fine studies on right-wing thought among Russian dissidents before *glasnost* and on national bolshevism. I benefited from them; they are mentioned in the bibliographical note at the end of this book. On the contemporary extreme right, whose history begins with the Gorbachev era, there is no comprehensive work so far and I entered uncharted waters. I was most fortunate to have the support of my colleague Valeri Solovei; as a result the problem that faced me was one of drowning, not of drought. I refer to the abundance of printed material.

Much of this source material is exceedingly rare; for many of the journals, not to mention the booklets and leaflets, students will look in vain even in specialized archives and collections. My debt to Mr. Solovei is very heavy indeed, and it is not limited to keeping me supplied with sources: He

7. S. Frank, *Nravstvennyi vodorazdel v russkoi revoliutsii* (Petrograd, April 1917).

answered innumerable queries and provided a detailed critique of my manuscript. Certain sections of this book (notably the chapter on the nationalist establishment) are almost as much his as they are mine. However, the ultimate draft was written by me. I believe that while he agrees with many of my formulations, he does not necessarily accept all of them.

Others who have given me the benefit of their advice with regard to specific questions in the historical section are Josef Frank, Gregori Freeze, Abraham Ascher, Hans Rogger, Robert Otto, Mikhail Epstein, Leonard Stanton, and Michael Hagemeister.

I always have difficulties with the transliteration since there is no unified system that makes sense to me; if there is some consistency in this book I owe it to the unrivaled expertise of my neighbor Ken Katzner. Kari Anderson, the librarian at the Center for Strategic & International Studies, kindly helped to obtain some rare books by way of various library loan schemes, and I also had the support of my friends Larissa and Frantisek Silnicki in the same context. I was helped by my assistants Aimee Breslow and Anne Truslow, and a little group of intelligent and industrious interns at CSIS— Sarah Despres, Marek Michalewski, Dimitri Osipov, Jon Kenny, and Nancy Oslo.

Part
One

BEFORE THE REVOLUTION

Chapter One

THE RUSSIAN IDEA AND MANIFEST DESTINY

PATRIOTISM—THE LOVE OF ONE'S HOMELAND—has existed since time immemorial, whereas nationalism as a doctrine, a system of values and beliefs, has its origins in the Romantic age. A Russian identity developed over many centuries; the early Russian literature, such as the Nestor Chronicle (*Povest vremennikh let*), and the *Tale of Igor's Campaigns* are works sui generis, not imitations of another culture; so is early Russian painting, so were the teachings of the Russian church.

Russians defended their land against the Teutonic Knights in the thirteenth century and, less successfully, against Mongols and Tatars in the centuries after. Ideology hardly played a role in all this. The famous pronouncement of the monk Filofei of Pskov (a monastery) in a "letter against the astronomers" that Moscow was the "third Rome" made only a limited impression on the rulers of the day and on public opinion, such as it was. It became only gradually, among some, an article of faith.[1] A little later the same century the idea of "Holy Russia" emerged.

Of all European countries Russia was the most isolated. According to reports by countless travelers, political, cultural, and social developments in other parts of Europe had largely bypassed it. Radical change came with the advent of Peter I; his policies of modernization and Westernization have

---

1. For the history of the idea of Moscow as the third Rome, see Leon Poliakov, *Moscou—Troisième Rome* (Paris, 1989).

been a bone of contention to this very day. From this date on, state and nation developed in Russia on different lines.

National consciousness has always evolved in opposition to foreign influences, and Russia, quite naturally, was no exception. The Old Believers regarded Peter as an agent of Satan in view of his reforms banning so many of the old customs and beliefs; being forced to cut their beards was only the ultimate indignity. But resentment was by no means restricted to the more backward classes. The political establishment was angry about the key role played by so many Germans at court, and in ruling the country as well as the army and the diplomatic service. Among the upper classes there was the fashion of imitating all things French, but this provoked a violent reaction among some patriots.

Many Russians resented that the history of their country was written—often in a detached and unpatriotic spirit—by Germans, that in their new Academy of Sciences foreigners dominated. Thus, in deliberate opposition to alien influences, a Russian school of literature developed, mainly in the theater, and the first Russian histories were written. Their authors were well-meaning men of no great talent, nor could they base themselves on rich and unbroken national traditions, as the French or the British and the Germans could. Thus, the patriotic playwrights were quickly forgotten. But the underlying sentiment—that the Russian people could make an important cultural contribution of their own—persisted, and there were even claims that "we are better and greater people than the Germans." Fonvizin (himself, as his name indicates, a Russian of recent origin) wrote that the Russians had more feeling, more heart, a greater capacity for love than most foreigners.[2]

On what evidence were such claims based? Partly on instinct, partly on the newly awakened interest in the Russian language, in the folk and folklore, in the habits, the sayings, and the songs of the people. Thus, the search for a national character got under way well before the Romantic age, as it did in Germany under the influence of Herder. This new spirit found its most eloquent expression in the writings of Nikolai Karamzin. While some of his contemporaries, such as Plavilshchikov went very far indeed in claiming that Russians were in almost every respect superior to all other peoples ("The Russian is capable of understanding everything. . . . Can any other people boast of such qualities?"), Karamzin in his great history and his famous memoir on Ancient and Modern Russia recognized that these were myths—but successful myths. Peter's predecessors had never lost the

2. Hans Rogger, *National Consciousness in Eighteenth-Century Russia* (Cambridge, Mass, 1960), p. 83.

conviction that an Orthodox Russian was the most perfect citizen and Holy Russia the foremost state in the world.

It was a delusion, but it greatly contributed to strengthening patriotism and the moral fiber of the country. The Petrine reforms, as Karamzin saw the matter, had deprived Russia of its Russianness and destroyed the unity of the nation. Peter had not realized that the national spirit constituted the moral strength of the people. Still, he had not succeeded altogether; the Russian spirit had not been eradicated and thus there was great hope for a national revival.

After Karamzin, nationalism became part of the official doctrine of the Russian state, but his writings also influenced the Slavophiles. Bureaucratic, conservative nationalism was the prevailing fashion at the beginning and again at the end of the nineteenth century, whereas the middle was dominated by the Slavophiles. The conservative, bureaucratic nationalists believed in slow, gradual, organic development. But since they took a pessimistic view of human nature and of the Russian people in general, they wanted as little development as possible. The bureaucratic nationalists took a dim view of the producers of panegyrics on the unspoiled national character, the purity and virtue of the Russian peasant past and present. As far as they were concerned the common people could not be trusted unless they obeyed God and the tsar. Love for the fatherland was fine, but autocracy was absolutely essential. Russians had to be protected from foreign (European) influences, not so much because they were foreign, but because they undermined belief in religion and the monarchy. Thus the famous formula of "Autocracy, Orthodoxy, and *Narodnost*" came into being, and it was surely no coincidence that *narodnost* came last in this list and was the most ambiguous of the three pillars of the regime. These bureaucratic nationalists were not cynics who believed, without personally sharing these sentiments, that nationalism (like religion) was good for the people. They were realists, and there was therefore little room for messianism and dreams in their view of the world. Many of them (including Konstantin Pobedonostsev, the procurator of the Holy Synod) admired England, but they also knew that the average Russian was less mature, less law-abiding than the average Briton, and that an English-style political system was therefore quite unsuitable for Russia and would be for a long time to come.

The firm belief that the Russian people was not interested in politics was shared by democratic Slavophiles like Ivan Aksakov, in whose thought "the people" was as important as the tsar. But Aksakov also believed that democracy had no place in Russia's life and history. All the Russian people wanted was rural autonomy; they did not have the desire to govern.

At the same time Aksakov was a firm believer in the freedom of expression, and this was bound to bring him into conflict with the bureaucratic nationalists, who were not even sure whether the Russian people could be trusted to read the Bible in Russian; they insisted therefore in keeping the religious services in Church Slavonic, which hardly anyone understood. Such a nationalism was perhaps closer to the real world than were the Romantic dreams of the Slavophiles. But it was unlikely to generate much enthusiasm among the educated classes, let alone among the "sons of the kitchen maids"—that is to say, the emerging intelligentsia.

To generalize about Slavophilism is difficult and potentially misleading; its leading proponents were few but strongly individualist. There was no Slavophile manifesto or program or party line. They disagreed about the proper attitude toward other nations, about their appraisal of Russia's past and present, about the aims of Russian foreign policy, about censorship, about the impact of capitalism on Russia, about the role of Peter I, and about a great many other topics. They were in broad agreement that the Russian people had a great future whereas the West was sinking, and that the West was up to no good as far as Russia was concerned; they were also convinced that over the past century and more, the Russian state had become too strong, whereas the people (and above all, the peasants) had been suppressed. While they were not fighting for greater political liberty, they thought there was not enough social justice and spiritual freedom. This brought them into occasional conflict with the authorities; a few of them were detained for short periods, and they had frequent disagreements with censors. Some Slavophiles were (or became) conservatives or even reactionaries *pur sang*, but others did not. While Slavophilism had strong political overtones, it was not primarily a political but a cultural movement; Slavophiles regarded Russia as a religious and metaphysical rather than a political problem. In the writings of the leading Slavophiles one can find arguments for and against the important questions of the day and this explains, at least in part, why the debate about the historical role of Slavophilism continues to this day and, for all one knows, may go on for a long time.

The Slavophiles were highly educated people; most of them knew Europe well—better, in fact, than some contemporary Russian democrats such as, for instance, Nikolai Chernychevsky. They were steeped in French and German culture; the poet and diplomat Fyodor Tyutchev wrote in a famous poem that Russia's boundaries extended from the Nile to the Neva, from the Elbe to China, from the Volga to the Euphrates, from the Ganges to the Danube. But at home he spoke French more often than Russian, and most of his correspondence was not in Russian either. Konstantin Aksakov was the most single-minded Slavophile, the one most given to glorifying Russia's past. His colleague Pogodin would agree with him—the Russian people were indeed marvelous, but only potentially. In reality they were at present quite horrid and beastly.

Slavophilism was, as the philosopher Nikolai Berdyaev once wrote, the first truly independent Russian ideology. But at the same time, at least among the first generation of Slavophiles, the emphasis on religion was even stronger than on the nation; the philosopher Aleksei Khomyakov was primarily a religious rather than a national thinker. "Autocracy" for these Slavophiles was little better than a necessary evil, and to "purge" Slavophilism of its religious-messianic content (as some latter-day Russian nationalists did) was to take away its very essence.

Even the negative attitude of the Slavophiles to the West (or rather to contemporary Western civilization) was predominantly religious in nature. They rejected the West first because Protestantism and, a fortiori, Catholicism were inferior to Orthodoxy and second because the West had become materialist and atheist. Orthodoxy alone had preserved its spiritual purity, its organic values; the Russian people were Christian not only in their church service but in their way of life. Therefore they had preserved their youth, whereas Europe was old, ill, and in a state of advanced decay.[3]

There was a populist element in Slavophilism which made its exponents view the domestic policies of the bureaucratic nationalists with grave forebodings. It is perhaps exaggerated to regard them, as some latter-day historians did, as the precursors of the *narodnik* ("populist") movement. For Ivan Aksakov the idea of a *zemski sobor*—that is to say, political reform by means of popular representation and a constitution—was absolutely essential. Toward the end of his life he regarded it as the last chance on the road to peaceful change in Russia and he wrote that Pobedonostsev and Katkov, the bureaucratic nationalists who opposed it, would ruin the country.

In later years the surviving Slavophiles, and also the second generation, became preoccupied with questions of foreign policy. This meant primarily support for the Southern Slavs in their struggle against the Ottoman Empire. There had never been sympathy for the Northern Slavs, notably the Poles, who belonged to the wrong religion and were considered ingrates in view of their lack of appreciation for the blessings of Russian rule and their constant struggle for self-determination. But if the Slavophiles showed much patriotism during the Crimean war, so did Westerners such

3. The literature on the Slavophiles is enormous. The most recent authoritative work is A. Walicki, *The Slavophile Controversy* (Oxford, England, 1975).

as Turgenev. In the First World War Pavel Milyukov, the great liberal critic of Slavophilism, was as ardent an advocate of seizing Tsargrad (Constantinople) as the Slavophiles. The Slavophiles supported Russian expansion in Central Asia, and some of their leaders came to believe that Germany and Austria were their main enemies in Europe. This was in contrast to their earlier conviction that they had most to fear from Catholic France, the main agent of revolutionary ferment in the West. Almost without exception the Slavophiles were firmly convinced (as Tyutchev wrote his sister) "that there is no single trend in the West which would not conspire against Russia, especially against its future, and would not try to harm us." Or Dostoyevsky: "Europe has a remarkable dislike for us and has never liked us. She has never considered us as one of her own . . . but only as vexatious newcomers."

The idea of Western Russophobia goes far back in history and it was one of the chief motives of Slavophilism—the suspicion that the West was plotting against Russia and holding it in contempt, openly or secretly. This was certainly unjust with regard to the German right, which throughout the nineteenth century thought of the alliance with Russia as the base of its foreign policy, and which, on an ideological level, always favored an antirevolutionary alliance with tsarist autocracy. These issues are not of purely antiquarian interest, for they were to resurface in the thinking of the Russian right toward the end of the twentieth century.

Of the latter-day Slavophiles, Konstantin Leontiev and Nikolai Danilevsky are usually mentioned in the same breath, though they had little in common. Both were scientists by training; Leontiev later on entered the diplomatic service and became passionately involved in religion. He spent a year in the famous Mount Athos monastery and eventually took vows and settled in a monastery near Moscow, where he died. He differed in many respects from the earlier Slavophiles; while sharing the fear that Russia would be infected by European decay he saw the answer in a harsh, autocratic regime, based on the Byzantine tradition and fervent religious faith. He had no time for idealizing either the Russian peasantry or the other Slav peoples.

Leontiev was no nationalist in the customary sense, because nationalism, as he saw it, was Western in inspiration, modernist, and even liberal—and thus in contradiction to the religious and autocratic Russian tradition. For the same reason he opposed the aggressive foreign policy of the Slavophiles in the Balkans and the domestic Russification in the Baltic countries and elsewhere. As long as the ruling stratum in the Baltic provinces had been loyal to the tsar, why compel them to conform as far as their language and culture were concerned?

Leontiev's views were frequently dismissed as obscurantist by his fellow Slavophiles, but they were so obscurantist as to be almost modern. Toward the end of his life he seems to have reached the conclusion that since Western capitalism and liberalism had no future in Russia and since the Eastern Orthodox (Byzantine) civilization could not be revived either, the only future for Russia was in some form of state socialism, which would provide the necessary measure of discipline (and repression) without which the whole fabric of society would come apart. Leontiev was a deeply pessimistic thinker; he thought the glorification of Russia's past a mere delusion and the dreams about Russia's future a mere chimera. The best one could hope for was to preserve the status quo with all its imperfections.

His literary and political views are interesting, often in contradiction to mainstream Slavophilism; he preferred Tolstoy to Dostoyevsky both as a writer and as a patriot. As a conservative he despised Slavophilism, because it was modernist, democratic, vulgar, and potentially dangerous. But Leontiev's influence in his lifetime was very limited; after his death his teachings were mainly of interest to theologians and historians of ideas.[4]

Danilevsky, on the other hand, was widely read and enthusiastically welcomed in his time; his magnum opus, *Russia and Europe,* was translated into various Western languages and reappeared, albeit in an abridged version, under *glasnost.* Like Dostoyevsky, Danilevsky began life as a political radical, and in some ways he always remained one; he became the most eloquent spokesman of the believers in a Russian imperial mission. He has been compared with Spengler as well as with Stalin, but the grain of truth in these parallels should not be exaggerated. Like Spengler he believed in the rise and decline of civilizations; like Stalin he envisaged a totalitarian system of sorts, but it was, of course, quite remote from the practices of twentieth-century totalitarians. He was united with the Slavophiles in the belief in the decay of the West, the conviction that there would be a long and bloody struggle with Europe, out of which Russia would emerge victorious, and also a certain populist agrarian socialism. He was more modern in approach than most other Slavophiles; thus, he had no hesitation introducing to Russia Western advances in technologies and science. He was only opposed to copying alien cultural and political models—such as parliamentary democracy, the class struggle, Western plutocratic imperialism—in contrast to the Russian tradition of political and spiritual unity. His

4. But in the general renaissance of Slavophilism in the nineties Leontiev was not forgotten. In 1991, on the occasion of the hundredth anniversary of his death, articles about and by Leontiev were published by *Nash Sovremennik,* 12 (1991), in *Russkii Vestnik,* 31 (1991), and in other organs of the conservatives.

advocacy of expansion was motivated by a feeling of a world-historical mission.[5]

The concept of a historical mission leads by necessity to Dostoyevsky, by far the most influential of the Slavophiles and also the most difficult to fathom. In the Russophile renaissance in the 1980s Dostoyevsky plays a crucial role, and his influence has by no means been restricted to the right. *Besy* ("The Possessed"), the great anti-utopian novel of 1871 on the likely consequences of socialism, has been equally often invoked by the liberals.

Western students of Dostoyevsky have been fascinated by his great novels and have endlessly commented on them. But they have never quite known what to make of his political journalism, specifically *The Diary of a Writer*. In his political writings Dostoyevsky all too often appears a warmonger, a rabid chauvinist, a blind supporter of autocracy, a bitter hater of Poles, Jews, and foreigners in general. True, the more outrageous statements are often accompanied by all kinds of reservations—references to Russia's pan-human mission, to the fraternal love of mankind in general. But these did not always sound convincing even at their most tolerant, as in the famous speech on Pushkin's anniversary (1880), when Dostoyevsky tried to bring about a reconciliation between Westerners and Slavophiles. Dostoyevsky's ideas have been regarded by some Western commentators as little more than exalted rubbish, vague phrases that brought about unprecedented scenes of emotional fraternization (as at the Pushkin festival) but had no lasting effect whatsoever.

It is tempting to regard Dostoyevsky's political journalism as a temporary aberration, just as the journalistic efforts of other great writers should not be taken too seriously. But it is useful to recall that this journalism was very influential at the time. In the words of one of his friends,

> Dostoyevsky's fame was not caused by his prison sentence, not by *The House of the Dead,* not even by his novels—at least not primarily by them—but by *The Diary of a Writer*. It was the *Diary* that made his name known to all of Russia, made him the teacher and idol of youth, yes, and not only of youth but of all those tortured by the questions that Heine called "accursed."[6]

Dostoyevsky's nationalist thought developed through his association with the *pochvenniki,* the native-soil conservatives, sometimes in consonance with, at other times in contradiction to mainstream Slavophilism.

---

5. Danilevsky's book was banned after 1917, but an abridged version was republished in Moscow in 1991.

6. Elena Stakenshneider, *F. M. Dostoyevsky v vospominanya Sovremennikov* (Moscow, 1964), vol. 2, p. 307. Quoted in Joseph Frank, *Through the Russian Prism* (Princeton, N.J., 1990), p. 153.

Not too much should be made of these internal quarrels, if only because the views of both sides changed over the years. Religion, to give but one example, figured much less prominently in Dostoyevsky's thought in the 1860s than in later years.

The *pochvenniki* (the very term was to reappear in the 1970s) were an antirationalist group of believers in organic growth rather than in revolutionary change. They were anticapitalist and felt that Russia's innate sense of fraternity guaranteed inner unity and social harmony.[7] In this respect the Russian nation was an "extraordinary phenomenon" (Dostoyevsky's words), and its character did not resemble the character of any other European people. One of Dostoyevsky's ever recurring themes was that every people believed that the salvation of mankind depended on it, that it existed in order to stand at the head of the peoples. It ceased to be a great people the moment it lost the belief that it alone was the repository of truth.

Dostoyevsky believed that the Russians were the only God-bearing people and would save the world—they were the body of God. Only Orthodoxy had preserved the divine image of Christ in all its purity, and it could therefore act as a guide for other peoples in a world that had lost its way.

Unlike some of the Slavophiles, the *pochvenniki* did not believe that the Petrine reforms had been an unmitigated disaster, nor did they claim that the educated classes had betrayed the common people, who had remained the only bearer of the national traditions.

With the *pochvenniki* and the Slavophiles, Dostoyevsky believed in the union of the tsar with the people as the most effective bulwark against the bourgeois West which also made Russia virtually immune to revolutionary temptations. He predicted that all the great European powers would be destroyed because they would be undermined from within by the unsatisfied democratic aspirations of their lower classes. In Russia, on the other hand, this could not happen because the people were happy and were becoming even more so as time passed by. Thus, only one colossus—Russia—would remain in Europe, and this might come to pass even much earlier than people thought. But at the same time there was Dostoyevsky's great fear of revolution—which was, after all, what *Besy—The Possessed*—was all about.

The inner contradictions in Dostoyevsky's thinking are more striking than the consistency in his views. He frequently invoked the universal, all-embracing humanity of the Russian people and maintained that true Russianness was the capacity to absorb all precious European values. But

7. Wayne Dowler, *Dostoyevsky, Grigorev and Native Soil Conservatism* (Toronto, 1982), p. 80.

the constant chauvinistic drumbeating, the calls to make war against the Turks and to conquer Constantinople, the attacks on the Catholic church were not in line with this humanitarian ideal. Dostoyevsky wrote in his notebook in 1863 that nationality was not the final goal of mankind and that only in universal humanity could it lead a full and harmonious life. But this could be attained only through emphasis on the unique *natsionalnost* of every people. The universal human values were a distant ideal, and in the meantime it seemed permissible to go rather far in stressing national exclusivity *(samobytnost)* and attacking the enemies, real and imaginary, of the nation.

Dostoyevsky's anti-Semitism is of interest in this context. At times he denied it, and it could indeed be argued (as Joseph Frank has done) that Dostoyevsky hated Poles even more than he did Jews and that in any case anti-Semitism was a logical component of his general xenophobia. (He hated and feared the kulaks as much as the "Yids.") But there still remains a riddle: The Poles, the Jesuits, the Turks were real antagonists and could perhaps be considered potential threats by watchful Russian patriots. But in the 1870s the Jews were neither among the leaders of the Russian revolutionary movement, nor had they any significant influence on Russian social and cultural life, nor were they in the front rank of politics or economic life. Very few Jews lived outside the Pale of Settlement. It is not certain whether Dostoyevsky (or Ivan Aksakov, the most anti-Semitic of the Slavophiles) ever met a Jew in the flesh or talked to one; they certainly did not know any Jews well. There are no Jews among the leading characters in Dostoyevsky's novels. Why should a weak, oppressed, and relatively small minority have provoked such fears and violent feelings, as bloodsuckers and vampires? There is no obvious answer; perhaps the Jews were an abstraction or a potential competitor of the Russians for the role of the Chosen People. But taken the real conditions in which the "Chosen People" lived at the time it is not easy to be satisfied with an explanation of this kind.

The same syndrome was to recur on the Russian right one hundred years later. At a time when ethnic Russians were persecuted and expelled from many parts of the Soviet Union, from Lithuania to Central Asia, from Moldova to the Caucasus, the spokesmen and thinkers of the Russian right were preoccupied not with the real dangers facing their compatriots but with the single-minded concentration on "Zionists," many of whom had no dearer wish than to leave Russia.

Dostoyevsky's views on religion have attracted several generations of thinkers, Russian and non-Russian; they have been of interest to the existentialists and generally speaking to all those preoccupied with faith and evil. Dostoyevsky has fascinated the contemporary right because of his obiter dicta on foreigners, bourgeois, Westerners, socialists, Catholics, and Jews. But this cult is based, at least in part, on a misunderstanding and it is of limited political efficacy. With all his doubts and self-torment, Dostoyevsky was essentially a religious writer, more occupied with sin and goodness, with faith, madness, and mystery, than with the future of the Russian empire.

Nor is the "Russian idea," as Dostoyevsky envisaged it, of much use to the Russian right. True, it implies opposition to futile attempts to copy Europe, to live according to national principles developed by other peoples and alien to the Russian tradition. But it also meant that Russia's world-historical role was "pan-humanism," a synthesis of all the ideas developed by the West, reconciling otherwise antagonistic elements with an admixture of the Russian spirit. Dostoyevsky envisaged, in other words, a Westernism purified and raised to a higher level. Such ideas were far too complicated for the Russian right, just as Dostoyevsky's all-pervasive insistence on Russia's infinite capacity for harsh self-criticism was of no political help to them.

The Slavophiles had no lasting influence on the intelligentsia, which found it not even necessary to confront their ideas which they thought mere "police religion." The fact that the latter-day Slavophiles dropped many of their erstwhile radical ideas and moved closer to bureaucratic, state nationalism seemed to bear out the negative attitude of the left.

But the reception of Slavophile ideas was not too friendly even among those close to them by background. The most famous early criticism came from Cha'adayev, Pushkin's friend and mentor, with his stern warnings about the Slavophiles' arrogant apotheosis of the Russian people, who were in fact backward and self-isolated, lacking both past and future. At the end of Slavophilism there was Vladimir Solovyov, religious philosopher and poet, who bitterly criticized them for idealizing the Russian people. He attacked them for "zoological patriotism," for their gradual loss of religious and humanist content, which had been replaced by national egoism. Commenting on Danilevsky's *Russia and Europe,* he wrote:

> Our nationalism desires to destroy Turkey and Austria, to divide Germany, to annex Constantinople and, should an opportunity arise, even India. If, however, we are asked what we have to offer mankind as compensation for what we take and destroy, what cultural and spiritual principles we have contributed to world history, then we must either be silent or indulge in meaningless phrases.

By the end of the nineteenth century Slavophilism had faded away as an intellectual current. There were strong pan-Slavic feelings in the bureaucracy and the army, and there were right-wing monarchist writers such as Menshikov and Lev Tikhomirov, who had begun their political career with the terrorists of Narodnaya Volya. But it is difficult to think of a Russian Maurice Barrès or Charles Maurras. Berdyaev wrote in 1907 that "a conservative man of letters today is almost a contradiction in terms. . . ."

The nearest to a national revival on the philosophical level was the publication of *Landmarks (Vekhi)* in 1909. However, this volume was primarily concerned with the alienation ("dissociation," according to the vocabulary of 1909) between the state and the people. It dealt only in passing with the intellectuals' lack of patriotism. There were some harsh words, notably by Sergei Bulgakov, about the cosmopolitanism of the Russian intelligentsia, the absence of healthy national feeling. But this was merely regarded as one component among several of the intelligentsia's isolation from the people; less important than the fact that the intelligentsia had spurned Christ and embraced atheism.

The ideas of Russian nationalist thinkers throughout the nineteenth century are in most ways part of a worldwide phenomenon that began with political Romanticism. It was more marked in Germany than in France and Britain, because Germany was a latecomer among nations and felt a greater urge to prove to itself and others that it had a major contribution to make to world civilization. For Britain and France such a role was self-evident; Italy became nationalist after the turn of the century but set itself more modest aims prior to the advent of fascism. America, too, had its proponents of Manifest Destiny. If an extreme nationalist doctrine emerged in France toward the end of the century, this was probably a reaction to a lost war and the ensuing mood of defeatism. The pan-German leagues and similar groups were a specific manifestation of the zeitgeist and also were rooted in the feeling that, alone among the great powers, Germany had neither an empire comparable to Britain's and France's (or even Belgium's and Holland's) nor enough lebensraum in Europe.

The specific ingredient of the Russian idea was its religious content. The extreme nationalists in Germany and France would invoke the support of the deity, but more often than not stood in opposition to the church. In Russia, on the other hand, even extreme nationalism, as will be shown presently, developed largely under the umbrella of the church and with the blessings of the monarchy.

How to explain the relative weakness of the "Russian idea" among the intelligentsia? To ask the question is to answer it: If the Russian intelligentsia was in opposition to the existing order, that was not because the educated classes were innately more negative, destructive, antipatriotic than in other countries; in hours of danger they would still rally around the flag.

It was mainly rooted in the incapacity of the Russian political establishment to effect political and social change, in its reluctance to surrender any of its privileges, to broaden its base, and to integrate the intelligentsia. Thus, government and opposition became ever more polarized.

The Russian armies did fight for three years in the First World War, despite heavy losses. But eventually the breaking point was reached, and this led to the downfall of the system. Such a disaster could not possibly have occurred by accident. To this extent the Russian right was quite correct in its assessment. But it could not accept the obvious—that the debacle had been predominantly the responsibility of the tsar, his ministers, the whole state apparatus, and their policies over many years, which had Russia involved in a war for which it was not prepared and that it could not win. And so the search got under way, as it did in defeated Germany one year later, for the "sinister forces," the "hidden hand," that had administered the "stab in the back" that had led to the catastrophe.

THE BLACK HUNDRED AND THE EMERGENCE OF THE RUSSIAN RIGHT

A RUSSIAN CONSERVATIVE-NATIONALIST PARTY in Russia emerged only around the turn of the last century. The reasons seem obvious: In an autocratically ruled state there were no political parties. The government traditionally argued that it had a monopoly of political action and looked with suspicion on independent activities, which were considered divisive and were, as a result, discouraged or even banned by the authorities.[1] There were nevertheless a few such attempts on a small scale, such as the "Holy Brotherhood" of the early 1880s. But they did not amount to much and were considered, rightly or wrongly, as mere manifestations of "police patriotism." This changed only with the appearance of the "Black Hundred" at the time of tsarism's acute crisis in 1904–1905.

The Black Hundred are a unique phenomenon in the history of twentieth-century politics. Like the Action Française, it was a halfway house between the old-fashioned reactionary movements of the nineteenth century and the right-wing populist (fascist) parties of the twentieth. With their strong ties to monarchy and church they largely belonged to the past, but unlike the earlier conservative groups they were no longer elitist. Having understood the crucial importance of mobilizing the masses, they were the harbingers of political parties of a new type. One of the most influential

1. Hans Rogger, "The Formation of the Russian Right 1906–1909," in *Californian Slavic Studies*, vol. 3, (1964), p. 66ff.

leaders of the movement wrote years later that in spirit this Russian movement was almost similar to national socialism.[2]

However, the Black Hundred are by no means of historical interest only. Their message was not forgotten among Russian right-wing émigrés after 1917, and when, under Gorbachev, freedom of political expression returned to Russia, the Black Hundred were among the first to benefit from glasnost.[3] The message that Russia could be saved only by the formation of an organization on the lines of the Union of Russian People ("SRN," to use its Russian initials) was voiced after 1987 often and on various levels of political sophistication.[4]

Black Hundred is a somewhat vague catchall term for various extreme right-wing groups that existed between, roughly speaking, the turn of the century and 1917. Even before that there had been influential writers— such as V. A. Gringmut, Pavel Bulatsel, Mikhail Menshikov, and Sergei Sharapov—who had bitterly attacked not only the rising tide of revolution but liberalism and capitalism, the disloyal minorities, such as the Poles, the Finns, the Baltic Germans, and above all the Jews.

The names of these publicists had been wholly forgotten during the Soviet period, except perhaps by a few specialists in the history of late tsarism. No one bothered to discuss or refute them. After 1987 most of them were rediscovered by a new generation of writers on the extreme right.[5]

True, they by no means constituted a common front. Thus, to give but one example, Sharapov, who was strongly anti-German, openly accused Menshikov of being an Austrian agent.

Menshikov is of interest in this context because he was the first to preach racial anti-Semitism, in contrast to the earlier, mainly religious species.[6] As he saw it, the race problem was the most crucial facing Russia

2. N. Markov, *Der Kampf der dunklen Mächte* (Erfurt, Germany, 1935), p. 4. A member of the tsarist Duma, Markov II, as he was known, worked for the Nazis after Hitler's rise to power.

3. The "Union of Russian People" was refounded in a meeting at the House of the Soviet Army in Moscow on August 1, 1990; its new program was published in *Russkie vedomosti,* 4 (1991).

4. Viktor Ostretsov, *Polozhenie del,* 3 (1991). At the same time, a highbrow spokesman for the extreme right, Vadim Kozhinov, expressed support (*Moskovskaya pravda,* October 4, 1991); earlier on, the Black Hundred label had been generally rejected by the right, because it had acquired a negative connotation over time.

5. For a revival of Gringmut, see *Domostroi,* 31, (1991). For the Menshikov renaissance, see *Slovo,* 9 (1991); *Russkii Vestnik,* 1 (1991); *Kuban,* 9 (1989), and the republication of his diaries in *Rossiskii arkhiv* 1992 and *Tretii rim,* 7 (1991).

6. His ideas were mainly derived from Houston Stewart Chamberlain, whom he frequently quoted. There was the usual problem: While Chamberlain was a racist, he did not think highly of the non-Germanic races. . . .

at the time. He seems not to have been quite aware of the implications of his message. For to preach racial exclusivity in a multinational empire was, at the very least, asking for serious trouble.

The first major organized group to emerge from among these far-right circles was the Russkoye Sobranie ("Russian Association") which came into being in late 1900 and was initially wholly preoccupied with Russian history and art, but gradually became politicized. Among its leaders were well-known members of the aristocracy such as Princes Golitsyn, Apraksin, and Shakhovskoi, as well as bishops such as Serafim, university professors, and publicists, as well as a sprinkling of generals and high government officials. Russkoye Sobranie opened branches in the following years in major cities, mainly in southern Russia but also in Warsaw and Kazan. It was relatively weakly represented in the universities and had few followers among students. Nor was it strong among the middle class; most landowners had not much interest in it, either. When in October 1905 a tsarist manifesto gave the country a measure of political freedom, Russkoye Sobranie appeared in public with a political manifesto that expressed fervent belief in monarchy and church and demanded special anti-Jewish laws "in view of the Jewish hostility to Christianity and the non-Jewish nationals as well as their [Jews'] aspirations to world power."

Such an elitist group of like-minded personalities, well known and well connected in society, seemed quite powerless to stem the rising revolutionary tide; it ought to be recalled that these were the years of the Russo-Japanese War and the first Russian revolution. The country became more and more polarized, and on the right there was much fear that the whole system would collapse. Hence a greater readiness to support all kinds of extreme right-wing ideas and groups that had been rejected in the past.

In this critical period two new parties were founded, first the Union of Russian People ("Lyudei") in March 1906, and in October of that year the Soyuz Russkovo Naroda (or SRN). They were almost identical in the composition of their leadership, except that the leadership of the SRN from the beginning was in the hands of a man who had not been politically active earlier on, the physician Dubrovin, who showed greater energy and tactical flair than any of his precursors. He established direct contact with top government and administrative figures, explaining that the old system could be saved only by a patriotic mass movement; that for this purpose both financial resources and political and police support were needed; and that his movement would engage in both mass action and individual terrorism. These proposals met with the approval of certain key members of the bureaucracy and the extreme right-wingers among the ministers. The tsar himself gave the SRN (to whom he had been introduced by Grand

Duke Nikolai Nikolayevich) his blessing; he had quite independently reached the conclusion that international Jewry, through its two wings, Jewish capitalism and Jewish socialism—the Marx-Rothschild alliance—was fomenting revolution aiming to overthrow his regime. This campaign, he knew, was orchestrated by the Alliance Israelite Universelle, and its immediate aim was the introduction of universal, equal, direct and secret suffrage, which would by necessity lead to revolution.

The tsar was bitterly disappointed with the helplessness and inactivity of the other right-wing organizations; hence his sympathy for the SRN. As Georges Louis, the French ambassador to Russia, was later to write: "The Black Hundred are ruling the country and the government obeys them because it knows the emperor is inclined to sympathize with them." Orders were given to print the SRN's appeals for pogroms on the state printing presses, and millions of rubles were passed on to the group. In late 1905 Dubrovin began to mobilize mass support through sympathizers in the clergy and in patriotic organizations as well as the police and local administrations. This proved to be easier than could have been expected; the message of the SRN fell on fertile ground.

Where did the SRN find its political and social base?[7] The term "Okhotny Ryad" has frequently been used by contemporaries to define the state of mind that helped to spread the message of the Black Hundred. Okhotny Ryad is a well-known quarter in the center of Moscow which later housed Gosplan, the unfortunate Soviet state planning authority. The historical Okhotny Ryad totally disappeared in the Communist period; at the turn of the century it housed Moscow's game and meat market. It was inhabited by owners of small shops, usually first-generation Muscovites, rough and not well educated, who had arrived from their villages to make the most of the opportunities there. At the same time they were bewildered and afraid because of the pace of social change and the rapid economic ups and downs. They were staunch believers in monarchy and church; they tended to hate the intelligentsia and the non-Russian minorities because

7. The history of the SRN has not yet been written. Hans Rogger's essays on the subject are of importance; H. D. Löwe, *Antisemitismus und reaktionäre Utopie* (Hamburg, 1978), contains interesting material. There are doctoral dissertations by Robert Edelmann (Columbia University, 1974) and Don Rawson (University of Washington, 1971). Most of the material in Russian can be found only in contemporary newspapers and periodicals. A first serious attempt at analysis was V. Levitsky, "Pravya Partii," in L. Martov et al., *Obsbeshvennie dvizhenie* (St. Petersburg, 1913), vol. 3. Under *glasnost* many documents concerning the program of the SRN have been reprinted, as well as a brief history by V. Osetrov, *Chernaya sotnya i krasnaya sotnya* (Moscow, 1991). A million copies of this wholly laudatory booklet were printed by the military publishing house in 1990. A more detailed book by the same writer had been announced but publication was delayed following a lawsuit on the grounds of racial incitement.

these were disturbing the peace and the social equilibrium. To say that this was the lower lower middle class would be correct, but would also be to say very little, for Okhotny Ryad was more of a mindset than a social category.

At the same time, the SRN (like its predecessors) counted among its members leading representatives of the aristocracy; in addition to those already mentioned one comes across the names Urussov, Meshshersky, Sheremetev, and Gagarin, all well-known aristocrats. From among the higher clergy, bishops Hermogen of Saratov and Antony of Volhynia should be mentioned. There were a few academics and intellectuals, such as the well-known historian Ilovaisky, and A. A. Maikov, the son of the famous poet.[8]

Comparing the Action Française with the Black Hundred, one finds distinct differences; the former had its mainstay among the upper middle class and the universities, whereas the latter was a curious mixture of the aristocracy, the more backward sections of the petite bourgeoisie, and the flotsam and jetsam of the big cities. Generalizations about the Black Hundred are difficult because conditions and membership varied from region to region. At the height of its influence, in 1906–1907, it had some three thousand branches. It was stronger in southern Russia than in other parts of the country. Membership was more or less uncontrolled: Anyone paying a fifty-kopek annual fee could join. (Only Jews could not, even if they had converted.[9]) Some members of the Black Hundred were perhaps high-minded idealists who had joined the movement because they saw their ideals and values threatened by the onslaught of dangerous and destructive revolutionaries.

But the public image of the organization was not that of a group of unselfish idealists. Count Witte, the former prime minister, wrote in his memoirs that "the Union was a body made up of plain thieves and hooligans": "The aims of the Black Hundred are usually selfish and of the lowest character. Their stomachs and pockets dictate their aspirations. They are typical murderers from the dark alleys." Of their leaders he wrote: "Decent people do not shake their hands and avoid their society." Witte was one of the main bugbears of the Black Hundred, and they had planned to assassinate him. In contrast, Stolypin, who could not possibly be suspected of liberal aberrations, was a hero of the right. However, he too gave orders to the Odessa local administration to disarm and disband most of the Black Hundred units. The most recent Black Hundred historian com-

8. He was the author of a pamphlet, *Revoliutsionery i chernosotentsy* (St. Petersburg, 1907).

9. According to paragraph 15 of the constitution of the SRN. Ostretsov, p. 30.

plains that even after Stolypin the ministry continued to withhold its regular subsidies from the Black Hundred and that the commander of the Odessa Military District "persecuted" these patriots in 1916–1917; the governors of Astrakhan and Irkutsk and other high officials are reported to have behaved in a similar unpatriotic fashion.[10] The Black Hundred were not unduly bothered by receiving financial support from the government; if the revolutionaries were financed by world capitalism, it was only natural that the patriotic forces should ask for the assistance of their own government.

Since most of the generals and governors reluctant to help the SRN were neither liberals nor radicals, what was the reason for their lack of enthusiasm? In some places the criminal element seems to have prevailed among the Black Hundred. Very few officials were inclined to take extreme measures against a short, sharp pogrom putting Jews and left-wingers in their place. But if these pogroms got out of hand, if they turned into the plundering of shops, if general order was affected, the authorities could not tolerate it. Odessa was a prime example, for the local Black Hundred had established a reign of terror that lasted for almost two years and that affected industry, trade, and life in general.

The Black Hundred have entered history mainly as the perpetrators of the anti-Jewish pogroms of 1905–1906. The pogroms got under way in late October 1905, as counterdemonstrations against celebrations by left-wing organizations hailing the tsar's October manifesto, which promised a democratic constitution. There were three hundred victims of the pogrom in Odessa; a hundred and twenty were killed in Yekaterinoslav, forty-six in Kiev, eighty in Bialystok (in 1906), not counting the thousands injured. Altogether, there were some seven hundred such pogroms, only twenty-four outside the Pale of Settlement and none in Poland and Lithuania, where the Black Hundred were hardly represented. Various parliamentary inquiry committees found that the local authorities were frequently involved; in some places where the Black Hundred did not exist (such as Ciedlec) the pogrom was carried out by the police single-handed; the same seems to be true with regard to Orsha, as well as Simferopol and Feodosiya. It was virtually impossible to establish to what extent pogroms were spontaneous and to what degree they were carefully planned and organized. Obviously, there would have been no pogroms but for latent, widespread, and violent anti-Semitism. Equally, the perpetrators would not have dared to take to the streets, to kill, and to burn but for the existence of some form of organization and the belief that the tsar, the bureaucracy, and the church were, at the very least, not opposed to the attacks.

10. Ibid., pp. 30–31.

It ought to be recalled, however, that there had been pogroms well before the appearance of the Black Hundred on the scene: Pogroms had taken place in the southern and eastern Ukraine in 1881 and on a major scale in Kishinev and Gomel in 1903, again before the appearance of the Black Hundred. In these as in other cases, the immediate reason was incitement by local propagandists, which fell on fertile ground. Last, mention should be made of the fact that the most murderous pogroms took place in 1919 during the civil war (for instance, in Proskurov, with seventeen hundred killed) long after the Black Hundred had ceased to exist.[11]

Two latter-day interpretations of the pogroms ought to be mentioned in passing. According to Soviet Communist historiography the attacks were as much directed against the left as against Jews; workers seldom, if ever, took part in them. In fact there were few attacks against left-wingers, and working-class elements (particularly railway workers) frequently played a prominent part in the pogroms.

According to the Black Hundred version, the SRN "never, under any circumstances, appealed for the murder of anyone"; the clashes between the Russian population and the Jews were always provoked by well-armed Jewish fighters who attacked the unarmed Russian population.[12] Seen in this light, the pogroms were mere acts of self-defense against "brutalized, predatory, and insatiable Judea," in the words of a contemporary Black Hundred periodical. But for this "counterattack" the tsarist system would have crumbled.[13]

The Black Hundred also engaged in individual terror, such as the murders of the Duma deputies Gertsenstein and Jollos; they claimed in their defense that a great many more patriotic figures had been killed by left-wing terrorists. The choice of victims is difficult to fathom: Gertsenstein, for instance, was not an ardent revolutionary but a right-wing Kadet (Liberal) of Jewish origin who had converted many years earlier. He was one of the country's leading experts on agricultural problems. However, he was one of the representatives of the capital in Parliament, and the idea that a Jew, even a convert, should represent Moscow seems to have been intolerable to the Black Hundred.

The revolutionary ferment abated toward the end of 1906; so did counter-revolutionary activities. Among the Black Hundred differences of opinion arose, not so much on ideological lines but as the result of

---

11. For a thoughtful investigation of the origins and circumstances of the pogroms of 1905 and 1919, see J. D. Klier and S. Lambroza, eds., *Pogroms* (Cambridge, Mass., 1992).

12. Ostretsov, pp. 22–23.

13. Ibid., p. 24.

individual leaders' conflicting ambitions. The Moscow branch of the SRN became independent; Vladimir Mitrofanovich Purishkevich, a Bessarabian landowner, founded his "Union of the Archangel Michael," with its main backing in Odessa, Bessarabia and other southern Russian cities. The rest of the SNR split between followers of Dr. Dubrovin and Markov II. They denounced each other to the government for lack of patriotism and even philosemitism as emerged when the state archives were opened after 1917. The authorities, by and large, reduced their allocations, and the attempts of the SNR to engage in socioeconomic ventures (such as the establishment of schools, agricultural cooperatives, and savings-and-loan institutions) were unsuccessful. An anti-alcohol campaign got under way, but if it had any effect this was not reflected in statistics concerning the consumption of alcohol.

Of the leaders of the SRN, Dubrovin and Purishkevich died soon after the Revolution. Dubrovin had been the better organizer, but he was strongly disliked even by his collaborators. Boris Nikolsky, a St. Petersburg law professor and a mainstay of the SRN at the university, called him a "vile parasite" and a "coarse, repulsive animal." Nevertheless, Dubrovin seems to have had his qualities as an organizer at a time when other leading figures on the extreme right just kept talking about the need to do something.

Purishkevich was the most flamboyant personality in this camp and nationally known as a Duma deputy. He was of humble origin; his grandfather had been a poor village priest. But wealth had somehow come to the family; Purishkevich became a most outspoken defender of the monarchy and aristocracy. He had graduated from university with a dissertation on oligarchic rebellions in ancient Greece. In 1900, at the age of thirty, he became special assistant to Plehve, the minister of the interior. There were likely to be disturbances and scandals wherever he appeared whether in Parliament, in a restaurant, or even at the theater, protesting against a performance of Oscar Wilde's *Salomé*.[14] He was adept at causing commotion, and there was method behind apparent madness: Being basically opposed to the parliamentary system, he wanted to discredit the Duma. The SRN as such had not participated in the elections to the first Duma, but individual leaders did. Like Dr. Goebbels he tried to break the system from within; like Goebbels he wrote poetry and novels.

Millions in government money passed through Purishkevich's hands between 1906 and 1917. In later years the bureaucracy trusted him more

14. There is a short Soviet biography of Purishkevich by S. Lyubosh, *Russkii fashist* (Leningrad, 1925), which says that he set the style ten years before fascism arose in Europe (p. 29) and that he was intellectually and morally head and shoulders above the other extreme right-wingers.

than it did Dr. Dubrovin. As one of his political enemies said, many right-wingers accepted bribes, but Purishkevich was the only one to deliver the goods.

Purishkevich usually played the role of the lone wolf. When war broke out he was fiercely anti-German, whereas most other Black Hundred leaders, realizing that Russia was too weak to sustain a prolonged war, wanted an alliance with Germany against Britain, France, and China. During the war Purishkevich seems to have realized that he was fighting for a lost cause in view of the incompetence and imbecility of the court and of the ruling classes in general. When he returned from a visit to the front in late 1916 he made a sensational speech in the Duma that got great applause from everyone but the extreme right. Russia, he thought, could be saved only by extreme action. He participated in the murder of Rasputin, firing the shots that eventually killed the monk. Purishkevich was arrested after the Revolution, but was released or succeeded in escaping and went to the south, where he died in 1920.

The third Black Hundred leader of some stature was Markov II, also a gifted Duma orator. He was a landowner from the Kursk area and proud of allegedly resembling Peter the Great in his appearance. He lacked, however, Purishkevich's flair and charisma as well as his political intelligence. His anti-Semitism was radical; in a speech prior to 1917 he predicted that all Jews, down to the last, would be killed in the coming pogroms, whereas Purishkevich merely wanted to resettle them in the Kolyma region. Markov II played a somewhat shady part in émigré politics, settled in Germany, entered the service of the Nazis, and was last seen toward the end of the war. All trace of him is lost after 1945.

After the abdication of the tsar and the March revolution, the Black Hundred were banned, and an official investigation into their activities clarified much that had been obscure earlier on. There had been no secret as far as SRN doctrine was concerned. It was based on traditional tsarist doctrine: "Orthodoxy, autocracy *("samoderzhavie")* and *narodnost* (an untranslatable term, meaning in this context something akin to a popular monarchy). According to Black Hundred ideology the bureaucracy had somehow spoiled relations between the tsar and the people, and ways and means had to be found to reestablish direct links between the ruler and his subjects. The Black Hundred were against the very concept of parliamentarism; a parliament meant the existence of political parties, and thus perpetual conflict, whereas for the SRN the unity of the people was the supreme value.

They advocated the convocation of a *sobor* ("assembly") on the lines of similar such assemblies in Russian history, whose function was limited, however, to advising the tsar and which had no decisive power. Only true Russians, not *inorodnye* (those of foreign origin) could be members of a *sobor*. Mention has been made of the fact that according to the constitution of the SRN no one of Jewish origin could be a member; other non-Russians could join only if their election was approved unanimously. While women could, according to the bylaws, be members, they were barred from taking any leading position (paragraph 17 of the SRN's constitution).[15]

Parts of the SRN's program were seemingly radical; the group advocated limiting the working week, raising the living standard of peasants, and making cheap credits available to peasants; it even supported some kind of agrarian reform. These radical sections of the program had been adopted under pressure from workers' and peasants' delegates and they became, in later years, something of an embarrassment for the SRN. Some leaders argued that they were not really needed: Russian workers were better protected than those in the capitalist world because power in the West was in the hands of Jewish exploiters, whereas in Russia it (still) was in the hands of the tsar, the friend of the working class.[16]

As the leaders of the Black Hundred and other thinkers of the far right saw it, most of the damage and ferment had been caused by Russia's urbanization and industrialization, which had entered a new, accelerated phase in the 1890s. As in other fascist movements the town symbolized rootlessness, decadence, revolutionary change, whereas a true national rejuvenation of the country could take place only in the village. At the same time, even the most extreme right-wingers realized that a strong Russia (such as they desired) needed a developed industry. In this respect, as in others, they faced a dilemma for which they had no answer. They opposed not only banking and the gold standard, but even Stolypin's agrarian reforms, because these put an end to the traditional communes, the *obshchina,* and favored the emergence of well-to-do peasants, the kulaks. While Lenin regarded the Stolypin reforms as a real socioeconomic alternative—which, if successful, might have prevented the success of the Bolshevik revolution in 1917—and while for the right under *glasnost* Stolypin became the greatest hero in recent Russian history, for the Black Hundred, he was

15. In fact a significant proportion of the publicists and supporters of the Black Hundred were not of Russian origin. This is true with regard to Purishkevich (who was of Moldovian, that is to say Romanian, origin); Gringmut (a converted Jew); Butmi de Katzman (who dedicated his edition of the *Protocols* to the SRN); Krushevan (a member of the Duma and editor of *Bessarabets*); General Kaulbars; Levendal; Engelgard; Plehve; Pelikan; General Rand; Richter-Shvanebach; and others. Among those who continued the Black Hundred tradition in the emigration after 1917 one finds names such as Vinberg and Graf Leuchtenberg in prominent places.

16. Loewe, *Antisemitismus,* p. 124

at best a dubious ally, at worst a Mason and a dangerous enemy.

An important difference between the SRN and the traditional right was the single-minded concentration of the former on the Jewish issue. No one on the right liked the Jews and favored equal rights for them. But for the traditional right-wing parties, all of which had been anti-Semitic to some extent, the "Jewish problem" had been just one of a number of issues, domestic and foreign, such as Slavophilism, foreign political expansion (especially toward the south), the strengthening of the Russian armed forces, and so on. The Black Hundred, on the other hand, had no sympathy for their fellow Slavs; they were suspicious of all foreigners. (France and Britain, as they saw it, had been "Judaized.") The Black Hundred were isolationists and favored a reduction of the military budget, above all that of the navy. They concentrated their fire against the Jews, who were the source of all evil in holy Russia. All Jews were revolutionaries and all revolutionaries were Jews. At the same time all Jews were capitalists and all capitalists were either Jews or tools in the hands of Jews. The Jewish revolutionaries wanted to undermine and overthrow the existing order so as to facilitate the installation of the rule of the Jewish capitalists.

This thesis of the conformity of interests between Jewish revolutionaries and Jewish capitalists became one of the main planks of Nazism. There was perhaps one important difference: It is doubtful whether Hitler and Goebbels, with all their anti-Semitism, truly believed in this preposterous theory, which they used simply because they thought it efficacious from a propagandistic point of view. There is no reason to doubt that the Markovs, Dubrovins, et al., truly believed in it. While the Black Hundred did attack left-wing parties physically and in their propaganda, their main campaigns were always directed against the liberal groups (such as the Kadets) and the capitalists. The militant workers were misguided but honest people, who might be led back to Black Hundred patriotism; the capitalists (as distinct from the big landowners) were the really dangerous enemy and were beyond redemption.

There was an enormous distance between this image of the all-powerful Jew and the reality of millions of desperately poor Jews huddled together in the "Pale of Settlement." There were few Jewish capitalists at the time; there was a small Jewish middle class, and the number of Jews in Moscow and St. Petersburg was tiny. (There were no pogroms in Moscow simply because there were no potential victims.) But the physical absence of Jews did not bother the Black Hundred: The Jew was the Antichrist, absent and yet omnipresent, a powerful myth helping to mobilize ignorant masses.

But with all this the SRN never became a leading force in the country. It could count on the sympathies of perhaps 10 percent, in some places up to 15 or 20 percent of the people. They were militants, very much in the public eye, but they were never near to achieving a political breakthrough.

The Black Hundred split after 1907 and the movement became organizationally much weaker, but a reservoir of goodwill continued to exist. Dozens of newspapers and periodicals, mostly of a local character, continued to appear. The Black Hundred also found support in *Novoye vremya* and other mainstream conservative publications, in periodicals sponsored by the army during the war, in church publications, and even in *Pravitelstvenny vestnik*, the official organ of the Russian government.

The ruling classes and high society were divided from the beginning about the role of the Black Hundred. The tsar was an almost fanatical supporter, calling them a "shining example of justice and order to all men"; his wife stuck with them to the very end. If there was a political difference between tsar and tsarina it concerned the authenticity of the *Protocols*. Stolypin had ordered two high police officials, Martynov and Vasiliev, to investigate the authenticity of the *Protocols*. The investigators had reached the conclusion that they were a forgery. Whereupon Nikolai gave an order that the *Protocols* were no longer to be used, "since it was impossible to pursue a pure aim by impure means"! Alexandra Fedorovna, his wife, continued to believe in their authenticity.[17]

Count Witte hated and despised the Black Hundred and was high on their list of enemies. Stolypin's attitude was more complicated. He regarded them as a cause of unrest and instability and acted decisively when they threatened public order. Kokovtsev, prime minister from 1911, followed a similar line, whereas Makarov, minister of the interior at the time of the Beilis trial (Kiev, 1913), supported SRN activities; so did Durnovo, one of his predecessors, as well as Trepov, who held many high positions in government. There was opposition against the Black Hundred among the finance ministers, and generally speaking, among all those who had to deal with Russia's industrial and commercial development. They knew that to carry out the Black Hundred's ideas about a return to medieval conditions was neither feasible nor desirable, and their program quite irrelevant to Russia's real problems. The pogroms made it more difficult to get credits abroad and, generally speaking, created a climate of uncertainty not conducive to prosperity. The same was true, broadly speaking, with regard to the Foreign Ministry bureaucracy; unlike the SRN ministry officials were not isolationists and could not ignore what the outside world was thinking of Russia.

17. Vl. Burtsev, *Protokoly tsionskikh mudretsov* (Paris, 1938), pp. 106–107. Reprinted, Moscow, 1991.

Some general observations concerning the SRN should complete this brief survey. It was much stronger in the west and south of Russia than in the center and east and it was very weak in the countryside. The first government subsidy was given by Stolypin—some 150,000 rubles mainly for publications. But it also emerged from letters written by Purishkevich that Stolypin was, on the whole, reluctant to give support to the SRN.[18] The largest individual supporter was Poluboyarinova, the widow of a wealthy publisher, who over the years had given some 500,000 rubles to the organization. In later years more substantial sums, about 1.5 million rubles, were given by the authorities to Purishkevich and Markov II for distribution among their groups.

Last, the constant dissent and intrigues among the SRN leadership eventually brought about the collapse of the movement. Thus, in Moscow the archpriest Vostorgov, who had founded the branch, constantly fought his rival Orlov; the rivalry between Pelikan and Konovnitsyn destroyed the movement in Odessa.

The SRN did on occasion show a certain amount of independence, as in its demand that the tsar should be nearer to the people—an old Slavophile notion—or in its attacks against the bureaucracy (including even the head of the Holy Synod of the Orthodox church), which was impeding close ties between the tsar and the people. It did use populist slogans and tactics, but in the final analysis the SRN remained part and parcel of the system that provided it with money and political support. It did not produce a leader on the Hitlerian scale but continued to regard the tsar as its supreme authority. In brief, unlike the Nazis or the Italian fascists it was never wholly independent; it did not break with the establishment and had no ambitions to become a party of a new type. It went beyond religion toward racism, but it never visualized cutting its ties to organized religion. On the contrary, religion remained its central plank. Racialism, pure and simple, would not have done in a country in which half the population was not of Russian origin. The SRN could have opted for "Little Russia," but this would have run counter to their nationalist aspirations. Or they could have envisaged the expulsion or extermination of all non-Russians from Russia, but such a solution was too radical for a party that though it was moving in the direction of fascism, was as yet very far from reaching this indistinct goal.

18. *Soyuz russkovo naroda* (Moscow, 1929), p. 164.

THE APPEARANCE OF THE PROTOCOLS AND THE GREAT MASONIC PLOT

RUSSIAN PATRIOTS FREQUENTLY DIFFERED about the reasons for the Bolshevik Revolution of 1917, but all agreed that it was an unmitigated disaster: *gibel rossii*—the ruin of Russia. A few were to change their views later on, but this was, as yet, years ahead. The right-wingers thought that the Revolution was mainly the fault of the utopian and destructive attitudes of the intellectuals. But harsh words were also said about the Russian people in general, who (as Struve once put it) supported the Revolution so that they could work less (or could steal) without facing the consequences. Others blamed the people for having turned against religion and the state and for not having developed a true national consciousness. But the monarchy did not escape blame either for its share in the responsibility for the catastrophe. Some, like Berdyaev, at one time blamed the West, as the Slavophiles had done before, for importing alien ideas, which had caused much of the harm. There were calls for a spiritual revival in which religious nationalism would play the central role.

However, these soul-searchings were confined, on the whole, to a relatively small group of intellectuals. Among the majority of the Revolution's opponents, especially those who took up arms against it, it was more common to look for a tangible enemy, a hidden hand, a criminal, all-powerful gang of plotters. And since the changes had been so radical, since institutions that had been in existence for centuries disappeared almost overnight, no explanation was too farfetched to escape scrutiny as a possible master key to these inexplicable events. Everyone had known of the tsar before 1917, but only very few had ever heard of Lenin and Trotsky, let alone their chief aides. Where had they come from? Whose interest did they really serve? Such a reaction has been by no means uncommon in the annals of mankind; in Germany the revolution had been much less radical, yet there was the same inclination to believe in the existence of a "hidden hand," a giant conspiracy.

There are countries that seem particularly prone to being influenced by conspiracy theories; Russia has been traditionally receptive to them, but so are the United States and the Mediterranean countries. In fact, some believers can be found in virtually every country. Some conspiracy theories are traditionally limited to the fringes of society; others tend to become at times the prevailing intellectual fashion.

Such explanations were intellectually not quite satisfactory. Even if the Revolution had been no more than a plot, how was one to explain that the Bolsheviks prevailed over their enemies in the civil war? Those who opposed Bolshevism on purely nationalist grounds faced a further ideological difficulty. The slogan of the White movement had been "For a united and indivisible Russia"—and under the Communists, particularly under Stalin, Russia was certainly indivisible and also increasingly militarily strong. Obviously, there must have been some deeper reason for the Revolution's success.

But not many people form their political opinions on purely rational and logical grounds, and it was much more comfortable and less painful to believe in the guilt of foreigners than to engage in soul-searching, to admit that the tsarist regime had been shortsighted, inefficient, morally corrupt, and obscurantist or that there had been a lack of moral fiber. In the context of this disaster the old propaganda of the Black Hundred about a world conspiracy of Jews, Masons, and foreign agents acquired a new credibility that it did not have before. Was it not a fact that there were many foreign names behind the aliases of the leading Bolsheviks and the heads of the other revolutionary parties?

There was some truth in the allegations about the prominent role of Jews and other foreigners among the new leaders. Since the Jews in Russia had been the object of much oppression, it was only natural that many of them should join the revolutionary parties, which promised to overthrow the regime that had been the cause of their sufferings, including the murder of many of them. That the Bolsheviks had a lesser percentage of Jews than the other revolutionary parties made little difference as far as the anti-Bolsheviks were concerned. Nor were they impressed by the fact that all the Bolshevik leaders had renounced Judaism and felt themselves Russian, that in any case they were removed from positions of leadership not long after the revolution, and that, lastly, the percentage of Jews among the émigrés from Russia was also far larger than it should have been according to their percentage of the general population. "Jewish bolshevism" became the enemy par excellence of the right, and all kinds of unlikely stories were circulated: The Russian Revolution had been financed by the New York banking house of Kuhn, Loeb & Company. If it could be shown that Jacob Schiff—Kuhn, Loeb's head—acting on behalf of the New York plutocrats, had paid the Communists, it followed that the Revolution was the work of aliens, not of native revolutionaries. The same stories were used in Nazi propaganda after 1933, but there is much reason to doubt that the Nazis ever believed them; their attitude was more cynical.

This propaganda was useful because it demonstrated that there was a common front of Jewish Communists and Jewish millionaires, both working for the same end: Jewish world rule. There was not a shred of truth in this or in the many similar canards, but neither court verdicts nor the unanimous opinion of reputable historians, showing in detail how, when, and by whom these forgeries were concocted, have put an end to them.

Thus Trotsky and Sverdlov became the foremost villains of the Russian Revolution, not Lenin or Stalin or Dzerzhinsky. Little did it matter that Sverdlov had died less than two years after the Revolution and that Trotsky no longer influenced events after 1923, and was deported from the Soviet Union in 1929. They were still held responsible for events that occurred ten, twenty, even fifty years after their demise.

But politically, conspiracy-theory propaganda was not very effective; those sponsoring and broadcasting it were defeated in the struggle for power in Russia.

History is full of fantasies, delusions, and lies, and it would be possible to dismiss these specific inventions as mere curiosities but for two circumstances. If the conspiracy theories had no impact in Russia at the time, they provided inspiration in the development of Nazi doctrine, especially during the latter's early phase. I have described elsewhere how Germans and Russians of the extreme right became Hitler's mentors by conveying the *Protocols of the Elders of Zion* from Russia to Germany in 1918, and how this propaganda fell on more fertile ground in Germany at the time than it had in Russia.[1] By one of these strange twists of history, German anti-Semitic doctrine, which had been exported to Russia in the 1880s, was reimported from Russia to Germany after the First World War. But this

---

1. W. Laqueur, *Russia and Germany* (London, 1965; rev. ed. New Brunswick, N.J., 1990), chapters 4–6.

matter belongs to German rather than Russian history and is therefore of no direct relevance in our story. More relevant in the present context is the fact that after an eclipse of more than seventy years the slogans of the extreme right of 1918 resurfaced in a Russia shaken by deep convulsions in 1990.

At the core of this conspiracy doctrine were the *Protocols of the Elders of Zion*. The complicated history of this best-selling book and all of the literature based on it have been analyzed in exhaustive detail. But the basic ideas underlying the *Protocols* are so central to the present-day ideology of the far right in Russia that they ought to be summarized yet another time in briefest detail.[2]

The *Protocols* have several precursors: Wilhelm Marr, once a leading socialist, wrote a pamphlet in Switzerland in 1879 in which he predicted not only the victory of Jewry over Germandom but also a Jewish revolutionary attempt to overthrow the tsarist regime. But this warning fell on deaf ears. More successful was the "Speech of the Chief Rabbi" by Hermann Goedzsche, another German writer, once a diplomat, who had to leave the service for dishonorable conduct and under the pen name "Sir John Ratcliff" became a prolific writer of pulp fiction. The "Speech," part of a larger novel called *Biarritz*, described a scene in the Jewish cemetery of Prague where the Sanhedrin, the supreme Jewish body (which was last heard of eighteen hundred years ago) met every hundred years to discuss the Jewish plan for world domination. The "Speech" was taken up by the Russian government and reprinted in hundreds of thousands, perhaps millions of copies. So was another brochure, by "Major Osman Bey Kibridzli Zade," who claimed that the revolutionary movement in Russia was headed by the Alliance Israelite Universelle, a charity organization established in Paris in 1860 to defend Jewish communities against ritual-murder accusations in various parts of the world and allegedly sponsored by the Rothschilds. Osman Bey had even more startling information to offer: He maintained that the Jews had already set up an army to cordon off Russia. The rabbis of East Germany were its officers and Bamberger, the chief rabbi of Königsberg, served as the commander in chief. "Osman Bey" was the pseudonym of a Romanian apostate from Judaism named Milliner, who

2. The most authoritative account is still Norman Cohn, *Warrant for Genocide* (London, 1967); a Russian edition was published in Moscow in 1991. See also Laqueur, *Russia and Germany*, chapters 5–6. The most complete and up-to-date Western biobibliography of Sergei Nilus, the key figure in the dissemination of the *Protocols*, is Michael Hagemeister, "Wer war Sergei Nilus?" In *Ostkirchliche Studien* (March 1991). Among recent Russian right-wing writers, A. Strishev ought to be mentioned (*Tsar kolokol* 6 [1990]; *Moskovskii Literator,* 32–33 [1990], *Veche,* [36, Munich, 1989]). The collected works of Sergei Nilus were republished in Moscow in 1991–1992; most of them are on subjects other than the *Protocols*.

tried without much success to blackmail international personalities: He promised to keep them out of his revelations if they paid him.

When Tsar Nikolai II read this booklet he added in his hand, "I fully share the opinions here expressed." The belief in the leading role of the Alliance lingered on for many years; it again appeared in the writings of Alfred Rosenberg, the chief Nazi ideologist after the First World War.

There existed some other precursors of the *Protocols,* which pretended to be the verbatim record of twenty-four secret meetings of the heads of the world Jewish conspiracy, giving an outline of their intentions. It was their declared aim to destroy all states and build on the ruins a Jewish world empire to be headed by an emperor of the line of David. The conspirators' main tools were democracy, liberalism, and socialism. They had been behind all the upheavals in history, including the French Revolution. They supported demands for the freedom of the individual and they were also behind the class struggle. All political assassinations and all major strikes were organized by them. They induced workers to become alcoholics and created chaotic conditions by increasing food prices and spreading infectious diseases. They already constituted a secret world government, but since their power was as yet incomplete they incited peoples against each other to provoke a world war.

There was, however, a great difference between their tactics, used to gain world power, and their real, long-term aims. The Elders were by no means democrats or liberals. Real happiness in the future world order would not be brought about by democratic principles but, on the contrary, by blind obedience to authority. Only a small section of the population would receive education under the new order. Furthermore, it would be the honorable duty of all citizens to spy on each other. The new government would put down without mercy all those who opposed it; its former co-conspirators, such as the Masons, would be liquidated, some killed, others exiled to primitive settlements overseas.

But what if the non-Jews discovered this diabolical conspiracy in time to thwart it? What if they turned against the Jews once they had realized that all disasters and intrigues were part of the Elders' strategic master plan? Against this last eventuality the Elders had a horrible weapon: Soon (this was written before the turn of the century) all capitals would have a network of underground railways. In case of danger, the Elders would blow up the cities from the underground tunnels, and all government offices and archives—and all the non-Jews—would perish and their prosperity be destroyed.

This ultimate weapon was too farfetched even for the credulity of the Russian and German editors of the *Protocols.* The Russian edition added a footnote observing that there were as yet no such underground tunnels in Russia, but international committees were already at work to sponsor their construction. The German editor, Theodor Fritsch, noted that common sense revolted against the idea. It was probably a manner of speaking, he said, by which the author wanted to emphasize that the Jews would not be deterred from using even the most horrible weapons to achieve their aims.

The attitude of the extreme right toward the *Protocols* after 1985 has shown on occasion similar reservations. The fundamentalists selling the *Protocols* in front of Moscow subway stations and churches have argued that they were the literal truth. Those catering for a more sophisticated public have conceded that the book cannot be considered, strictly speaking, a historical document, but is merely an "artistic expression" of views widely held at the time. The editors of a Russian literary magazine publishing the *Protocols* in 1991 introduced them as follows: "We do not share the ideology of the *Protocols* and fully admit the possibility that the Zionists did not write them." Nevertheless, it was their duty to publish them so that "readers could form their own opinion."[3] To be on the safe side, the editors preceded the *Protocols* in each issue with an article by a distinguished Russian philosopher of Jewish origin, Semyon Frank.

According to its early version the conspiracy was based on an anonymous, amorphous organization—the "Sanhedrin," an alliance between the Jews and the Masons. Later the Alliance Israelite Universelle became the main culprit, but after about 1920 the Alliance disappeared and the chief role was attributed to the world Zionist movement. There were several variations; according to one school of thought, the *spiritus rector* was Ahad Ha'am (Asher Ginzburg), an Odessa cultural philosopher who happened to be a sharp critic of political Zionism, a fact that seems to have been unknown to the anti-Semites.

The conspiracy theory of history, meaning the conviction that there is a central conspiracy behind all the world's evils and discontents, is probably as old as historiography. At times it appears as a deep persecution mania afflicting individuals and whole peoples. In the modern age the Puritan revolution in England, as well as the French Revolution, were attributed to a conspiracy of philosophers, Illuminati, and Freemasons. Jews appeared as members of this coalition only with the publication in 1869 of a book by the French nobleman Gougenot des Mousseaux, *Le Juif, le judaisme et la judaisation des peuples chrêtiens,* which was translated into German by Alfred Rosenberg. By 1880 the belief in a world conspiracy began to gain

3. M. Nazarov, in *Nash sovremennik,* 12 (1991), p. 152; editorial note in *Kuban,* 2 (1991), p. 87.

ground among the extreme right in France, Germany, and Russia; the *Protocols* were merely part of this tradition, a text concocted by Rachkovsky, the head of tsarist intelligence in France, in collaboration with some agents and supporters.

The first Russian edition was brought out in Kishinev by Butmi de Katzman and Kruzhevan, two individuals of Bessarabian origin. The second and more important one was published by Sergei Nilus, a Russian playboy who after spending several years in France underwent a religious conversion and retired to one of Russia's leading monasteries. In Nilus's case the *Protocols* were part of a far more ambitious work, *The Big in the Small,* an incredible gallimaufry of religious quotations, exact predictions about the coming of the Antichrist, and symbolic drawings of stars and snakes. Nilus's first edition of the *Protocols* was brought out by the court printers in Tsarskoye Selo, a later one by the printing shop of Troitse-Sergeyeva Lavra, Russia's foremost monastery. But there is no evidence that either the court or the Holy Synod of the Orthodox church helped to promote the *Protocols*. Nor did the Nazis in later years like Nilus's religious fanaticism. As Gregor Schwartz-Bostunich, a Russian émigré and the missing link between the Black Hundred and the Nazis, wrote: "Nilus's work was an immortal achievement, but ideologically we remain astronomically remote from a man who really expected the coming of the Antichrist and for whom the medieval devil was a reality."[4]

The early reception of the *Protocols* in Russia was disappointing; even the Russian right was reluctant to endorse it. Jews in Russia were a downtrodden minority, living for the most part in abject poverty. They bore no resemblance to the rich and all-powerful Jews described in the *Protocols*. Only after the Revolution was there a change, and apocalyptic events called for a convincing answer. Was it not a fact that Jews were suddenly in prominent positions in Russian and German politics as well as in the economic and cultural life of these countries? That the forgeries were primitive did not really matter. As one contemporary author put it, the ignorant believed them because they were ignorant, and the partially intelligent because it was for the good of the reactionary cause to do so.

The literature generated by the *Protocols* flourished in many countries throughout the 1920s and 1930s. Among Russian émigrés it led to some very extreme manifestations such as the writings of Fyodor Viktorovich Vinberg, a former colonel in the tsarist army, turned writer and philosopher

---

4. G. Schwartz-Bostunich, *Jüdischer Imperialismus,* p. 359. This Kiev-born Russian became a high-ranking SS officer, a confidant of Hitler, and one of the Nazis' chief authorities on the Talmud, ritual murder, and Freemasonry. See Laqueur, *Russia and Germany,* pp. 134–37.

in the Berlin emigration. He wrote that the late and lamented tsar had mistakenly idealized the Russian people, who in reality were a good-for-nothing lot and deserved to be punished for having betrayed the tsar. They were an "anthropoid herd," a blind, senseless mass, a multifaced brute that understood nothing but its crudest materialist needs. Three-quarters of all Christians were already caught in the Judeo-Masonic web; all the global gold reserves were in their hands, and also three-quarters of the world press.

Given these dismal facts, was there hope for salvation? Vinberg believed there was, for there existed aside from the higher anti-Semitism also a lower anti-Semitism, which was "God-given" and came from the depths of the people (sic!) It would cut the Gordian knot by destroying the Jews, the Judaized, and everything smacking of Judaism. The nest of the vipers had to be destroyed so that no trace was left.[5] Vinberg was a true precursor of the Final Solution, even though at the time (he died in 1927) few paid attention to his ravings. He had a few younger followers in his day, former lieutenants and captains in the tsarist army. The best known was Shabelsky-Bork, who shot Vladimir Nabokov (the father of the famous writer) at a political meeting in Berlin in 1922. The killer was arrested but released under the Nazis. After the war, like other like-minded individuals he escaped to Latin America.[6]

In the beginning the Zionists did not figure at all in the conspiracy by the Elders; the first World Zionist Congress took place only in 1897 and during the decade after this event few people knew even about its existence. After the Bolshevik revolution, the Russian far right claimed that it had been the result of a conspiracy between the Germans and the Jews—much to the annoyance of the German right-wing extremists, who wanted to make use of the Protocols but declared that the "German connection" was arrant nonsense. In 1920 Winston Churchill, who had believed for a short while in a global Bolshevik plot (in which the Jews played a leading part) published an article in which he stressed the obvious fact that Zionism and communism were bitter enemies.[7] The Russian anti-Semites did not, however, accept this, either out of ignorance or because it did not fit their

5. F. Vinberg, Krestny put (Munich, 1921), pp. 240–65. On Vinberg, see Jane Burbank, Intelligentsia and Revolution (New York, 1986), pp. 171–77, and Laqueur, Russia and Germany, pp. 127–30. Similar views were expressed in the writings of Markov II, Schwartz-Bostunich, N. D. Zhevakhov, E. Brant, and other émigré writers.

6. Shabelsky-Bork's writings were published posthumously by a publishing house of the Orthodox church in the United States.

7. "The struggle which is now beginning between the Zionists and the Bolshevik Jews is little less than a struggle for the soul of the Jewish people." Illustrated Sunday Herald (London, February 1920).

preconceived motions. However, even in the literature of the *Protocols* published in the 1920s and 1930s, Zionism did not play any significant role, and it was only after the establishment of the state of Israel that the connection between Zionism and communism was made. Zionism was accused at one and the same time of having inspired and executed the Revolution, and of anti-Sovietism.

There were conspiracy theorists among the Russian émigrés who cast their nets in different directions, discovering a hidden hand in all kinds of likely, and more often, unlikely organizations, such as the World Council of Churches, the League of Nations, the Trilateral Commission, the Bilderberg conferences, the Vatican, the Baptists, the YMCA, and even the Boy Scouts. When conspiracy theories had their second coming in Russia in the 1990s, the Fabian Society, H. G. Wells, and Kibbo Kift (the British woodcraft movement of the 1920s) were added to the list.[8]) But above all, interest was focused on Masonic influences in Russia and world politics, and it is to this red herring that we ought to turn now.

The Global Conspiracy

The idea of a global conspiracy by Freemasons to subjugate all mankind has been part and parcel of Russian extreme right-wing doctrine for a long time. This image of Freemasonry is very distant from the ideas of respecting the dignity of all human beings, the tolerance, and the willingness to help that gave birth centuries ago to Masonic lodges in various countries, first, apparently, in Britain. In its modern form Freemasonry came into being in the early decades of the eighteenth century. Throughout history a great many prominent personalities have been Masons—not only George Washington and Benjamin Franklin, Franklin Roosevelt and Harry Truman, not only British and Prussian kings, French presidents and prime ministers, but also many leading writers and composers, including Goethe, Haydn, and Mozart—and, last but not least, men of the left such as Salvador Allende. Masonry has attracted suspicion from the early days of its existence, partly because of its secretiveness and strange rituals, but mainly, no doubt, because of the proclivity among many people to believe in the existence of a "hidden hand." Prominent among the enemies of Masonry was the

8. A. Dugin, "Anatomia mondialisma," *Den,* 16 (1991). Dugin, formerly a leading figure in Pamyat, subsequently became an important ideologist of the far right, writing on neoconservatism, neopaganism, sex, and the radicals, often deriving his inspiration from Julius Evola, the Italian fascist ideologist. In September 1992 the first issue of Dugin's own journal *Elementy* was published, devoted to the promotion of his brand of geopolitics and combating "mondialism." *Éléments* was the name of the theoretical organ of the French New Right.

Catholic church, which regarded it as a dangerous competitor; the first anti-Masonic bull, issued by Pope Clement XII in 1738, was followed by countless subsequent condemnations.[9] The main points of accusation were that the lodges accepted members of different religious confessions and that Freemasonry undermined the peace of mind of individuals and political stability.

Freemasonry has been banned by virtually all dictatorships, including the fascist regimes, the Communist countries, and Franco's Spain. It was outlawed in tsarist Russia in 1822, and new lodges came into being there only toward the end of the century. The idea that the Puritan revolution in England was engineered by a secret society was widespread at the time. Later on, at the time of the French Revolution, the concept of a triple conspiracy (of philosophers, Freemasons, and Illuminati) produced by the Abbé Barruel and the Chevalier de Malet found many converts among antirevolutionaries. Jews were not included in the list of fellow conspirators simply because they did not yet play any part in European (or American) politics. This innovation came only in 1869, with the publication of the book by Gougenot des Mousseaux which we have already mentioned and which proved conclusively—to those willing to believe—that there indeed existed a giant conspiracy to subvert all cherished values: Christianity, monarchy, patriotism, internal peace. Since then there has been a flood of publications in all major languages belaboring this theme. After the turn of the century, when the Zionist movement came into being, the Jews became the main partners of the Masons in the conspiracy. Yet others maintained that *Zhidomasonstvo* ("Jewmasonry," as it was called in Russia) was not even specifically Jewish, since the Jews belonging to it were *deraciné,* uprooted cosmopolitans.

Among the Russian right these ideas fell on fertile ground. There were certain obstacles to overcome, since many heroes of Russian history, such as General Suvorov, Marshal Kutuzov, and the Decembrists, had been Masons, as had Pushkin and countless other Russian writers. Nor could anyone in his right mind argue that Jews played any significant political role under tsarism. But on the other hand, Jews were prominent in the revolutionary movement and also in the economic development of the country, and for this reason it came as no surprise that the revolution of 1905 was attributed by some to Masons and Jews.[10] The conspiracy theory of history

9. Until 1972 Masons were excommunicated according to canon law.

10. Some of the spadework for this propaganda was done by foreigners such as the Czech clergyman Rudolf Vrba (*Die Revolution in Russland* [two vols.; Prague, 1907–1908]); his message was eagerly absorbed in Russia.

found its most famous expression in the infamous *Protocols of the Elders of Zion*. But the *Protocols* were apparently not deemed sufficient; a somewhat more sophisticated version of the theory was needed. Against this background, anti-Masonic literature became a major industry among Russian émigrés in the 1920s and 1930s. After 1987 these theories were disinterred by the extreme right in Russia and became part and parcel of its contemporary ideology.

It is only fair to add that similar propaganda appeared elsewhere; among the Nazis there was a very active anti-Masonic literature, with General Erich Ludendorff as its best-known proponent, and the Gestapo had a special department dealing with it. The neo-Nazi movement has continued the anti-Masonic tradition, and there have been recurrent accusations against Masonic activities in England, America, Italy, and other countries. However, in Russia anti-Masonic doctrine acquired greater popularity than almost anywhere else.

After the Second World War there was in the West a decline in the extent and intensity of anti-Masonic literature, just as there was less interest in anti-Semitism. However, both among Russian émigrés and subsequently inside the Soviet Union, some specialized studies continued to appear. This refers above all to the writings of Grigorii Aronson, George Katkov, and Nina Berberova, based to a large extent on the recollections of Russian émigrés.[11] None of these writers had any sympathy for the *Zhidomasonstvo* conspiracy theories. But they were convinced that since so many members of the Provisional Government (March–November 1917) had been members of Masonic lodges, the impact of Freemasons on the course of events must have been greater than was generally assumed by earlier historians. Katkov came to far-reaching conclusions about the influence of the Masons, which are almost certainly exaggerated. Berberova, on the other hand, was more cautious, stressing that far from being radicals the Masons among the members of the Provisional Government had all along been opposed to revolution and that, in any case, many of their opponents—including the tsar himself; Lopuchin, the head of the police; and a great many White generals—were or had been Masons at one time or another. Unless it could be shown that Masonic solidarity had not only existed, but had decisively shaped the course of events, the fact that Alexander Kerensky and some of his ministers had belonged to a lodge was of no historical consequence.

The Masonic theme began to preoccupy several Soviet writers and historians during the late Brezhnev period. Among them was the novelist

11. G. Aronson, *Rossiya nakanune revoliutsii* (New York, 1962). G. Katkov, *Russia 1917,* (London, 1969). Nina Berberova, *Lyudi i lozhi* (Moscow, 1990).

Valentin Pikul; their works were considered entertainment (the Soviet equivalent of political thrillers) and seldom even reviewed, but found an enormous readership. Pikul was at one time probably the most widely read author, alive or dead, in the Soviet Union with the exception of Alexandre Dumas. More surprisingly perhaps, two professional historians, N. N. Yakovlev and V. I. Startsev, also became interested in the subject, and while their findings were controversial, to say the least, they were tolerated and perhaps even encouraged by the party ideological authorities.[12] Neither Yakovlev nor Startsev made any major discoveries; they used the material assembled by contemporary émigré writers (and before, in the 1920s, by writers such as S. Melgunov) and accordingly rewrote Soviet history. If hitherto it had been accepted that a bourgeois conspiracy had led to March 1917 and the downfall of the tsarist regime, the accents were now put differently: It had been a Masonic rather than a bourgeois plot.

Historians have submitted this thesis to minute analysis and reached the conclusion that while there were Masons in Russia in 1916–1917, there was no "Masonic problem." There was therefore no good reason to revise the more or less accepted thesis about Freemasonry as a *quantité négligeable*.[13] However, even if it is assumed for argument's sake that the assertions about the crucial role played by Masonry in 1917 were wholly correct, they still would not have been of great use to the extreme right in Russia seventy-four years after the event. As political ammunition it was simply not effective. For within a few months the plotters of February 1917 found themselves in exile, powerless and miserable.

Stronger medicine was needed: "evidence" pointing to a worldwide conspiracy concerning not just one country and one year but omnipresent, omnipotent, and omnidestructive. Hence the reappearance of the fantasies of the extreme right-wingers within the Russian emigration in the 1920s, who, in turn, had drawn their inspiration from like-minded spirits in nineteenth-century France and Germany. Little did it matter that the stories now resuscitated had been invented by novelists with a rich imagination or by international swindlers like Leo Taxil, who toward the end of his life had freely admitted that his "facts" had been a mere hoax.

12. N. N. Yakovlev, *1 August 1914* (Moscow, 1974); V. I. Startsev, *Revoliutsia i vlast* (Moscow, 1978) and *Vnutrennaya Politika Vremenenogo Pravitelstva* (Leningrad 1980).

    Yakovlev became subsequently something of an embarrassment to the Russian right as the author of *Ts.R.U. protiv S.S.S.R.* ("The CIA Against the Soviet Union") (Moscow, 2nd ed., 1980). This pamphlet had quite obviously been commissioned by some very high authority and caused a scandal because it engaged in long diatribes against such "foreign agents and traitors" as Sinyavsky, Galanskov, Ginsburg, and, most prominently, Solzhenitsyn. He relates his conversations with Andropov and work for the KGB in detail in *Molodaya Gvardiya*, 8, 1992, p. 147.

13. A. Ya. Avrekh, *Masony i revoliutsia* (Moscow, 1990), p. 342.

According to the new-old version of *Zhidomasonstvo* which reemerged in 1987–1988, all modern history had been a seamless conspiracy against religion, authority, national values. The conspiracy began with the French Revolution and continued with the revolutions of 1830 and 1848. The mysterious death of Tsar Alexander I in 1825 was probably connected with the fact that while he had been a Mason in his younger years, he later defected and even banned the lodges in Russia.[14] The Crimean war was an anti-Russian Masonic intrigue; so were virtually all other nineteenth-century wars, and the First World War. Palmerston, Disraeli, and in all probability also Bismarck were Masons; Bismarck in any case was a puppet manipulated by his financier, the Jew Bleichroeder, and his boss, the emperor, also a former Mason.

The Russian revolutions of 1917 were engineered by Masons from various countries including Lord Milner (representing the Rothschild interests), the German banking house of Warburg, the American bankers Schiff and Kuhn (who also financed Trotsky), and the senior German official Ulrich von Brockdorff-Rantzau (later foreign minister), who gave money to Parvus, a leading Russian–German–Jewish socialist and businessman, who passed it on to Lenin. According to this version of history, the German government, which financed Lenin's sealed train from Switzerland to the Finland station, merely acted on behalf of international Freemasons rather than on its own initiative.

The conspiring Masons were helped by renegade Russians—Masons—like Sazonov (the foreign minister) and generals such as Brusilov, Krimov, Russkii, and Gurko.[15]

And so the argument continues: To the present day, all of Russian and world history has been a story of terror and fraud, up to and including the establishment in Moscow of a Jewish-Masonic presence, in the form of the all-powerful American B'nai B'rith lodge, in 1990.[16] These American Jewish Masons wanted not merely to build a new temple of King Solomon in the holy Russian capital but to establish their domination over the Russian people once and for ever.

These were certainly frightening prospects and it is easy to understand that at least some people, not burdened by a deeper knowledge of politics,

---

14. There is an enormous literature in this vein. Virtually every issue of *Nash sovremennik* and *Molodaya gvardiya* after 1987 has devoted at least one article to this subject, not to mention the smaller publications of these circles. It would be well-nigh impossible to provide an exhaustive bibliography. Many of the examples quoted are from Pyotr Lanin (a professional historian) "Tainie pruzhiny istorii," *Molodaya gvardiya,* 7 and 8 (1991).

15. Lanin, "Tainie . . . ," *Molodaya Gvardiya,* 8, p. 257.

16. Ibid., pp. 260 ff.

would come to believe that now, for the first time, they had reached an understanding of the mainsprings of world history. Others, to be sure, might ask inconvenient questions: If the key figures on both sides were all Masons, why did they quarrel in the first place? The frequent answer is that these conflicts, revolutions, and wars were a mere make-believe to mislead simple people. But this is not easy to accept—after all, there were always winners and losers, and why, for instance, should the Russian Masons so often be on the side of the losers? To make their case more convincing, the fighters against *Zhidomasonstvo*, like their predecessors of the 1920s, use a number of stratagems, which can be briefly summarized as follows.

1. They imply a Masonic solidarity that never existed between Masons from different countries and lodges—which, in reality, had nothing in common and even competed with each other.

2. They include in their fantasies not merely true Masonic lodges but all secret or semi-secret societies. A prime example is the Thule society in Munich in 1920, a small group of right-wing sectarians preaching proto-Nazi doctrines. Rudolf Hess was probably a member of this group for a few months, hence the conclusion that Hitler must have been also a Mason. (In reality Hitler was as fierce an opponent of Masonry as the Soviet foes of *Zhidomasonstvo*, and this is true for all other Nazi leaders of importance.)

3. On the flimsiest of evidence, statesmen and public figures who never belonged to a lodge are branded as Masons. Thus, Bismarck becomes a Mason because in a contemporary painting he is depicted embracing Shuvalov, the Russian ambassador to Germany, in something resembling a "Masonic embrace." Kiwanis, Rotarians, Lions, and members of the Ancient Order of Hibernians are considered part of the conspiracy.

4. In a similar way Jewish blood is attributed to "pure Aryans" such as Kerensky, the head of the Provisional Government, whose "real name" is said to have been Kirbis, and Victor Chernov, the head of the Socialist Revolutionary party, who was allegedly named Zuckermann. These inventions date back to the 1920s, but there are also some innovative practices. Mikhail Gorbachev, Raissa Gorbachev, Yeltsin, Yakovlev, Arbatov, and virtually all other leading figures of the *glasnost-perestroika* period have been declared Jews. So were Evtushenko and Solzhenitsyn (whose real name was said to have been "Solzhenitser"), and even Alla Pugacheva, the most famous rock star of the time.

5. However, the proponents of the Masonic-Jewish theory of history still face one major hurdle in their attempts to gain true credibility. Their audience might be fascinated by the fact that Garibaldi and Mazzini were Masons, but how relevant is this to the present-day situation in Russia? Unless it can be shown that the Bolsheviks too, were part of this giant

global conspiracy, the arguments will not be effective. Since no one has been able so far to show that Lenin and Stalin and Trotsky (or Khrushchev and Brezhnev and Kaganovich) belonged to the Grand Orient or some other such lodge, this remains the Achilles' heel of the doctrine. True, some ideologists of the extreme right claim to have found that at least one Old Bolshevik was a member of a lodge prior to 1917: Skvortsov-Stepanov, whose name is known now only to a few experts specializing in the history of the Communist Party of the Soviet Union. They also allege that Bukharin and Radek, Lenin's companions, were "indirectly" connected with the lodges, which presumably means that they had acquaintances who were Masons, which, alas, means little or nothing.

In brief, there are logical difficulties. But they do not prevent the proponents of *Zhidomasonstvo* from returning to this topic time and time again, assuming that there always will be a receptive audience fascinated by stories about the "hidden hand," be the hand that of the Mafia or that of the Masonic plotters, even though the last Russian masonic lodge (in Paris) was closed in the early 1970s for want of members, and some small new lodges were opened in Russia only in 1991. Nevertheless, "the Judeo-Masonic" lobby still remains the shadow government of the Soviet Union; its main aim is to discredit the Communist ideological and economic system and to seize the top position in the state apparatus.[17]

Conspiracy theories of history have been for a long time part of Russian political psychology; the Bolsheviks had little to learn in this respect from the extreme right. The allegations against the countless "enemies of the people," from the 1930s to the Doctors' Plot, were, after all, in the same vein, and on occasion even the identity of the enemies has been the same (Kuhn, Loeb, Schiff—and "Wall Street" in general). Anti-Masonic writings have been encouraged by the party apparatus up to the most recent past.[18] The main difference between the Communist approach and that of the extreme right was that the villains of Communist *Zhidomasonstvo* also included the Russian right-wing émigrés such as Generals Krasnov, Biskupsky, Skoropadsky, and Petliura (the Ukrainian civil war leader), some of whom subsequently became Nazi collaborators.

An illustration of the true significance and the limits of Russian Masonry's power is given in Roman Gul's autobiography *Ya unes Rossiyu,*[19] a work frequently quoted in Russia under *glasnost*. Gul, a well-known

17. *Russkoye delo* (Petrograd), 2 (1991).

18. For instance, Lolli Zamoisky, *Za fasadom masonskogo khrama* (Moscow, 1990), a book that could, with a few changes, have appeared twenty or thirty years earlier.

19. Two vols. (New York, 1984).

émigré writer, arrived in Paris in 1933, having been arrested for a while by the Nazis following their accession to power. He had great difficulty in obtaining a French residence permit, and friends advised him to get in touch with one Margulis, the head of a lodge, who had been for a short time a minister in one of the White governments. Margulis advised him to join a Masonic lodge, in the belief that in view of the close links between French and Russian Masons, it would be easy to assist the stateless and homeless Gul. Gul notes dryly that the Masons could not help him; the mighty lodges, which could allegedly trigger revolutions at the drop of a hat, were quite powerless to obtain a routine document for one of their members.[20]

More recently, the term *Masonophobia* has entered the Russian language. A Russian psychiatrist has described a public appearance by Nikolai Burlyaev, a well-known Russian actor, in a Moscow church. Burlyaev at a certain stage in his life reached the conclusion that Mikhail Lermontov was not killed in a duel by a fellow officer whom he had offended (the hitherto accepted version), but fell victim to a Judeo-Masonic conspiracy. Burlyaev produced a movie on these lines, which was widely derided. In his public appearance Burlyaev tried to justify his approach.

Mikhail Buyanov, the psychiatrist, sadly reached the conclusion that while *Masonophobia* was a kind of ideological madness, characterized by various fears and extreme suspicion akin to delirious zealotry or perhaps paranoia, it was well beyond the competence of the medical profession to extend help in such cases. The psychological type tending toward such mental defects had always existed, and probably always would.[21] It is easy to ridicule the fantasies of the proponents of *Zhidomasonstvo*, but since they are articles of faith it is pointless rationally to discuss them; they are immune to critical investigation and refutation. Not many people of education will accept them but they are, after all, not intended mainly for educated people's consumption.

20. Gul, *Rossiyu,* vol. 2, pp. 179–88.

21. Mikhail Buyanov, "Masonofobia," *Novoye vremya* 42 (1991).

Chapter Four

"DAMN THEE, BLACK DEVIL": THE ORTHODOX CHURCH AND THE RADICAL RIGHT

WHAT ROLE DID THE ORTHODOX CHURCH PLAY in the rise of the Black Hundred and in the emergence of an extreme right-wing ideology? Most Christian churches, not only in Russia, were gravitating around the turn of the last century toward conservative, right-wing parties for obvious historical reasons: The church was not just closely identified with the political establishment, it was part of it; its interests and ideas were those of the establishment. Those who challenged the existing order were rationalists, unbelievers, enemies of state and church. True, in every country there were some farsighted churchmen who understood that if the church wanted to retain its influence, it had to move with the times, and that this, in view of the rapid cultural and social change, involved church reform. But by and large, the antireform forces were stronger and the pace of change in all Christian churches, outside some intellectual circles, was slow up to the end of the Second World War.

The identification of church and state was nowhere more pronounced than in Russia; the Orthodox church was the handmaiden of the tsarist regime. This shielded the church from competition with other denominations, but the price to be paid was enormous. The great majority of the intelligentsia had lost interest in religion; in all classes, even among the peasants, there was a great measure of contempt for the stupidity, the venality, and the low moral standards of the clergy. The devastating picture presented in Tolstoy's *Resurrection* corresponded more with public views than did Dostoyevsky's Father Zosima. There were few more faithful supporters of the political order than the writer Nikolai Leskov. Yet again, the picture drawn by Leskov of one of the central figures in the church at the time, Ioann of Kronstadt, was devastating.[1]

The estrangement between society and church began well before radicalism had an impact on the Russian intelligentsia. Pushkin had apparently never heard of his contemporary Serafim of Saransk—the central religious figure of his time—and vice versa; they would not have been very interested, had they known of each other. Nor had any tsar since Peter I shown great interest in religion; some, like Nikolai II, became devout followers of faith healers, but this was a far cry from true religion. The Orthodox church was extremely formalistic and rigid, emphasizing the minutiae of the liturgy and the observation of various commandments. It had a wonderful ritual, but the appeal to the heart was not of equal importance. The singing in church was uplifting, but hardly anyone understood the words, because they were in (modified) Church Slavonic. There was talk about Christian love, humility, and charity but the preoccupation with superstition, evil spirits, and Satan himself was equally pronounced. True, at all times throughout the last two centuries there had been devout, truly religious church leaders and followers. Many Russians in search of a spiritual home went to monasteries such as Optina Pustyn, not far from Moscow, to sit at the feet of *startsy*, to unburden their souls, and to look for spiritual guidance. After 1905 some prominent intellectuals were reconverted to the Orthodox church and there were some hesitant steps toward church reform. Various church commissions were convened, but when the Revolution came in 1917 not much progress had been made.

The ideology of the extreme right in Russia drew heavily on certain religious elements. Specifically, this refers to the identity of state (and nationalism) and church. This tradition goes back a long time; Sergei of Radonezh, the best-known and most popular of all Russian saints, is revered not so much because of his specific spiritual qualities—he is a largely legendary figure, who left no record in writing—but for the fact that he blessed Prince Dmitri and his warriors on the eve of the battle of Kulikovo, the great victory over the Tatars. Sergei was a national hero, and one of the founders of the union between church and state which was so characteristic of Russian history and had such fateful consequences.[2]

1. In *Polunochniki* ("Midnight Talks"), 1891; also his *Cathedral People* and Pomyalovsky's *Sketches of a Seminary* (1855–1863). Leskov's grandfather had been a priest.

2. The six hundredth anniversary of the death of Sergei of Radonezh, in 1992, was an occasion for major celebration in the church and among the Russian right.

Another central issue was the apocalyptic-eschatological element in church thinking. Around the middle of the nineteenth century, Fyodor Bukharev, a cleric and religious thinker trying to interpret the book of Revelation, wrote about Russia's specific mission in the world; this mission, said Bukharev, included the liberation of Near Eastern peoples from the Muslim yoke. These ideas were rejected by the church at the time, but the symbols and concepts of the book of Revelation—the pale horse and the star called wormwood, the four beasts, the great dragon and the great serpent, the war in heaven, the mark of the beast, the great power of the devil, whose time is short and who is therefore full of anger—all this continued to have a major impact on religious thinking right up to the Revolution on the most primitive and the most sophisticated levels. Without this apocalyptic element it is very difficult to understand the reception of the *Protocols of the Elders of Zion* and similar propagandistic writings. Whereas in Bukharev's day apocalyptic thought had been in an essentially optimistic vein (Russia's liberating mission) it became more and more a matter of gloom and foreboding as the century drew to its close. Apocalypticism became fashionable in Russian literature, as witness Bryusov's *Pale Horse*, Rozanov's *Apocalypse of Our Time*, Solovyov's *A Story of the Antichrist*, and Andrei Bely's *Vision of the Coming Kingdom of the Beast*. It is difficult to decide whether this was a slightly belated manifestation of fin-de-sièclism, or whether there was something specifically Russian in this mood; for similar poems and novels about the end of the world being at hand appeared also in other countries. But there was certainly better reason to feel apprehensive in Russia than elsewhere.

Part of the clergy freely uttered their feelings of doom. Ioann of Kronstadt, the best-known and most beloved churchman of his time, wrote in 1907, not long before his death, that the tsardom was close to collapse. If things remained as they were, if godless people and reckless anarchists remained unpunished, and if Russia would not cleanse itself, it would be destroyed as so many ancient kingdoms had been, for its godlessness and lawlessness.

The *starets* (Elder) Varsonofi of Optina Pustyn (who was the spiritual adviser of Sergei Nilus of *Protocols* fame) had proclaimed a few years earlier that terrible times were ahead, that the Antichrist had appeared but that the world had not recognized him, that the networks of the devil could be seen from the monastery, that soon most altars would be destroyed.

At this stage a quandary facing the historian should be noted. There are no written records in this as in some other cases; one has to rely on such unreliable sources as Nilus and his biographer Strezhev. Varsonofi may have expressed such views but there is no certainty that he did; Nilus made him sound too much like his own ravings.[3]

To give yet another example, Black Hundred literature would invoke the authority of Serafim of Saransk to the effect that there was no redemption for Jews and similar sinners. It is very doubtful whether St. Serafim ever said anything to this effect. But he did say that the Jews were a holy people and pleasing to God.[4]

There have been similar warnings by revivalist preachers at almost all times and in most countries, but they have appeared at the margins of church and society, and their impact has been ephemeral in modern times. In Russia, on the other hand, the response was far greater; Ioann was not an eccentric but a leading authority on prayer, a model churchman, and a *thaumaturg* (a faith healer). He was more widely known than the patriarch himself despite his lowly status in the hierarchy; he was a "black," secular, married priest and could therefore not aspire to be promoted to the higher echelons of the church. When Chekhov wrote a friend about his trip to Sakhalin, he reported that he had seen in every house a picture of Father Ioann, who was also a honorary member of the Union of Russian People and the first to consecrate their flags.[5]

He was born in 1829 in a poor village in northern Russia, in a family that had had close ties with the church for many generations. He had great difficulty in learning as a child, but found refuge in prayer early on. He received his higher education at the St. Petersburg religious academy, graduating without distinction at the bottom of his class. He decided not to become a monk; having been appointed priest at the cathedral of Kronstadt he married the daughter of his predecessor, but vowed sexual abstinence—much to the chagrin of his wife, who complained to his superior.

Kronstadt, which was the port of St. Petersburg, was at the time a difficult place; it contained poor people, beggars, and the homeless who had been expelled from St. Petersburg. Ioann soon showed his great ability

3. *Veche (Novgorod)*, 7 (1991), p. 16. Varsonofi (Pavel Plachankov), a former Cossack colonel and a gentleman of independent means, became a monk relatively late in life and was *skete* superior of Optina from 1906 to 1912. Leonard J. Stanton, *Optina Pustyn in the Russian Literary Imagination* (New York, 1992), p. 21; for the faking of evidence, see pp. 280–300.

4. Alexander Nezhny, *Ogonyok* 45 (1991), reports that this did not prevent the church in 1991 from inviting the new Black Hundred from Moscow and Nizhni Novgorod to act as a guard of honor at the rededication of the shrine of St. Serafim in Diveyevo.

5. There is a substantial literature on Ioann Sergeyev (his original name). The most detailed works are Alla Selawry, *Johannes von Kronstadt, Starez Russlands* (Basel, 1981); A. Semanov Tian-Shansky, *Otets Ioann Kronstadsky* (New York, 1955); I. K. Sursky, *Otets Ioann Kronstadsky*, 2 vols. (Belgrade, 1938–1941).

as a preacher, spiritual adviser, and teacher. He attracted the poor to the church; the children adored him; wherever he appeared in the streets, masses of people would follow him. He asked for (and obtained) the help of the rich for social work—homes for the poor, schools, hostels, and hospitals. Kronstadt became a model of churchly success, and since Ioann also acquired fame as a faith healer, sick people all over Russia turned to him. On some days he would receive six thousand letters and telegrams asking for his blessing. When he traveled, special train compartments and river steamers were put at his disposal, and strong police units had to guide him through the masses. No politician, not even the tsar enjoyed a similar genuine popularity at the time. When Alexander III died in the Crimea in 1894 he called for Ioann to be with him at his deathbed.

Some of his writings were published. The great religious scholar Georgi Fedotov has called him a genius of prayer and a teacher of prayer.[6] Prayer, as Ioann saw it, was the "constant feeling of our infirmity or spiritual poverty, the sanctification of the soul, the foretaste of future blessedness, angelic bliss, the heavenly rain, refreshing watering and fertilizing the ground of the soul, the power and strength of the soul and body, the purifying and freshening of the mental air, the enlightenment of the countenance, the hour of the spirit, the golden link, uniting the creature to the Creator. . . ."

Like other Orthodox preachers, Ioann was also heavily preoccupied with the forces of darkness. He wrote that the young and those leading the life of the sinful world tended to believe that there was a devil somewhere, but that he was not in any way near them and that his wickedness did not concern them. Only the older and wiser knew that Satan was a heavy burden, pitiless, injuring all.

There is nothing in Ioann's writing that had not been said before; his strength was not in his ideas or in the written word but in his personality. There was more than a streak of mysticism in him, and some of his superiors, including Pobedonostsev, distrusted him, rightly as it would appear, for even in his lifetime his closest followers, the Ioannity, declared his divinity. They thought of him as a new Christ, and established yet another religious sect; the house where he had been born became a shrine attracting many pilgrims.

Father Ioann disclaimed any interest in politics. Yet he was an active participant in the affairs of the day, and his politics were those of the extreme right. He was an implacable foe of all those challenging authority, not just the revolutionaries (for whom he asked the most severe punish-

6. G. Fedotov, *A Treasury of Russian Spirituality* (New York, 1948), p. 346.

ment) but even those advocating moderate, liberal reform. This brought him into conflict with public opinion and at the time of the sailors' revolt in Kronstadt in 1905–1906 he had to leave town temporarily. However, this did not in any way affect his popularity among the common people. A naïve man and a religious fundamentalist, he genuinely believed that his views were above politics; the alliance between church and state was for him not a political but a religious article of faith. When the Kishinev pogrom occurred, well before the Revolution of 1905, he was at first critical of the blood libel. But after an emissary had been sent to give him certain explanations, he justified the pogrom, apologizing for his earlier misinterpretation.

How to justify the murder of children and old people against the background of Christian love? Ioann obviously thought that the Jews were tools of Satan and as such not worthy of compassion. He belonged to the bitterest foes of Tolstoy, a critic of the Orthodox church establishment, and his followers for whom he thought no punishment was severe enough.

Ioann died in 1908, but his fame lived on. While synods of the Orthodox church in Russia, despite considerable pressure, have so far not canonized him, he has been a central figure in religious practice in the Orthodox church in America, whose publishing house is named after him.

In the religious revival now taking place in Russia, Ioann is one of the main figures, constantly invoked, in particular by the extreme right. It could well be that many are attracted by Ioann the great man of prayer, but for others it is precisely his extreme and uncompromising views that make him a revered and saintly figure, a national as well as a church hero. In any case Ioann of Kronstadt is essential to our understanding of the attitude of wide circles inside the church toward the extreme right.

The church as such wanted to remain distant from politics. While (as Professor G. Freeze has put it) Nikolai's regime played upon popular religious sentiment to "resacralize autocracy and bolster its legitimacy," the church had been moving toward greater autonomy since the middle of the nineteenth century. Thus it was left to local bishops to deal with the Black Hundred.

No one knows with any certainty what the political preferences of Russia's forty thousand priests were. Certainly not all of them were conservative: Some of the leading church journals were critical of the government and despised the Black Hundred. Among the priests who were members of the first and second Duma, a majority were liberal or relatively liberal. Of the forty-nine priests elected to the third Duma, more than half belonged to the extreme right. There were unrest and strikes in most theological seminaries. Dr. Dubrovin accused Metropolitan Antony of St.

Petersburg of harboring dangerous radicals and criticized him for refusing to officiate at meetings of the Black Hundred. (Antony had declared: "I consider you terrorists. . . .")[7]

Yet Antony was by no means a liberal; he had excommunicated Tolstoy. By and large the Holy Synod was cautiously conservative, and became more so after 1906. It ordered bishops to punish priests who had been too radical. Archbishop Yakov of Yaroslavl, who had shown coldness toward the SRN, was transferred to an out-of-the-way diocese. Broadly speaking, the lower clergy tended to be more critical of government policies, whereas the majority of the supreme leadership was conservative, and some were open supporters of the far right. Among these were Vladimir of Moscow, Aleksei of Taurida, Flavian of Kiev, and particularly Anatoli of Volhynia and Hermogen of Saratov.

It was owing to the support of this wing of the church that the Black Hundred received a flying start. Their publications, such as the *Pochayevski listok*, issued at Pochayev monastery in Volhynia, preached in every issue that reform was sinful and that the Jews were plotters trying to weaken the Russian state, so that the great Jewish international financiers could enslave the Russian people.[8] After the Bialystok pogrom *Pochayevski listok* reported that the Jews themselves had arranged the bloodbath, a theme that was taken up by Black Hundred authors in 1990. A typical issue of this periodical (and of the daily newspaper *Pochayevskie izvestiya*) would carry a banner headline such as "The Jews, Our Enslavers and Despoilers"; there were pamphlets entitled "The Enemies of the Human Race," which argued that the Jews were striving for world domination with the aid of the Masons, the intelligentsia, and the revolutionary parties by means of secrecy, lying, trickery, hypocrisy, and treason.[9] Among many other things, they were responsible for the defeat of the Russian armies in the war against Japan. These were in all essential points the basic tenets of Black Hundred propaganda.

It would be tedious to engage in a more detailed analysis of the sayings and writings of certain church leaders from their pulpits and their press organs. Many of these publications were not just tendentious but inflam-

7. Quoted in John S. Curtiss, *Church and State in Russia: The Last Years of the Empire, 1900–1917* (New York, 1940), p. 210.

8. The driving force was the monk Iliodor (Trufanov). A Don Cossack, he was originally a close associate of Rasputin but later fell out with him and published a violent attack, "The Mad Monk of Russia." Iliodor was exiled to Tsaritsyn, where he became the object of a hysterical cult, mainly among women. He was eventually defrocked and emigrated to America, where he died in 1958.

9. Many more examples appear in Curtiss, *Church and State*, pp. 254ff.

matory, calls for pogroms and bloodshed. Ioann of Kronstadt in one of his sermons in 1906 also said that the Jews brought the pogroms upon themselves; the pogrom was the hand of God punishing them for their grievous sins against the government. Thus the Black Hundred could act with good conscience; not only did they have the backing of the tsar, they were carrying out a mission on behalf of God. In one of his writings the monk Iliodor described a vision of a battle between two camps. The one was the army of the Black Hundred; the other consisted of many classes and races, but the Jews were always prominent and in front. Eventually God appeared and together with the angels and saints led the Black Hundred to victory over Satan's band, killing them or forcing them to flee.

Such preaching and visions eventually became an embarrassment for the Holy Synod, which in a special resolution (dated February 1907) denounced the activities of Iliodor and his protectors as unworthy of the Holy Church. (It took, however, another five years to bring him to heel.) But at almost the same time (in March 1908) the synod passed another resolution encouraging the bishops not just to permit but to bless the participation of the clergy in the activities of the SRN.[10]

To summarize the attitude of the church during the critical years: Most church leaders certainly gravitated to the right; the Black Hundred as such were never condemned. The lower clergy was divided; many remained neutral; some helped those persecuted by the tsarist authorities and the Black Hundred. The SRN had the support of an influential segment of the clergy and without this support they would not have been a force of any consequence.

At the same time a religious revival took place, but largely outside the church; neither Dostoyevsky nor Solovyov, its two most influential thinkers, were professional theologians. Dostoyevsky pointed out the polarity in Russian religious life most succinctly in the juxtaposition of Father Zosima and Father Ferapont in the *Brothers Karamazov*. The former represented *sophia*, the holy wisdom of all-embracing love, a black cleric; the other stood for the formalist, ascetic, fear-striking and fear-stricken religion.[11] But while Dostoyevsky the religious thinker clearly sympathized with Zosima, as an aggressive nationalist and commentator he clearly preferred Ferapont. While not sentimentally pro-Jewish, Solovyov's attitude was altogether different. He wrote that as a Slav, he felt a great guilt in the presence of Jews and would like to expiate it:

10. Ibid., pp. 272–73.

11. On the polarity see N. Zernov, *The Religious Renaissance of the Twentieth Century* (London, 1963), and the works of K. Mochulsky and others on Dostoyevsky. For a survey of the literature, see Sven Linner, *Starets Zosima* (Stockholm, 1973).

The Jewish question is essentially a question of truth and justice. Justice is trampled on the face of the Jews because there is not even the slightest excuse for the persecution to which they have been subjected; the accusations leveled against them by the anti-Semites fail to hold up even under the most lenient criticism—they are, for the most part, wicked lies.[12]

It is not surprising that present-day right-wing ideologists have little use for Solovyov, whereas Dostoyevsky, the political publicist not the religious thinker, is invoked on many occasions.

The new religious thinking continued with the publication of *Vekhi*, with Berdyaev, Sergei Bulgakov, and other now world-famous religious thinkers. But their influence was greater in the West than inside the Orthodox church. To many Orthodox believers these new converts were suspect for a number of reasons: They put too much emphasis on personal, spiritual freedom, which, their critics claimed, was not in the tradition of the church. They were too much influenced by Western thinking and while they were Russian nationalists, their nationalism was not extreme enough. They were too much preoccupied with meditations about religion and too little with the discipline of the church. Above all, their cardinal sin was ecumenism; they were too well disposed toward other Christian churches, not insistent enough on the exclusive mission of Eastern Orthodoxy. From the beginning to this very day these religious thinkers have been bitterly attacked by the Black Hundred element in the Orthodox church and treated with suspicion by mainstream Orthodox leadership. A writer named Bulatovich argued in 1909 that *Vekhi* was the work of seven Russo-Jewish *intelligenty*. Bulgakov, as Bulatovich saw it, was correct in diagnosing with Dostoyevsky that a legion of devils had entered the gigantic body of Russia and shaken it into convulsions, tormenting and mutilating it. But he had identified the wrong devils, "for the name of the legion is Jew."[13] There leads a direct line from this kind of thinking to a comment published in 1991 in a journal of the extreme right in Moscow: "I hope that archpriest Alexander Men has atoned for his sin of ecumenism through his death. For as St. Serafim taught, there is no way for a Jew to salvation other than to share the martyrdom of our Lord."[14] (Alexander Men was an archpriest of (half) Jewish origin, the author of many important theological works. He was killed in 1990 in a village near Moscow in circumstances that have not

12. V. Solovyov, *Stati po yevreiskomu voprosu* (Berlin, 1925), p. 48.

13. *Russkoye znamya* (1909), quoted in Christopher Reed, *Religion, Revolution and the Russian Intelligentsia 1900–1912* (London, 1979); for a scurrilous present-day attack on Berdyaev, see *Slovo*, 9 (1991), p. 72.

14. A Udabov in *Russkoye voskresenie* 4 (12) (1991). On the same page of the journal the following statement appears: "When Dostoyevsky said that beauty will save the world he meant, no doubt, the beauty of Russian arms" (I. Kobrin).

been clarified, possibly by an assassin of the extreme right.)

These are, needless to say, extreme voices and it would be misleading to generalize on the basis of the writings of a handful of fanatics. Present-day political attitudes of the church will preoccupy us later on; there is much evidence that the problems facing the Orthodox church around the turn of the century have not disappeared. The relationship between the church and the extreme right is still a legitimate subject for investigation and discussion. Before turning to other topics, mention should be made of one strand of thought that is specifically Russian inasmuch as contemporary right-wing thought is concerned: the preoccupation with Satanism. It is clearly pre-fascist and its origins and function should be reviewed, however briefly.

Satan and the Antichrist

The most important link between Black Hundred doctrine and the Ortho-dox church, and the issue essential for an understanding of the ideology of the extreme right, is the idea of Satan and the coming of Antichrist. The concept of conflict between the forces of good and evil exists in many religions; in the Manichaean religions it is, of course, more pronounced than in others. In Judaism and Christianity Satan is a malignant power that hates God and seeks to destroy all that God has created. In the New Testament Satan becomes even more sinister and powerful, a central figure, under the direct inspiration of the devil. According to early Christian writers he would appear just before the Second Coming of Christ, stay in power for three and a half years (either 1,260 or 1,290 days), rule with an iron rod and then be defeated by Christ. According to early commentators he would be a Jew, the son of a whore of the tribe of Dan. According to some other writers the Antichrist would be a reincarnation of Nero, and according to Wycliffe, Hus, and Luther, there was much reason to believe that the Roman pope was, in fact, the Antichrist.

These ideas played a very important role in the medieval writings of the Russian Orthodox church and also in its iconography. Very often the devil appeared as a snake, but frequently as a dragon, sometimes as a lion, an ape, a wolf, or a goat.[15] The devil would often be depicted as a Jew, but not seldom as a black man (an allusion to the kingdom of darkness). Sometimes he would appear as a monk, or even in the figure of Christ. According to yet other sources he will be a seven-headed beast, waging war against the faithful, defeating many kings. All but a few staunch believers would be

15. T. A. Riazanovsky, *Demonologia v drevnerusskoi literature* (Moscow, 1915), pp. 47 ff.

deceived by him, but he could be identified by the number of the beast: 666. Shortly before his final defeat he will rebuild the temple of Solomon, destroyed by the Romans.

The propaganda material of the Black Hundred from the beginning to the present day is replete with references to the Book of Revelation and various apocryphal writings referring to the coming of Antichrist. Indeed, without a knowledge of these sources it is difficult to understand either pictures (the "beast" in various fantastic appearances) or text.[16]

The coming of the Antichrist was predicted in Western Europe for the year 1000, and later on for 1184, 1186, 1229, 1345, 1385, 1516, and other dates in between.[17] It was said that he would subvert Christianity by terror, miracles, fraud, and false teaching, making war against the saints. There were unending discussions as to the origins of the Antichrist, his nature, and the ways of his defeat (by Christ or by one of Christ's agents such as the Archangel Michael). The most important supporters of the Antichrist were the Jews, for having rejected Jesus they were prone to be deceived more easily than others.

In the sixteenth century (at the very latest) the theme of the Antichrist began to fade in the West; some theologians regarded him as an institution rather than a person, others thought that he would never be entirely defeated. The dogma of Lucifer has not been disavowed in the Catholic church, and indeed cannot be. But in actual fact little use has been made of it. The church has recognized diabolical machinations only on the rarest occasions over the last centuries.

For the humanists and also some latter-day theologians the devil became a grotesque and comic figure (Ben Jonson's *The Devil Is an Ass*). But among many Russians there was no room for such levity. Like Dostoyevsky's Stavrogin they believed in a personal devil not just an allegory. Nor were they willing to entertain *apokatastasis*—the idea voiced by Origen, one of the most influential church fathers, that there was salvation even for the devil and the evil spirits.[18]

In addition to the devil and Satan the Orthodox church has been

---

16. Thus, to give but one example, one writer noted that it was not by accident that the first issue of *Ogonyok*, the liberal weekly published after the coup of August 1991 featured the number 666 on its front page. *Polozhenie del* 3 (1991). Virtually all recent periodicals of the extreme right, such as *Puls tushina, Nashe,* and *Pamyat,* have drawings reminiscent of Hieronymus Bosch, Breughel, or Doré ("Satan enthroned in Hell") and earlier such artists—executed, alas, with less mastery.

17. R. K. Emerson, *Antichrist in the Middle Ages* (Seattle, 1981), p. 54.

18. These teachings were banned by church councils in the sixth century. J. B. Russell, *Satan* (Ithaca, N.Y., 1981), pp. 144ff. Russell's four volumes on diabology are the most authoritative work now available. Unfortunately, he deals with the Eastern churches only in passing.

heavily preoccupied with the existence of innumerable demons (*besy*, as in the title of Dostoyevsky's novel). These demons tormented men and women by causing illnesses (including madness) and also afflicted people spiritually. Most Russian saints, including Serafim, reported terrible torment caused by demons—without, however, specifying details. Women and monks were most likely to be affected by demonic or Satanic forces.[19] On occasion the demons would tempt men and women, often sexually, but also in other ways, as by inducing them to consume alcohol. For reasons that are not entirely obvious, wandering clowns and musicians (*skomorokhy*) were also frequently considered servants of Satan.

There was no way to exorcise demons except through prayer and the help of the Archangel Michael. The belief in the coming of the Antichrist was particularly strong in Russia before the year 1492, when seven thousand years had allegedly passed since the creation of the universe.

Some of the elements of Russian demonology go back to pre-Christian times; others reached Russia by way of Byzantium. But there was also a certain Bogomil influence.[20] While at one time the belief in Satan and demons was fairly universal in Christian Europe, it has persisted longer and more strongly in Russia than elsewhere and it has taken on pronounced political overtones over the last hundred and fifty years.

Small sects believing in Satanism or, conversely, the existence of an all-powerful hidden hand, continue to exist in many lands, but they nowhere constitute a political force of any importance. The decisive element in Nazism was not religious superstition but a pseudo-scientific racial theory; Hitler and his paladins never felt fear of the overwhelming strength of some hostile sinister force, and the idea of the coming of the Antichrist was far from them. True, certain Nazi and fascist ideas were religious in origin, but fascism moved several major steps beyond these origins, shedding in the process most of the commandments as well as the taboos of Christianity.

In Russia, on the other hand, for reasons that may not be readily explicable, the medieval tradition has proved stronger. For a not inconsiderable part of the population the preoccupation with Satan and his demons seems to have been as strong as that with God and his angels. This obsession was widespread under Stalin, when omnipresent demons—in the guise of saboteurs, spies, and other enemies—put up a last desperate stand

19. Riazanovsky, *Demonologia*, pp. 61ff. On pagan demons, see V. Mansikka, *Die Religion der Ostslaven* (Helsinki, 1922).

20. The Bogomils believed that the creation of earth had been delegated by God to Satan. All of creation was basically evil, except things spiritual.

before the final victory of socialism. (Stalin's doctrine that the class struggle would become sharper with the gradual victory of socialism may well have been derived from the idea of the last desperate stand of Satan.)

In recent years many elements of demonology, and the belief in the Antichrist, have been resurrected in the doctrine of the Russian far right, not just in the abstract, but with reference to concrete political enemies, the sinister forces representing Satan. Paradoxically, the destruction of communism has provoked a reaction in these circles that much resembles the reaction to the victory of communism in 1917. Both times radical change was interpreted as the work of the devil. Satan brought communism to power in 1917, and Satan destroyed it in 1991. It remains an open question whether this is merely another manifestation of religious fundamentalism—*nullus diabolus, nullus redemptor* ("no devil, no god")—or whether, as Freud and others have thought, the belief in the devil is yet another case of negative projection—seeing in others the very same negative elements we refuse to recognize in ourselves.[21]

---

21. Jung, as so often, took a divergent position; the modern tendency to dismiss the devil was merely the fear of facing the reality of evil.

Part Two

COMMUNISM AND NATIONALISM, 1917–1987

Chapter Five

SOVIET PATRIOTISM

THE BOLSHEVIK REVOLUTION OF 1917 was led by men who believed in proletarian internationalism; they thought it the first of a series of uprisings culminating in the world revolution. The anthem of the new era was the "Internationale"; written by a Frenchman, it did not mention Russia or the Russian people, but stated that there would be a total break with the past and that the future belonged to mankind, not to any one people. Russian nationalism was out of fashion; the traditional heroes and symbols of the former regime were derided and discarded, the nobility decimated, the church persecuted.

But with all this it soon appeared that the new rulers had no desire to sacrifice Russia on the altar of a world revolution that did not materialize. Nor had they any wish to liquidate the Russian empire. Finland, the Baltic countries, and Poland gained independence, but this was inevitable given Russia's military weakness at the time. On the other hand, the Red Army invaded the Ukraine, Georgia, Central Asia, and the Far East, liquidating separatist movements. Many hundreds of officers of the old tsarist army fought with the Reds, not because they were enamored of Lenin and Trotsky, but because they vaguely felt that in the long run communism was the best hope for a resurgence of a strong Russia. Among the émigrés in the 1920s there was a growing belief that internationalism was a passing phase and that the Bolsheviks, whether they wanted to or not—Hegel's famous "cunning of reason"—were becoming good Russian patriots in the course of time. True, some of the more extravagantly stated expectations were premature; the process was to take considerably longer than some thought. The church was still persecuted, the heroes of Russian history still denigrated, and among the key figures of the regime there were still too many men of non-Russian origin.

But the long-term trend was unmistakable. Once Stalin had proclaimed the building of socialism in one country, the reemergence of patriotism was inevitable. True, it was now called "Soviet patriotism," but in fact it led to the restoration of Russian traditions and values. The "nihilistic" (Marxist) attitude to Russian history was frowned upon, many cultural traditions were restored, *rodina* ("fatherland") came to be as frequently invoked as socialism. True, the retreat from international to national socialism was not unconnected with the emergence of similar such movements in other parts of Europe, notably in Germany. But whatever the reason, the non-Russians who had been so prominent during the Revolution and the civil war gradually disappeared and were replaced by Molotov and Voroshilov, and later by Zhdanov and Malenkov. The supreme leader, to be sure, was still a Georgian, but his Russian patriotism was second to no one's. More and more frequently he would denounce the former negative attitudes to the traditions of the great Russian people.

Even before the outbreak of the Second World War Stalin had gone well beyond Lenin in rehabilitating Russian nationalism. Lenin had always maintained that there were two Russian cultural traditions: the radical-democratic trend, to which bolshevism was the heir, and the reactionary trend, conservative and monarchist, from which Communists had to dissociate themselves. But under Stalin not only was Peter I, the great reformer, rehabilitated, but so were Dmitri Donskoi, Ivan Kalita, Ivan IV ("the Terrible") and all those with the historical merit of expanding Russia's borders and making it a great power. As one student of Soviet patriotism has noted, tsarist patriotic historians had dealt with Ivan IV in an excessively objective and even cosmopolitan—that is to say, critical—spirit, compared with the post-1940 Soviet version, which was almost uncritically enthusiastic.[1]

The nineteenth-century tsars still remained in the bad books of the regime, but their generals, such as Suvorov and Kutuzov, became heroes to be emulated. By 1938 the study of Russian had become compulsory all over the Soviet Union, and with a very few exceptions the non-Russian languages had to be written in the Cyrillic alphabet. When Hitler gave the

1. This refers to Ilovaisky's *History of Russia*. See Frederick Barghoorn, *Soviet Russian Nationalism* (New York, 1956), p. 216.

order to attack the Soviet Union in June 1941 and Russia had to fight for her national existence, this became the "Great Patriotic War," even though Marx had decided that workers had no fatherland. Stalin addressed the Russian people not as comrades but as brothers and sisters, calling them to resist the invader as Dmitri Donskoi, Minin and Pozharsky, and the defenders of Holy Russia against Napoleon had done. Slavic solidarity was invoked and the Orthodox church welcomed as an ally against the Germans.

When the war against Germany ended, Stalin proclaimed that it had been won mainly owing to the courage and the other sterling qualities of the great Russian people, and after Japan's defeat he said that this was the revenge for tsarist Russia's defeat in 1905. No wonder that a great many foreign observers, including Russian émigrés, reached the conclusion that the Soviet Union had moved full circle back to the traditions of Russian nationalism.

Events between 1945 and Stalin's death seemed to confirm such an appraisal. True, there was no move toward greater freedom, as many had expected, but the emphasis on Russian nationalism certainly became ever more pronounced: This was the age of the struggle against "cosmopolitanism" in which kowtowing to the West became a cardinal sin. Historians and writers, composers and painters, philosophers and scientists were denounced because they had not fully done justice to the leading role of Russian culture in the past. Russian priority in most scientific and technological fields was claimed, including the invention of the telephone and radio. It was said that Russian scientists had traditionally shown excessive respect toward foreigners, whereas most Westerners, except for a few progressives, had shown disdain toward Russian culture and the Russian people. Westerners had always claimed (and were claiming now), that Russia was a backward country; thus they tried to undermine the Russian people's spirit of patriotic pride.

This, then, was the party line during the late Stalinist era, propagated in countless editorials and echoed in books, plays, and movies. It is certain that not all such propaganda was believed by the Russian people, let alone the intelligentsia, but it was understood that this was the official doctrine, from which no open dissent was permitted. Among the victims of this xenophobic campaign were not a few who had been singled out simply because they were not of Russian descent, even though they had never uttered a word critical of Russian history or culture.

Even an extreme Russian nationalist could not have found fault with Soviet communism in 1950 as far as its patriotic fervor was concerned. Whatever its other sins of commission or omission, Soviet patriotism to all intents and purposes was Russian patriotism. While Russian patriotic traditions were encouraged in every way, no such encouragement was given (except halfheartedly and for short periods) to the other peoples of the Soviet Union. According to official doctrine they owed a debt to the Russians; even if they had been annexed by force, this had been, at least in retrospect, a positive development. For, as a result, they had become part of the most progressive union of peoples, headed by the benevolent elder brother, who, as the new anthem announced, "merged for ever the unbreakable union of free republics."

Whether Russia gained or lost as the result of the imposed union is immaterial. In many instances it had to support the weaker younger brethren: A price had to be paid for an imperial mission. But belief in this mission was strong, and the Russian leadership was willing to put up with the burden. There was, of course, opposition to Russian tutelage among the subject nations; it is impossible to judge how strong that dissent was at the time because the secret police saw to it that there were no open manifestations of discontent.

The non-Russian republics were doubly unfree—ruled by a tyrannical system, and furthermore by one that was essentially foreign. Nevertheless, separatist aspirations were probably not as widespread and intense as in later years, except in the formerly independent nations such as the Baltic states. There was a feeling at the time that belonging to a prestigious club had certain advantages. Furthermore, in the post-Stalin period the local leadership in the non-Russian republics was given a much freer hand—which, more often than not, was used for personal gain by these leaders. Sympathy vanished in the same measure as the "club" lost its prestige. Similar developments have taken place in other parts of the world; no one wants to belong to a club that has no power, no influence, and no prestige, and which can provide no benefits.

Looking back on Stalin's rule, one can see that Russian nationalists should have been, by and large, satisfied with the positive achievements of his reign. Many of them were, but others were still unhappy, for Marxism-Leninism continued to be the official state ideology, to which at least lip service had to be paid on every occasion. Since Marx was a German Jew and Lenin a *déraciné* Russian, this was clearly an unsatisfactory state of affairs. The spiritual values and ideals of the regime were still not those of eternal Russia.

By no means had all the pillars of the old regime been rehabilitated; the monarchy was still derided and the church was barely tolerated. No attention was paid to old monuments and churches bearing evidence of the glories of old Russia. The old Russian village, the eternal font of Russianism, had disappeared under the Communist regime. The young generation was educated in a spirit of materialism and not imbued with the values of old Russia. While Jews had disappeared from key positions in government and party (and, of course, from the army and the KGB) there were still too many of them in cultural and scientific life, and their impact was thought to be nefarious.

In brief, while bolshevism had turned into national socialism it was in many respects an uneasy and unsatisfactory compromise. The Soviet regime was not willing to admit that the overthrow of the tsarist regime and the Bolshevik revolution had been national disasters and that the wrong side had been victorious in the civil war.

Thus it came as no surprise that in the years after Stalin's death—and particularly in the 1960s, as the political reins were loosened—a revival of Russian nationalism took place on various levels. Gradually, a Russian party and something akin to a new Russian ideology emerged. This revival was by no means monolithic; it took place inside established organizations and journals, among dissidents and their samizdat. Some of the new nationalists were conservative, even essentially monarchist, while others gravitated toward national bolshevism—that is to say, a new synthesis between traditional Russian nationalism and Leninism-Stalinism. Some were Christian-religious, but among others there was a renaissance of neopagan thought. Some nationalists envisaged a new Russia that was free and democratic, even if it did not necessarily emulate the Western model of parliamentary democracy. Others preached unbridled chauvinism, racialism, even fascism, and had nothing but contempt for democratic ideas and institutions. Some of the dissidents of the right who fell foul of the regime were arrested and spent years in labor camps, but most did not, in contrast to the dissidents of the left. Dissident nationalist writers or painters would be subjected on occasion to criticism for straying too far from the party line, but most were not excluded from their professional associations. Was this because the right-wing nationalist deviation was considered less dangerous than the liberal-democratic? The history of the Soviet Union between 1935 and 1985 has shown that the system could integrate Russian nationalism without suffering any harm. It could not coexist with the ideas propagated by the democratic dissidents, because these undermined the very foundations of the regime.

It is interesting to compare the different treatment meted out to the academicians Sakharov and Shafarevich. Shafarevich had written a radical critique of socialism, which was published in the 1970s in Paris, as well as many similar essays. He signed various appeals by dissidents. Yet he was left in peace, whereas Sakharov, whose ideas at the time were those of a Western Social Democrat who did not reject socialism per se, was subjected to many years of relentless persecution. Sakharov wanted freedom for Russia; Shafarevich stood for a great, powerful Russia. The latter could be accommodated; the former was unacceptable.

The nationalists, unlike the liberals, had well-wishers and protectors among the supreme party leadership. The same is true with regard to the army command and in particular the political directorate of the Soviet army. The ideas propagated by the right appealed to the generals and marshals. These ideas were far more likely to inculcate a spirit of patriotism in young recruits than was the synthetic Leninist doctrine of the party, which had its uses as a liturgy on occasions of state but had lost all emotional appeal. The nationalist revival took place, as has been mentioned, both within the Soviet establishment and among dissident groups, and its main components ought to be reviewed in the following.

Religion

Religion has traditionally played a central part in Russian national ideology. To be Russian, Dostoyevsky said, is to be Orthodox. It was therefore not by accident that, parallel with the nationalist revival of the 1960s and 1970s, a religious resurgence took place. Not all who became active in church affairs gravitated to the right, nor was the reverse the case, but there was a significant overlap. Very often it is impossible to state with any certainty whether the inspiration of a certain individual or patriotic group was primarily religious or primarily nationalist.

The renewed interest in religion took various forms. Among intellectuals it became fashionable to collect icons and to display them in one's home; religious shrines were restored; books were published dealing with the Russian religious tradition and expressing regret that it had been destroyed by a crude, materialist, antireligious policy.

This revival took place outside the established church, which was firmly controlled by the party and the KGB. The patriarchate did not make serious efforts to extend its freedom of action and for this reason as well as for its close collaboration with the authorities it was attacked by the activists of the 1960s, such as Solzhenitsyn and the priests Yakunin, Dudko, and Eshelman.[2]

The truly important dissident Christian groups—such as VSKHSON, the All-Russian Social Christian Union for the Liberation of the People,

2. It is only fair to mention that when Metropolitan Nikolai tried to protest in 1960 against the party's increasingly stringent control of the church, he was unceremoniously deposed and replaced by a more pliable churchman. For a general historical survey of the period see Jane Ellis, *The Russian Orthodox Church: A Contemporary History* (London, 1986).

which had some thirty members and perhaps the same number of sympathizers—were not under the umbrella of the church. There was a Religious-
Philosophical Seminary in Moscow, and sundry small right-wing groups
headed by men such as Genadi Shimanov and Leonid Borodin, who were
to play a role of some significance under *glasnost*. The most important
journal was *Veche*, edited in the 1970s by Vladimir Osipov; its politics were
centrist, combining the demand for political freedom with Russian nationalist views in the tradition of the Slavophiles and Dostoyevsky. *Veche* was
not a monolithic journal but provided a platform to writers of different
persuasions.[3]

One essay that created a considerable commotion and provoked much
contradiction was written by "V. Gorsky": "Russian Messianism and the
New National Consciousness," a powerful and remarkably prophetic critique of both populism (communism) and Russian messianism. As the
author saw it, the messianic concept had gradually lost its religious content
and transformed itself into the idea of a "Great Russia," of Russians being
the only God-fearing people in the whole world, slated to revive and save
the world. According to Gorsky:

> Overcoming the national-messianic temptation is Russia's first and foremost task.
> Russia will not be able to rid itself of despotism until it rejects the idea of national
> greatness. For this reason it is not "national renaissance," but the struggle for freedom
> and spiritual values that must become the central creative idea of our future.[4]

The author foresaw the emergence of separatist, centrifugal forces which
would lead to the collapse of the Soviet empire: Not only the satellite
nations but the Baltic countries, the Ukraine, the Caucasus, and the people
of Central Asia would, without fail, demand their right to break away and
depart from the notorious "indissoluble union."

Such remarkably prophetic views were anathema to many Christian
dissidents such as Solzhenitsyn and Borodin who polemicized against
Gorsky. They rejected the charge of national messianism, arguing that the
Russian Revolution had taken place mainly because of foreign influences;
among its militant alien elements Jews, above all, had been very prominent.
It had nothing to do with the Russian ideological tradition but had occurred because a break with national conservatism had taken place. If

3. Other important publications were the *Vestnik* and *Mnogaya leta,* a collection of essays edited
by Shimanov. The *Vestnik* appeared in Paris but published articles written by authors living in
Russia. The same is true with regard to the Munich *Veche* of the 1980s, which was more
right-wing in inspiration than the samizdat journal by the same name.

4. *Vestnik,* 97, originally published in the samizdat collection *Metanoia 2.* An English translation
appeared in M. Meerson-Aksenov and Boris Shragin, *The Political, Social and Religious Thought
of Russian Samizdat* (Belmont, Mass., 1977), pp. 353–93.

Gorsky was putting the blame on the Russian national idea, he was guilty of the same sin the Bolsheviks had committed all along—denationalization, at a time when only nationalism could bring about a spiritual renaissance of the fatherland. Seen from this perspective, Russian messianism and Russophilism were a bugbear, a red herring; the real enemy was rootless cosmopolitanism. The task of a true patriot was to cultivate respect for the Russian national heritage, to promote the restoration of traditional Russian culture, and to encourage love of the fatherland and the Orthodox church.

Some critics went even further and expressed doubts whether Gorsky and other liberal Christian writers were really Russians by origin because their views were so remote from the feelings of a true Russian patriot. Some right-wing radicals reached the conclusion that the Soviet leadership, with all its sins and its antireligious bias, was ideologically closer to them than were the liberal, pro-Western, antireligious dissidents. (In the same way, a Catholic believer in liberation theology would find more in common with a Communist than with a fellow Christian who held conservative views.) The radicals called for a rapprochement between church and state, in which the majority of concessions would admittedly have to be made by the rulers since church activities were under such tight control.

The Communist party, needless to say, never responded to these overtures, but the groundwork was thus laid for the rapprochement that took place in the Gorbachev era between two wholly different camps—the conservative nationalists and the neo-Stalinists, who had little in common, except common enemies.

Nationalism was not the only issue confronting *Veche* and the other thinkers involved in the revival of religious values. There was the question of "modernism," which preoccupied all contemporary religions to some extent. Purely political problems such as the "Yellow Peril" played a part, as did the question of nationalities and above all, of the Jews. Attitudes toward other Christian churches, primarily the Catholic, were widely discussed. China need not preoccupy us in the present context; it was certainly not a religious problem. The nationalities issue was of greater consequence. As the editors of *Veche* told its (Jewish) readers "The term 'Russian' does not at all signify 'anti-Semitic.'" On the contrary, they expressed sympathy for the Jewish national movement—with, however, three important provisos: "Where it does not aspire to a privileged position in Russia, where it is not infused with racism, and where it does not hope for the world rule of the Chosen People."[5]

5. Quoted in J. Dunlop, *Faces of Contemporary Russian Nationalism* (Princeton, N.J., 1983), p. 152.

During the last two generations there have been numerous Jewish converts to the Orthodox church, and though unlike in the Catholic church, not one has risen to a position of eminence in the ecclesiastical hierarchy, some of them were certainly welcomed in the community and played a part of some importance in the debates of the 1960s and 1970s. Most converts from Judaism belonged to the liberal and modernist wing of the church and therefore aroused the ire of the more conservative elements. While the editors of *Veche* were willing to welcome the Jewish national movement, many others in the ranks of the church regarded "Zionism" as an abomination, the work of Satan and the greatest menace to the Russian people—*civitas diaboli*. Even moderate Christian thinkers felt that though Jews had been removed from all key positions in government, many of them were still living better than the average Russian. As they saw it, historically the attitude of the Russian people toward the Jews was not blameless, but Jews too bore a substantial responsibility for Russia's misfortunes after 1917.

The other Slav nationalities were by and large regarded as brothers in spirit and fate. Christian dissidents expressed the hope that these feelings were reciprocated and that the Slavs would stay together in a future Russia. A few were more pessimistic and expressed the view that in view of past coercion there was great resentment against Russians, that the unity had been forced, and that the liquidation of the empire, however regrettable, was probably the only possible solution. Solzhenitsyn, too, reached this conclusion, albeit only many years later.

Orthodox attitudes toward Rome had always been hostile to a certain extent; some church leaders regarded Catholicism as an unwelcome competitor, even though Catholic influence outside the Ukraine was almost nonexistent; others considered Catholicism a danger greater even than atheism. Some Christian dissidents tended to favor an improvement of relations with Rome, but the majority were averse to it, as were the Orthodox establishment and the fundamentalists. Some regarded ecumenism as a mortal sin. A believing Catholic could not be a true son of the fatherland, for his loyalty was to a foreign authority. There was less suspicion with regard to the Protestant sects and the Old Believers. The Protestants had no center abroad to which they were linked and the Old Believers were, of course, a purely Russian phenomenon. They did not constitute a danger because their influence had shrunk in recent decades (and their organization was heavily penetrated by the KGB). At the same time, some warned against idealizing the Old Believers to the detriment of the Orthodox church.

But the main issue confronting dissident Christians (to repeat it once again) was the relationship with the state, the struggle for more religious freedom, the freedom to imbue the young generation with Christian and patriotic values. What kind of future Russia did the Christian dissidents envisage? There were almost as many concepts as there were believers. VSKHSON and *Veche* certainly believed in personal freedom, in the equality of citizens before the law, in freedom of assembly and information. Some of the Christian dissidents were in favor of a monarchy, but they stood for the monarchic system or idea rather than a specific candidate. They did not advocate a theocracy, but accepted the separation of church and state. A supreme council governing the country (according to their blueprint) would, however, be given a veto over any law or action not corresponding to the basic principles of the Social-Christian order.[6] One-third of the council's members were to come from the church hierarchy. They were opposed to a parliamentary system because it seemed not suitable to Russian conditions; in this respect there was a basic difference between the Christian party in Russia and the German Christian Democratic Union or the Italian Demochristians who had opted for a parliamentary regime. Instead, the Christian dissidents favored some form of corporatism, which was vague and resembled in some respects the solidarism of the NTS (about which more later), in others the social teaching of the Catholic church, and in yet others Mussolini's doctrines about the corporate state. *Veche* and VSKHSON were critical of the West in the tradition of the Slavophiles and Dostoyevsky: The West was materialist; the West lacked Russia's idealism and spiritualism, its feeling of dedication; and Russophobia was never far from the surface in many Western circles.

However, criticism of the West (and Western religion) in these circles was restrained, whereas on the margins of the Christian revival far more extreme views were expressed by Genadi Shimanov, Evgeni Vagin, and others. Their extremism manifested itself not so much in religious fanaticism but in more vociferous anti-Westernism, belief in "Satanism," a Masonic-Jewish world conspiracy and the existence of an organized campaign of Russophobia. Some of these extremists gravitated toward national bolshevism; they hoped for an eventual understanding between party, state, and religious establishment. Others, such as Shimanov, were convinced that the established church was as bankrupt as the other state and party institutions and that there could be no religious rebirth without a nationalist revival. Yet others proposed a monarchy more or less in line with the tsarist system.

6. The constitution of the "All-Union Christian-Social Union" (Paris 1975), as quoted in Yanov, *The Russian Challenge*, p. 92.

It ought to be mentioned at least in passing that twentieth-century Russian religious thinkers such as Berdyaev, Bulgakov, and Pavel Florensky (who died in a Soviet camp) were held in higher esteem in the West than inside the Soviet Union. The fundamentalists of the Orthodox church disliked these "modernists" with their "Sophian" heresies, and to the conservatives outside the church they were deeply suspect. They thought modernism a plot of crypto-Masonic intellectuals whose true inspiration was un-Russian—Rosicrucian, Theosophical, even Satanist.[7]

Seen in retrospect, the relative weakness of Christian thought during the last decades of Soviet power is not easy to explain. The church had a reservoir of many millions of religious believers, and in view of the decomposition of Communist ideology and the longing for spiritual certainties, as well as the traditional weakness of Western political ideas in Russia, they almost had a monopoly. Yet the foundations were still not laid for a major Christian revival. The Orthodox church had been deeply penetrated by the state security organs and not only had acted as an informer but, as in the case of trials of dissident Christians, had supported the Communist persecution of religion. But there were many honest and devoted priests and the fact that there was much collaboration at the top cannot by itself explain why the church did not exude a greater appeal than it did.

Could it be that religious feeling was not, in the final analysis, as deep in this materialist society as is generally believed? Among many, there was a genuine desire to believe, and the ritual of the Orthodox church was as impressive as ever. True, there was competition—Theosophy both Russian and Western, all kinds of sects of Far Eastern and para-religious derivation. The fashions resembled those prevailing in the West in the 1960s and 1970s. There was probably a good deal of curiosity rather than a deep faith among some new churchgoers. As for the patriots who believed in the necessity of a nationalist-religious synthesis, it is next to impossible to state with any certainty which part of their inspiration was the stronger. Osipov, one of the key figures in the religious revival said: "I am a religious person. Christus and his religious doctrines are to me in the last resort preferable to nationalism. But I know the soul of the contemporary Russian: The national element in him is at the present time more vital and evident than the religious one."[8]

7. An example of this wholly negative attitude is Igor Smirnov, "Filosofia smuty," in *Nash sovremennik,* 11 (1991). For an interesting combination of the Theosophical and Satanic motives, see the work of the writer Yuri Mamleyev, who emigrated from Russia in 1974.

8. After 1987 Osipov became a leader of one of the monarchist groups, the "Renaissance" faction.

Chapter Six

FASCISM AND THE RUSSIAN EMIGRATION

FASCISM HAD A CONSIDERABLE IMPACT in the Russian émigré community in the late 1920s and the 1930s. Fascism and German national socialism seemed the most uncompromising anticommunist forces; dynamic movements, they appealed to the young generation. They promised action and quick results, very much in contrast to the unending debates of the West European parliamentary regimes and also to the ineffectual organizations established by the older generation of Russian émigrés. The Russian liberals and socialists continued to defend the democracies, as did some Christian thinkers such as G. P. Fedotov. But sympathies for the fascist critique of the parliamentary system could easily be detected not just among spokesmen for the conservatives of whom Struve was probably the most influential, but also among people at the center of the political spectrum such as N. Timasheff. Fascism seemed to be the wave of the future, whereas democracy appeared to be on the road to the often invoked dustbin of history.

The propaganda of the monarchist-conservative circles also adjusted itself to the new fascist doctrine. True, fascism did not make it easy for the Russian right; the Hitler-Stalin pact came as a shock, and the invasion of the Soviet Union in 1941, while welcomed by some, raised troubling questions for others: Was the Nazi invasion merely part of the promised struggle to destroy communism? Or was it perhaps also, or even mainly, a war against the Russian people, the prelude to German expansion in the

East? Some émigrés were not troubled; Metropolitan Serafim in Paris, Count Grabbe, the ataman of the Don Cossacks, the writers Merezhkovsky and Hippius, and sundry Russian generals in Paris welcomed the Nazi invasion as a "crusade against Judeo-Masonic bolshevism" and called on all Russians to collaborate. As they saw it, only Nazi Germany could reawaken Russia.[1]

But others, including the White general Anton Denikin, had their doubts and passed word among their fellow countrymen that collaboration with the invaders could not be recommended in good conscience. Many preferred to wait and see; a few opted for active resistance against fascism.

Several new organizations came into being in the 1920s, mainly consisting of members of the younger generation, militant in approach, acutely aware that the older émigrés had failed to make any significant progress in their struggle against bolshevism. These groups were particularly responsive to the appeal of fascism and three of them ought to be singled out for more than cursory mention.[2] The smallest and most bizarre group was the Young Russians (Mladorossitsi) movement, headed by a very young man named Alexander Kazem Bek, a scion of an aristocratic family that had migrated from Persia to Russia in the early nineteenth century and had become wholly Russified. Aged twenty-one, Kazem Bek was elected head of a student group in Paris that advocated a new kind of totalitarian monarchy, the struggle against Masonry and international capital, a life of "blood, fire, and sacrifice." Kazem Bek accepted all the trappings of fascism—uniforms, military discipline, and adulation of the leader; his followers welcomed him in his public appearances with repeated shouts of "Glava!"—"The Führer!"—raising their right arms. According to Kazem Bek, the old regime was not to be restored because it had become rotten to the core, eaten by philistinism, bourgeois greed, "drugs and syphilis." Seen in this light the treatment meted out to the old regime by the Bolsheviks had been justified. The apocalypse of 1917 and the civil war had been a catastrophe, but a necessary one.

These views were not as heretical as they might appear at first sight, and they found support in the mainstream of the Russian émigré community: Struve offered the Young Russians space in his periodical; Kyrill, the chief Romanov pretender (who had moved to Paris from Germany) gave them his blessing; and they counted two grand dukes among their members.

---

1. A political history of the Russian émigré community has not yet been written. Some details about collaboration between Russian émigrés in France and the Nazis are given in Robert H. Johnston, *New Mecca, New Babylon* (Kingston and Montreal, 1988), pp. 165–70.

2. About Russian émigré collaboration with the Nazis in Germany after 1933, see Robert C. Williams, *Culture in Exile* (Ithaca, N.Y., 1972), pp. 332–52.

However, Kazem Bek's adulation of Mussolini (and later of Hitler) was coupled with admiration for Stalin. Under Stalin, Soviet communism had advanced from internationalism to national socialism; Stalin and his followers were moving toward the acceptance of values that were also those of the Young Russians.[3] If so, why did the Young Russians not return to the Soviet Union or at least enter an alliance with the Communists?

The dilemma of the Russian nationalists of the extreme right after Stalin's rise to power has been described by no one better than by G. P. Fedotov, the religious thinker who wrote in 1935 that the liberals opposed Soviet power because it had stamped out freedom, and the democrats because the Communists had enslaved the people. The socialists were against bolshevism because it was a travesty of socialist ideals, whereas religious people could not accept it because atheism had become the new state religion.

Decent nonparty émigrés could not accept the system because it was producing people without decency and conscience. But, Fedotov continued, for a nationalist émigré *pur sang* there was no reason to hate the bolsheviks. His continued opposition was based on a misinterpretation, and as this misunderstanding was cleared up, yesterday's (anti-Soviet) activists would turn into *vozvrazhentsy,* re-emigrants.[4] Elsewhere Fedotov noted that if yesterday one could merely speculate about a nascent Soviet fascism, today it was already a fait accompli. The correct label for the Soviet system was "national socialist."

Fedotov's generalizations were perhaps a little sweeping, glossing over certain differences between the two totalitarian systems. But he put his finger on a real problem—and given the time when these predictions were made, they were remarkably prescient. As far as Kazem Bek's personal fate (about which more below) was concerned, they were certainly prophetic.

Kazem Bek advocated a synthesis of the old order and the new, a monarchy headed by Grand Duke Kyrill and based to a large extent on Soviet institutions—a Bolshevik (or at least a "social") monarchy. This idea also found other proponents in the 1930s such as the philosopher and theologian Ivan Il'in and a recent émigré named Ivan Solonevich. Kazem

---

3. For Kazem Bek's views, *K molodoi Rossii* (Paris, 1928), as well as *Rossiya mladorossy i emigratsia* (Paris, n d.) and the periodicals *Bodrost* and *Mladorosskaya iskra*. A short review of his political career is given in Nicholas Hayes, "Kazem Bek and the Young Russian Revolution," *Slavic Review* (June 1980), pp. 265–68, and there are interesting references in V. S. Varshavsky, *Nezamechennoye pokolenie* (New York, 1956), as well in Johnston, *New Mecca,* and Roman Gul's autobiography.

4. G. P. Fedotov, "Novyi idol," first published in *Sovremennie zapiski,* 57 (1935), reprinted in Fedotov, *Tyazhba o Rossii* (Paris, 1982), pp. 182–98.

Bek admired Stalinism; he believed that a dictatorship supported by the people *(vozhdism)* was the ideal form of government for Russia. But he claimed that whereas Stalin had done an excellent demolition job, doing away with the antinationalist old guard of Bolshevism, he was probably not up to the building of a new society. For this purpose a new generation, a new elite with new ideas, was needed—and it would be spearheaded by the Young Russians. Like Trotsky, Kazem Bek regarded Stalin as another Bonaparte, with the new Brumaire just around the corner.

The Young Russians' doctrine was full of inconsistencies, which did not particularly bother them, since they had nothing but contempt for ideologies and intellectuals. They knew instinctively what they wanted: a national revolution, a great Russia, a strong army. They frequently announced the emergence of a new style and a new morality, but never tried to elaborate on this. They were fascinated by Hitler and their leader went to Berlin in September 1933 for a conference to discuss closer cooperation with the Russian Nazi party in Germany (ROND). If relations with the Nazis subsequently became strained, this mainly had to do with the fact that the Nazis did not trust Kazem Bek because of his national-Bolshevik inclinations.

The Young Russians were xenophobic and racist ("Every foreigner is our enemy"), believing in the supremacy of the white race and, of course, a Russian imperialist mission. They denied charges, of anti-Semitism, but according to their program all Jews had to be removed from Russian public life. From the Eurasians the Young Russians borrowed the idea that Russia's main mission was in Asia. But at the same time Russia was to be the bulwark of the West against the "Yellow Peril."

By 1939 the Young Russians were on the decline. The other émigrés regarded their bombast with scorn mixed with suspicion; they were frequently called the "second Soviet party." Their activities were no longer prominently featured in the media, and the number of their followers was shrinking. They still admired Mussolini, but Hitler had been a disappointment; the Hitler-Stalin pact caused a great deal of disorientation in their ranks. By 1939 Kazem Bek had even discovered that the Nazis had territorial designs in Eastern Europe, which would conflict with Russia's interests. When the Second World War broke out, he advised his followers to support the Western democracies. After the war he found his way to the United States, but in 1956 (leaving his family behind) he disappeared rather suddenly—to resurface, after a few months, in Moscow. It appeared that he had been a Soviet agent for some considerable time; to this day it is not known whether this connection dates back to the period before World War II. In Moscow Kazem Bek found employment as one of the secretaries of the Patriarch of the Orthodox church and as a contributor to the journal of the Moscow patriarchate. He died in Moscow in 1977.[5]

The influence of the Young Russians was limited by and large to Paris and a few other French cities. Politically, the movement never amounted to very much. Kazem Bek claimed tens of thousands of supporters, whereas their number was never more than two thousand. The Young Russians are mainly of symptomatic interest, strongly influenced by fascism while also discovering surprising affinities with Stalinism.

In retrospect, the fate of Kazem Bek is less surprising than it appeared at the time: He ended up where he belonged. While at one time or another the Soviets found in the Russian emigration agents of influence who eventually returned to the Soviet Union, it is significant that no Menshevik and only one Socialist Revolutionary (Sukhomlin) returned to Stalinist Russia after having secretly served Moscow for years. The incidence of re-emigration on the right was considerably higher. No contemporary gave a better explanation than Fedotov, writing in 1938:

> Despotism and the totalitarian state appeared to be a strong internal temptation for many Christian souls. Hitler is not just an ally but the ideal of a Russian leader. Not only the "staff captains" [see n. 6, below] but a whole assembly of bishops [of Karlovats in Yugoslavia] welcomes this enemy of Christianity and affirms that the whole of Orthodox Russia is praying for him. If you read this, life no longer seems liveable. Again, as in the days of the October Revolution, one suffers from being a Russian; one suffers because bolshevism, like leprosy, is eating up the body of Russia. What can we call this process by which the Russian emigration is afflicted, except Bolshevization?[6]

This powerful indictment needs some words of explanation. Fedotov did not, of course, refer to the whole Russian émigré community but to those who influenced public opinion and were the most vociferous enemies of the Soviet system. He had in mind, above all, Ivan Solonevich's views, which had growing support among the clergy and the émigré media. As far as they were concerned, an alliance with Hitler was not a mere tactical maneuver but a spiritual necessity on the road to Russia's regeneration. Once upon a time, as Fedotov saw it, the fight of the White émigrés had been conducted as a struggle for an indivisible Russia; now the émigrés were willing to carve Russia up and give it to the enemy. The struggle had been

---

5. N. Hayes, "Kazem Bek," p. 268.

6. "Nash pozor" ("Our Shame"), originally published November 15, 1938, in *Novaya Rossiya*. Reprinted in G. P. Fedotov, *Zashita rossii* (New York, 1988), p. 20ff. "Staff captains" refers to Ivan Solonevich's movement, about which more below; the Karlovats synod was one of the two spiritual centers of the Russian émigré church.

conducted for religion and the tsar. But many monarchists now held the monarchy in contempt as a relic of the past. As for religion, Solonevich had blurted out that it was not necessary either. The only aim was "to beat the Bolsheviks." But they were beginning to realize that Stalin had undercut their ideological premises: "For what do you fight? You like fascism? But Russia presents the most consistent form of fascism, and Stalin has pronounced the slogan of a great and powerful Russia."[7]

Ivan Lukyanovich Solonevich, who made such a powerful impression on the Russian emigration, began his career in tsarist Russia as a champion wrestler and a contributor to a journal of the extreme right. Together with his brother and their families they had escaped from Russia over the Finnish border in 1934. The story of their adventure and their second book *(Russia in a Concentration Camp)* became international best-sellers. Ivan Solonevich published articles in the liberal and centrist émigré press, but within two years he veered to the right, joining a conspirational group of tsarist former army officers (mostly lieutenants and captains) based mainly in Bulgaria, who aimed at infiltrating both the Soviet Union and the existing political groupings in the Russian emigration. They were more or less openly fascist in their outlook, and at the same time heavily penetrated by Soviet agents. Since they contributed very substantially to the political disintegration of the Russian émigré community, Solonevich was suspected early on of being a Soviet agent. But this was never proven and it was probably wrong. He certainly accepted German money and tried to ingratiate himself with the Nazis. But he was too independent to be their favorite candidate for leadership—inasmuch as any such leader was needed by them in the first place. For this reason Solonevich's dreams never materialized. After the war he found himself in Argentina, where he died in 1953 and where some of his friends still publish a news sheet devoted to his memory.

There would be no particular reason to deal with this figure, who might have been no more than a minor footnote to the history of Russian emigration, but for the fact that Solonevich was rediscovered by the extreme right in the Soviet Union under *glasnost* and became one of its spiritual mentors. Together with other fascist, pro-fascist, and para-fascist thinkers of the 1930s he has entered the pantheon of the Russian right.[8] His biography was suitably rewritten. Thus, he was "compelled" to move from Bulgaria to Germany (by whom?) and he did what he could to

7. Ibid., p. 205.

8. He has been widely reprinted and quoted, by Igor Shafarevich, *Molodaya gvardiya,* 6 and 12 (1989). For Solonevich as a martyr, see *Russkii vestnik,* 18 (1991). Large sections of his work were published in *Nash sovremennik,* 5 (1990) and elsewhere—for example, *Polozhenie del,* 3 (1991) and *Politika,* 14 (1991).

counteract the suicidal Russophobic propaganda of the Germans. His final canonization as one of the chief saints of the new Russian right was on the occasion of his hundredth birthday, in 1991.[9]

The Fascist Party

Russian fascist parties existed in the 1930s in Germany and Manchuria and there was also a tiny group in the United States. The most numerous was the one in Harbin, Manchuria, which found its first followers among students and graduates of the local law faculty. They were instrumental in publishing the *Protocols of the Elders of Zion* and gave lectures about the misdeeds of the Masons in Russia and elsewhere. They were attracted by the exploits of Italian and German fascism and got the support of a former tsarist general, V. D. Kozmin, to act as a respectable figurehead. This was the beginning of the RFO (Russian Fascist Organization) which later became the RFP (Russian Fascist Party) and issued regular publications such as *Nash put* and *Natsia*.

After his arrival from the Soviet Union, Konstantin Rodzayevsky became the leader of the RFP. Aged twenty-four, this dynamic young man pushed the tsarist general aside and from 1931 until the arrival of the Soviet army in 1945 headed this small movement. The RFO copied the Nazis in every respect—uniforms, the wide display of swastikas, the reprinting of cartoons from *Der Stürmer*.[10] Early on they began to concentrate their attacks not against Stalin but against Kaganovich; like some Nazi commentators, they professed to regard him as the true ruler of the Soviet Union, or, in any case, as a more convenient target.

However, the Manchurian fascists suffered from two fatal weaknesses. The appeal of fascism in Europe rested to a decisive degree on its ability to mobilize the masses, millions of them. But Harbin and Man-chou-li, the other major town in Manchuria, were backwaters and the number of émigrés there was small. In their assemblies and marches a few dozen, at most a few hundred appeared—always the same faces. At best Rodzayevsky could hope for a quick German (or Japanese) victory over the Soviet Union, and the division of the country between them, perhaps along the river Yenisei. But this was not a very inviting prospect for a Russian patriot. He also assumed—there was no limit to his naïveté—that a "national

9. Igor Dyakov in *Nash Sovremennik,* 11 (1991).

10. Yu. Melnikov (pseud.), "Russkie fashisti v Manchurii," in *Problemy dalnego vostoka* 2 and 3 (1991). The most detailed account is John J. Stephan, *The Russian Fascists* (New York, 1978).

government" would be imposed by the occupiers, with him at the head.

But the RFP suffered from yet another weakness. It was entirely the tool of the Japanese army, or to be precise of the intelligence department of the Kwantung Army, which was at the time in effective charge of Manchuria. This was not the mendacious allegation of some political enemies, but the gist of an official report prepared by a highly placed SS official (and noted Russian expert), Dr. Otto Braeutigam. Without such political and financial aid the RFP would not have been able to exist. A high price had to be paid for this dependence; one was close collaboration with Cossack Ataman Semyonov, one of the most notorious figures of the civil war, who had settled in Manchuria. Semyonov was a man of the extreme right but was not very impressed by Nazism and fascism, which he considered of little relevance to Russia; instead he relied on Cossack solidarity. Many of his erstwhile followers had settled in Manchuria.[11] In fact, outside Harbin his groups were stronger than Rodzayevsky's, and the Japanese seemed to have trusted him slightly more than they did the RFO.

Semyonov and Rodzayevsky were condemned to death at the same trial in August 1946. One year earlier Rodzayevsky had sadly admitted that his whole struggle had been based on a misunderstanding: "Stalinism is exactly what we mistakenly called 'Russian fascism.' It is our Russian fascism cleansed of extremes, illusions and errors."[12] Subsequently, he wrote a letter to Stalin in which he expressed regret for his misdeeds and the hope of being permitted to serve his fatherland and its leader. He wanted to establish a Soviet fifth column abroad, made up of his former fellow fascists.[13] The offer was not accepted.

While other émigré groups of the extreme right and of fascist orientation were rehabilitated in later years by the extreme right in the Soviet Union, Rodzayevsky's group did not fare well; it had been too closely tied to its foreign masters. It developed no original ideas but merely copied those emanating from Berlin and Rome.

The same is true, a fortiori, with regard to Anastas Vosniyatsky's VFO (All-Russian Fascist Organization), founded in 1933 in Windham County, Connecticut. Vosniyatsky was born in Warsaw in 1898; his most important achievement in life was his marriage to Marion Stephens, née Marion Buckingham Ream, an American heiress twenty-one years older than he. The Chicago-based Reams had made an enormous fortune in grain and livestock. Vosniyatsky could have spent the rest of his life comfortably as

11. Stephan, *The Russian Fascists*, pp. 160–61.

12. Pyotr Balukshin, *Final v kitae* (San Francisco, 1959), vol. 2, p. 129.

13. Ibid., p. 133.

a Connecticut squire, but he had political ambitions, and, like many of his generation, he believed that fascism was the wave of the future. Unlike all other émigré politicians he had a great deal of money at his disposal.

Nevertheless, his forays into politics were farcical. But for the exaggerations of the American media, which announced that fifty thousand fascists were training on his Connecticut farm, no one would have taken notice of him. He established contact with the German Nazi *Bund* and with Rodzayevsky in Harbin. But in the last resort his activities were of even less importance than those of the Manchurian fascists. He died in obscurity in St. Petersburg, Florida, in 1965. His story has been told and there is no need to go over it again.[14]

NTS

Far more interesting and more influential was the NTS, which first emerged among younger members of the émigré community in Yugoslavia in the late 1920s. Of all the Russian émigré groups the NTS is the only one still in existence; under *glasnost* it was permitted to open an office in Moscow. We shall deal only with its early activities; its controversial history since 1945 has been the subject of much comment but is of no relevance in the present context. Its full name was Natsionalniy Trudovoi Soyuz Novogo Pokoleniya ("National Labor Union of the New Generation") and it was better known for many years as the Novo Pokolentsy, "New Generationists." Its first congress took place in 1930, where V. M. Baidalakov, a Don Cossack, was elected president.

Among the early participants we find several aristocrats such as Duke Leuchtenberg and Count Volkonsky, but the central figures from the beginning and for many years to come were little-known men such as R. P. Ronchevsky, V. D. Poremsky, A. S. Kazantsev, and M. A. Georgevsky, a professor, somewhat older than the others, who was the chief ideologist during the early period. The central aim of the new movement was to continue the struggle for the "White idea"—but in ways somewhat different from those of the older generation.[15] Like the other nationalists the NTS stood for a great and strong Russia, for freedom, and for releasing the peasants from the kolkhoz system. But these basic tenets were common to

---

14. Stephan, *The Russian Fascists.*

15. The most important sources for this period of NTS history are its periodical, *Za Rossiyu,* and the autobiographies of B. Pryanizhnikov (*Novopokolentsy* [Silver Spring, Md., 1986]) and Stolypin, *Na Sluzhbe Rossii,* Frankfurt, n.d.

virtually all right-wing groups in the emigration, and the NTS was to grope for many years for some more specific orientation. Unlike the Young Russians it took ideological problems seriously, and every few years it adopted a new program (1930, 1931, 1935, 1938, 1940, 1944—not counting the various postwar programs). Its basic political philosophy during the early years was solidarism. This doctrine was by no means identical with the social teachings of the Catholic church which went by the same name. Solidarism according to the NTS thinkers was a synthesis of activism, idealism, and nationalism. It deliberately contrasted itself with Marxism by emphasizing the importance of ideas (and idealism); it stressed the significance of the nation as the most important organic framework of all human endeavor. The stress on activism was a little unclear; it was probably meant to be something akin to the Marxist unity of theory and practice.

Solidarism saw itself as the antithesis of the class struggle. Relations between classes were to be harmonious, with a strong state as the supreme arbiter. This implied the rejection of both "excessive" liberal individualism and Western pluralism. There was to be freedom in the future Russia, but not unlimited freedom; nor did the NTS envisage a multiparty capitalist system. Key industries were to be state-owned. Lastly, religion was to be of central importance in the future order, with the Orthodox church in a dominant position.[16]

In later years NTS leaders argued that they had been greatly influenced by Khomyakov's concept of *sobornost,* which played a key role in the thinking of the Slavophiles and is frequently invoked by the Russian right to this day. The term, which goes back to sixteenth-century Russian political culture, is virtually untranslatable and means something akin to "national unity and cooperation." Another thinker who influenced the early NTS and who was probably the first to use the term "solidarism" at the time was the émigré legal philosopher G. Gins.[17]

The NTS political philosophy shows a deliberate attempt to escape the confines of the counterrevolutionary camp, to move beyond the old disputes of the Bolsheviks and their enemies. In this respect NTS was not, however, quite consistent. Thus, in 1935 the NTS proclaimed that it regarded itself as the successor of General Kornilov, the military leader who wanted to stage a coup against Kerensky's government in July 1917 but

16. A good short summary of early NTS doctrine, based on its various programs, is given in C. Andreyev, *Vlassov and the Russian Liberation Movement.*

17. NTS old-timers such as A. Artyemov, Y. Trushnovich, and R. Redlich have published their recollections on the ideas and politics of the movement in *Posev,* 1990–91. They are of interest, but tend to leave out events and activities that appear embarrassing in retrospect.

failed. In later programs this reference was dropped.[18] On the other hand, the wartime program included various provisions apparently inserted following the influx of new (Soviet) refugees and prisoners of war. There it was claimed that the NTS was to resurrect the revolutionary spirit of 1917 for the benefit of the people. The 1944 program also included anti-Jewish passages: All non-Russian nationalities would be part of the nation, except the Jews, who would be free to emigrate if they were willing to leave their property behind. Otherwise they would be resettled in specially designated areas.[19] In later years it was argued that the anti-Jewish sections had been inserted under Nazi pressure. But the historian C. Andreyev rightly notes that the NTS claims to have been an illegal party in Germany (and some of its members were jailed), and that it is not readily obvious why an underground organization should have bowed to pressure.

An examination of NTS publications well before the outbreak of the war shows considerable emphasis on the "Jewish character" of Bolshevik rule in the Soviet Union, and this at a time when very few Jews were left among the Communist leaders. Marxism, the NTS said, was a typical product of German Jewry, and as for the February Revolution of 1917, it could well have been the result of a "Judeo-Masonic conspiracy." True, the NTS, in contrast to other groups of the far right, thought that this probably was a factor of secondary importance.[20]

During the 1930s the NTS's attitude toward fascism was in principle, favorable. As Georgievsky wrote in 1935: "We see in national socialism an idea based on service and the national interest, and in Italian fascism, gravitating toward solidarism, convincing proof as far as the feasibility and the eventual success of our struggle is concerned."[21] With democracy in retreat all over Europe, it was only natural (as a leading NTS member put it many years later), that the NTS should find itself in the same camp as the various fascisms.[22] The NTS periodical published articles in praise of Nazism, but equally of Austrian corporatism, the Spanish Falange, and Italian fascism, and it found a particular affinity with Antonio Salazar's Portugal.

18. Andreyev, *Vlassov*, p. 190.

19. *Skhema natsionalnogo trudovogo soyuza* (Berlin, 1944), pp. 43ff.

20. The historical record of the NTS was the subject of many polemical exchanges after 1945. See, for instance, the State Department publication "The Russian Solidarist Movement," External Research Paper Series 3, no. 76 (Washington, D.C., 1951), and the writings of Boris Dvinov. Also the collection of essays *Protiv techenia* I (New York, n.d. [1953?]).

21. Quoted in Pryanizhnikov, *Novopokolentsy*, p. 41. After the war various attempts were made to rewrite prewar NTS history, which need not, however, preoccupy us here.

22. Ibid.

There is no doubt that fascism had a significant influence on the ideological program of the NTS. Unlike the Russian fascists in Harbin they did not, however, ape Nazism; they refrained from copying its cruder manifestations and they were, in the final analysis, more in the authoritarian than the fascist-totalitarian mold.

This did not prevent close cooperation with Nazi Germany. The Novopokolentsy knew that this was the only power capable of defeating Stalin's Russia. (They cooperated equally closely up to August 1939 with the Polish General Staff.) Some of the leading members of NTS went to Berlin, where German intelligence put a printing shop at their disposal to publish a periodical to be smuggled into the Soviet Union. Collaboration became considerably closer during the war years and many NTS members, such as Roman Redlich, Tenserov, and Poremsky, went to occupied Russia in various capacities to work for Rosenberg's Eastern Ministry. According to postwar NTS publications, they had to conceal their Russian origins; but this is stretching credulity too far. Their German employers knew, of course, with whom they were dealing. While officially, the German branch of NTS had dissolved itself in 1938, the NTS leadership had moved to Berlin during the war years and some of their leading figures such as Poremsky, Vergun, and Kazantsev joined the editorial board of *Novoye Slovo,* the official pro-Nazi daily newspaper in Berlin. Later on, during the war NTS closely cooperated with ROA, the Vlassov army. The political program of ROA was influenced by NTS, and many individual Russian prisoners of war joined the NTS.

In view of all this it is difficult to agree with the post-1945 NTS version of its own history, that its policy was to constitute a "third force," not with Stalin, not with Hitler but with "our own people," and that the NTS was on collision course with the two giants.

With all the ideological proximity between NTS and the Nazis, the solidarists never became a fully fledged fascist party, and it was possible after 1945 to claim that they had all along acted according to their own political agenda. They had simply used the Nazis, just as Lenin had used the German emperor's government in 1917 so as to make his way back to Russia. While NTS rejected liberal democracy and envisaged an authoritarian regime for Russia, they had never practiced the cult of a *Führer,* nor did they like the anti-Christian attitude of the Nazis. Above all, they came to realize, as the war went on, that the kind of Russia the Nazis envisaged in their "New Order" was very different from their own image and intentions. In brief, they became painfully aware that the Nazis were not just anti-Communist but also anti-Russian. It had been one of the basic tenets of the White movement that a post-Bolshevik Russia should be united and indivisible. The Nazis had very different plans for Russia; as the war went on, they preferred to deal with Ukrainians and other minorities rather than with the Russians.

NTS probably sent more propaganda material to the Soviet Union before, during, and after the war than any other émigré faction. However, it did not have any measurable impact, partly because the Soviet security apparatus was so effective, but also because NTS doctrine, which had been developed in the West, did not appeal very much to Russians. Soviet reality was not receptive to ideas that had been nurtured in different circumstances. Thus, even under *glasnost*, when NTS could more or less freely import its journals and books, the group did not draw much response. Perhaps decades of indoctrination about the NTS as a mere instrument of enemy forces—first the Germans, later the Americans—had been successful. True, there would be the occasional comment to the effect that solidarism was the only idea that could possibly save Russia.[23] There should be fewer strikes, the new class of industrial entrepreneurs should have a say, and everyone should believe in a strong Russian state (*gosudarstvennost*).

By and large, individual thinkers such as Professor Ivan Il'in had a larger impact than the programs and manifestos of the NTS. Ivan Il'in had been a philosophy professor in Moscow, a student of Hegel and Hermann Cohen, before the Revolution. He was exiled together with a group of leading thinkers, including Berdyaev, in 1922. More than most of his colleagues he took part in the daily political struggle, as—among other things—editor of a journal called *Russkii kolokol*. Though he did not belong to the younger generation, he became a close friend of NTS, with which he differed only on one major issue. While Il'in was, or became, a convinced monarchist, NTS always tried to stay out of the dispute over whether the coming Russia should be a republic or a monarchy.

Il'in's articles and books have been more widely republished by the Russian right under *glasnost* than those of any other émigré thinker. This is not easy to understand, for others—such as P. B. Struve, who also became a monarchist—were undoubtedly more profound and original thinkers. Perhaps Il'in's popularity is the result of his undiminishing enthusiasm, the extremism that permeates all his writings, and the fact that he appealed to a less highbrow public.

About the content of his writings there is not much to say. He wrote that the "White idea" did not aim at the restoration of the old order, that

---

23. Mikhail Kislink, head of Kemerovo district, quoted by TASS, October 15, 1991. The NTS cooperated with Osipov's group, about which more below, and it had an outlet for its views in certain local journals such as *Sever* (Petrozavodsk).

Russian culture had always developed on lines different from the West; that Russia needed "organic democracy," not formal or mechanist as in the West, or as preached by the Russian intelligentsia for generations. What "organic" freedom was, Il'in never made quite clear; he was firmly convinced that a monarchy had always been the best political order for Russia. Rebels against authority had always been wrong; Lenin was "Pugachev with a university degree."[24]

In 1926 Il'in became the center of a heated debate following the publication of his book *On Resisting Evil by Force* (republished in Moscow in 1991). This was ostensibly a polemic against the Tolstoyan doctrine of nonresistance against evil. Since there were few, if any, Tolstoyans among the émigrés, the message was interpreted as an appeal to use their own weapons against the Bolsheviks. This was received with enthusiasm by the extreme right and also by some leading clergymen. But the message was rejected by most thinkers of the center, including S. Hippius and S. Frank. Berdyaev wrote on this occasion that a Chekist (the precursor of the KGB) operating on behalf of God was worse than a Chekist working for the devil.[25]

Il'in left Germany in 1935 for Switzerland, where he died in 1954. His admirers have described him as an antifascist, which he certainly was not; his books were widely published in Germany even after 1933. But he certainly was not a Nazi in spirit; he was an old-fashioned conservative monarchist. Il'in never tried to be a populist or to be "modern" in any other way, which makes the Il'in revival, compared with the relatively scant response to NTS in contemporary Russia, all the more puzzling.

24: Pugachev was a late-eighteenth-century leader of rebelling peasants. Il'in's writings have been widely reprinted in Russia in the organs of the conservatives as well as those of the extreme right—for instance, *Tretii rim* 5 (1991); *Russkii vestnik,* 18–27 (1991); *Russkoe tovarichestvo,* 3 (1991). Some of his books have also been republished.

25. For a summary of this debate, N. Poltoratsky, *Ivan Aleksandrovich Il'in* (Tenafly, N.J., 1985) pp. 129–37; "On Resisting Evil by Force" was published in installments in *Slovo,* 5–8 (1991).

Chapter Seven

THE RUSSIAN PARTY AND NATIONAL BOLSHEVISM

DURING THE 1970S A "RUSSIAN PARTY" EMERGED on the Soviet intellectual scene. It did not have any significant political impact at the time, because power was as yet firmly in Communist hands. One could, however, point to a variety of straws in the wind; the most obvious and interesting were the emergence of a school of "village writers" and the debate on Slavophilism. Not unexpectedly, the leading ideologists of the Russian party of the 1970s were to play an important role in the emergence of a new right after 1985.

Soviet writers were able to write more realistically about life in the village than about any other aspect of Soviet society. The origins of this school go back to the essays of Vladimir Ovechkin and Efim Dorosh in the late Stalin period. Fyodor Abramov, Vasili Shukshin, and Valentin Rasputin, the village writers of northern Russia and Siberia, were among the most gifted writers of the 1960 and 1970s. Written with insight, passion, and literary mastery, their stories dealt with the fate of ordinary people far away from the centers of power and culture. There is a striking similarity in the general atmosphere and also the denouement of novels such as Viktor Astafiev's *Pastukh i pastukha* ("Shepherd and Shepherdess"), Shukshin's *Kalina krasnaya* ("Red Guelder Rose") and Rasputin's *Farewell to Matyora* and *Pozhar* ("Fire"), to mention but the best known. The theme is of the loneliness of the human beings in life and death in the heart of Russia. It is not "blood-and-soil" *(Blut und Boden)* literature, Nazi style, embellishing the past and painting the present in rosy colors: Conditions are far from idyllic. Abramov's villagers are much of the time nasty to each other. There is no attempt to hide the moral deterioration in the country-side and the small cities that results from the breaking up of old communities and the introduction of modern technology. These works were written in a deeply pessimistic spirit; there is no chauvinism and xenophobia, only some ridicule of city folk.[1]

Vasili Belov wrote with deep love about village life in the old Russia that survived up to the time of collectivization. With much feeling he described the old craftsmen (with such outlandish names as Ivan Afrikanovich) and beggars of old Russia, the close ties to nature, and the often charming superstitions of the peasants, with their quaint customs and house spirits. His heroes are uneducated and poor, but essentially peaceful, living in harmony with themselves and the cosmos. For Belov, as for most village writers, the big city is an unfriendly and threatening, even dangerous place; the houses are big and anonymous, the people cold and silent. Belov was born in a village near Vologda, Soloukhin near Vladimir, in truly old Russia. Soloukhin's Russia is that of many thousands of churches and monasteries, of saint-day feasts, church bells, village weddings and funerals, holy men and holy fools. He was preoccupied with the beauties of nature and architecture and he did more than anyone else to promote the preservation of icons and old churches. If Soloukhin had a favorite Western writer it seems to have been Knut Hamsun, and this was no accident: Hamsun's heroes are uncorrupted by civilization; they have escaped the soulless environment of the city and materialism, modern industry, and the American (Western) way of life. The Hamsun parallel is, alas, ominous, considering the record of that great writer under the German occupation of his country.

Both Astafiev and Rasputin were born in Siberia and stayed there all their lives. Their world is that of the big forests, the taiga, the mighty rivers, and the descendants of the pioneers. Rasputin's novels are permeated with deep melancholy. *Pozhar*, for example, describes the moral decline of a small town. The warehouses burn, but instead of trying to put out the fire, the locals engage in an orgy of looting and even killing. These people have no roots and no loyalty; they make money, drink, and steal. The story is told by Ivan Petrovich, a militiaman; at the end he decides to leave the town, having lost his home. But he has little hope of finding a new home elsewhere in Russia where people still have moral standards and care about each other, where the difference between good and evil is still clear. In

---

1. One of the village writers' precursors, Efim Dorosh, was a Jew.

Farewell to Matryona, his earlier and more famous book, people also lose their home, albeit for a different reason; this is the story of the last days of an island-settlement in the Angara River that is going to disappear as the result of technological progress, in the form of a giant hydroelectrical station.

There is gloom in most of the village writers' works, and it is easy to understand why. Not only has traditional village life disappeared under Soviet rule, but also nature has systematically been despoiled and ruined; the standard of living, especially in the non–Black Earth regions of northern Russia, is abysmally low. The countryside is depopulated; those who remain are, by and large, the weak and those lacking initiative. But the village writers nevertheless expressed sadness about this lost world. If their critics wrote of them mockingly as "peasant-lovers" and quoted Marx on the "idiocy of rural life," they replied that the idiocy of urban life had become even more glaring.

What were the politics of the village writers prior to *glasnost?* Though they wrote quite freely about the true state of affairs in the Russian country-side, by and large they were tolerated by the party censors; Soloukhin was criticized for going too far in praising the Orthodox church, but he suffered no real harm; soon after this criticism, the Lenin Prize was awarded to him. The village writers were patriots who felt acute pain over the irretrievable loss suffered by rural Russia. They had great respect for old traditions, customs, and religion (sometimes pagan), and they shared the conviction that life a hundred years earlier had been better. They were deeply skeptical about progress, had no admiration for the urban intelligentsia, and acutely disliked modern mass culture as imported from the West and eagerly absorbed by the young generation in the cities. Most of them were not party members, but not one of them stood in open opposition to the party line. On the contrary, quite a few were members of the executive of the Writers' Union and, when necessary, they paid respect to the party's role in Soviet history, even though the realities they described in their novels did not really warrant this—after all, the party had been responsible for collec-tivization. In brief, these loyal citizens were unpolitical, or at least had opted out of active politics and kept their true political convictions for themselves and their closest friends. Some of them published their works in journals, such as *Nash sovremennik,* that had acquired a conservative reputation. Others (including Abramov, Belov, Shukshin, Yashin and Zaly-gin) were published by *Novy mir.* Not one of them became a dissident or thought of publishing his work in samizdat or abroad.

With *glasnost* and *perestroika* there came the politicization of the village writers. From carpenters building a bathhouse in the village, Vasili Belov moved on to the intellectuals in the sinful city. His next novel (*Vse vperyod*-"Everything Is Still Ahead") opens in the Place Pigalle, Paris, where the heroine, a fickle Russian woman, watches a pornographic film. This, with iron logic, leads to her moral corruption. She leaves her Russian husband and becomes the wife of a Jewish villain. But if Paris is sinful, Moscow is no better, a nightmare of metal, glass, rubber, the smell of gasoline, and too many foreigners. Something devilish is going on: the systematic poisoning of the Russian soul and body by means of alcohol and drugs, by rampant sexploitation, by the actions of Jews and other cosmopolitans, emissaries of Satan. (President Kennedy also has a hand in poisoning the Russian people.) Belov offers a diagnosis: In order to destroy a people one does not need hydrogen bombs. It is enough to subvert them, to make children quarrel with their parents, to set women against men. It is not easy, but it can be done. What saved Russia in the past? The *izba*, the peasant hut. If Russia goes under, it won't be because of Pershing missiles but because of the disappearance of the peasants' huts. The same disgust manifests itself in Belov's essays. Even in his native Vologda he had to watch rock groups and nearly nude stripteasers shaking their bellies and hips.

If this had been merely the case of a talented writer moving out of his native habitat, pontificating about a world alien to him, and producing a grotesque caricature, the case of Belov would not be of wider interest. But it was part of a wider phenomenon: the gradual move to the right, even the extreme right, of a whole group of writers. Some of the ideas they voiced under *glasnost* must have been there before; it is unlikely that they were converted from one month to the next. But their ideological turn is still something of a puzzle; it cannot simply be explained with reference to limited horizons and the resentment a bunch of provincials feels for the capital. And it is difficult to understand because neither Belov (in Vologda), nor Rasputin (who makes his home in Irkutsk), nor the other village writers can possibly have met in their native surroundings many Jews, Masons, Satanists, foreign agents, or cosmopolitans. The manifestations of cultural modernism that they detested so much; the Moscow intellectuals whom they abhorred; the Russophobia they decried—all these cannot possibly have been part of their own experience. They knew about them mainly from hearsay.

In Germany, in the United States, and in other countries, writers and artists living outside the metropolitan areas have traditionally resented their colleagues (and critics) in the center, who are responsible for setting the literary and artistic agenda, deciding what work of art should succeed, influential in the publishing houses and the media. But the Soviet village writers were not deprived children but part of the elite. They were held in the highest esteem; millions of copies of their works were printed; they were the recipients of Lenin and Stalin prizes and became "Heroes of Socialist Labor," members of the Supreme Soviet, and so on. Equally puzzling was the strange political alliance they entered; it included veteran Communists and military writers who had no enthusiasm for old churches (or for villages in general), and even the literary functionaries whom they had professed to despise in earlier years.

Why should Gorbachev's policies and the writings of the liberals have provoked such a violent reaction? Why did the creative work of many village writers come virtually to an end, at least temporarily in 1987? Why did they turn instead to political speeches, essays, polemics, appeals? We shall have to deal with these questions later on, but fairness demands that we note that not all of them turned in this direction.

Some of the leading village writers (such as Abramov, Yashin, Lipatov, and Shukshin) were no longer alive when *glasnost* came; it is unlikely that all of these would have joined Belov and Rasputin on the road to extremism.[2] Other notable writers—for example, Sergei Zalygin, Victor Astafiev, Boris Mozhayev—were still active but refused to follow their erstwhile comrades on the road to the extreme right.

The best known representative of the democratic-patriotic camp was the academician Dmitri Likhachev, the grand old man of early Russian literature and history. Before the turn of the century, when Milyukov wrote his famous essay on the disintegration of the Slavophile camp, he mentioned the philosopher Vladimir Solovyov as the spokesman of the Slavophile left, in contradiction to the various right-wingers. Solovyov replied that to the best of his knowledge he was the only member of the Slavophile left and that he was eager to resign from this position. It has been argued that Likhachev's position among the patriots was similar, but the parallel is not quite correct. There were others, such as Sergei Averintsev, another academician and a student of religion, and Sergei Zalygin, who became editor of *Novy mir* and made it a bulwark of enlightened nationalism. They did not share the extremists' hatreds and fears, nor did they think that military dictatorship was a panacea for Russia's ills. They viewed with displeasure the new alliance between the patriots of the right with old Stalinists and racists. Some still cooperated with erstwhile comrades: Zalygin invited leading writers such as Belov to write for *Novy mir*. Others took a more uncompromising line vis-à-vis chauvinism; for example, Likhachev maintained on many occasions that there was a basic distinction between

2. Abramov had a bad attack of anticosmopolitanism as a young man, but reportedly regretted it in later years.

patriotism (the love of one's own country) and nationalism (the hatred of other countries).[3] He was among the foremost preservationists and ecologists, resisting the derouting of the Siberian rivers; he fought for the publication of patriotic works, such as Nikolai Karamzin's *History of Russia,* which had been suppressed ever since the revolution. But he was not willing to make common cause with those who espoused obscurantism and chauvinism. This led, under *glasnost,* to open conflict between the democratic All-Union Cultural Foundation of which he was president, and the nationalists' Cultural Fund, presided over by Peter Proskurin.[4]

A patriotic revival was only to be expected in view of the decline of Marxist-Leninist ideology. In a similar way, the division between conservative nationalists and liberal-democratic ones was also a foregone conclusion. The main field of battle in the 1960s had been certain journals specializing in the theory of literature, such as *Voprosy literaturi,* and magazines such as *Nash sovremennik* and *Molodaya gvardiya,* which were again to play a leading role after 1985 in the emergence of the new Russian right.

The patriotic spirit had manifested itself even earlier, in the exhibitions of the painter Ilya Glazunov, who was preoccupied with religious motifs (such as the return of the Prodigal Son) and the traditional heroes from Russia's past (Kulikovo, Tsarevich Dmitri). Glazunov was a fine craftsman, and there were no modernist aberrations in his work—it was socialist realism turned inside out. The cognoscenti derided it, but masses of people streamed to see his pictures, and while he was gently upbraided by some official party critics (and while some of his pictures could not be shown publicly prior to *glasnost*) he had his supporters in the leadership and no sanctions were taken against him. Dmitri Vasiliev, the leader of Pamyat, worked with him for a while, but the two did not get on well.

In the late 1960s some nationalist and religious dissidents were rediscovering the Slavophiles; within a short time similar stirrings could be detected in the official literary magazines, sometimes in the form of impassioned, if primitive, appeals (Shalmayev), at other times on a higher level of sophistication (Lobanov, Kozhinov). The argument ran, briefly, as follows: First of all, Russia had become a spiritually empty, Americanized country. Its old, traditional values were ignored or despised. As a result Russian society had become materialistic, philistine, rootless, open to all

3. D. Likhachev, *O Russkom* (Moscow, 1989). Originally published in *Novy mir* ten years earlier.

4. Proskurin is the author of an epopee of Russian life during and after the last war. Stalin appears in his work in a rather favorable light and there is a palpable element of xenophobia. In his travelogues Proskurin claimed, inter alia, that the average Englishman cannot afford to make a call from a public phone booth.

kinds of negative, cosmopolitan influences. This was an "antibourgeois" critique resembling the right-wing *Kultur Kritiker* in the West. True, the country had become stronger economically and from a military point of view. But a whole internal dimension was missing—the national patrimony, the roots, all that was specifically Russian in nature, national character, ideals and idealism, the peasantry as the cradle of the national culture. And without all this Russia was becoming an empty shell.

A second basic tenet of the nationalists was the thesis of the "single stream" of Russian history and culture, which was, of course, in total contradiction to Leninism. According to Lenin (and prevailing official ideology) there had been a progressive trend in Russian history and culture, which was to serve as a lodestar for communism. Among the progressives were Peter the Great (at least in part); the rebels against tsarist tyranny; literary figures such as Herzen, Chernyshevsky, and Gorky. On the other side of the barricade there had been most of the tsars, the oppressors and exploiters, the reactionaries and religious obscurantists, and it was from this part of the national heritage that progressive Russians had to dissociate themselves. Most of the neo-Slavophiles had to tread cautiously on this ground; they thought very little of the progressive tradition and the heroes praised by Plekhanov and Lenin. In their public stance they were willing to accept a compromise: The progressive traditions were fine and should not be discarded, but the peasants, the church (as a fighter for national unity), Dostoyevsky, and the Slavophiles had also to be given their due at long last.

Such views, whether one agreed with them or not, would not have been considered particularly shocking in any other country. But the Soviet Union at the time was still a totalitarian society and no major deviation from the official ideology could be tolerated. For to accept a "single stream" approach in these conditions would not have meant merely to do justice to the monarchy, the church, and other enemies of the Revolution and of socialism; it would also have had far-reaching repercussions concerning the present situation. It would have meant that both the Reds and the Whites had a good case in the civil war. If both Nicholas II and Lenin had been right, there should not have been a revolution in the first place, and perhaps something in between bolshevism and the monarchy should have emerged. One of the new nationalist factions, the National Bolshevik trend, did in fact advocate an approach on broadly these lines.

A reply had to be given to the heretics, but considering the magnitude of the heresy it was surprisingly mild, even halfhearted, and it enabled the nationalists to fight on. Their position was made easier as a result of the fact that they had not frontally attacked bolshevism. On the contrary, they tried hard and not unsuccessfully to adjust to the party line. Thus Kozhinov dwelt at great length on Dostoyevsky as a critic of bourgeois society; Lobanov pointed to *Besy* as a horrible example of the Americanization of the soul; and Lanshikov, yet another ideologist of the right, argued that the very fact that the Bolshevik Revolution had taken place in Russia was the most striking demonstration that Russia had a unique historical mission. Ostensibly, the nationalists steered clear of politics; theirs was, as far as they were concerned, a purely cultural debate. They freely quoted Marx, Lenin, and Brezhnev to buttress their arguments. They did not invoke the issue of the brutal murder of the last tsar's family or the persecution of the church after 1917 or the horrible excesses of collectivization. There was plenty of anti-Zionist and anti-Masonic propaganda but it did not go beyond the official party line; the crimes had all been the fault of Trotsky and other cosmopolitans, not of Lenin and hardly of Stalin. Their loyalty to the Soviet state, to Marxism-Leninism, was not in question.

Did the nationalists' worldview radically change between, say, 1970 and 1990? Originally they had believed (or professed to believe) in the overall positive role of the Communist party. Had they been sworn enemies of communism all along and had they simply used Aesopian language before *glasnost*, so as not to get into conflict with censorship? Why had they not opted for samizdat? If the fate of the nation was at stake, surely some of them should have shown a little more courage.

It is not easy to provide an answer with any assurance. Some leading members of the "nationalist party" were old Communists; Sergei Vikulin, the editor of *Nash sovremennik*, had made a modest name for himself with stories on village life distinguished by a notable embellishment of reality. Anatoli Ivanov, the editor of *Molodaya gvardiya*, had engaged in antireligious propaganda at a time when such exercises were no longer mandatory. But other leading representatives of the conservatives (such as Kozhinov) had, for all one knows, always been patriots who had paid only a minimum of lip service to the party line.[5]

If they failed to opt for a confrontation with their ideological foes in the party leadership, it was probably because they feared losing their literary outlets. Even under Communist censorship they could, after all, do some good for their cause. If they had behaved like Solzhenitsyn or Borodin they would have found themselves outside Russia, or in prison and deprived of the ability to publish. This risk they did not want to accept.

Censorship made Aesopian language de rigueur. When one of the

---

5. But the minimum was still quite substantial. Thus Kozhinov wrote a long programmatic article (*Nash sovremennik* 10, [1986]), on the *Leninist* concept of national culture, in which he expressed unreserved approval; almost half the citations were to Lenin's collected works.

nationalists wanted to express dismay about the war in Afghanistan, he had to refer to Trotsky's aggressive strategies rather than call a spade by its rightful name. In discussing the Slavophiles, they constantly had to emphasize the progressive character of these thinkers (as demonstrated by their insistence on agrarian reform) and to explain away as of no consequence clearly obscurantist utterances. Those who were religious believers, such as Soloukhin, had to make it known from time to time that they were atheists in their innermost heart. They would attack Pasternak and Tvardovsky when the authorities asked for it, but seldom Stalin and never Lenin. Dissimulation became their second nature. They were not the stuff of which heroes and martyrs are made.

Sometimes their Aesopianism went so far as to obscure their intentions. Thus the writing of most of the conservatives constantly referred to the battle of Kulikovo (1380) as a turning point in Russian history. At Kulikovo, Dmitri Donskoi, duke of Moscow, defeated a Tatar army; but, as students of Russian history knew, the battle was in no way decisive. The Tatars came back, sacked Moscow, and kept the Russian principalities under their rule for almost another two hundred years. It has been argued that the real target of the Russian nationalists citing Kulikovo was not the Tatars, but the "cosmopolitan coalition" of Russia's foes. This, if true, was a farfetched way to identify one's enemies; one could not be quite certain what the nationalists had in mind, and there must have been more straightforward ways to broadcast their message.

Another feature that emerged from the writings of the nationalists was that while they greatly admired Russia's historical and cultural traditions, they were not really as knowledgeable about them as they should have been. True, these topics were not widely taught, nor was the literature readily available. Whatever the reason, if one of them referred to "Nil Sarovski," this was comparable to a Catholic mentioning St. Augustine of Assisi. The nationalists' beliefs, in short, were intense, but they seem to have been more clear in their minds about their enemies than about their national traditions, values, and ideals.

Everything considered, the nationalists did not do badly in their running battle with the liberals inside and outside the party apparatus. True, they suffered setbacks; under Brezhnev and Chernenko they fared better than under Andropov. Editors were replaced from time to time, but their seats were taken by like-minded people. Russian messianism had to be played down for certain periods, but on the whole the nationalists maintained and even extended and fortified their positions. Roman Gazeta, the only publishing house producing mass editions on cheap paper and at a very low price, brought out writers from the nationalist camp almost exclusively.

Their ideological foes, on the other hand, were defeated. Alexander Yakovlev, acting head of the ideological department of the Central Committee, launched a broadside in 1972 against the "antihistoricism of the Russophiles," criticizing their cult of religion and taking the side of the nineteenth-century revolutionary democrats against the conservatives. As a result Yakovlev found himself exiled for many years as ambassador to Canada, and it took Gorbachev's rise to power for him to return to Moscow. Subsequently Yakovlev became a member of the Politburo and the chief bogeyman of the Russophiles, even though he seldom intervened in the ideological debate between nationalists and liberal democrats. Perhaps the nationalists were right to dislike him, because alone in the political leadership he was a man of both knowledge and firm convictions; not an extremist, not an uncritical pro-Westerner; a Russian patriot; but at the same time a democrat in the tradition of the nineteenth-century Russian intelligentsia, who had no sympathy for chauvinism and religious obscurantism.

Nash sovremennik prevailed in the conflict with the liberal *Novy mir* which ended with the ouster of Tvardovsky (the editor in chief) and virtually his whole crew. *Novy mir* had sharply criticized writings by leading New Right spokesmen, and while this was not the only reason for its downfall, it was undoubtedly one of the main causes. It showed that while the party leadership had no wish to adopt in toto nationalist doctrine as it emerged from the pages of *Nash sovremennik* and *Molodaya gvardiya,* and while it expected the right wing not to exceed certain limits as far as Marxism-Leninism was concerned, it considered the "liberals" a far more alien and potentially dangerous element. Both *Novy mir* and *Molodaya gvardiya* were purged in 1969–1970. But while the latter resumed its editorial policy within a year as if nothing had happened, *Novy mir* was effectively silenced for twenty years.[6] A crucial role in the downfall of *Novy mir* was played by the "letter of the eleven"—an open letter published in *Ogonyok* in 1969 in which some leading literary figures came out openly in defense of the views that had been voiced in *Molodaya gvardiya.*[7] All eleven were, as far as can be established, members in good standing of the Communist party. They would have hardly signed this manifesto without encouragement from above. The letter meant that Russian nationalism (again within well-known limits) had received official sanction. And also it

6. John Dunlop, *The Faces of Contemporary Russian Nationalism* (Princeton, N.J., 1983), pp. 221–41.

7. This letter was to play an important role in the ideological polemics under *glasnost* in 1989–1990.

meant that the foundation was laid for a nationalist-Communist alliance, which twenty years later emerged as a political reality.

Solzhenitsyn and Friends

One of the crucial influences on the development of the Soviet right in the 1960s and 1970s was Alexander Solzhenitsyn. Until the late 1960s Solzhenitsyn's fame rested on his novels, published in *Novy mir* or in samizdat. Those close to him must have known his political views; he agreed with the liberal Sakharov on some issues and disagreed on others. When he brought *Ivan Denisovich,* his famous first novel, to a Moscow literary magazine, his seemingly obvious choice was *Novy mir,* the bulwark of the "liberals," who enthusiastically welcomed him. The idea of taking it to one of the conservative mouthpieces seems not even to have occurred to him. In later years he quarreled with *Novy mir,* but this had more to do with questions of editing and style, and above all with Solzhenitsyn's conviction that *Novy mir* did not fight hard enough to get his stories released by the censors. (This was an unfair charge; the embattled *Novy mir* went as far as it possibly could in difficult conditions.) At one point, as a sign of protest, he took his stories to the journals of the right, which despite some promises did nothing for him. On the contrary, among the harshest critics of Solzhenitsyn while he was in the Soviet Union were the conservatives and some of the nationalists, including prominent church leaders, whereas the *obrazovanshchina*— the intelligentsia, which he was to deride so much in later years—was his main champion.

Solzhenitsyn's political views began to emerge clearly from "Live Not by Lies," his open letter to the Soviet leaders, and the collection of essays *From Under the Rubble.* But "Live Not by Lies" dealt mainly with the issues of freedom, repentance, and the moral regeneration of the Soviet people. *From Under the Rubble* contained some criticism of the intelligentsia ("the smatterers"). Solzhenitsyn singled out those who believed that "overcoming the national messianic delusion was Russia's most urgent task." But he also attacked the National Bolsheviks, and if this collection of essays expressed the views of a few conservatives, liberal nationalists such as Karabanov and Agursky were also represented.

"Live Not by Lies," written in his Zurich exile, was Solzhenitsyn's appraisal of the world situation. It makes strange reading in retrospect: The West was on its knees (this was the title of one of the subsections); war with China was seemingly inevitable (another subtitle); the world faced an immediate dangerous grain shortage. There were other such predictions, which were not borne out by subsequent events. At the same time the letter included astute comments and suggestions, such as the need for radical change in the countryside; the village, once the mainstay of Russian civilization, had become its chief weakness. The misery of urban life was singled out for comment, as were the ecological disasters and the need to cast off Marxist-Leninist ideology, which had become altogether irrelevant. Marxism-Leninism generated permanent conflict with the outside world, was sapping Russia's strength at home, and, generally speaking, perpetuated the system of permanent lies. Solzhenitsyn proposed the abolition of the draft, which was unlikely to endear him to the right.

What was the ideological alternative, in Solzhenitsyn's view? Some kind of enlightened authoritarian regime based on the Soviets, for a grass-roots democracy was simply not attainable in Russia in the near future. He regarded Christianity as the only living force able to help Russia on the road to spiritual healing, but he wanted no special privileges for the church. His was an appeal for kindheartedness, for love of one's own people, against political and economic gigantism, for encouraging the inner moral development of the Russian people. It later emerged that there had been an earlier version of the "Letter" more critical of the West and more laudatory of the Slavophiles.

Solzhenitsyn's views, though moderately stated, were not welcomed by the liberal dissidents. Sakharov, in a reply, noted—as usual—Solzhenitsyn's greatness as a novelist but took exception to what he regarded as the latter's excessively nationalistic views. Even if stated only by implication, their assumption was that Western ideas were at the bottom of Russia's evils and that meaningful democracy was impossible in Russia. Sakharov also discovered a latent xenophobic streak in the "Letter," as well as a concentration on the suffering of the Russian people, ignoring the torment of others.[8]

After Solzhenitsyn's forcible deportation from the Soviet Union his political comments, as in his famous Harvard speech and in many interviews and occasional essays, became less moderate. There was a certain inconsistency: He believed that Russia's crisis was essentially spiritual rather than political in nature, but he still went on commenting on many political issues of the day. He realized that his main function was that of a creative writer (*The Red Wheel* series was well under way) but in his first years in exile he still let himself be distracted on frequent occasions to deliver his political

8. There is much literature on the development of Solzhenitsyn's views over the years. The most authoritative and balanced survey is Michael Scammel's massive Solzhenitsyn biography (New York, 1984). The most systematic outline is Dora Shturman, *Gorodu i miru* (Urbi et Orbi) (Paris and New York, 1988), which is very much in sympathy with Solzhenitsyn.

obiter dicta. His speeches became more strident, and there was the recurring notion that the West was terribly weak and did not even begin to realize the extent of the Russian danger. (The notion that hardly any Westerner was capable of understanding Russia was widespread among Russian émigrés. It was probably provoked by some misguided publications by certain Western Sovietologists, but there were also deep-seated differences of opinion concerning the interpretation of Russian history.)

Generally speaking, Solzhenitsyn and many other Russians came to the West intellectually quite unprepared, and hence unable, to understand the mainsprings of Western culture and politics. The cultural isolation to which they had been subjected manifested itself all too clearly. There was often a grain of truth in his publicistic writings, on some occasions more than on others. On the decadence of the West and in the attacks against "our pluralists" (i.e., Russian liberal dissidents) Solzhenitsyn's ire was provoked by those in the West who put much or most of the blame on the Russian element in the misfortunes that had befallen his country, rather than on the impact of bolshevism, an alien (Western) ideology imported against the wish of the people. But Solzhenitsyn usually weakened his case by exaggeration and lack of balance.

This was also true with regard to some of his political fiction, most notably in *Lenin in Zurich*. The intention of demystifying Lenin was praiseworthy, as a novel it was powerful, but read as history it was seriously flawed and in some respects downright misleading. Boris Souvarine, who had known Lenin, whose knowledge of the Soviet period was much deeper than Solzhenitsyn's and whose anticommunism predated the novelist's by several decades, rightly pointed to some of the main weaknesses: Lenin's trip via Germany to Russia in 1917 had never been secret. Parvus-Helphand (the ideologist of the "permanent revolution"), who appeared in the novel as Lenin's evil guru and Svengali, had never had any real influence on him; in fact, Lenin had detested him.

According to Solzhenitsyn only one-quarter of Lenin's ancestry was Russian, but what did it matter? After all, the tsar had even less Russian blood in his veins, and two-thirds of the Russian aristocracy was of foreign origin, not to mention Pushkin, Lermontov, and many other stars in the Russian firmament. Solzhenitsyn could argue that as a novelist he could take certain artistic liberties with historical facts. But his critics were also right in maintaining that Solzhenitsyn was producing a new mythology, which was far from the historical truth.

Some of Solzhenitsyn's critics clearly overshot their target when in the heat of the polemic they referred to him as a new fundamentalist ayatollah preaching Pravoslav fascism. But having entered the fray with strong views,

Solzhenitsyn could not reasonably expect uncritical acceptance of his political philosophy. He had never used the language of the Black Hundred, nor had he preached the establishment of a theocracy. But he attacked the liberals and Westerners, the "antipatriots," without mercy, and they naturally repaid him in the same coin. Much as he hated bolshevism, he was a product of the Soviet system; his psychology, as one critic has said, bears the stamp of the best and loftiest of human qualities, but also of war, concentration camp, and totalitarianism. His way of arguing with political enemies was influenced by his upbringing and the milieu in which he had lived most of his life. He was not well versed in Western thought, nor did he make a great effort to learn, occupied as he was with his enormous literary project. He shielded himself from all new influences. No wonder, then, that his long stay in the West merely confirmed his prejudices, just as Dostoyevsky's visit to London, and his inspection tour of the Crystal Palace, had confirmed his assumption about the coming victory of a materialist civilization—and the proximity of the apocalypse.

Of Solzhenitsyn's erstwhile friends and well-wishers in Moscow, some parted ways with him early on. Lakshin of the *Novy mir* editorial board wrote that Solzhenitsyn did not recognize equality in spiritual matters, that he was writing in the tradition of hagiography, with his own life as the exemplary one.

Some of his former comrades in arms went over to the extreme right. One such was Igor Shafarevich, a capable mathematician who had been made a professor at the age of twenty-one and eventually became a corresponding and then a full member of the Academy of Sciences. Shafarevich the political essayist was not quite in the same league as Solzhenitsyn. As a writer he was rather plodding; his "Socialism as a Phenomenon of World History" reminded unkind critics of the reinvention of the wheel several millennia after the event. Relentlessly, over 384 pages he marshaled excerpts from the 168 books he had read on the subject, proving that socialism had always been a bad idea with disastrous consequences. Considering that the book was written at a time when Marxism-Leninism was the state religion in the Soviet Union, it was perhaps a remarkable manifestation of critical thought. But it did not contain anything that reasonably well-informed Western readers did not know. Furthermore, the selectiveness of the sources and the one-sidedness of the approach were not compatible with scholarliness and objectivity. As a polemical tract the book had its merits but it was not a work of lasting value.

Shafarevich acquired true fame as the result of the publication of *Russophobia,* a much smaller book. First written around 1980 and later updated, it became accessible to a wider circle of readers only in 1990, following the publication of the manuscript in installments in *Nash sov-remennik* and other periodicals of the right such as the Munich *Veche*.[9]

Shafarevich's basic thesis is that there exists a "small people" *(malyi narod)* that has been trying throughout history to manipulate the "great people," to decide its fate for it, to destroy religious and national values in Russian life. As typical examples of the campaigns of the "small people" to distract popular attention from the really important issues, the author mentions Voltaire's protest against the Catholic church in connection with a witchcraft trial, the Dreyfus affair, and the Beilis trial (in which in 1913 a Kiev Jewish tailor was accused of ritual murder, and subsequently acquitted). Typical representatives of the "small people were Heinrich Heine, mainly in view of his "dirty attacks against Christianity," and the Hebrew poet Bialik (best known for his lament after the Kishinev pogrom). The "small people" want to denigrate Russia in a systematic way, attribute to it a serf mentality, deny all its historical achievements. They aim at turning it into a Western-style liberal democracy. This would be tantamount to a spiritual occupation of Russia and eventually perhaps also physical occupation by the "small people" and the West.

The "small people" consists mainly, though not exclusively, of Jewish intellectuals, anti-Russian, rootlessly cosmopolitan, destructive elements—a "ferment of decomposition," in the phrase of a nineteenth-century German historian. Shafarevich got his inspiration concerning the "small people" from August Cochin, the historian of the French revolution who died on the field of battle in the First World War. Cochin investigated the groundwork laid for revolution by various literary and philosophical circles under the *ancien régime*.

However, it is not readily obvious in what way these circles and individuals, from Voltaire to the Encyclopedists, could shed light on the situation in Russia. They certainly could not be charged with a lack of patriotism; the troops of the French Revolution were marching, after all, to the tune "Allons, enfants de la patrie."[10] Shafarevich's predilection for

9. There exist various versions of this book, some expurgated. The most recent one is *Est li u Rossii budushshe?* (Moscow 1991).

10. An original twist to Shafarevich's ideas was given by Evgenii Vagin, a monarchist who left the Soviet Union and settled in Italy after having spent several years in the gulag. Vagin suggested the term "mondialism" to define the ideology and the political aims of the *"malyi narod"* (*Slovo,* 10 [1991]; see also L. Okhotin in *Den,* 7 [1991]). This refers to the establishment of a plutocratic world government, antinationalist, antireligious on the lines of Bilderberg, the world federalists, Fukujama-Kojéve; a highbrow and updated version of the *Protocols of the Elders of Zion.* Vagin had been a leader of VSKHSON, the Christian dissident group, and after his emigration edited *Veche* in Munich, an extreme right-wing organ. The word "mondialism" was probably first coined by the French *Nouvelle Droite.*

monarchies and his aversion for democrats constitute a legitimate point of view. But since monarchs and monarchists are not necessarily greater patriots than their opponents, Shafarevich's reasoning is not easy to follow.

The concept of Russophobia goes back to the Slavophiles and writers such as Tyutchev, but the enemies in question at the time were British imperialism, the Catholic church, European liberals—hardly the "small people," which had no political influence. It is, of course, true that throughout history both foreigners and Russians have expressed negative views of many features of Russian history and politics: Many reports by foreign travelers to Russia were not flattering; and there were some very negative, exaggerated accounts by Baltic Germans such as Victor Hehn.[11] But similar views were expressed by native sons, including leading Russian thinkers who cannot possibly be accused of antipatriotism; from Pushkin, Lermontov, and Cha'adayev to Chernychevsky and Gorky. Some of the harshest comments on the Russian people were made by leaders of the extreme right after the Revolution of 1917: The Russian people were scum because they had betrayed the tsar. Every Russian schoolchild knows Lermontov's poem "Land of Masters, land of Slaves," yet Shafarevich directs his attacks against émigré periodicals of which not one in a thousand Russians has ever heard. Shafarevich could have argued (but never did) that what is permissible to a Lermontov and Cha'adayev is not permissible to Jews and other "aliens" who have no real roots in Russia. His indignation was selective, and as a result he received much acclaim in like-minded circles but was ridiculed by the liberal intelligentsia.

What can be said in Shafarevich's defense? Throughout Russian history, parts of the liberal and radical intelligentsia have been alienated from the state and have never regarded it as the embodiment of the national spirit. They have been accused of destructive attitudes, of general negativism, of the desire to destroy rather than to build. Dostoyevsky wrote about the alienation of the intelligentsia at great length and the famous "Landmarks" *(Vekhi)* of 1909 is devoted to this theme. This alienation is certainly regrettable from the point of view of a Russian patriot, but it leaves open the question of responsibility. It could hardly be argued that the tsarist regime tried very hard to integrate the intelligentsia (let alone national minorities) in the conduct of affairs of state. In any case there is something strange, even pathological, in the extreme sensitiveness shown by those seeing a mortal sin in all and any criticism of the nation and putting all the blame for what went wrong in Russia on foreigners.

Throughout modern history there have been Anglophobia, Franco-

11. V. Hehn, *De moribus Ruthenorum* (Stuttgart, 1892).

phobia, Germanophobia, and a great deal of anti-Americanism, some of it justified, some tasteless and stupid. Yet normal British, French, German, and American citizens have shrugged off attacks of this kind as a matter of no particular consequence. How is one to explain why in Russia such sensitivity has been, at least in some circles, so much greater than it has anywhere else? It is a question that certainly deserves careful study.

An Interim Balance

Russian patriotic writers with little sympathy for the chauvinists in their country have argued for a long time that the West tends to exaggerate the importance of the Black Hundred and their ideology, and even more the role of their successors such as Pamyat. Russians have claimed that this has been done with the intention to discredit Russian conservatives and patriots, and the "Russian idea" in general.

These complaints deserve to be taken seriously, and we shall have to refer to them again in the course of this study. The Black Hundred and their successors certainly had no monopoly as far as Russian patriotism is concerned, just as the Bolsheviks on the left had no monopoly on socialism. Before 1917 (and after 1988) there were Social Democrats, Socialist Revolutionaries, and various liberal groups, all of which were of far greater consequence on the ideological (and much of the time also on the political) level. To some extent the complaints of the moderate Russian nationalists are justified. Much ink was spilled between 1987 and 1992 about Pamyat and about impending pogroms; but the only pogroms that took place were directed against Russians, Armenians, and Mesket Turks.

However, experience in other countries has shown that at a time of political and economic crisis, marginal fascist or para-fascist groups may suddenly assume a role of considerable importance; sometimes they may emerge as a decisive force in politics. It was this fear, rather than the actual danger or the wish to calumniate the Russian national idea, that provoked interest in the extremist, chauvinist groups. Nor can it be argued that their influence was wholly imaginary under late tsarism. Nikolai II, after all, subscribed to much of their program, and so did certain other key figures within his administration. It cannot be seriously denied that toward the end of his life Stalin believed in a Jewish conspiracy against him—hence the Doctors' Plot and the campaign against "cosmopolitans." In the 1970s and 1980s similar ideas had supporters in the Politburo; otherwise the so-called "anti-Zionist campaign" would not have been launched.

How central was (and is) the idea of a Judeo-Masonic conspiracy to the doctrines of the extreme right, and to what extent was (and is) it believed? Why did it have a renaissance under *glasnost*? For the lunatic fringe, as in other countries, a conspiracy theory was absolutely crucial; one cannot understand fringe thinking without it. It was probably more intensely believed in Russia than in other countries, including Nazi Germany. Hitler, Goebbels, Goering, and their ilk thought the Jews racially inferior and hated and despised them; but they never believed in a giant plot.

There were some Nazis who did, but these were not figures of great consequence; the great believer in a Masonic conspiracy was General Ludendorff, a political lightweight who became something of an embarrassment for the Nazis. Among the politically more sophisticated leaders in Russia as in Germany there was the feeling that the *Protocols* and the other conspiracy theories should not be taken at face value.

However, there was suspicion, even among intellectuals, that there was no smoke without fire. Perhaps there was some truth in the sensational revelations? In any case, the *Protocols* had their use as a propaganda weapon, but they were certainly not a firm article of belief for serious persons. The *Protocols* as such, while mentioned in Nazi propaganda and published in the Third Reich, were never officially endorsed by it. In Russia after 1917 and again in the late 1980s and 1990s there seems to have been greater willingness to accept them. This may be connected with the presence of many Jews in the new political elite for some years after 1917; they offered an easy target. But there were no Jews among the leaders of the 1980s, so this explanation does not seem quite satisfactory. Russian acceptance of the *Protocols* was undoubtedly connected with the occurrence of sudden cataclysmal events in 1917, as in 1990–1991, which paved the way for all kinds of farfetched theories. In the same way there was a revival of astrology and other occult "sciences."

How widely was *zhidomasonstvo* believed? Was Russian public opinion more chauvinist, anti-Semitic, and xenophobic than French or German around the turn of the last century? There was more anti-Semitism in France at the time than in Germany, and probably not less in Germany than in Russia. True, there were no pogroms in Western and Central Europe, but the pogroms were limited to certain sections of society, and most of them took place outside Russia proper. Despite official and popular anti-Semitism in the Soviet Union there was a great deal of intermingling in the 1970s and 1980s. Jews played an important part in cultural life and there was a high percentage of intermarriage. Though many Jews left, this was seldom because of acute anti-Semitism. Thus, while dealing with the manifestations of *zhidomasonstvo* it is vital to keep in mind that it affected certain parts of Soviet society but not others.

Furthermore, the leaders and gurus of even the most radical sects were aware that conspiracy theories could never be the whole content of their doctrine. Hatred and suspicion are powerful instincts, but they are not sufficient; something more positive was needed, as it had been in Nazi Germany and fascist Italy. Among these positive elements are national traditions that should be revived: the church; the cult of the village, where Russianness had developed over the centuries. It includes ecological concerns, the preservation of the natural habitat, the forests that had been destroyed, the lakes that had been poisoned, the old buildings that had turned into ruins. It means attention to all the negative features that had afflicted wide sections of Russian society: crime, alcoholism, the dissolution of the family, the lack of idealism among the young generation.

All the nationalist groups, moderate and extreme alike, have tried to imbue their fellow citizens, and above all the young, with spiritual values. They celebrated the battle of Kulikovo and the heroic deeds of Minin and Pozharsky; they commemorated Suvorov, Kutuzov, and other military leaders. They rediscovered Stolypin. They opposed the rerouting of the Siberian rivers ("the project of the century") and some of them volunteered to rebuild historical monuments in their spare time. There was a great reservoir of goodwill; the various societies dedicated to the preservation of the Russian environment had millions of members.

But, however dear the old Russian village was to the heart of Russian patriots, it had disappeared, and probably it was also too late to save some of the rivers or Lake Aral. The young had only limited interest in the battles of past centuries and the military leaders of past ages. The struggle against alcoholism was by and large a failure—and in any case, as with many of the other good causes, there was nothing specific rightwing about it. Readings from Pushkin and Lermontov attracted big crowds. But not many poems lent themselves to patriotic indoctrination such as the extreme right wanted: Pushkin's warning to those who calumniated Russia, his "Moscow: How much there is in this sound for every Russian" and his "Onegin rides; for he shall see Holy Russia"; Lermontov's "Borodino"; Viazemsky's "Holy Russia—Providence foretold her path"; and a bit of Tyutchev. But on the whole the great Russian writers were more interested in nature and the private sphere and the ultimate questions of human existence. If they wrote about the government and society of their country they were frequently bitterly critical. Some were "Westerners," others pacifists and downright unpatriotic such as Tolstoy. Even Dostoyevsky wrote about religious faith and pan-humanism much of the time. In the circumstances, there was a strong temptation to fall back on conspirational delusions, such as the belief that Lermontov had been killed by Freemasons and Jews.[12]

There was a Russian school of painters and there were Russian composers whose work was deeply imbued with the spirit of their homeland. But these great masters were in no way the the monopoly of the far right, nor even of the moderate nationalists. They were part and parcel of Russian culture and, to a certain extent, of all mankind.

While *zhidomasonstvo* was, by and large, limited to the extreme groups, it had certain ideological repercussions among more moderate nationalists. The moderates did not believe the cruder manifestations of the *Protocols* and similar conspiracy theories. But they did suspect that there was widespread Russophobia and a concerted effort to denigrate the "Russian idea." The idea that "the whole world is lined up against us" has appeared in various times in many places, and there is probably no people that has not been subject to phobias. But why should Russians have reacted so much more violently against negative comment than citizens of other countries facing similar criticism? At a time when in certain parts of the former Soviet Union Russians were beaten up merely for speaking Russian, why should educated men of the Russian right have disinterred forgotten poems of the 1920s in which tactless remarks were made on certain heroes of Russian history?[13] There is no obvious answer to this question.

12. This was the thesis of Ivan Burlayev's movie *Lermontov*, which was derided by the cognoscenti and virtually all critics but became a cult film of the right.

13. This refers, for instance, to the poems of Pavel Kogan and Jack Altgausen, poets of the 1920s and 1930s. Kogan was instrumental in informing on a friend, the famous physicist Lev Landau, who but for Kapitsa's intervention, would have perished as a result. Kogan was killed in the Second World War. Deriding Russian heroes was fashionable at the time; the prime movers were not Kogan but Pokrovsky and Demyan Bednyi, of true Russian stock.

Chapter Eight

JUDAISM WITHOUT A MASK

AN ESSENTIAL INGREDIENT in the development of the ideology of the extreme right in the postwar period was anti-Semitism. In contrast to other components it developed predominantly inside the government and not within the dissident fringe. Zionism had been considered an enemy in the Soviet Union ever since the Revolution of 1917. In the early 1920s the last independent Zionist (and Jewish) groups were dissolved and the militants arrested. For several decades after, Zionism and the Jews did not feature prominently in Soviet policy and propaganda—which was only natural, in view of the very limited importance of Zionism in world politics.

There was discrimination against Jews in the 1930s and during the war; most of those in leading positions were purged. But no open attacks took place and even the "anticosmopolitan campaign," which got under way in the late 1940s, was not directed against Jews per se; care was taken to include a few ethnic Russians among those accused of "cosmopolitan" crimes. The destruction of Yiddish culture and the execution of most Yiddish writers could not be interpreted as anti-Zionist, for Zionists never had any use for Yiddish. It was, of course, a manifestation of anti-Semitism. But only during the last months of Stalin's life, with the arrest of the Jewish doctors accused of poisoning and trying to kill the Russian leadership, were all restraints dropped. Stalin intended to deport all Jews from Russia to points north of the Arctic Circle—following the request of some leading Jewish figures that this be done. Immediately after Stalin's death, the surviving physicians were released from prison and the plans for deportation were shelved.

In 1948 the Soviet government was among the first to recognize the state of Israel, and while Soviet attitudes toward the Jewish state rapidly cooled, relations remained more or less normal up to 1967, when Moscow broke off diplomatic ties following the Six Day War. Throughout the 1950s and 1960s the party line toward Zionism and Israel was hostile, but there was no particular emphasis, either quantitative or qualitative, on these topics. If Israel was depicted in a very unfavorable light, the same was true, broadly speaking, with regard to the United States and most other Western countries.

It was only in the middle sixties that a new kind of literature came into being which, while ostensibly "anti-Zionist," did not really aim its attacks at the world Zionist movement or the state of Israel but set itself different targets. (A specialized anti-Israeli literature continued to appear, but this was quite obviously written for a different and much smaller public.) "Anti-Zionism" was a code word for attacks on Jews and Judaism in general, and also on various other causes and people, usually of a liberal or social-democratic orientation. The first shot was fired with the publication of Trofim Kichko's *Judaism Without Embellishment* in 1963, and the campaign gathered further momentum around 1970. Thereafter, every year a dozen books and hundreds of articles were published, relentlessly spreading the same message, which was, briefly, as follows: The idea of Judaism is the idea of world fascism. The Old Testament was fascist; so were Moses, King Solomon, and virtually all other Jewish leaders from the very beginning. The Jews had always been chauvinist aggressors and mass murderers; they were parasites who had never created anything new, original, and valuable. They had always sought to destroy and subjugate other peoples, and in particular the Russians. Their aim was the domination of the whole world through deceit, corruption (material and spiritual), and mass murder. The Jews had been the pioneers of capitalism and every other evil cause in history; they were in the forefront of anticommunism and nourished a burning hatred of Russian culture ("Russophobia"). Hitler and the other Nazi leaders had been mere puppets in their hands; they had incited Hitler to make war against the Soviet Union in 1941. They had connived with Hitler at the destruction of certain groups of poor Jews during the Second World War, but the number of Jews killed had been grossly exaggerated. The aim of this intrigue was to get international sanction for the establishment of the state of Israel. But Israel was a mere sideshow; the real aim was world domination. Now that the Jews had subverted and gotten hold of all key positions in the United States and the other Western countries, the only major obstacle to the ultimate Zionist victory was the Soviet Union.[1]

From time to time a few of these books and authors were criticized for going too far, and Kichko's work was even temporarily withdrawn following intervention by some foreign Communist parties that found the text (and perhaps even more, the *Stürmer*-style cartoons) embarrassing. But the "anti-Zionist" propaganda had powerful protectors; notwithstanding minor setbacks it continued full steam and over the years became even more outspoken and radical. If there had been certain taboos in the beginning, most of these were eventually dropped. By the early 1980s it was legitimate to argue that there had never been anti-Jewish pogroms in tsarist Russia, but merely legitimate acts of self-defense against Jewish provocations. This was not how Lenin had commented on these events, but it had become safe to ignore Lenin and the shibboleths of "proletarian internationalism." As Romanenko wrote in 1986, anti-Semitism could not exist by definition in the Soviet Union; therefore no punches had to be pulled in attacking the Jews. If Hitler had been a mere Jewish puppet, no wonder virtually all Western politicians were either Jews, or of Jewish origin, or under Jewish influence. The same was true for all the big corporations, the banks, the media, and, generally speaking, all key positions, except possibly in Japan and China.

This, then, was the general tenor of the new literature on Jews and Judaism. It also covered quite a few groups and individuals that were not Jewish at all—such as, for instance, the Jehovah's Witnesses. For, as these Russian writers saw it, only Zionists would have chosen such a name voluntarily. In addition, there was a considerable amount of fiction catering to a public unlikely to read political tracts. Typical examples were the novels by Ivan Shevtsov, a former professional army officer. The main villain in his best known work was a Jew, who murdered and disemboweled his mother to gain her inheritance; he later subjected to the same treatment a beautiful young Russian teenager whom he had first seduced and then turned into a drug addict. In between he engaged in anti-Soviet propaganda, writing articles and plays.[2]

It is clear from this literature that the target was not a small state in the Middle East whose existence was of some limited interest to Soviet policy-

1. Among the outstanding works in this flood of literature were the writings of V. Begun, Lev Korneyev, V. Bolshakov, Yevgeni Yevseyev, V. Emelyanov, Yu. Ivanov, V. I. Kiselev, and A. Z. Romanenko, whose *O klassovoi sushshnosti Tsionisma* appeared in Leningrad in 1986.

2. Various Soviet publications denounced these books, and even *Pravda* called them "ideologically vicious and artistically weak." But up to 1990, hundreds of thousands of copies were still reprinted by the publishing house of the Soviet armed forces. And there were other novels of the same kind.

makers. If so, what were the aims of this "anti-Zionism"? It is not at all easy to provide a satisfactory answer. If these writers and those backing them were really motivated by a deep, burning hate of the Jews they should have welcomed the opportunity to get rid of them. For they certainly did not want the assimilation of Russian Jewry, which would further poison their genetic font. But they opposed a Jewish exodus from the Soviet Union.

Did they really believe that Judaism and Zionism were essentially fascist and rabidly anticommunist in nature? This is highly doubtful, for under *glasnost* the accusations against Jews suddenly changed; the main charge was no longer that Jews were anticommunist, but on the contrary that they had been prominently involved in the Bolshevik party before, during, and after the Revolution and thus had brought untold misery on the Russian people. In brief, many anti-Semitic authors had been anticommunist all along, though they had to hide it. But this had not made the supposedly anticommunist Jews any more attractive to them.

The official anti-Zionist literature prior to 1986 could not be openly anti-Marxist, even though the fact that Karl Marx was a German Jew by origin had been no secret. On the contrary, the anti-Semites used the classics of Marxism-Leninism to buttress their case. Their arguments were essentially those of the Black Hundred, but they could not openly state their sources; instead, they had to write about the "class essence" of Judaism while they really meant the Jews' race. It was, no doubt, frustrating to have to use code words such as "Zionism" when the real target was quite obvious. Anti-Semitism is not a rational phenomenon, and the endeavor to look for rational explanations has seldom been altogether satisfactory.

When in the 1920s a disproportionate number of Jews had been in positions of political influence, popular anti-Semitism had not been particularly intense. In his lifetime Trotsky had not been more hated than other Bolshevik leaders—except, of course, by the Stalinists. It was only fifty years after his assassination that Trotsky and other Jewish Communists of his generation, such as Sverdlov, became monsters of mythical proportions. True, in the 1920s the dictatorship would not permit open manifestations of anti-Semitism, but this alone does not explain the riddle. Punishment in such cases was never very severe, and if popular feeling in this respect had been overwhelmingly strong, this would have shown itself one way or another. Yet it seldom did. Whatever the reasons, in the 1980s the Jews were disliked in some circles, hated in others, and these emotions were fanned by influential persons in the Soviet Union. There is no reason to assume that Khrushchev, Brezhnev and Andropov were rabid anti-Semites;

they probably did not particularly like Jews but nor did Jewish issues obsess them. If so, who were the forces encouraging the sustained anti-Jewish campaign?

The political directorate of the Soviet armed forces was certainly one of the main supporters of the "anti-Zionists" even though making war against Israel cannot possibly have been high on the agenda of the Soviet General Staff. There were individual leaders on the Central Committee and in the KGB who thought that as the efficacy of official Soviet ideology was palpably declining, the image of a new enemy had to be bolstered, and for various reasons the Jews seemed more vulnerable than others in this respect. Others regarded anti-Zionism as a useful counterweight against liberals and above all dissidents. It was certainly no accident that dissidents permitted to leave were in most cases allowed to leave only for Israel, quite irrespective of whether they were of Jewish origin. The political establishment wanted the general public to believe that all liberals and Jews were "Zionists" at heart. A considerable effort was invested in this campaign, but its effect at the time was limited. In large parts of Russia and in large sections of the population it had hardly any impact at all.

This was not due to philosemitism but to the unwillingness to regard the Jewish problem as one of overwhelming importance. Even among the right-wing dissidents, the Jewish issue did not always figure at the very top. True, in the right-wingers' blueprints for a Russian renaissance there was not much room for "Russian-speaking people" (another code term widely used) who were not of ethnic Russian origin. The right-wingers would favor, more or less openly, the emigration of most Russian Jews, or alternatively, perhaps, the establishment of a Jewish autonomous republic inside the Soviet Union but far away from the Russian heartland. But in the ideological writings of the Russian right the Jewish question was usually just one out of several problems that had to be confronted. Was this, perhaps, because the official anti-Zionist campaign had preempted the subject? Even Igor Shafarevich did not touch upon this issue in writings published before 1986, though it would have been less risky to do so than to attack socialism *tout court*. Even the chief organs of "anti-Zionism" would publish an occasional Jewish author, as indeed some of them did even under *glasnost*, were it only to show that they were not racialists after all.

Seen in retrospect the main historical role of the anti-Zionist campaign—which, beginning in the middle 1960s lasted for almost a quarter of a century—was to provide some continuity between the old anti-Semitism and the new. As the era of *glasnost* dawned, most of the champions of the anti-Zionist drive could be found in the camp of the extreme right.

They could now draw upon the spadework done in earlier years. As restrictions disappeared after 1986, the code words were dropped; a spade could safely be called a spade and no longer an agricultural implement.

True, even after 1986 many opponents of the Jews would deny that they were anti-Semites, referring to the fact that the Arabs were also Semites and that they had nothing against them. But this argument was not exactly novel: Beginning in 1935, the Ministry of Propaganda in Nazi Germany had issued instructions not to use the term "anti-Semitism" because it was offensive to Arabs. The last issue of the standard work on the subject, the *Handbuch der Judenfrage* (1944) stated *expressis verbis* that the concept "anti-Semitism" was "unsuitable because there are other people with Semitic languages such as the Arabs who stand in complete opposition to the Jews."[3]

---

3. On the use of the term "anti-Semitism" in the ninteenth and twentieth centuries, see M. Zimmermann, *Wilhelm Marr: The Patriarch of Antisemitism.* (New York, 1986), pp. 114–15.

NEOPAGANISM AND THE MYTH OF THE GOLDEN AGE

ONE CENTRAL DEMAND of the new Russian nationalism was full freedom for the Orthodox church. As Koshelev had reminded his fellow Slavophiles almost a hundred and fifty years earlier, "without Orthodoxy our *narodnost* is mere rubbish." A few nationalists admitted that they were not religious believers, or, more usually, would simply refrain from commenting on religion. On the other hand, not all religious believers subscribed to a nationalist ideology. And last, there were some, especially among the extreme right, who turned against Christianity and propagated instead a pagan religion that had allegedly been practiced in Russia's distant past.

Very little is known about Russia's pre-Christian past, but this did not deter some nationalists: They freely used myths and even outright forgeries. Such practices are not unknown in the history of other peoples. Ossian's poetry agitated all of Europe toward the end of the eighteenth century; it was written by Macpherson, a Scotsman who pretended that it dated back to the ancient history of Ireland and Scotland. The Czechs had their Königinhofer manuscript, allegedly a thousand years old but manufactured in fact by a nineteenth-century patriot. It needed a man of Masaryk's stature to expose the forgery. The German SS had a special department called *Ahnenerbe* systematically collecting (and manufacturing) evidence of the splendor of pagan Germany.[1]

1. Michael Kater's study *Ahnenerbe* (Stuttgart, 1974), provides a critical review of these activities. Hitler was not much interested, but Himmler gave the enterprise his most ardent

Similar forgeries became fashionable in certain Russian national circles. The most famous of these was the *Book of Vlas*. The existence of this document was first made known in 1953 in an obscure San Francisco journal called *Zhar-ptitsa* ("Firebird"). It announced that before the advent of Christianity there was a great civilization in Russia, dating back to about 1000 B.C. The *Book of Vlas* was said to be a chronicle by pagan priests, dealing with the exploits of the dynasts then ruling Russia; Bravlin, Skoten, Svetoyar, Oleg, and Igor the Older. They allegedly fought the Varagians, Byzantium, and above all the Khazars, who had adopted Judaism.

Unfortunately, the original document no longer existed; it had been in the possession of a colonel named Izenbeck and had been copied by a friend before its disappearance in Nazi-occupied Belgium in World War II. In 1957 an ex-Russian then living in Australia sent a copy of the book (or rather a fragment of a book) to the Soviet Academy in Moscow. The circumstances of the discovery were suspect, to put it mildly, and the Moscow experts, having examined it, said that there was no doubt in their minds. It was a forgery, probably produced by A. I. Sulekadzev, an early-nineteenth-century specialist in forgeries—one of which, incidentally, was called the *Song of Vlas*. Others thought that the forgery was of more recent date and was the work of a certain Yuri Mirolyubov, a chemist and amateur historian from Kiev, who had left the city with the retreating Germans in 1944.[2]

With this the story should have rested, but almost twenty years later it was taken up by a certain Dr. V. Skurlatov who in a series of articles went well beyond the original claims of the *Book of Vlas*. According to his interpretation, the Russians were the descendants of Aryans (or rather "Oriyans") and had come from India and Central Asia about 1000 B.C. Thus the Russians were the first Indo-European or Indo-Aryan people; through the Phoenicians all European culture had come from them. *Vlas* was given wide publicity in leading Soviet journals (albeit popular ones, not those written by and for specialists); it was hailed as a priceless monument of world culture, a pinnacle of the creativity of the Russian folk.

---

support. Mussolini was even less interested in this kind of historical myth-making, but then Italy with its rich Roman past could easily afford to stick to the facts, whereas the fascist movements in some of the smaller European countries, such as Romania, were almost desperate in the search for a glorious heritage.

2. The complicated detective story of the origins of the *Book of Vlas* and its subsequent fate has been put together with great thoroughness by Maya Kaganska, "The Book of Vlas: The Saga of a Forgery," in *Jews and Jewish Topics in Soviet and East European Publications*, 4 (1986), pp. 3–27. This essay also includes a full bibliography of all the publications for and against *Vlas* prior to 1986. On the same subject see also L. Poliakov, *Continent* (November 1987).

Behind the campaign promoting the *Book of Vlas* was one individual who on and off has played an important role in the recent history of the ultra-nationalist camp: Valeri Skurlatov. He first became known in the 1960s, when he distributed among Komsomol leaders and activists of the Moscow party executive a document called "A Code of Morals," which called for the branding and sterilization of Russian women who had sexual intercourse with foreigners. He also demanded the preparing of the young generation for the "mortal struggle" ahead connected with the cosmic mission of the Russian people.[3] Skurlatov suggested corporal punishment for young people disobeying his "code," and he also noted in passing that there was no baser occupation than that of a thinker, an intellectual.

Skurlatov's suggestions caused a minor scandal; he was excluded from the Communist party, but his career suffered no lasting harm. Within ten years he was back in the public eye as a doctor of history, a title much more infrequently bestowed in Russia than in the West, the author of a book entitled *Zionism and Apartheid*. But his main assignment during these years was to popularize *Vlas* under his own name and various pseudonyms. The main intention behind this exercise was not just to show that a great Russian culture had existed thousands of years before such a civilization had arisen elsewhere; Skurlatov also wanted to demonstrate that the Russians were the Aryan people par excellence, that they were a race of supermen who had practiced a cult of warriors and at the same time excelled in virtually all fields of cultural endeavor. They were the light bearers, forever fighting the forces of darkness.

Skurlatov was not successful in persuading the historians, but he spread his gospel through novelists such as Chivilikhin, millions of copies of whose very long novel-essay *Pamyat* ("Memory") were printed in the 1970s and early 1980s. It dealt with the Aryan origins of the Russian people. There was a determined effort in influential circles to give the widest circulation to this book, which had few literary merits and was no joy to read except for the greatest enthusiasts. Skurlatov also had some success among the writers of science fiction, a very popular genre in the Soviet Union. A dozen stories and novels were published between 1976 and 1985 that in one way or another took up the ideas he propagated.[4]

This campaign was by no means a private initiative pursued by an

3. An English translation of this document appears in A. Yanov, *The New Russian Right* (Berkeley, Calif., 1978), pp. 170–72. In the 1990s Skurlatov reappeared as the central figure in various parties and "committees of national salvation." For speculations concerning his real motives and those of his backers, see *Arkhiv samizdat* 6589, June 28, 1991 (RFE/RL)

4. For a listing of these novels and short summaries of their contents, see Kaganska, "The Book of Vlas," pp. 21–24.

eccentric. Skurlatov found considerable support among the fraternity of "anti-Semitologists"; one of the most prominent, Korneyev, wrote that only Jews and those under their influence would disbelieve the message of the *Book of Vlas.* Another "expert," named Emelyanov, declared in 1974 that while the Old Testament was essentially fascist, the New Testament, at least in part, acted as a corrective. Emelyanov had started his career, like Korneyev and other anti-Zionists, at the Institute of Oriental Studies. (Korneyev was by profession a specialist in Malagasy literature.) Emelyanov's work was interrupted for a number of years after he murdered his wife and dismembered her body. (We shall deal with this part of his career later on.) When he was released from a mental institution in the late 1980s his advocacy of paganism had become outspoken and radical. A bitter attack in the form of an open letter to the head of the Orthodox church provoked anger among some of his erstwhile comrades-in-arms.

In 1991 some organs of the extreme right published excerpts from Alfred Rosenberg's *Myth of the Twentieth Century,* the bible of Nazi anti-Christianism. Such frankness was laudable, inasmuch as it recognized an intellectual debt that earlier on had not been acknowledged. But it involved the neopaganists in all kind of inconsistencies, since it was not easy to combine elements of Leninism with Nazi ideology. To provide but one illustration: In 1991, *Istoki,* the organ of one of the extremist groups, published an editorial by V. Prishchepenko, a well-known Moscow neo-Bolshevik, under the title "The Witchhunt Has Gotten Under Way!"[5]

Prishchepenko had acquired a certain reputation in the 1970s as a supporter of Skurlatov; he was the author of a study in which he maintained that there had been a pre-Christian Russian order of knights well in advance of Western medieval knighthood. But he had remained a Bolshevik at heart and in his 1991 article he compared the Yeltsin "witchhunt" with Hitler's following the burning of the *Reichstag* in 1933. Hitler, it was said, was a Mason, a lackey of the banker Mendelssohn, and the worst enemy of the Russian people. Yet page three of the same journal was devoted to a speech by Goebbels on "The Theory and Practice of Bolshevism," originally delivered at the 1936 Nuremberg Party Congress. If Hitler was the worst enemy of the Russian people, Goebbels was apparently a good friend—and the last page of the same journal was devoted to excerpts from the *Book of Vlas.* . . .[6]

5. This referred to the arrest of the leaders of the coup of August 1991. *Istoki,* 5 (1991).

6. The influence of the *Book of Vlas* extended to right-wing extremist circles that rejected Emelyanov's neopaganism and derided his competence with regard to historical issues. (Emelyanov's degree was in economics rather than history.) *Rodnye Prostory* (Leningrad) 1 (1991).

The appearance of *Vlas* and similar forgeries (myths, in more polite language) should not have come as a surprise: It runs like a red thread through the ideological history of the extreme right, from the *Protocols* on. Is it a powerful myth? There are reasons for doubt, because the national idea in Russia has been closely connected with Christianity and from a political point of view a frontal attack on it was unwise, to say the least. Hitler disliked the church but trod very carefully in dealing with it. Mussolini, though not a believer, always tried to be on good terms with the Vatican. But the appearance of Aryan neopaganism did show that not all Russian nationalists were Christian believers and that at least some of them derived their inspiration from very different sources.

Why the need for this pagan myth? This question takes us back to a debate about Russia's national origins that has been raging for a long time, and not only among those specializing in early medieval history. According to the Nestor Chronicle, the Slav tribes of Kievan Rus had invited the Germanic Varangians from Scandinavia to be their princes: "Our land is great and rich, but there is no order in it. Come and rule over us!"

This, if true, would have been a unique case, without parallel in the history of humanity, in the words of Karamzin, the first major Russian historian. Some of the Slavophiles explained it with reference to the early Russians' democratic feeling and lack of national prejudices. However, the very idea that foreigners were needed to restore order in the Russian house cannot have been a pleasant one for Russian patriots; hence the long-standing dispute between Nestorists and anti-Nestorists, those rejecting this unpatriotic version of early Russian history.

The ethnic origin of the Slavs has been not just a historical issue but a highly charged political question. Some Slavophiles tended to discover Slavic influences in all ages and all over the globe, and Dostoyevsky in his pre-Slavophile period wrote of Khomyakov the Slavophile that he would prove irrefutably that Adam too was a Slav who lived in Russia. The propagation of the *Book of Vlas* is a belated and grotesque example of a tradition that goes back for a long time.

Part Three

VILLAINS GALORE—
THE POSTCOMMUNIST AGE

Chapter Ten

THE IDEOLOGY OF THE NEW RIGHT (1)

RUSSIAN CONSERVATIVES BELIEVE that the history of their country has always followed a course different from that of Europe. For a long time Russia was a backward country—mainly because it acted as a bulwark against Mongols, Tatars, and other invaders from the East. Europe did not come to Russia's help in these wars but, on the contrary, isolated it and erected all kind of barriers. About the radical Petrine reforms opinions differ: Few conservatives reject them altogether, but many believe that the innovations could have been introduced over a longer period and without causing so many traumas. As Russia continued to expand into Asia and the Caucasus during the eighteenth and nineteenth centuries, it was a civilizing force not an imperialist aggressor.

Russian power increased rapidly. It became the strongest military force on the Continent; without its contribution Napoleon would not have been defeated. There were setbacks, such as the Crimean War, but these were far from decisive. The industrial revolution occurred later in Russia than it did in the West. But as a result Russia was spared some of the worst features of the industrial revolution and modernization that occurred in the West. With the liberation of the serfs the stage was set for rapid growth in agriculture. At the turn of the last century, Russia produced as much grain as all the American countries taken together; it was the granary of Europe. There were years of starvation, but they were not remotely as bad as under Stalin. At the same time Russia's industrial growth between 1885 and 1914

(5.7 percent per annum) was greater than in any other country. If in 1855 there were 855 miles of railroad, this had risen to 17,000 in 1885 and 48,000 by 1914. Both the direct and the indirect tax burdens were considerably lower in tsarist Russia than in the West. While the country was still poor on a per-capita basis, its social legislation (for instance with regard to working hours and child labor) was quite progressive in comparison with the rest of the world. The diet of the Russian worker and peasant in 1913 was better than in 1991. Some 70 percent of the population was literate when the First World War broke out, and but for the war and the ensuing turmoil, illiteracy would probably have been stamped out in the 1920s. School attendance had been mandatory since 1908; the fees in institutions of higher education were considerably lower than elsewhere.

Foreign observers predicted further stormy growth, given the intrinsic wealth of the country; some went as far as to claim that by the end of the twentieth century Russia would be the world's leading economic power. Demographers estimated that by 1948 the tsarist empire would count 348 million inhabitants. Russian culture, at least the works produced by its best representatives, had achieved world renown; writers such as Tolstoy and Dostoyevsky had no equals in other countries.

Seen in this light Russian history was very different from the Marxists' version, which portrayed a backward, downtrodden, abysmally poor, and unhappy country. In brief, the Revolution and Soviet power were not just a moral and political disaster, but had most unfortunate demographic, economic, and social consequences.

But such views leave out a great deal and provide a one-sided and distorted picture. True, Russia expanded in various directions and became militarily powerful. But it did little to integrate the non-Russian nationalities; its rulers opposed all aspirations to even cultural autonomy and limited self-government. Economic growth rates were impressive, but mainly because the starting point was so low; these are the so-called benefits of backwardness. Furthermore, economic development resulted mainly from the initiative of Westernizers such as Count Witte (whom the Russian nationalists detested), Bunge, his predecessor, and Stolypin (whom they liked more, but whose social policy they still opposed). Jews and other "aliens" played a central role in the modernization of Russia.

Above all, the main pillars of the regime were anything but solid. The autocrats, with the exception of Alexander II, showed little statesmanship and foresight. They believed that the people were not ready (and probably would never be) to take a larger share in governing the country. As a result, the monarchs and their entourage became more and more isolated from the people. "Society"—that is to say, the intelligentsia, much of the middle class, and even sections of the nobility—were opposed to tsarist rule. The church counted for less in this context than is commonly assumed; it was little more than a government department. There were nationalist politicians of stature who recognized the need for a more dynamic policy, but the monarch allowed them little freedom of action, and then only reluctantly and in times of crisis.

No serious attempt was made by the rulers to achieve a greater measure of social cohesion and unity. Much has been said by conservative thinkers in condemnation of the utopian, destructive radicalism of the Russian intelligentsia throughout the nineteenth century and leading up to the Revolution. But such alienation did not come by accident—Alexander III always referred to the "rotten intelligentsia" trying to meddle in affairs of state. If there was no legal outlet for the political energies of the intelligentsia and wide sections of the general population, those energies were bound to explode; by contrast, in the West they were contained and made productive.

There were many warning signs well before 1917—the Crimean War, the terrorist campaigns, the Revolution of 1905, the defeat in the war against Japan—but they were not heeded. A case could perhaps be made in favor of the proposition that monarchy was the best form of government for Russia. But even confirmed monarchists found it increasingly difficult to accept that the individuals who were at the helm had the necessary qualifications to fulfil their mission.

The two heroes of the right were Stolypin and Nikolai II, the "Martyr Tsar." Solzhenitsyn greatly contributed to the Stolypin renaissance with the publication of his historical novels in the 1970s and 1980s; under *glasnost,* hundreds of thousands of copies of Stolypin's speeches were published, as biographies and commemorative articles appeared.[1]

Arkady Stolypin (1861–1911) first became known as a strict, efficient, and incorruptible governor (of Grodno and later Saratov districts). In 1906 he was made minister of the interior, and the year after, prime minister. He was undoubtedly the most intelligent and forceful Russian statesman of the late tsarist period. The left hated him because of his ruthless repression of the revolutionary movement and his dissolution of Parliament. At the same time they recognized that if the agrarian reforms initiated by him had been pushed forward with equal energy after his assassination, and if there had been another decade or two of peaceful development, as Stolypin hoped

---

1. For present-day eulogies of Stolypin see, for instance, "Prorok," *Volya Rossii* (Yekaterinburg), 2 (1991), and the report on the Stolypin lectures in St. Petersburg: *Nashe Vremya,* 6 (1991).

and prayed for, the revolutionary movement would have lost much of its momentum. The slogan "Land for the peasants" would no longer have been effective, and the October Revolution might never have happened.

In a round-table debate that took place in Moscow in 1991 on the reasons for the limited appeal of the patriotic movement, Y. D. Rechkalov referred to its orthodoxy and its tendency to view Russian history through mythological spectacles: Only a practicing member of the Orthodox church could be a true Russian; the market and democracy were evil by definition. References to the last tsar had to be in the style of sugary wall paintings. Stolypin, according to the same school of thought, was a fundamentalist of tsarist autocracy, who spent every minute of his life racking his brain as to how to strengthen autocracy.

But the real Stolypin, as Rechkalov noted, advocated an enlightened patriotism that was fully aware of the advantages and values of a constitution. He wanted twenty years of peace, not to improve and intensify police control, but to implant among the people a civic spirit, to educate them toward abiding by the law, and thus to create the preconditions of a more democratic system. Stolypin's conservative contemporaries were quite aware of his long-term intentions and for this reason he was bitterly attacked by the extreme right for undermining and even destroying tsarism, the church, the collectivist spirit of the Russian people, and so on.[2]

Stolypin was a vigorous leader, and a fine speaker in the Duma; his sincerity and reliability were acknowledged even by his political enemies. In the beginning he was trusted by the tsar, but Nikolai II's attitude changed over the years as the result not only of the constant pressure exerted by Stolypin to get necessary decisions made by a hesitant monarch, but also of the intrigues of the courtiers and of the tsar's wife, who wanted to get rid of him. After Stolypin's murder by Bagrov, a revolutionary turned police agent (and a Jew converted to Christianity) Alexandra told his successor not to mention to her the name of the man who had "overshadowed her husband."

Some of Stolypin's winged sayings were reinvoked under *glasnost*. The liberals and revolutionaries, he said, wanted great shocks, whereas he stood for a great Russia; "We have to give freedom to the Russian people, but first the Russian people have to be worthy of freedom"; "Policy must take care of the sound and the strong, not the drunken and the weak." Thus a legend spread, that, but for Stolypin's murder, all would have been well, and that he was killed by the same Satanic forces that were responsible for Russia's downfall in general.

2. "Prosveshchennyy patriotizm . . ." *Moskva,* 5 (1991), p. 9.

Indeed, the circumstances of Stolypin's murder are not entirely clear to this day, but there is no reason to assume that Russia's fate would have been different but for his assassination. It was only a question of a little time until his enemies at court would have effected his resignation; he had offended too many politicians, his political base was too narrow, he had too often threatened to resign, his health had deteriorated. Furthermore, his policies were by no means all successful and enlightened; in his attitude toward the non-Russian nationalities there was much less elasticity and willingness to compromise than there was in his socio-economic strategy. They would never share his ideas of a "Great Russia." He could not bring about a reconciliation and sooner or later there would have been acute conflict and probably an explosion. In brief, the hopes attached to Stolypin rest on slender factual evidence.

The hopes attached to the last tsar seem even more misplaced in retrospect. He was a handsome, charming, inoffensive, and shy young man when he came to power; outwardly imperturbable, he was indecisive at heart and not very bright. He adored his wife and loved his family; as a figurehead, like some of his European cousins, he would probably have done exceedingly well. It was his misfortune that he ascended to the throne at a time of crisis and that he persuaded himself (and was pushed by his wife) to play an active, indeed the central, role in Russian politics. For such a role he was wholly unsuitable; his reign began and ended in disaster. The best possible case that can be made in retrospect is that he was a well-meaning but weak man who surrounded himself with bad advisers. The horrible murder of the tsar and his family was a crime by any standards, but Nikolai was no more a saint (which he became in the eyes of the right) than other political leaders.[3]

The circumstances of the murder of the tsar's family have not been clarified sufficiently to this day. Since they continue to play an important role in the thinking of the "Russian party," the issues involved ought to be reviewed, however briefly.

The statements published by the Bolsheviks at the time were palpably mendacious: that the tsar had been executed on July 16, 1918 in Yekaterinburg (Sverdlovsk) whereas his family had been transferred to a safe place elsewhere. The more detailed reports by White investigators (Sokolov) and Soviet spokesmen (Bykov) seemed to agree on the essential facts: The tsar's

3. A devastating appraisal of Nikolai II's character and intellectual capacity can be found in the diary of M. Menshikov, the most extreme conservative writer of the time. The entry in question was written in April 1918, under the impression that the tsar had been killed. Menshikov believed that almost anyone with a minimum of common sense and stature could have saved the country. *Russkii vestnik,* 20 (1991).

whole family, as well as other persons, had been killed on that date in the Ipatiev house.[4] However, no human remains were found in the cellar of the house or nearby, and soon rumors began to spread that at least one member of the family (the famous Anastasia)—and perhaps others, too—had miraculously escaped. Such folklore is frequent in Russian history following the death of an emperor; it can be taken for granted that no one did escape. But there were major inconsistencies with regard to key issues, such as who gave the order and why, and who executed it.

It seems likely that the local Soviet authorities were afraid that the tsar would be liberated by the White armies, which were on the offensive at the time. It is equally possible that an order was given by Moscow; but if so, it is unlikely that instructions came from Sverdlov (as the right-wing version claims). On a matter of such importance Lenin would have been consulted, if not the whole Politburo. Trotsky, for once, could not be made responsible, for he was away at the front. Following the same version, the line of command was Sverdlov, Goloshekin (the head of the local Soviet security), Yurovsky (the commander of the unit acting as a prison guard to the tsar's family). All three were Jews, and furthermore, an inscription was discovered on the wall, a (mis)quotation from Heine:

> *Belsazar ward in selbiger Nacht*
> *von seinen Knechten umgebracht.*

According to the official version, Yurovsky, the key person, was an Old Bolshevik. But further investigation showed that in the very same year when he was reported to have joined the Communist party, he had in fact converted to Christianity in Berlin—and furthermore, tried to make a small fortune as a businessman. This was not in conformity with the image of an Old Bolshevik, and there were similar discrepancies with regard to the identity of the guards.[5] According to some sources they were Latvian soldiers, according to others Austro-Hungarian prisoners of war; in some accounts they have been described as members of the Socialist Revolutionary party, in others as nonparty individuals.

According to an account by Bruce Lockhart, the famous British agent in Moscow, the Russian people showed no interest in the fate of the tsar

---

4. Right-wing circles have demanded for some time that this building be made a national shrine, and Boris Yeltsin has been bitterly attacked because he had the house demolished (following instructions from Brezhnev) when he was party secretary at Sverdlovsk (Yekaterinburg). *Russkoye znamya*, 1 (1991). *Russkoye znamya* was the main organ of the Black Hundred in 1906, and the new journal regards itself as its namesake's legitimate heir.

5. According to a very recent theory, which is as likely (or unlikely) as previous ones, Yurovsky was not really Yurovsky but Stanislav Unshlikht, a well-known Old Bolshevik, and a Polish nobleman by origin. Unshlikht's nickname in the party was "Yurovsky," and in later years he became one of the heads of the Cheka—the secret police. *Strana i mir,* 6 (1991), pp. 106–129.

at the time. But to extremists his murder has remained an issue of crucial significance, a case not just of revenge but of ritual murder. The theme prominently appeared all along in sections of the émigré press, and after 1987 also in Russia.

If the October Revolution was an unmitigated disaster, what of the February Revolution and the abdication of the tsar, which had preceded it?

Many monarchists and right-wingers agree that it was the source of the evil and those responsible. But by early 1917 the tsarist regime had been thoroughly discredited and was virtually isolated as far as public opinion was concerned. Not only had Milyukov, the Kadet leader, attacked treason high up in a speech of unprecedented ferocity, but Purishkevich, the spokesman of the contemporary extreme right, was equally scathing about the state of affairs. While the right, following Solzhenitsyn, seems to imply that the February Revolution should never have taken place, it does not suggest that the prevailing lack of purpose at the top could have possibly continued.

Only the extreme right condemns the abdication of the tsar without reservation. Under *glasnost* there was considerable interest in the civil war period and most of the key publications—such as Denikin's memoirs, Krasnov's novels, and the *Archive of the Russian Revolution* (originally published in Berlin in the 1920s)—have been reissued in Moscow. While the National Bolsheviks have tended to take a balanced approach, finding good and evil in both camps of the civil war, the traditional right came to identify itself entirely with the Whites and, once the shackles of Communist censorship were removed, found nothing but fault and crime on the side of the Reds.

Formerly the rightists had not dared to express such views even by implication. Was it just a matter of censorship, or had there been a genuine change of heart in their midst after 1985? We have been dealing in passing with this issue. Many right-wingers, including the editors of the main right-wing journals, had been members of the Communist party. There is reason to believe that they had joined the party not just to acquire protective coloring and enhance their careers. In other words, there might have been a genuine conversion, or at least a radicalization of views, among some of them. They do not deny that the Whites, too, engaged in terrorism, but, as they see it, much less so than the Bolsheviks, who were the first to terrorize the population on a mass scale.

But why were the Whites defeated in the civil war?[6] Was it just because the Communists were more ruthless and more united? At one stage, in

---

6. Mr. M. Bernstam of Stanford (California), in an article reprinted by *Molodaya gvardiya* 56 (1992), has argued that the Reds were supported by "alien" forces such as Latvian units. But it should be added in fairness that the Whites were supported by the Western Allies and Japan.

October 1919, victory seemed within reach of the Whites; how, then, to explain their sudden collapse? The obvious answer is that most peasants did not relish the prospect that the big landowners would return and reclaim the land that had been distributed. Nor were the non-Russians, who constituted about half the population of the Russian empire, attracted by nationalist slogans about the "one and indivisible Russia." There were other reasons, but those we have adduced were sufficient to make the victory of the White armies very unlikely. The Whites claimed in later years that the aim of their movement was never mere counterrevolution, restoration of the status quo ante. But they never clarified their political aims, beyond their hostility to bolshevism, and this narrowly confined their appeal.

If Kerensky and Milyukov, the head of the Provisional Government and its foreign minister respectively, were anathema to the monarchists living abroad, this did not change after 1987. There was no sympathy in these circles for the parties of the center, for those advocating parliamentary democracy, let alone social democracy. With the advent of *glasnost* the heritage of the Russian emigration was rediscovered by the Russian right, and to a certain extent revived and reembraced. The beginnings of this trend can be traced back by about a decade; since the late 1970s there has been renewed interest in the émigrés and an evident desire to rehabilitate at least some of the political enemies of sixty years earlier.[7]

There were some startling parallels between the spirit of the Communist, pre-*glasnost* rehabilitations and the views of the extreme right. Neither the party nor the ultra-right was interested in the rehabilitation of liberals, the leftists, or the non–ethnic Russian émigrés.[8] The common denominator was Russian patriotism. Little did it matter that the liberals and the Mensheviks had been by and large consistent foes of fascism as well as of Stalinism, and that on the right there had been, by contrast, frequent vacillations in both respects: Among those who returned after 1945, or at least expressed a willingness to cooperate with Stalin's Russia, there had been very few democrats. The one major difference was that the pre-1985 rehabilitations predominantly concerned the first wave of immigrants—

7. L. K. Shkarenkov, *Agoniya beloy emigratsii* (Moscow, 1986); A. L. Afanasiev, *Polyn v chuzhikh polyakh* (Minsk, 1985).

8. Most Russian émigrés were not grand dukes, nor did they belong to the far right. The leading daily newspapers of the emigration, such as *Posledniya novosti* (Paris, 1920–1940) and *Novoye russkoye slovo* (New York), the leading periodicals, such as *Sovremennye zapiski* (Paris) and *Volya rossii* (Prague) were left of center. Their editors and contributors were not rehabilitated; the Russian right has not shown any interest in figures such as Pavel Milyukov, Victor Chernov, Alexander Kerensky, or Mark Vishniak, who were (and are) considered enemies of Russia and "traitors" to this day.

those who had left during the Revolution or the civil war—whereas those who had collaborated with Germany in the war or had left their homeland in the war's wake were still considered traitors and beyond redemption. Rehabilitations under Brezhnev included in their welcome outstanding cultural figures (such as, for instance, Stravinsky) who were not known for their pronounced political views, whereas confirmed anticommunists remained beyond the pale.

The attitude of the right wing after 1987 was different in this respect. Even extreme émigré anticommunists were welcomed. There was dissent within the right with regard to such figures as General Vlasov, head of the Russian Volunteer army in 1943–45, who for some conservatives, especially former war veterans, remained a traitor; there were long and inconclusive debates about his historical role.[9] The attitude of the leading journals of the right was inconsistent in this respect. On the one hand, they bitterly denounced Daniel Granin's *Zubr,* about a leading (apolitical) geneticist, who was sent to Germany in the 1920s to continue his studies and decided to remain there under Hitler when it appeared that many of his close relations had perished in the purge. (He was seized by the Soviets in 1945, permitted to continue his work in a gulag laboratory, and ultimately rehabilitated.) The same journals gave wide acclaim to émigré politicians who had collaborated with the Nazis by choice rather than necessity.

What Cultural Heritage for the Right?

Like the Bolsheviks eighty years earlier, the new Russian right posed the question: What part of our cultural heritage do we accept, and from what do we dissociate ourselves? The more enlightened among right-wingers tried to cast their net as wide as possible. The lunatic fringe tried to exclude virtually everyone who had not belonged to the Black Hundred—and since not many cultural figures *had* belonged, they were left with a very small heritage, including a few forgotten writers such as Shabelskaya and Krestovsky.[10]

There was general agreement that Pushkin, Lermontov, and Gogol were an inalienable part of the Russian cultural heritage. Pushkin's non-

9. For the case against Vlasov, see General M. Gareyev, "O Mifakh . . ." in *Voenno-istoricheskii zhurnal,* 4 (1991).

10. Shabelskaya, an actress and Russian femme fatale, was the author of *Satanisty 20' go veka* and the mother of the officer who shot Vladimir Nabokov's father in Berlin in 1922. Krestovsky was the Russian Eugène Sue; he wrote about the sewers of St. Petersburg and late in life developed a special interest in the Jewish underworld.

Russian racial provenance was ignored, and certain of his (and Lermontov's) poems that seemed unpatriotic were declared apocryphal. The greatest of all Russian writers and thinkers was Dostoyevsky; all of his birthdays were elaborately celebrated. The attitude toward Tolstoy, on the other hand, while not negative, was much cooler. Through his writings he had undermined the tsarist government and the church; he had been a pacifist, showing no interest in Russia's historical mission; and he demonstrated other unhealthy tendencies.

A similar attitude prevailed with regard to Turgenyev and Chekhov; they were not *personae non gratae*, but they had been too Western in inspiration and had done little to educate the Russian people in a spirit of patriotism.

Once one reaches the twentieth century, problems grow worse. For many on the right, Esenin was the great idol. He had much to recommend him: A young man of impeccable peasant background, he had been a shepherd in his youth. He had great talent and after his death fell out of favor in the Soviet Union. The fact that he criticized the American way of life and predicted the "collapse of the skyscrapers" also endeared him to the right. He was the bard of the Russian village, of hay-making, of peaceful landscapes, of the Virgin Mary and Jesus walking through the fields. But he was also a playboy and hooligan, a poet of prostitutes and drunken brawls, and the author of blasphemous verse about Christ.

Esenin had welcomed the Revolution but later wrote that he felt a stranger in his native land. Like Mayakovsky, he took his own life; as in Mayakovsky's case there are rumors to this day that he was either killed or driven to suicide.[11] As so often, much of the guilt was attributed to Trotsky, even though Trotsky, appreciating Esenin's great talent, had been one of his well-wishers among the Communist leaders.

The Russian right has traditionally idolized the peasantry in the same way as the Bolsheviks have paid homage to the working class. The peasantry has been the only true bearer and guarantor of the Russian idea; all other classes have been parasites, or at best uncertain allies. Seen in this light the Esenin cult of the new Russian right is not a matter of surprise, because these were precisely the ideas of Esenin and of his friend and mentor

11. Bukharin's negative comments on Esenin are often adduced in this context, but they appeared two years after the death of the poet. Allegations that Esenin was killed persist. See "Ubiistvo Yesenina," *V Bloknot patriota,* 1 (1990), Leningrad. *Moskovskii literator,* (1992) announced the establishment of a committee to clarify the circumstances of the death of S. A. Esenin. It has been recently alleged that Alexander Blok, too, was murdered (poisoned) by leading Bolshevik intellectuals. (V. Soloukhin, *Literaturnaya Rossiya,* 4 [1992]). The evidence is ludicrous.

Kluyev, the peasant writers par excellence when they took literary St. Petersburg by storm on the eve of the First World War.

How genuine was this *style russe*? Had it come straight from the Russian village? There was certainly an element of bogus rural simplicity in it. As Khodasevich, one of the great Russian critics, put it with the benefit of hindsight, the birth of the "Russian idea" took place not in the middle of a birch forest but in the *chambre séparée* of a St. Petersburg French restaurant—"a little Orthodoxy, a little flagellant sectarianism, a little revolution, a little chauvinism . . ."[12]

Attempts have been made to claim for the extreme right some other great poets of the early twentieth century. Blok did write about the battle of Kulikovo, and his poems contain certain Slavophile themes. He believed in the coming apocalypse, and on at least one occasion said that he "hated the bourgeois, the devil, and the liberals." He also spoke of Western civilization as an old and dying world. All of this endeared him to the truly patriotic. But his name suggests that he is not of purely Russian stock; and he suffered from general weltschmerz and misanthropy ("Man disgusts me and life is horrible"). Furthermore, his sympathies were with the Socialist Revolutionaries, and in one of his long poems, which is featured in all Soviet anthologies, he expressed sympathy with the Revolution.

Andrei Belyi, another leading poet of the time, wrote about the resurrection of Christ in Russia and about "Rossiya, Rossiya, Rossiya, messiya gryadushchevo dnya" ("O Russia, the messiah of the coming day"). And he denounced "soulless materialism." But he was also a follower of Rudolph Steiner and of Theosophy—which, in the folklore of the Russian right, is almost as reprehensible as the Masonic conspiracy.

This leaves the right with some fine writers, such as Voloshin, Kluyev, and Khlebnikov—who were not, however, among the very greatest. Kluyev (1887–1933), the first of the peasant writers, was certainly a nationalist, and so was Khlebnikov; but there was too much eroticism in the former and too much modernism in the latter to make them of much use for patriotic indoctrination. Of the émigré writers, Ivan Bunin, the most famous, is widely admired on all sides of the political spectrum, but he was "too cold," he wrote critically about the Russian peasant, and he disliked Dos-

---

12. V. Khodasevich, "Yesenin," *Sovremennye zapiski*, vol. 27 (1926). See also Fritz Merau, *Sergej Jessenin* (Leipzig, 1992), pp. 66–71. A few years later Yesenin, like Blok and some other friends, opted for revolutionary destructivism, whereas Gorky, the main bugbear of the right, warned against mindless destruction. As an idol of the Russian right Yesenin has serious flaws. He wrote one friend (A. Mariengof) that the only people in Russia who had appreciated his work were young Jewish girls, and to another (V. Nasedkin) he said that Trotsky was the ideal, most accomplished human being (autumn 1925).

toyevsky. Balmont and Sologub with all their other merits belonged for many years to the school known as "Russian decadence." Ivan Shmelev and Igor Severyanin were politically acceptable, but not writers of the very highest order.

This leaves, paradoxically, two Soviet writers, Mikhail Sholokhov and Leonid Leonov. But Sholokhov was an establishment figure par excellence, even though some of his writings were unpublishable for a long time. He wrote more realistically about the collectivization of agriculture than most of his contemporaries, but he did in the end accept and approve it. His behavior toward dissidents such as Solzhenitsyn showed that he either lacked character and courage, or thoroughly identified himself with whatever outrages were committed by the political leadership. Furthermore, *And Quiet Flows the Don* is so much more accomplished than Sholokhov's other works that its authorship has been disputed, and the controversy has not ceased to this day.

Leonov's best work was done in the 1920s when he was a Communist fellow-traveler; his later books were written in full conformity with the party line and while there are traces of Dostoyevskyan influences, his patriotism was entirely in line with the official ideology of the period.

With all their ideological weaknesses, these and some other writers have been claimed, albeit selectively, by the Russian right. But their work does not explain what *Russkost,* (Russianness) really is and what kind of truly Russian culture the Russian party wants to prevail. True, the Slavophiles wrote about the matter in their day, but their visions refer almost exclusively to the past; Dostoyevsky's remarks on the subject are also rooted in the last century. Some contemporary Russian writers have argued that life once upon a time in Russia (and particularly in the Russian village) was more harmonious than it is at present. But even they conceded that this world of yesterday cannot be restored.

What message does the right have for the present age? Paradoxically, most of the thinking and writing about what is Russian has come not from the right but from the liberal-patriotic camp—from Berdyaev, Fedotov, and Likhachev—and is, for a variety of reasons, quite unacceptable for the extreme right. Of the nationalism of the far right, Berdyaev wrote that it was barbaric and stupid, pagan and immoral in inspiration, full of Eastern wildness and darkness, "an orgy of the old Russian dissoluteness."[13]

Those who more recently have tried to define Russian patriotism have produced little but vague generalities. According to Shafarevich, patriotism is the awareness of specific values, and the instinct to preserve one's national identity. Therefore the extinction of patriotism is the best indicator of the

13. N. Berdyaev, "O russkom natsionalnom," *Slovo* (Dec. 7, 1908).

beginning of the end of a people, their transformation from a living entity to a dead machine. According to Valentin Rasputin, *russkost* (like Germandom and the French spirit) is simply the nation's general direction, which it received when coming of age. This trend might be artistic, or religious, or pragmatic. But every nation has something specific on top of the universal human qualities and it is called to develop and fertilize that toward which it has a specific inclination.[14]

There is nothing specifically Russian in these ideas; they are derived from Hegel, and particularly from Herder, who had, however, not political but cultural traditions in mind. Attempts to define what is specifically Russian are bound to be unsatisfactory, if only because there is usually more than one "national character" or idea—which is bound, furthermore, to change from time to time.

Fedotov, in an interesting attempt to define what is specifically Russian, points to the "superfluous people", to the wanderer *(skitalets)* and the builder, to a Moscow-type and a Western-type Russian, to unrestricted freedom *(volnost)* and sectarian rebelliousness, to gloom and childishness, to religiosity, and many other features for which one cannot find a common denominator.[15]

But why is it so important to establish what is specifically Russian? It would be difficult to think of any major British or French thinker who has given much time and thought to similar preoccupations. What was, and is, specifically French is obvious and has been instinctively understood; there has been no need to define and articulate it. Germany has been the only major country that has at times been similarly preoccupied with a search for its national identity, and the search has resulted in not very helpful obiter dicta such as Richard Wagner's famous "To be German means to do something for its own sake."

These agonizing searches for a well-defined national identity (and destiny) could well be a manifestation of weakness and uncertainty in nations that only recently attained full independence or that for some other reason seem to believe that their past performance on the world-historical scene has not been equal to other peoples', that think, rightly or wrongly, that their promise has not been fulfilled. Such a search shows unhappiness with one's own history. *Russkost,* as a critic has noted, has no contemporary content but refers with longing to the past, often the distant past.[16] There certainly is a danger of getting lost in the myths of faraway ages. While the

---

14. I. Shafarevich, *Politika,* March 1991; Rasputin quoted by A. Strelyani, "Pesni zapadnykh Slavyan," *Literaturnaya gazeta* (August 8, 1991).

15. G. P. Fedotov, "Russkii chelovek," *Russkiye zapiski,* 3 (1938).

16. V. Khlestkin, "Kamo gryadeshiy," *Obshchestvennye nauki,* 3 (1989).

Russians have nothing comparable to the Nibelungen, there are plenty of knights in shining armor—the various Mstislavs and Rostislavs and their heroic feats as described in the epics of the early Middle Ages. When French people refer to their country, it is usually in terms of *la belle France;* the English invoke merry old England; the Germans speak of *treudeutsch* (truly German). Only Russian nationalists invoke an ideal that is not aesthetic or ethical or political but moral-religious, the ideal of "Holy Russia."[17]

The Economic Visions of Russian Nationalism

The Russian right has traditionally shown little interest in economic policy. It has all along expressed its strong dislikes but it has hardly ever presented viable alternatives. In a famous letter of 1990, which was signed by seventy-four Russian writers and cultural figures and is one of the main manifestos of the Russian right, there are many references to Nazism, Zionism, Russophobia, patriotism, and so on, but not a single reference to the national economy, and this at a time of major crisis.[18]

The same is true with regard to many conservative movements in other parts of the world and also with regard to fascism. But there are basic differences. Conservative resistance to industrialization has been not as powerful in the West as it has been in Russia. Nor have the problems been as acute: There was no need to make a new beginning, here and now. In tsarist Russia the conservatives were by and large against industrialization, against the emergence of the new class of industrialists, entrepreneurs, and bankers which they rightly regarded as a danger to their vision of Russia. The right wing knew, of course, that the basic support for tsarism came from the countryside. Rightists correctly assumed that greater economic freedom would sooner or later result in a greater measure of political freedom, which they abhorred. If Russia had to be developed and modernized, it should be done by the bureaucracy. However, the state had neither the technical competence nor the money to undertake this task. It could supervise, promote, and brake, but it could not play the role of entrepreneur and investor. Thus the bourgeoisie, rather than the working class, became the main enemy of the conservatives, who preached a common front against "capitalist exploitation." But these attitudes found no major echo in the villages and none at all in the cities.

The pre-1914 anticapitalism of the Russian right is still of interest,

17. V. Solovyov, *Polnoye sobraniye sochinenii,* III, p. 50, n.d.

18. The letter was originally published in *Literaturnaya Rossiya,* 9 (1990), and was reprinted in *Nash Sovremennik,* 4 (1990), and elsewhere.

because the motif and the argument have remained more or less the same to this day: The market, a capitalist system, is not suitable for Russia. This has been preached on various levels of sophistication. Genadi Shimanov, a leader of the extreme right both before and during *perestroika*, has argued that capitalism from the days of the Old Testament to Rothschild and beyond has been an invention of the Jews, who also invented communism. Their domination over world finance was, and is, the key to their domination over the world.[19]

On a somewhat less emotional level of debate, it has been argued that Russia is not suited for a capitalist system simply because the Russian ethic is not Protestant, nor Calvinist, nor even Catholic, but Orthodox.[20] Max Weber, Sombart, and even Arnold Toynbee appear as witnesses for the prosecution. The fact that Japan is producing products of even higher quality than those of the Christian West is explained by the survival and intensity of national tradition in that country. Since Russian psychology and moral values differ radically from those of West *and* East, capitalism is bound to fail in Russia in any case. It would merely turn Russia into a Third World country.

The market, in brief, is not a panacea for Russia's ills but, on the contrary, a trap. But what cure do the conservatives have for the state of the economy? One looks in vain for clear answers in the writings of the best-known right-wing publicists of the *perestroika* period, Mikhail Antonov and Sergei Kurginyan.

Antonov made his first appearance some twenty-five years ago, among the Christian dissenters. He had made a study of the social teachings of the Slavophiles and advocated something akin to the deindustrialization of Russia and the transfer of vital industries to Siberia, a suggestion that was not greeted with joy by the natives of Siberia.

Antonov had been a member of the Communist party, but according to his own account had reached the conclusion by the middle 1960s that Marxism was a doctrine deeply alien to the Russian people.[21] In fact, the conversion seems to have taken place somewhat later, for in the 1960s Antonov still proclaimed that only a "combination of Russian Orthodoxy and Leninism could give the Russian people a world outlook capable of synthesizing centuries of experience as a nation."[22] It is revealing that not only Soviet liberals but also many right-wingers continued to stake their

19. "O tainoi prirode kapitalizma," *Veche* (Novgorod), 10 (1991).

20. Yu. Borodai, "Pochemu Pravoslavnym ne goditsya Protestanskii kapitalizm," *Nash sovremennik*, 10 (1990).

21. *Voskresenye* (August 1990).

22. L. Alexeyeva, *Soviet Dissent* (Middletown, 1985).

claims for Lenin and Leninism right up to 1988 and even beyond. Those of the right juxtaposed the good Lenin to the bad Trotsky, who despised and hated the Russian people.

At one time Antonov had been detained, but he was rehabilitated in the late 1970s. With the dawn of *glasnost* he published a number of long, well-written programmatic articles in mainstream conservative journals such as *Molodaya gvardiya* and *Nash sovremennik.*

Some of his criticism was well taken, as for instance with regard to the irredeemable ecological damage that had been caused by forced industrialization. But these observations had been made by many others before, and once it came to practical suggestions, the author was clearly at a loss. He argued that Russia could not possibly aspire to a living standard comparable to the West's or the Far East's. This was not necessarily a disaster, for Russia's ideals and values were not those of the West and Japan; its values were spiritual, not materialistic. An ascetic life was closer to Russian hearts than the Western consumer society. To the extent that these ideals had been forgotten, Russian workers and peasants would have to be reimbued with them; the bureaucracy would have to be purged of the criminal elements that had penetrated it. As a result the economic performance of the country, and living standards, would improve. In Antonov's view the economic malaise was a moral rather than an economic problem.

Antonov was an honored member of the right. In 1989 he became president of a new organization devoted to the preservation of Russian cultural traditions. But his message was not taken quite seriously even among like-minded people. N. N. Lysenko, president of the Republican People's Party (RNPR), referred to it as the "bucolic-Pravoslav-moral economics," implying that Russian workers would hardly show much enthusiasm for harder work and longer hours, or for queues for shoddy goods, as the result of more intensive patriotic indoctrination.[23]

Sergei Kurginyan became famous as the author of a number of equally long articles and the editor of a book called *Post-Perestroika* in which he showed considerable literary erudition. In the course of one article he would quote not only Shakespeare, Goethe, and Dostoyevsky but also Spengler, Toynbee, Gödel, Swedenborg and Jakob Böhme. His training had been as an actor and he continued to be the director of the Moscow experimental theater Na Doskakh ("On the Boards"). He also had a science degree; under *glasnost* he became the head of the Experimental

---

23. *Nashe vremya*, 7–8 (1991). Lysenko's proposal for overcoming the crisis was the establishment of a great state credit institute which was to sponsor and support all kinds of small enterprises.

Creative Center, a Moscow politological think tank that had a certain influence; on some occasions it was quoted by Pavlov, the onetime prime minister, and by other highly placed Communist officials.[24]

Like Antonov, Kurginyan was strong on criticism—mainly directed against the advisers of Gorbachev and Yeltsin and their foreign helpers. But as in the case of Antonov, one looks in vain for detailed, constructive ideas and an alternative concept. To be precise, he had a surfeit of ideas, often causing giddiness among his audience. In contrast to Antonov, Kurginyan called his approach neoconservative or neotraditional, and the "authoritarian" label did not frighten him.

As Kurginyan the patriot-technocrat saw it, the situation was very bad and the people had to be told the truth. Modernization had to be carried out without dependence on foreign credits. This could obviously be done only if the state continued to play a decisive role in the country's economy, with the imposition of discipline from above and a great deal of indoctrination. But since Kurginyan, unlike Antonov, was not an ethnic Russian, the Slavophiles could not appeal to him in equal measure and the patriotism advocated by him had to be different in character—*gosudarstvenny*, "statist," with the state rather than the people as the highest authority.

Kurginyan is a past master in the preparation of scenarios that reveal an exceedingly fertile mind, and on occasion he makes astute observations; but he shows neither logic nor consistency. He has preached at one and the same time the modernization of Soviet society, with the application of the most recent technologies—and a return to the social teachings of early Christianity and Islam. He proposed *perestroika* on the basis of a monastic-ascetic metareligion combining spiritual communism with Christianity (both fundamentalist and Teilhardian), Russian patriotism, anti-Westernism, Third Worldism, and, generally speaking, the consolidation of all healthy forces in society. Kurginyan finds his models in the settlements of the Dukhobors, a Russian religious sect, and also in Cossack communities. Kurginyan's scenarios found admirers in 1990–1991 among Communists as well as in the state bureaucracy and the security forces. His critics have derided him as a charlatan, purveying a weird and wholly incompatible mixture of technocratic pragmatism, communism, and chauvinism.[25]

24. Kurginyan's original articles appeared in *Literaturnaya Rossiya*, 26, 27, 28, 35 (1989); subsequently his essays were also published in *Den; Moskovskaya pravda* ("A political Quadrille, or the Pact with the Black Pudel"—a reference to Goethe's *Faust* [June 8, 1991]); *Moskva*, 9 (1991), and in many other journals. See also "Pravaya alternativa," *Postfactum*, 1/2 (1991), pp. 10–12 and several booklets published in 1992 such as *Rossiya i Mir*.

25. *Nezavisimaya gazeta*, February 19, 1991; Victor Yasman, "Elite Think Tank Prepares Post-Perestroika Strategy," *Report on the USSR* (May 24, 1991).

Kurginyan's views have provoked bitter criticism in some right-wing extremist circles. He has been attacked as a false prophet, a proponent of state capitalism who ignores the spiritual potential of the Russian people and, generally speaking, proposes Masonic-Jewish-mondialist views. His attacker defended Nazi economic policies in the course of this polemic:

The decisive factor accounting for the broad support for the Nazi idea was the enormous anger among the [German] people caused by the total Zionization of the German press and the ruin of the German economy caused by the evil machinations of the *Zhidomasonstvo,* the Communists, and the social democrats of all hues.

Where Hitler went wrong was when he followed Zionist inspiration and decided to fulfill his ambitions through territorial expansion.[26]

The most influential voice heard on the subject of Russia's reconstruction was, of course, Solzhenitsyn's. Solzhenitsyn differed on one essential point from Antonov and Kurginyan inasmuch as he freely admitted that he had no expert economic knowledge and could give no prescriptions as to how to effect the transition from state ownership to private enterprise.[27] He agreed with other conservative writers that it would be criminally wrong and dangerous to sell to foreigners Russia's mineral wealth or its forests. Nor would it be right to permit limitless concentration of capital, which would result in some new form of monopolism. It would be equally wrong if the pressure of the profit motive became too strong, for this would adversely affect the health of society.

Solzhenitsyn opposed the transfer of foreign economic models to Russia, but at the same time conceded that seventy years of indoctrination to the effect that owning property and hired labor were something evil had very negative consequences for the well-being of the Russian people. Solzhenitsyn favored encouraging small enterprises, and he placed his hope in Russian workmanship, once the government yoke was removed. If the Japanese had managed to build a strong economy by virtue of their workers' high morale, Russia too, should be able to succeed.

Solzhenitsyn has been attacked by nationalist extremists for supporting, in one of his earlier books, some kind of "moral socialism," when in fact socialism was an invention of the devil, rooted in jealousy and not in the spiritual depth of Christianity.[28] Whatever Solzhenitsyn's views of twenty years ago, both Antonov and Kurginyan dropped the "socialist" label much later on. Antonov declared in 1989 that only socialist organizations

26. N. P. Goryachev, *Otechestvo* (December 1991).

27. *Kak nam obustroit Rossiyu?* (Paris, 1990), p. 18.

28. V. Krivorotov in *Kuban,* 1 (1991), p. 80; the reference is to Solzhenitsyn's *Cancer Ward.*

and individuals supporting the Communist party policy of *perestroika* were welcome in his organization,[29] and Kurginyan also favored some form of national or state socialism. The National Bolsheviks of the right have gone even further, trying to enlist Lenin (the democrat, enemy of the bureaucracy, and architect of a classless society) in the reconstruction of Russia that they envisage.[30]

Just as there has been no unanimity among the liberals with regard to economic policies, there has been a wide spectrum of opinions among the right. There is agreement that *perestroika* has been a failure and that only criminals, speculators, and similar destructive elements have benefited from the (limited) opportunities that opened up under Gorbachev.[31] *"Koopera-tor"* became a synonym for "thief" in these circles, and it was taken for granted that the Mafia had a stranglehold on the Soviet economy. Such an assessment of the situation was not, perhaps, entirely wrong, but it left open crucial questions on which the right could not agree: Was privatization wrong in principle, or only in the haphazard and inconsistent way it was carried out?[32]

The Russian right agreed unanimously that Stalin's collectivization had been a gigantic disaster resulting in the destruction of the traditional Russian village. Much of the blame was attributed to Yakovlev (né Epstein), a party leader of Jewish origin who had in reality played a secondary role (he was not a member of the Politburo). One would assume that the moment the development of independent initiative in the countryside became possible again, the conservatives would welcome it with enthusiasm. But this was by no means the case; just as the conservatives of 1906 had never really liked Stolypin's reforms breaking up the *obshchina,* those of 1990 saw mainly dangers in following similar actions. Anatoly Salutsky, a right-wing publicist of Jewish origin, acquired notoriety as the result of an unending series of articles in which he accused one of the reformers, the academician Zaslavskaya, of helping to destroy Soviet villages in the 1970s. But when opportunity arose Salutsky was not among those supporting the privatization of agriculture. And there were many like him.[33]

It is instructive to compare the economic doctrines of Nazism (and the German "conservative revolution" of 1929–1933) with those of the Rus-

29. "Na positsiyakh sotsializma," *Moskovskii literator* (March 24, 1989).

30. V. Litov, "S Leninym pobezhdat!" *Molodaya gvardiya,* 4 and 5 (1990).

31. A. Sergeyev, "Entsiklopediya kriminalnoi burzhuazii," *Nash sovremennik,* 4 (1990).

32. A Kuzmich, "Katastrofa Rossii, mif ili realnost?" *Voskresenye* 6 and 7 (1991).

33. "Otkrytoe pismo Akademiku Zaslavskoi," *Moskovskii literator* (April 14, 1989).

sian right. Both the Nazis and the Russian right believed in the primacy of politics over economics; both were to some extent anticapitalist, at least as far as doctrine was concerned. Early Nazi economic doctrine, developed by Feder and later discarded, included the death penalty for usurers and black marketeers (paragraph 12 of the Nazi program) as well as the nationalization of all "trusts" (para. 13). It favored agriculture over industry and regarded banks with much suspicion. Vasili Belov's characterization (in *Vse vperedi*) of the "traditional Russian village as the keeper of the national flame" is just what Hitler wrote in *Mein Kampf,* that a healthy stock of small holders has been at all times the best means to prevent social ills.[34]

This was not entirely wrong; the true problem was that the traditional village had disappeared in the wake of the revolution in agriculture. Early Nazi doctrine was based on certain fantasies concerning "breaking the servitude of the prime rate" and the distinction between "creative" (industrial) and "parasitic" (finance) capitalism. These slogans were purely demagogic and were discarded after 1933 without much ado. Both the Nazis and the German revolutionary conservatives believed in private initiative and property while envisaging a larger role for the state in the national economy than had been the practice earlier on. This was in some respects a German version of Keynesianism. On the eve of the takeover the Nazis had an economic program to tackle the crisis that was perfectly realistic, proved to be relatively successful, and earned them much political credit later on.[35]

But there was at least one fundamental difference: The problem facing the Nazis was to get an economy that had stalled going again. The infrastructure still existed—the factories, a skilled workforce, a network of communications. The Russian right faced an infinitely more difficult challenge: to replace a system that had proved to be unworkable. A return to the old system was possible in Germany with relatively minor modifications. In Russia it seemed possible, if at all, only as a short-term palliative.

The Russian New Right

In 1990 the first references appeared in Russian publications to a "Russian New Right" and Russian "neoconservatism." Among the first to use the term was the writer Alexander Prokhanov. Others were Sergei Kurginyan

34. *Mein Kampf* (Munich, 1930), p. 151.

35. A. Barkai, *Das Wirtschaftssystem des National Sozialismus* (Frankfurt, 1988); W. Hock, *Deutscher Antikapitalismus* (Frankfurt, 1960).

and Alexander Dugin. Prokhanov had begun his literary career among the liberals; he was a protégé of Yuri Trifonov. Later on he became fascinated by the army and wrote several books on the campaigns in Afghanistan, which earned him the sobriquet "the Nightingale of the General Staff." A man of great energy and amazing literary output, Prokhanov gradually moved into the front rank of organizers and officials of the literary scene. With the support of the chief political directorate of the armed forces he began to edit the weekly *Den* ("Day") as an answer to the liberal *Literaturnaya gazeta*. After the failed coup of 1991 *Den* carried the tag line "The Paper of the Spiritual Opposition." Kurginyan's progress from actor and director to head of a Moscow think tank specializing in scientific prognosticism has been mentioned; Dugin, an erstwhile member of Pamyat, has defined himself as "metaphysician and geopolitician."[36]

It is difficult to write about the "New Right" because of its inchoate character; when they invoke "neoconservatism" this has nothing to do with neoconservatism as understood in common usage in the United States. On the other hand they have liberally borrowed from French *Nouvelle Droite* ideology. The Russian New Rightists are certainly Russian patriots and stand for a strong Russia. They are antiliberal and antidemocratic and have no sympathy for what they regard as mushy outpourings about humanism and human rights: According to Prokhanov there is nothing about human rights in the Ten Commandments, a proposition that will be disputed by other readers of that text ("Thou shall not kill").[37]

In contrast to the Old Right which, as New Rightists see it, has no future, they are less interested in the past but concentrate on problems of Russia's domestic and foreign policy. They regard dictatorship as essential for the survival of the country; they favor a strong, centralized state apparatus and equally strong security forces. While they do not a priori reject the market, they seem to believe that for a long time to come the state will have to play a decisive role in the recovery and transformation of the country. They think that the extreme right's traditional preoccupations with Satanism, the Masonic-Jewish conspiracy, and so on are of no great relevance to the modern world, and while they pay lip service to the role of the church, they do not regard it as an ally of much promise. They prefer the old partocracy to the new liberals but believe that new ideas are needed to

36. *Den*, January 10, 1992. The term "New Right" is also claimed by some members of the social-Christian dissidents of the 1960s, such as E. Vagin (*Nash Sovremennik* 4 [1992]). In the present context our concern is with a more recent group of publicists whose mouthpiece is, above all, *Den*.

37. Prokhanov in *Vek XX i mir*, 11 (1991), p. 23.

replace Marxism-Leninism (and old-fashioned Russian nationalism) and that they are called to infuse these new ideas.

Dugin and Prokhanov have been fascinated by Alain de Benoist and the members of the French *Nouvelle Droite,* whom they regard as the Western equivalent to the Russian *pochvenniki.* They share the French right-wing fascination with early cultures and with Jung (to the extent that they are familiar with him), as well as a philosophy of nature based on mystical religiosity, and some refined form of racism. They believe that the Eurasian school of thought, to which the Russian New Right belongs, has many affinities with the French *Nouvelle Droite.*

Since very little is known about the *Nouvelle Droite*'s doctrines outside France, some of its basic tenets ought to be mentioned, however briefly. Benoist, the *maître-penseur* of this group, stresses the essential function of an aristocratic elite consisting of "heroic political fighters," one of Julius Evola's (the late fascist thinker) pet concepts. From Konrad Lorenz the concepts of aggression and of the territorial imperative as normal human features have been borrowed; the *Nouvelle Droite* also stresses the hierarchical structure of societies. Its doctrine is neopaganism, said to be more spiritual than Judeo-Christian monotheism, which has led to the uprooting of society under the guise of liberalism, democracy, and ultimately socialism. The *Nouvelle Droite*'s opposition to the Enlightenment and to rational thought is near total.

They regard the nation as the supreme value; any mixture or integration between races is an unmitigated evil, because it leads to decadence and "ethnocide," a key concept for the New Right in France as in Germany and Russia. But the French New Right rejects the charge of racism; its watchword is "ethnopluralism." It puts politics above economic considerations (the "primacy of politics"), and instinct and mythical thought above rational thinking. It is anti-intellectual and anticapitalist, preaching a "third way" between capitalism and communism. Their slogan is the "conservative revolution" in contrast to traditional restorative conservatism. It is pro-German and anti-American.

Students of Western intellectual thought will find traces of Nietzsche, Pareto, Sorel, and the ever-present Evola, as well as of European right-wing thinkers of the 1930s, in this doctrine. In Western Europe it is in many ways a repeat performance, with only a few novel ideas, and as far as these are concerned suspicion is called for. "Ethnopluralism" may have its uses as an intellectual argument to fend off unpleasant accusations, but does the New Right really believe in it? If it wants to be politically active, which is its ultimate aim, its obvious appeal is to the voters for the sundry National

Fronts, and for them ethnopluralism is, of course, anathema. While the French New Right has not, on the whole, invoked the classic conspiracy theories and has kept its distance from the Khaddafis and Louis Farrakhans, other, less sophisticated European rightists, including the Russians, have had no such scruples and stressed their affinity with all radicals who do not belong to the left.

Much of this mixture has been heady stuff for the Russian right-wing ideologists precisely because the right-wing political tradition has never been represented in Russia. They have been borrowing from it quite indiscriminately in recent years.[38] The New Right as an intellectual fashion in France lasted altogether for a few years; today its influence is minute.

Does "revolutionary conservatism" have a future in Russia?[39] Dugin believes that time is on the side of "our people," that New Right thought in the near future will be the most popular and widespread ideology in Russia, and that after its victory in Russia it will spread to other European countries. He has stated that the old right-wing doctrine is archaic; a return to a monarchical system or to Slavophilism is impossible without an ideological *metanoia*.[40]

Furthermore, the Old Right has needlessly limited its appeal because of its xenophobia. In fact, "our people" (as seen by Dugin) are not only Russians, but also the traditionalists among the smaller nations who recognize the danger of separatism on one hand and "mondialism" on the other.[41] While Dugin could well be right, emphasizing the essentially conservative frame of mind of Russia and other European nations, he clearly overrates the appeal of the New Right, both in Western Europe and in the East: A swing of the political pendulum to the right is far more likely to enhance the strength of populist, xenophobic forces than the geopolitical thinkers of the New Right. Much of the speculation on the traditional common ideals, values, and interests of Western Europe and Russia clearly

38. For a survey of *Nouvelle Droite* thinking, the writings of de Benoist should be consulted as well as the periodical *éléments* and the publications of the Copernic publishing house. For a good summary and excellent bibliography, see Gress-Jäschke-Schönke's *Neue Rechte and Rechtsextremismus in Europa* (Opladen, 1990), and Wolfgang Kowalsky, *Kulturrevolution* (Opladen, 1991).

39. According to Dugin the term was first used by the Slavophile Yuri Samarin, later by Dostoyevsky and Konstantin Leontiev.

40. *Metanoia* is a theological concept referring to total spiritual repentance in preparation for the coming of the Kingdom of God and salvation (Matthew 3:8 and 14:17; Mark 1:15).

41. "Vremya rabotaet na nashikh," *Politika* (September 1991). *Politika* has also published long interviews with Alain de Benoist, Robert Stoikers, and other Western ideologists of the New Right.

belongs to the realm of fantasy or is based on ignorance.[42]

Kurginyan and in particular Dugin have contributed to the new doctrine a violent anti-Americanism and above all the concept of the "state of emergency" *(chrezvychaynoye polozhenye)*. Kurginyan has claimed that all along he has been the ideologist of the "state of emergency," that is to say of a nondemocratic political solution. This is a rehash of the ideas of Carl Schmitt, the very learned and equally muddleheaded German political philosopher of the 1920s, who analyzed in detail the weaknesses of modern democracy, particularly if confronted with serious problems and perils. It is unlikely that Kurginyan ever read the early Schmitt. But Dugin apparently did, and fully accepted Schmitt's thesis that all politics is based on a friend-foe dichotomy. In foreign affairs Dugin stands for a Continental empire extending from Vladivostok to Dublin, as a counterweight to America and "Atlanticism." America is the enemy par excellence, a chimera, an anti-organic, transplanted civilization, lacking sacral state tradition, lacking civilization, and attempting nevertheless to impose its anti-ethnic, antitraditionalist "Babylonian" model on other continents.[43]

Dugin seems not to have visited America, nor have most of the other ideologists of the far right—which no doubt makes it easier to generalize on a subject of such complexity. The rightists' anti-American ideas are not new; they were spelled out in detail by the German extreme right in the 1930s. The Russian New Right frequently invokes such terms as "geopolitical" and "mondialist," even though their interpretation is by no means clear. Prokhanov has referred on occasion to America as Russia's eternal enemy, but like Kurginyan he seems to regard domestic politics as of greater urgency at the present stage.[44] The Russian New Right may one day find itself in a position of some influence. At the present time it is more an abstraction then a political reality.

42. To give but one example: Dugin includes Spengler, Othmar Spann, Werner Sombart, and Carl Schmitt among the leading thinkers of the German conservative revolution and claims that they were without exception staunch Russophiles. Nothing could have been further from their true beliefs. *Politika* (September 1991).

43. Dugin's infatuation with Julius Evola, whom he quotes on many occasions, has been noted. Evola (1898–1974), originally a Dadaist, became a leading fascist and neofascist ideologist, a follower of Alfred Rosenberg and disciple of the extreme German right. He fled to Germany after Mussolini was overthrown, was severely injured and paralyzed in the bombing of Vienna in 1945, but continued to publish. Some of his antimodernist and antidemocratic writings had a considerable impact on the European New Right.

44. *Den* has, however, stressed that it is not just a specific Russian phenomenon but part of a general continental (European and Asian) trend to which Le Pen and the Belgian journal *Vouloir* belong, as do the New Right and the extreme right in countries such as Britain, Germany, India, etc. *Den,* December 29, 1991.

Foreign Policy

Russian nationalists have been divided for a long time between those standing for a strong and indivisible Russia, and others, such as Solzhenitsyn, who regarded the old Soviet empire an intolerable burden. But even the latter had hoped that the new Russia emerging from Purgatory would include the Ukraine, Byelorussia, and northern Kazakhstan. They were not prepared for the disintegration that took place in 1991, as a result of which even the existence of the old RSFSR was threatened by further separatist pressures. They are unlikely to accept willingly this state of affairs, nor will many others who do not normally subscribe to a conservative worldview.

The Russian right woke up very late to the dangers facing it. While Kozhinov, one of its most erudite and eloquent spokesmen, published long articles arguing that the Khazar yoke was more dangerous than the Tatar and Mongol threat,[45] the Baltic countries, Moldova, and the Caucasus slipped away from Russian rule. While *Molodaya gvardiya* and *Nash sovremennik* fulminated against the Judeo-Masonic plot in 1917, the Ukraine and Central Asia declared their independence. It was a truly amazing case of political blindness, of invoking imaginary threats and ignoring real dangers. One day the more thoughtful thinkers of the right will, no doubt, try to establish how such fatal misjudgments could have occurred.

It is too early to speculate how Russian nationalists will explain the disaster that took place in 1991 and how they will react—whether by blaming the traditional culprits, by accepting the new realities, or by trying to regain at least some of the territories that have been lost. The shock has been so great, the changes so far-reaching—undoing centuries of Russian history—that it is difficult at the present time to assess the views of the right on foreign policy. For a long time to come domestic issues may well receive greater attention than foreign affairs.

The right has been united in its belief that Russia needs a strong army to maintain its rightful place in the world, and some of its leading spokesmen have argued for years that only the armed forces will be able to provide domestic leadership to prevent a descent into total chaos. According to some ideologists of the far right, the armed forces have not just been the shield of the nation, but also a major cultural force, the bearer of the people's morality.[46] The right has opposed disarmament and major cuts in

---

45. The Khazars were a Turkish tribe that established an empire in the Black Sea region in the fourth century and were converted to Judaism around A.D. 740. Khazar rule came to an end in the middle of the tenth century.

46. Karim Rash, "Armiya i Kultura," *Voenno-istoricheski zhurnal,* 9 (1989), p. 9.

the military budget. It has defended the armed forces (and often also the KGB) against attacks and this support has been reciprocated.

The right opposed Gorbachev's "New Thinking" for a variety of reasons, and they expressed great unhappiness even with the changes in official Soviet military doctrine in 1989–1990.[47] As they saw it, arms control worked in favor of the West. Through great efforts and sacrifices the Soviet Union had acquired a very strong strategic position. To squander it was tantamount to treason; hence the bitter attacks against Arbatov, Primakov, Burlatsky, and other advisers of Gorbachev. These men were by no means "liberals," let alone radicals, but they had come to realize that the Soviet economy could no longer sustain a military budget of such magnitude, and that, in any case, these allocations resulted in diminishing returns from a purely military point of view.

According to right-wing doctrine, it was wrong to assume that nuclear weapons would not play a decisive role in a coming war. At the same time, deep reductions in nuclear armament were bound to lead, sooner rather than later, to a "world government." This in the view of these circles is an American Trojan horse, the worst fate that can befall Russia, tantamount to a Western victory without a single battle.[48]

For the same reason the New Right opposed even the test bans (except the 1963 agreement). The tenor of the complaints about the changes in military doctrine was exceedingly bitter; the rightists saw their antagonists as "fifth columnists," infecting the country with some kind of political AIDS.[49] These debates were overtaken by the events of 1991. But the complaints and the arguments about the armed forces having been stabbed in the back are likely to persist.

Insofar as foreign policy proper is concerned, the right has traditionally distrusted and disliked the United States. This tradition goes back a long time before the revolution. Gorky, who for personal reasons received a less than cordial reception in puritan America, wrote eloquently about the "yellow devil" (Mammon) ruling the United States. For many years after 1945, America was described in Soviet propaganda as the greatest danger by far. True, there was also a pro-American trend of admiration and even exaggerated expectations on both the popular and the highbrow level, but the right wanted none of that. In its view, America is a materialist society, devoid of ideals and values, an artificial, synthetic nation which would

47. "Yadernyy shchit i natsionalnaya ideya," *Nash sovremennik* 10 (1991), p. 156 (Y. Katasonov).

48. Ibid., p. 152 (I. Shanin).

49. Ibid., p. 148 (A. N. Anisimov).

disintegrate sooner rather than later, partly because of its capitalist character but also because of a surfeit of egalitarianism and the absence of an elite. It is a sterile country that has never produced a culture of its own.

Such comments have been voiced for a long time by Western European critics, among them Adolf Hitler, who said: "There is more culture in one of Beethoven's symphonies than in the whole of American history." America is not considered a suitable partner for Russia in foreign politics. It is the main enemy even though there are no major bones of contention between the two countries as far as territory or economic competition or imperial ambition is concerned. According to the Russian right, America has tried systematically and not unsuccessfully to transform Russia into a satellite.[50]

Nor is there much love for China and Japan. There is some respect for Communist China, which seems to have managed its economic problems slightly better than Russia has and which succeeded in putting down the liberal challenge at home. But China is also the "Yellow Peril" that has always endangered Russia in Asia, the billion-plus horde that one day may expand to Siberia. Japan is admired for its national cohesion and economic achievements, but the cultural differences are so great as to prevent a real rapprochement, the territorial disputes quite apart. In contrast to the liberals, the right has bitterly opposed giving up any Russian territory at all, even that which, like the Kuriles, became part of the old Soviet Union only after 1945.[51]

Some on the right believe that there are better prospects for a strategic alliance with a rising Muslim empire, even if it should be fundamentalist in inspiration. But the Islamic world is far from united and many on the right suspect that the ambitions of Islam would soon collide with Russia's legitimate interests in Asia and possibly even in Europe. During the war in the Gulf in 1991, the Russian far right unanimously supported Iraq and denounced its own government for not dissociating itself from American and Western aggression.[52] Before the war broke out the extreme right

50. D. Katasonov, *Moskovskii literator,* 20 (December 1990). By summer of 1992 such views were voiced even by moderate right-wingers such as Nikolai Pavlov. *Nezavisimaya gazeta* (June 12, 1992).

51. For an illustration of anti-Japanese attitudes on the Russian right see the articles by Khorin and Sergeyev in *Russkii vestnik,* 28–29, 1991.

52. One illustration among many: "Agressia protiv Iraka prodolzhaetsia," *Polozhenie del,* May 1991. There were so many pro-Iraqi articles and the support was so enthusiastic that a good deal of speculation ensued as to whether this publicity was given free of charge. See also *Domostroi,* 2 (1991); *Den,* 2 (1991), *Pogranichnik* (Dec. 12, 1990; "Araviskaya avantyura detei Arbatova")

predicted that America was facing total disaster. After Saddam Hussein's defeat they argued that in view of the enormous American superiority it was disgraceful that the West had engaged in such unequal battle.

Some right-wing spokesmen argued at the time that good relations with the Muslim world would help Moscow to contain the separatist movement in the Soviet Muslim republics. Others, on the contrary, expressed a fear that Russia would undergo Islamization if the Central Asian republics remained part of the union.[53] This debate, too, was overtaken by events as the Central Asian republics seceded in 1991. There were enthusiastic articles in the nationalist journals about the political continuity in the Central Asian republics in 1990–1991, but this, too, changed in the year after.

There was no full agreement on correct policies at the time of the Persian Gulf crisis. Everyone agreed that the indirect help allegedly given by Gorbachev and Shevardnadze to the Americans was disgraceful. But whereas Kozhinov advocated an orientation toward the Third World (in accordance with some of Lenin's last writings), Shafarevich favored a Russian "Monroe doctrine" and an isolationist policy as long as the country had not recovered from its internal eclipse.[54]

The extreme right opposed the restoration of diplomatic ties with Israel, and it revived the long-defunct Russian-Palestinian Society, a remnant from tsarist days, which had originally engaged in religious and scientific (archeological) activities. However, these and similar initiatives were of exceedingly limited importance. The broader public hardly knew about them. In the main, right-wing attitudes were defensive and negative, accusing Gorbachev and, in particular, Shevardnadze of engaging in a wholesale giveaway of Russia's assets, territorial and military, and thus fatally weakening Russia's position as a great power.

This leaves the concepts of Eurasianism (to which we shall return later on) and the idea of a continental alliance. Eurasianism is, and always was, a nebulous idea from both a cultural and political point of view. Solovyov asked his friends whether, when they invoked the East, they wanted the Orient of Christ—or of Xerxes. Present-day Eurasians want neither Christ nor Xerxes nor Khomeini nor Khaddafi, but something that does not exist and therefore does not constitute a real alternative.

In this general context the theories of Lev Gumilev should be men-

---

53. Zabrodsky, *Moskva,* 7 (1991). For comments on subsequent events see A. Malshenko, "Islam i natsional kommunism," *Nezavisimaya gazeta* (March 12, 1992).

54. *Literaturnaya Rossiya,* 2 (1991). Their only idol apart from Saddam Hussein was President Milosevic of Serbia.

tioned, at least in passing. The son of Anna Akhmatova and the poet Nikolai Gumilev he developed some original concepts about ethnogenesis in general and the origins of Russia in particular. The ethnos, according to Gumilev, was biological in character and based on *passionarnost* ("instinct" or "drive"). He came close to advocating racial segregation.[55]

Gumilev's ideas appealed to the right because they had a certain amount in common with the Slavophiles' thought regarding the differences between the Russian ethnos and Europe, and because he also advocated a Eurasianism of sorts. Some of his works could not be published before 1987; they were popularized under *glasnost* by right-wing writers such as D. Balashev.[56] But Gumilev was also attacked from the right because of the stress he always put on the close relationship between Russia, the Tatars, and the Mongol Golden Horde. He suggested that the relations between Russia and her Eastern neighbors had been far more close and cordial than was generally assumed. Such claims were bound to offend believers in the purity of the Russian ethnos.[57]

The "continentalists," who are more numerous, stand for an all-European alliance based on a Berlin-Moscow axis as a counterweight to the United States with its overwhelming power. The argument in favor of a "Rapallo in reverse"—referring to the 1922 treaty, which was never consummated—runs, in brief, as follows: Germans and Russians have traditionally been good neighbors and close partners, complementing each other in various ways. True, on some occasions they have made war against each other, as in 1914 and 1941, but this had been the result of Western (and Judeo-Masonic) intrigues and in the end both these great nations had suffered. In 1922 Germany was the weaker partner in the alliance; today Russia is in bad shape.[58] But these are the transient ups and downs in the history of nations; sooner or later Russia will recover, and if they join forces, Germany and Russia will be the strongest power in Europe, perhaps in the whole world. Russian right-wing writers refer with satisfaction to an anti-

55. On Gumilev and the debate concerning his teachings, see Milan Hauer, *What Is Asia to Us?* (Boston, 1990), pp. 30–31. Gumilev died in June 1992.

56. *Literaturnaya Rossiya,* February 24, 1989. Some of Gumilev's writings are available in English translation; for instance, *Ethnogenesis and the Biosphere* (Moscow, 1990).

57. A. Kuzmin, in *Molodaya gvardiya,* 9 (1991), and Gumilev's reply in *Den,* 1 (1992). Also Gumilev, "Menya nazivayut Evraziitsem," *Nash sovremennik,* 1 (1991), and Guseva's bitter attack in *Russkii vestnik,* 27 (1991), charging him with falsifying the history of Russia and "spreading calumnies about our ancestors." *Russkii vestnik,* 15 (1992).

58. For arguments on these lines see, for instance: M. Alexander, *Literaturnaya Rossiya,* 26 (1990); E. Volodin, *Literaturnaya Rossiya,* 28 (1990). "We need a German-Russian alliance forever": N. Tverskov, *Golos rossii,* 1 (1991). The term "Moscow-Berlin Axis" was used by A. Fomenko, *Literaturnaya Rossiya,* 34 (1990), p. 19.

American mood in Germany and imply that there is also an ideological affinity between the two countries: Russia gravitates toward authoritarian rule, rather than democracy, and in Germany, too, one should not take the present parliamentarianism too seriously. As Vladimir Osipov has put it, Germany is basically a conservative country, which has not been affected by decomposition to the same extent as the rest of Europe or America.[59]

The authors of most of these historiosophical and "geopolitical" fantasies are nonspecialists with little if any knowledge of the world and intellectual life outside Russia. They are in the Spenglerian tradition of commenting on countries and peoples they have never seen. Thus there is a perennial tendency among them to overrate America's interest in Europe and to underrate the changes that have taken place in Germany since the Second World War. The lack of knowledge in depth and of empathy is combined with the discovery of conspiracies everywhere. The weekly *Den* proudly coined the term "conspiratology" for this new science, to which a permanent section in the paper is devoted.

Nineteenth-century Russian conservatives from the Slavophiles to Pobedonostsev had, as a rule, excellent knowledge of the West. It has been one of the sad consequences of the isolation of Russia since the Revolution of 1917 that even bitter enemies of bolshevism no longer understand the outside world. Their theories are rooted in a world of fantasies rather than in the realities of the modern world.

By and large we have restricted our survey to the far right without referring to its lunatic fringe. But such a fringe does exist; it has its meetings and publishes its journals; and the dividing line between these circles and the more respectable figures on the extreme right is not always easy to discern with the naked eye. The most extreme publications—such as, for instance, *Narodnoye delo* or *Russkie vedomosti*—show a heavy preoccupation with sexual themes. Thus it is argued that the white race (unlike the "colored") is not endangered by AIDS, and that a Russian woman who has intercourse with a black man or a Jew, even if only once, will no longer be able to give birth to a genetically "pure" Russian child, but will be the mother of a Jewish or black child.[60] It goes without saying that Rosenberg, Goebbels, and Mussolini have been widely published in this literature.

59. *Moskva,* 7 (1991).

60. *Narodnoye delo,* 1 (1992).

The Occult Sources of the Extreme Right

The sources of contemporary right-wing Russian thought can be traced back to the Slavophiles and Dostoyevsky, to the Orthodox church and (to a limited extent) to neopaganism. But there is yet another trend, often overlooked but as important as any of those mentioned. This is the esoteric tradition, the occult sciences, in particular astrology and other aspects of nonrational, nonanalytical thinking, drawn from ancient Indian sources, Nostradamus, spiritualism, parapsychology and the like. A survey of books published between 1988 and 1992 shows that the number of titles and the sizes of print runs of books and almanacs published during that period considerably exceeds the circulation of Karamzin's *History of Russia* and the other key works of the Russian national tradition, and equals, or perhaps even exceeds, that of the Bible and other religious writings.[61]

In the West as in the East this phenomenon has by and large been ignored. True, Jung once wrote that the high tide of astrology was now, not in the Middle Ages, and that it was "knocking on the doors of the universities." Fritz Saxl, the art historian, has noted the phenomenal rise of astrology; he interprets it, in part, as a return of paganism, typical of periods of great unrest, and has concluded that no historical period could be fully understood unless its unscientific tendencies were carefully studied.[62]

As far as academic thought is concerned, astrology has been out of fashion since the scientific revolution of the seventeenth century. But in England, and later in America, astrology was never quite dead. There was an occult revival in France in the late nineteenth century, and another in Germany just before and after the First World War; in Russia, too, these schools have been welcome for a long time. Several of the key figures— Madame Blavatsky (1831–1891), Gourdjieff, and Ouspenski—were of Russian origin, though they spent most of their lives outside their native country. The belief in faith healing has always been fashionable in Russia. The case of Rasputin is well known, as is the dependence of the tsar's family on this holy man. But he was only the best-known of a whole series of leading practitioners of faith healing. It was therefore no great surprise when this phenomenon reappeared in Russia in the 1960s, when even members of the Politburo were consulting fortune-tellers and faith healers.

61. To provide but one example: *Knizhnoye obozrenye*, 3 (1992), announced the publication of twenty-five new books under the heading "Philosophy, Sociology, Psychology, and Religion." Out of these, ten dealt with occult sciences. Whereas the average circulation of the nonoccult books was between ten and twenty thousand, fifty to one hundred thousand was the average for astrology and allied subjects.

62. Fritz Saxl, *Lectures* (London, 1957), vol. 1, p. 73.

However, the occult subculture was until recently kept apart from official ideology; *Pravda* would not publish horoscopes (as *Sovetskaya Rossiya* does in 1992), nor would *Kommunist* open its pages to discussions on Swedenborg and Rudolf Steiner. There were some scientific investigations into parapsychological phenomena, but this occurred in the West too.

While the occult sciences are prima facie unpolitical, their attraction for people subscribing to a rational Weltanschauung has been traditionally much weaker than for those believing that science was not in a position to provide answers to the truly important questions in life. The enormous revival of occultism in contemporary Russia is, in large part, a reaction to the "scientific" claims of yesteryear's official ideology, Marxism-Leninism.

As far as the Russian right is concerned, the belief in Satan and various demons that has been discussed earlier in our study is part of the occult tradition, for it goes far beyond the teaching of the church. But there are other influences, especially on the far right; a few typical examples will suffice to clarify their essence and appeal.

The belief in divination is widespread on the Russian right. Half of the December 1991 issue of *Russkoye voskresenye,* the organ of the Russian national-liberation movement, was devoted to translations from Nostradamus, according to whose prophecies the Satanists will be finally destroyed in the year 1999. These predictions are accompanied by a variety of medieval caricatures of animals and demons as well as pseudomathematical formulas.[63] *Puls tushina,* the leading anti-Semitic journal in Moscow, reported that a local Novosibirsk newspaper *(7 dnei)* reported the Chernobyl disaster ten days before the event.[64] True, such belief is not confined to the right: A publication of the Soviet Foreign Ministry reported that astrologers were the first to report in newspapers and on television that a coup d'état was possible in 1991 or 1992 but were dismissed as scaremongers.[65] But nowhere have such specific and far-reaching claims been made as in the journals of the extreme right. Thus, in the summer of 1991 both *Istoki* and *Voskresenye* published articles dealing with the mysterious death

63. *Russkoye voskresenye,* vol. 5, no. 13 (1991). However, Nostradamus was also discussed in popular scientific journals such as *Znaniye sila,* 11 (1991). There are no predictions about Russia, but about a country named Aquilon, which some followers of Nostradamus have construed as being Russia.

64. *Puls tushina,* 14 (1990). The author of the article later hanged himself. Needless to say, the case was treated as one of murder by *Puls tushina.*

65. Felix Velichko, "Astrology and Politics," *International Affairs* (November 1991), p. 96. The author also notes that the conspirators would have had somewhat better chances in July. It would be fair to note that many Western Sovietologists—not to mention Shevardnadze, Yakovlev, *et al.*—also expected a coup.

of some prominent Russian anti-Semites. The former article was entitled "How They Kill Us," the latter "The Riddle of a Murder Yet Undiscovered." Possibly they were written by the same person; one was signed "Astrologer," the other "Sharikov-Riesenschnauzer, astrologist."[66]

The articles deal with the suicide of Smirnov-Ostashvili, a Pamyat leader, and the death in a road accident of Evseev, a prominent ideologist of the same stripe. The argument of the author(s) runs briefly as follows: The figures 7 and 8 are considered propitious by people engaged in black magic. On February 7, 1990, *Literaturnaya gazeta* published an article accusing Smirnov-Ostashvili of various misdeeds. On February 10, 1990, Evseev had an accident; on the fifteenth ($15 = 7 + 8$!) he died. He was found injured by the traffic police at kilometer 78(!) of the Moscow ring road. Earlier that day the state attorney had initiated a legal action against Evseev under article 74 (incitement of racial hatred; again the 7!), which was discontinued because "ritual murder had already been committed." According to the astrologist, Evseev was either hypnotized by people engaged in black magic, or deceived and led into a trap by someone whom he thought an old friend, or killed by the physicians who, in an attempt to save him, cut his larynx ("so that he could not talk anymore.")

On the last picture of Ostashvili the clock shows ten; the tenth sign of the zodiac is Capricorn, which according to astrological tradition is auspicious for those holding secret power in the country—usually Mason-pederasts ("in the Soviet Union all Masons are pederasts")—because their idol is a little devil in the shape of a billygoat named Vafomet.[67] The author(s) considers the possibility that these nefarious actions might have been connected with a big anti-KGB campaign launched at the time but then dismisses the notion because a simple ritual murder seems more likely.

There is even more conclusive evidence. The murder was committed at eleven in the evening, which according to old Eastern tradition is the "hour of the dog." That provides a clue: When Rasputin and Nikolai II were killed, their dogs were also done away with. And *Ogonyok*, the leading liberal journal of the day, referred to Evseev shortly before his death as "Sharikov's children."[68] Further clues are provided by the signs of the zodiac. Each favors a certain people—the widder stands for Germany, the lion for Japan, the fishes for sundry island peoples, including the Jews *(sic)*. The same is true with regard to certain parts of the body. The calf stands for the face and the neck, the twins of Gemini for the waist, Aquarius for

---

66. *Istoki* (May 1991); *Voskresenye,* 7 (1991).

67. *Voskresenye,* 7 (1991).

68. A reference to M. Bulgakov's novel *The Heart of a Dog.*

the larynx. Since the doctors carrying out the postmortem cut Evseev's larynx, all the pieces in this Satanic puzzle fall into place. It clearly appears in what direction the bloody traces lead of the murder of two patriots—Evseev and Ostashvili.

This example conveys the flavor of the mentality and the arguments of the astrologists of the extreme right. One feels tempted to regard such ravings as an elaborate hoax; surely an astrologist choosing the pen name Riesenschnauzer-Sharikov cannot possibly have expected his arguments to be taken seriously. However, a sense of humor is not one of the outstanding features of the far right in any country, least of all in Russia.

There is no unanimity among the Russian right with regard to the various occult schools. One might have assumed that the doctrines of Madame Blavatsky should have appealed to the Russian right; she was Russian by origin and at one time volunteered to act as an agent of the Russian political police. She prominently referred in her works to India's wisdom, to the Swastika, and to the Aryan race. Her works, above all *The Secret Doctrine* (1888), were widely published in Russia under *glasnost.*[69] But the right kept its distance from Blavatsky, partly because she presented a syncretic religion colliding with the teachings of the Orthodox church. They are even less sympathetic toward the Rudolf Steiner school of Theosophy—largely, no doubt, because of the Jewish origin of its founder—and they have emphatically rejected the Rosicrucians and Swedenborg, the eighteenth-century Swedish engineer who was a pioneer of the primacy of extrasensory perception.

Again certain interesting parallels with the occult sources of German national socialism obtrude themselves. The Ariosophists of Germany and Austria picked from the rich variety of occult theories and practices those best fitting their political aspirations, and rejected or ignored the rest.[70] Himmler and other Nazi leaders were influenced by the Ariosophists. But in later years such influence declined; Hitler derided the sectarians of the right, whom he regarded as *Spinner*, faddists, who had no mass appeal and in fact impeded the unification of the German right with their unending internal squabbles. In some ways Hitler and the Russian far right faced similar dilemmas. Their Weltanschauung was irrational, utopian, anti-Western, antimodernist. But Hitler was sufficiently realistic to understand that

69. On the occasion of the hundredth anniversary of her death *Nauka i religiya*, once the leading atheist journal, devoted five articles to her memory (September 1991). A new Theosophical society was founded in Moscow in 1991.

70. N. Goodvick-Clarke, *The Occult Roots of Nazism* (Wellingborough, 1985), passim. G. Mosse, *The Crisis of German Ideology* (London, 1966), chapter 2. Above all, James Webb, *The Occult Establishment*, London, 1976.

a strong Germany could exist only if it were based on a strong army that was based in turn on a big and efficient industrial sector, not on occult fantasies. The *gosudarstvenniki*—statists—and National Bolsheviks among the Russian right understood this, but other groups found it exceedingly difficult to accept.

Chapter Eleven

THE IDEOLOGY OF THE NEW RIGHT (2)

THE ENEMIES OF THE RUSSIAN RIGHT, real and imaginary, are numerous. That the Russian right opposes Marxism goes without saying, but anti-Marxist polemics have not featured prominently in its publications, if only because the topic no longer seemed of particular interest. Anti-Marxism is widespread and has never been a right-wing monopoly. Marx did not think highly of the course of Russian history, and, with a few notable exceptions, he was not impressed by most of the Russians he had met. Tsarist Russia was, after all, the traditional enemy of the revolution, and this colored Marx's views in every respect. He was one of Britain's leading Russophobes in his time; his most offensive statements to this effect could not be published in the Soviet Union prior to *glasnost*. After 1987 some writers of the right used them with great relish.[1]

There were certain aspects of Marx's teachings that appealed to the Russian right, such as his anti-Jewish attitude, his antiliberalism, and his anticapitalism. If he despised Russians, he did not think highly of the Germans among whom he had grown up, and, generally speaking, he was inclined toward misanthropy. But from a Russian-nationalist point of view his positive sides were outweighed by his atheism, his advocacy of materialism, his internationalism, and his preaching of revolution. There is a tendency among Russian right-wingers not to take Marxism at face value but

1. For instance, V. Bondarenko, "Istoriya Rossii po Marksu," *Slovo* (February 1991).

to interpret its real aim in the light of yet another global conspiracy, Marx's real aim being not to help the workers and other exploited people (let alone to make mankind happy) but on the contrary, to add to human misery in accordance with the doctrine of Satanism. Having been a Christian in his youth, Marx later became a Satanist, according to this school of thought.[2] Marx is not considered one of the Elders of Zion, nor even a Mason, but a man possessed by demons. His whole life work was aimed at radical destruction, at the negation of all traditional values. Engels, on the other hand, was aware of the dangers of Satanism, but as a result of accepting liberal theology he came to collaborate closely with Marx.[3] On a higher level of sophistication, some intellectuals among the contemporary Russian right have tried to interpret the Marxist phenomenon on the lines of Bulgakov's famous essay, written in the early years of the century, on "Marx as a Religious Type."

Nor has Lenin been a central figure in the doctrine of the Russian right. The one major exception is a long essay by the writer V. Soloukhin, "Reading Lenin," in which the familiar points are made that Lenin was wrong on all major counts and is guilty of many crimes against the Russian people. This refers to the dictatorship he established against the express wish of the great majority of the Russian people; thus he unleashed a civil war and caused famine, untold suffering and destruction, and ultimately the disintegration of the Russian empire.[4] All these points had been made many times in the Western and the Russian émigré literature, but some were still novel in the Soviet context.

The demythologization of Lenin, as far as Russian readers were concerned, had begun with Solzhenitsyn's *Lenin in Zurich*. But the new version with Parvus-Helphand as Lenin's Svengali was about as dubious, where historical truth is concerned, as the old hagiography. The question of the German gold given to the Bolsheviks to finance their revolutionary propaganda had been widely debated in the West in the 1950s (and, in part, as early as 1917–1918) but, again, it was new to many Russians.

Much publicity was given by right-wing periodicals to instructions given by Lenin soon after the Revolution and intended to reduce the influence of the Orthodox church. The document in question had not been published before and it reflected badly on the traditional image of Lenin as essentially a tolerant man and a great humanist.

2. G. Marchenko, "Karl Marx," *Kuban*, 1 (1991), p. 41ff. The author is introduced as a "self-confessed Zionist."

3. *Ibid.*

4. *Rodina*, 10 (1989). The article was previously published in an émigré journal in Germany.

Last, there was the revelation that Blank, Lenin's maternal grandfather, was a converted Jew.[5] This, too was not a new discovery; the Russian writer Marietta Shaginian—and many Western biographers—had known it. Two Leningrad historians had discovered documentary evidence in 1964–1965, but their findings were suppressed. Nor was the issue of decisive importance.[6] Even under the Nuremberg laws in Nazi Germany, quarter-Jews were in most respects treated like full Aryans. But for many on the Russian right the discovery still appeared as confirmation of what they had suspected all along: that a real Russian would not have behaved as Lenin did.

Despite all these anti-Lenin revelations the Russian right did not persist in this propaganda theme. The right was not among those advocating closing down the mausoleum on Red Square. The attitude toward Lenin has not been remotely as negative as vis-à-vis Trotsky, Zinoviev, Sverdlov, and the other Jews in the leadership, even though Lenin was the undisputed leader of the Bolsheviks. With regard to Stalin, the approach of the right has been more positive than negative. The worst that even the extreme right has been saying about Stalin is that he was a half-Jew,[7] but since the same was alleged by these circles with regard to Hitler, Churchill, Roosevelt, and everyone else, and since the right also conceded that Stalin was an anti-Semite, the accusation was not particularly damaging.

For obvious reasons, mainstream Russian nationalist attitudes toward Stalin could not be too enthusiastic; Stalin was a topic best shunned. He could not possibly be one of the heroes of the national renaissance comparable to Sergei of Radonezh, Kutuzov, Stolypin, or Nikolai II. Nevertheless, his picture has been featured prominently on the front pages of nationalist publications;[8] and the National Bolsheviks have not been the only ones to jump to his defense against the attacks of the liberals.

The reasoning behind the defense of Stalin can be summarized as follows: While Lenin weakened Russia, overthrew tsarism, and undermined or destroyed all the pillars of Old Russia, Stalin was at heart a Russian nationalist; he made Russia a great power again, and ultimately a superpower. He restored many, though not all, of the old traditions. He committed grievous mistakes in his social policies and killed many Russian

5. M. Stein, "Genealogiya rod Ulyanovikh," originally published in *Literator* (Leningrad), 38 (1990), reprinted in *Slovo*, 11 (1991). About the Blank family in Zhitomir and Starokonstantinov, see V. Tsaplin, *Otechestvennie Arkhivy*, 2 (1992).

6. A reply to Soloukhin by the historians G. Bordiugov, V. Kozlov, and V. Loginov in *Istoriya i koniunktura* (Moscow, 1992), pp. 267ff.

7. G. Klimov, *Protokoly krasnykh mudretsov* (Globus, 1988), p. 226.

8. For instance, *Russkii vestnik*, 28–29 (1991).

patriots. But he won the war against Hitler, killed the old revolutionary guard, and relentlessly persecuted the "cosmopolitans." In retrospect, his record was mixed, but the fact that Russia was very strong, had so much international prestige, and was widely feared at the time of his death induced the right to discover many mitigating circumstances for Stalin's misdeeds.

What annoyed the New Right more than anything else was the liberals' relentless anti-Stalinist campaign and their heavy concentration on the purges of 1936–1938. During the collectivization of agriculture (1928–1931) many more Russians were killed. Hence the bitter attacks against Anatoli Rybakov, who had been a pioneer of anti-Stalinist literature with his *Children of the Arbat,* and against Trifonov and Evtushenko, who had also published Stalinist novels and poems in their youth. This appeared to them the height of duplicity and hypocrisy; the liberals, as they saw it, had no moral right to condemn Stalin and Stalinism.

I have dealt elsewhere, in some detail, with the assessment of Stalin by the Russian right after 1987.[9] All that need be said here is that the National Bolshevik right, from the Communist diehard Nina Andreyeva to *Molodaya Gvardiya,* stood up for his good name.

Former high officials in Stalin's administration, such as Benediktov, Malakhov, and even Molotov, published articles from which it emerged that Stalin was a hard but just taskmaster, that he had given young people a chance, that there had been much idealism and enthusiasm in his time, that moral standards had been infinitely higher.[10] If he had been compelled to take harsh measures against his enemies, that was mainly because these enemies threatened the survival of Russia and the Soviet regime. There had been many plots and conspiracies by enemies of the people, and any wavering on his part would have ended in disaster.[11] There were bound to be some (but not many) innocent victims in the process, but this was mainly the result of the bad advice Stalin had received from treacherous advisers such as Kaganovich.[12] Still, in the final analysis, Stalin emerged

9. W. Laqueur, *Stalin: The Glasnost Revelations* (New York, 1990), pp. 243ff.

10. Ivan Benediktov, *Molodaya gvardiya,* 4 (1989); G. Malakhov, *Molodaya gvardiya,* 4 (1988); Feliks Chuyev's conversations with Molotov were published in 1990.

11. *Polozhenie del,* 3 (1991).

12. Kaganovich was in 1990 the last survivor of Stalin's inner circle and became the main whipping boy of the right; after all, he had been the only Jew in this exclusive company. While Kaganovich's role was of considerable importance up to about 1937, he suffered an eclipse thereafter and no longer belonged to those closest to Stalin. He died in 1991, aged ninety-six. In the year before his death, several fake interviews with Kaganovich appeared in right-wing periodicals.

blemished from these attempts to save his honor, for as the supreme leader he bore the responsibility for picking such bad advisers.[13]

So much then for the National Bolsheviks. The mainstream nationalist version runs on somewhat different lines. It is not pro-Stalinist, but anti-anti-Stalinist, based on the assumption that a leader so much reviled by the liberals could not be all bad. As Vadim Kozhinov saw it, there were various things wrong with Stalinism, including the cult of the personality. It was, however, by no means a specifically Russian phenomenon, but was global in character, extending "from Madrid to Shanghai." The Stalin cult seized the masses and became a powerful political force. Furthermore, bolshevism was not a Russian phenomenon; aliens took a decisive part in its leadership. These foreigners had no love for Russia; they hated and despised it and merely wanted to use the Russian people as cannon fodder for the world revolution. Russian patriots need not mourn the fact that under Stalin many of these alien elements perished. At the same time great achievements were made by the Russian people under Stalin; the real tragedy consists in the fact that the greatest periods in history (such as the Renaissance) are also those in which many people are killed. Thus, the achievements under Stalin were made owing to the heroic efforts of the Russian people, whereas the crimes of Stalinism were committed mainly by foreigners.[14]

The right showed no enthusiasm in retrospect for Khrushchev, Brezhnev, and their acolytes, who had been faithful party members and manifested no interest in Russian national traditions. But at least these leaders had not squandered the heritage amassed by their predecessors throughout the centuries: Russia had remained a superpower up to the days of *perestroika* and *glasnost*. In retrospect, Khrushchev and Brezhnev appeared in a much more favorable light than Gorbachev or Shevardnadze, let alone the unspeakable Yakovlev.

The attitude of Russian right-wingers toward *perestroika* and *glasnost* was at first cautious and not entirely negative, but they were skeptical with regard to its success. Even the extreme right came up with slogans to the effect that they were the only true fighters for real reform, that they would help Gorbachev and above all Ligachev to save reform from the machina-

13. A. Barkashov, "Era rossii" (samizdat, 1991) for one of the many long lists of "alien" advisers.

14. A seminal article was V. Kozhinov, "Pravda i istina," *Nash sovremennik,* 4 (1988), followed by many similar essays by A. Lanshikov, V. Bondarenko, M. Lobanov, S. Kunayev, and others, in the same journal and in *Molodaya gvardiya* throughout 1989–1990. The publications of the extreme right and *Voenno-istoricheskii zhurnal* went further and claimed that the marshals and generals had indeed plotted against Stalin and Voroshilov and that the decapitation of the Red Army was therefore largely justified.

tions of the Mafia and the extremists of the left as well as the Russophobes. The right greatly preferred Ligachev to Gorbachev: The former was, quite obviously, a more conservative and cautious man, in less of a hurry to dismantle time-honored structures, institutions, and doctrines at home, and less eager to establish closer relations with the West. However, despite his Siberian background, Ligachev never became a true hero of the right. According to his background and mentality he was a loyal Communist party activist. If he criticized Gorbachev it was not because of Gorbachev's lack of patriotism but because of his deviation from the canons of Marxism-Leninism. Ligachev, for his part, shared some right-wing predilections—for instance, their taste for order and discipline and their aversion to cultural modernism. But he could not possibly go along with the unabashed anti-Marxist propaganda and the fervent support for the church and even the monarchy.

The attitude of the right toward Gorbachev became ever more hostile during 1989 and 1990 and reached its climax with the various barely veiled appeals to establish a new, military—or at least authoritarian—leadership.[15] This appeal was signed by leading party, government, and security figures as well as right-wing intellectuals such as Rasputin and Prokhanov. The manifesto stated, and the commentaries made it even more abundantly clear, that Gorbachev's policy was causing the total breakdown of Russian statehood (*gosudarstvennost*), that the transition to the market was disastrous, that the undermining in the media of the pillars of Soviet society (such as the army and the KGB) was suicidal, that "government policy was worse than Chernobyl," "tantamount to infecting the Russian body politic with spiritual AIDS."[16]

If the mainstream right attacked Gorbachev on matters of policy and principle, the extremists reviled him personally: It was reported that an old Turkish woman had been found who claimed that Gorbachev was her son. And in any case, it seemed quite obvious that his wife was not of truly Russian origins.

The Russian right faced problems from the very beginning with *glasnost*. They could not turn frontally against it; *glasnost*, after all, had been the watchword of some of the leading Slavophiles. Above all, it was owing to *glasnost* that they could voice for the first time their real views, having been confined for so many years to mere hints and implications. But *glasnost* also meant, of course, freedom of expression not only for them but in equal measure for their bitter enemies, those favoring a liberal and

15. "Slovo k narodu" appeared on July 23, 1991 in *Sovetskaya Rossiya* and *Moskovskaya pravda*.

16. N. Pozdnyakov, *Sovetskaya Rossiya* (July 30, 1991).

democratic Russia, in part on Western patterns. It was the victory of the pluralists—the *obrazovanshchina,* as Solzhenitsyn had called them.

It is difficult for a non-Russian (and perhaps also for many Russians) to understand how deeply suspicious the Russian right is of Russia's own intelligentsia.[17] As they see it, the intelligentsia is a typical Russian phenomenon, to be found only there—which is a half-truth. The intelligentsia, they claim, is almost wholly antipatriotic—always with the exception of its greatest representatives such as Pushkin, Dostoyevsky, Tolstoy, and so on, who were Russian geniuses, not dubious intellectuals.

How to explain the Russian right's great fear of the "horrible intelligentsia" (Nevzorov) which, it claims, is in total control of all the media?[18] The writers union of the Russian republic and the big Moscow publishing houses—Sovetskii Pisatel, Sovremennik, Knizhnaya Palata, Khudozhestvennaya Literatura—remained in the right wing's ownership. The professional organizations of Russian composers and painters remained, broadly speaking, in the same hands as before. If literary magazines such as *Znamya* and *Oktyabr* expressed the views of the liberals, *Molodaya gvardiya* and *Nash sovremennik* took a nationalist right-wing stand and *Novy mir* a position somewhere in the middle. Many literary magazines outside Moscow *(Sever, Kuban, Don)* belonged to the nationalists. If some television and radio programs gravitated toward the left, others expressed views closer to the center or the right.

The great fear thus remains inexplicable in the final analysis. Was it, perhaps, due to the suspicion that the nationalists would lose the young generation if the liberals were permitted to vent their views freely? Were they, unsure of their own arguments, attributing to left-wing intellectual reasoning magnetic qualities that the patriots lacked? Or was the fear the result of the old religious belief that the temptations of evil are very strong and have to be constantly resisted? For many on the right, their foes were not political opponents but represented Satan. The Russian right, like the right in other countries, regards it as the holy duty of the intellectuals to strengthen the national spirit, to praise the history of the Russian people, to defend them against their enemies, to preach adherence to traditional values. Any self-criticism is considered destructive, bordering on treason. The right has not the slightest understanding for or sympathy with the radical intellectuals who understand their role to be that of professional

---

17. See for instance V. Rasputin, "Intelligentsiya i patriotizm," *Moskva,* 2 (1991), or, on a lower level of sophistication, A. Nevzorov, "Yest takoe uzhaznoye poniatie, —intelligentsiya," *Narodnaya pravda,* 2 (November 1991).

18. Nevzorov, "Intelligentsiya."

critics, even of the conscience of the nation. It is known that on occasion, part of the intelligentsia has put itself in systematic opposition to the state and society and adopted consistently negative attitudes toward national traditions and the politics of the establishment in general. But this has happened during certain periods in Western countries such as the United States and Germany far more blatantly than it has in Russia, without causing a crisis of cosmic proportions. Mention has been made of the particular sensitivity of the Russian right toward incidents, or alleged incidents, of Russophobia. Russophobia (a subject to which we shall have to refer again) can be compared, broadly speaking, with anti-Americanism; and Russian arrivals to America—for example, Solzhenitsyn and Aksyonov—have expressed astonishment and shock at facing so much ill will and even hatred vis-à-vis the United States.[19] But in America, unlike among the self-conscious Russian right, such sentiments have been ignored or even been treated with ridicule.

Perhaps the central problem facing the Russian right was the fact that while it wanted, by and large, the dismantling of the Communist apparatus, it did not want all the old social structures to disappear, to be replaced by a new liberal-capitalist order, which it liked even less. The right wanted change, but controlled, limited, slow reforms. It stood for stability and continuity. For the alternative, as the right saw it, was a further uprooting of traditions; anarchy; possibly civil war. Having seen so many national values lost under Communist rule, the right feared that once Pandora's box was opened even the last remaining pillars of society—the family, public morality, patriotism, national discipline—would be subverted.

How to effect a transition to a more normal society (as the right saw it), culminating in a national renaissance? Democratization, quite obviously, was not the right answer, at least not democratization as preached and practiced in the West. The extreme right argued in their publications that democracy was a Jewish-Masonic invention intended to ruin Russia. *Zemshchina* frequently carried a tag line according to which democracy was the system prevailing in hell, whereas monarchy reigned supreme in heaven.

More moderate conservatives claimed that while in principle democracy was an admirable system, each country had to find, over time, the institutions that accorded with its history and traditions. There was no tradition of civic society in Russia, and it would take a long time to develop such institutions; as Solzhenitsyn had suggested, one should perhaps start with democracy on the local level.

The Russian right maintained that a transition from a totalitarian

19. Quoted in P. Hollander, *Anti-Americanism* (New York, 1992), p. 336.

(nihilist) regime to full democracy was impossible and would lead to disaster. The ideal solution was the establishment of an authoritarian-patriotic regime, which would give stability and provide the conditions for gradual change.[20]

It was the tragedy of the Russian right (and of Russia in general) that the developments after 1988 were unprecedented in history, that there were no parallels and paradigms, and political compasses did not exist. By late 1990 a sizeable part of the population and mainstream conservative groups (such as the Soyuz faction in the parliament) were arguing that there was no other way out of the impasse but authoritarianism: "The word need not frighten us, because there is authoritarianism and authoritarianism."[21] Singapore, Taiwan, and South Korea were prospering countries, certainly not democracies but also not Hitler- or Stalin-type dictatorships.

Colonels Alksnis and Petrushenko referred to the Chilean experience: When General Pinochet seized power, the country was on the brink of civil war; when he handed over the reins, the political, economic, and social climate was much better. This example did not lack piquancy because to the Soviet Union Pinochet had been one of the blackest of all international villains for many years, which had not, however, affected his popularity in some circles. Dr. Alexei Kiva, a Third World expert, explained why the Pinochet paradigm was unlikely to work in the Soviet Union.[22] Among the various reasons he adduced, only one should be noted: A crucial precondition for economic recovery was a drastic reduction of the defense budget. Yet the Soviet military continually claimed that the country's military power had become much weaker and that a rise in defense spending was therefore imperative.

Publicity was given to the writings of Adolf Hitler, Josef Goebbels, and Alfred Rosenberg by the extreme right, but these sectarian initiatives were not of much consequence.[23] Kurginyan publicized the "soft fascism" (his term) of the Strasser brothers, who had split with Hitler; Dugin promoted the ideas of Karl Haushofer, the father of (progressive) German geopoli-

20. Similar ideas about the impossibility of a sudden transition in Russia from totalitarianism to democracy had been voiced in 1989 by liberals such as A. Migranyan and I. Klyamkin.

21. B. Krotkov, *Rabochaya tribuna* (Jan. 31, 1991). A military dictatorship was said to be just around the corner: *Polozhenie del* (July 1991) and many other articles.

22. *Nezavisimaya gazeta* (English edition, April 1991), p. B. Elsewhere on the right it was argued that the pro-Pinochet enthusiasm was misplaced, mainly perhaps because of Pinochet's pro-American enthusiasm: *Den* (Jan. 26, 1992).

23. Thus *Istoki*, 5 (1991) published on its first page an article by S. I. Prishepenko, one of Moscow's leading neo-Bolsheviks, and on other pages of the magazine Goebbels's speech at the 1936 Nuremberg Party Congress on the "theory and practice of bolshevism."

tics—in contradistinction to Mackinder who had been an enemy, an early Atlanticist.[24] Elsewhere on the Russian right, General Franco found some admirers: In 1936–1939, he and the Spanish army loyal to him had saved Spain from a horrible fate.[25]

But these idols from foreign countries and distant periods were not of much relevance with regard to Russia after communism. Members of the old and new émigré generations contributed their advice. Mikhail Nazarov, a Masonic expert resident in Munich, warned the Russian public against American intrigues; had the Americans not been behind the coup of August 1991?[26] More sweeping were the contributions by Alexander Zinoviev and Eduard Limonov. The former, a distinguished expert in mathematical logic, had published several interesting if perverse books in the 1980s. His thesis was that Stalinism would last forever and was, in any case, the most suitable and satisfactory way of life for the Soviet Union. When his predictions were not borne out—most Russians seemed not to share this view—Zinoviev was evidently annoyed and in a series of articles called his fellow countrymen to a speedy return to the old system which, with all its drawbacks, was greatly preferable to *kata-stroika*—a term he had coined. "If the Western leaders had appointed their own man as the head of the Soviet government, he would not have caused as much harm to his country as Gorbachev." If the Revolution of 1917 had been a national catastrophe, so was Yeltsin's victory over the plotters, his establishment of a "gulag with a human face."[27]

Limonov, a younger writer who had made a name for himself with a sexually explicit semi-autobiographical novel describing the mores of the younger generation, admonished his fellow countrymen to show more patriotism, bitterly attacking the traitors at home and abroad who aimed at the destruction of the fatherland.[28] Having been exposed to Western ways for years, Limonov had reached the conclusion that in view of its Byzantine heritage Russia was an unsuitable ground for capitalism, which had its roots

24. Kurginyan in *Narodnaya Pravda* (November 1991); A. Dugin, *Den* (January 26, 1992). The author reminded his readers that Haushofer had met the Russian émigré Eurasians in Prague before World War II.

25. V. Kryukov, *Narodnoye delo*, 1 (1991).

26. "Lozh i pravda Avgusta 1991," *Literaturnaya Rossiya*, 43 (1991). Many on the Russian right (and some on the left) believed that the coup of August 1991 had been engineered by the Gorbachev liberals as a provocation. Some compared it with the burning of the Reichstag in February 1933: *Russkii Vestnik*, 20 (1991).

27. "Istoricheskaya tragediya," *Politika* 13 (September 1991). Eventually Zinoviev called for the overthrow "by all possible means" of the authorities: *Narodnaya pravda* (February 1992).

28. "Stukachestvo," *Sovetskaya Rossiya* (August 3, 1991).

in Calvinism.[29] The transformation of this sexually explicit young novelist who had rejected his native country was legitimate, as were the patriotic views he expressed. It was less intelligible, as Moscow critics pointed out, why patriots with such strong views about treason and other threats facing their country should fight for their ideas in Paris, Zurich, and Munich rather than return home. For one reason or another the Cassandras preferred life in the West, repulsive, miserable, and devoid of spiritual values as it was.

The unhappiness of the right-wing critics was shared in equal measure by many liberals, especially after the disintegration of the old Soviet Union following the coup of August 1991. As Denis Dragunsky wrote, Russia had won the fight against socialism only at the price of losing herself. And Alexander Tsypko, who had been one of the earliest and most emphatic of those who warned against the total dismemberment of the union, claimed that without the Ukraine and White Russia, Russia could not survive, just as the separatist states were not viable: "We have razed our state to the ground. . . . We destroyed all our own state structures."[30]

The essential difference between the liberals and the right was that the latter put all the blame on Gorbachev and Yeltsin, not on the plotters who had caused the earthquake. Furthermore, the right believed that the old empire, or much of it, could be reunited and maintained by military force alone.

The rapid deterioration of the situation in Russia in 1991–1992 was not conducive to a more sober, objective analysis of the roots of the evil and how to save the country. On the contrary, when after ten years Shafarevich reviewed his long essay on Russophobia he found no fault with either his analysis or his predictions of 1982.[31] Russophobia was the ideology of a certain layer of society, a minority arrogating to itself the right to speak for the whole people, trying to indoctrinate it with the belief that Russians were always crawling before a strong ruler. This was the reason for most, if not all, of Russia's misfortunes—the assumption being that if Sinyavsky had not written his literary essays on Pushkin and Gogol, if Grossman had not published *Fate and Life*, Russian history would have taken a different turning. The real culprit was not Stalin's cult of personality; Stalinism (as Kozhinov had shown) was a global phenomenon for which, not Russia, but Grossman and the other small Grossmans bore

29. *Sobesednik,* 45 (1990).

30. *Komsomolskaya pravda* (January 14, 1992); *Nezavisimaya gazeta* (January 9, 1992).

31. *Nash sovremennik,* 12 (1991). Many interviews with Shafarevich were published in 1990 and 1991. See, for instance, *Den,* 2 (1991); *Politika,* 7 (1991).

specific responsibility. The fact that leading Russian writers and thinkers from Pushkin and Lermontov on (including Polezhayev, who wrote "the people love the whip," and Vyazemsky, who coined the term *"kvasnoi patriotism"*) had been saying much harsher things about Russian history, was irrelevant. Either they had been misquoted, or it was not certain that they had really made these statements, or the statements were part of their "enigmatic Weltanschauung" (as in the case of Cha'adayev). *Quod licet Jovi, non licet bovi:* For Grossman to echo such views was an outrage and treason.

There is something to be said in favor of Shafarevich's claim that even if they have lived for generations in Russia, Jews are still considered guests by more than a few Russians and should behave tactfully. But the claim that "tactless" behavior on Jews' part had caused the national catastrophe was difficult to accept by any logical or other standard.

Why was Shafarevich's *Russophobia* so frequently quoted and hotly discussed? The question engaged Shafarevich, but the obvious answer seems not to have occurred to him. His book would have been ignored had it been written by a Pamyat leader such as Vasiliev or Yemelyanov; in fact, it would have been considered a relatively measured statement of certain nationalist complaints against the intelligentsia. It attracted so much attention only because it had been written by a corresponding member of the Academy of Sciences.

One of the main targets of Shafarevich's ire, and that of many other spokesmen of the right was Alexander Yanov, a historian and publicist who had emigrated from Russia to the United States in the 1970s and had published a number of articles and books about the new Russian right.[32] Yanov was one of the very few writers in the West who had paid attention— perhaps excessive attention—to the antidemocratic and aggressive character of some of the views that had been aired in the Soviet Union, both in samizdat and in mainstream publications, from the 1960s on. Yanov's particular conclusions were that but for active and massive Western support for the democratic elements in the Soviet Union, the victory of the extreme right was almost a foregone conclusion. Such a victory, as Yanov saw it, would constitute a grave danger to the West.

While Yanov's quotations were authentic and constituted an embarrassment for the Russian right, they were quite often presented in a breathless and somewhat sensationalist way; his was a one-dimensional intellectual history, and his political recommendations were more often than not impractical. It was perfectly true that some of the statements were

32. A. Yanov, *The Russian Idea and the Year 2000* (Oxford, England, 1987).

openly anti-Semitic and close to fascist in character, but the nuances were all too often missing, nor was it made clear that similar views were, after all, aired in many other countries. Last, Yanov did not clarify whether a certain statement represented the personal view of the writer and a few of his friends, or whether it expressed the mood and the considered opinion of tens of millions. Thus, he became an easy target of Shafarevich and Kozhinov, having allegedly called the West to occupy Russia in order to reeducate it (like MacArthur in Japan). Had Yanov not existed, the anti-Russophobe party would have invented him.

In the absence of a truly new Russian nationalist ideology in line with changing events, many right-wing spokesmen were bound to return, sooner or later, to anti-Jewish arguments. It appeared from time to time, to be sure, that the more enlightened spirits on the right were showing signs of boredom: All these arguments had been made before. Were the Jews really responsible for all of Russia's misfortunes? And who would take their place after their departure?

How important is the Jewish issue for the extremists of the right under *glasnost*? There had always been leading extremist figures who argued that relentless "zoological" anti-Semitism was not only intellectually mendacious but politically ineffective. Nikolai Leskov, one of the great Russian writers of the nineteenth century, could be charged neither with lack of patriotism nor with philosemitism, yet he wrote a long essay in 1883 in which he proved that many of the traditional accusations against the Jews in Russia were factually wrong. One of the central anti-Semitic charges was that the Jews had systematically poisoned the Russian people by organizing the distribution of vodka. If so, how was one to explain the fact that the incidence of drunkenness and crimes related to drunkenness was as high, or higher, outside the Pale of Settlement where no Jews lived?[33]

But the Russian right of 1990, otherwise very attentive to Leskov, chose to ignore him on this issue. Instead it preferred Vladimir Dal, the famous lexicographer. Dal's father was Danish, his mother German, but he was a staunch Russian patriot. At one time he published advertisements in the press to the effect that it was a malicious rumor to argue that he was not of Russian provenience. He is now better known for his four-volume lexicon, which has retained its value to the present day, than for his literary sketches. Dal gave his name to a long essay to the effect that the Jews were systematically committing ritual murder; he did not write it, but must have believed in its authenticity.[34] (It must be noted in passing that never in

33. N. Leskov, *Evrei v Rossii* (Moscow, 1990), pp. 12–13.

34. *Poiskaniya ob ubienii Evreami christianskikh mladentsev* . . . This book was first published in the 1850s; it is still sold at meetings of Zemshchina followers, at Vaganskoye cemetery. It was

history has a Russian court found a Jew guilty of ritual murder.) The Dal essay became the staple diet of certain journals of the right, such as *Zemshchina*, which quoted from it in virtually every issue.[35] At moments of weakness they would invoke the authority of Lev Tikhomirov, a nineteenth-century terrorist-turned-monarchist who claimed that ritual murder was possibly committed only by a small Jewish sect, the Hasidim, and that most Jews did not even know about it.

In the 1930s there was no more radical, uncompromising voice on the émigré right than Ivan Solonevich, who had recently departed Russia and knew Soviet realities better than most of his colleagues of the first wave. Solonevich called the theory of the Judeo-Masonic conspiracy stupid and harmful. It was not true that the Jews wanted and needed the Communist revolution; they had achieved full equality in the March revolution of 1917. Since most of them were tradespeople or craftsmen, they were bound to suffer in a Communist regime. In the nineteenth century, the Russian aristocracy and the intelligentsia had been far more important in paving the way for the Revolution than the Jews had. The American Jew Schiff had allegedly given money to the Bolsheviks. But even if this was true, the Russian millionaire Savva Morozov, not to mention the German government, had given much more. True, in the beginning there had been many Jews in the Soviet administration, because the Russians did not like these jobs or were not competent to fill them, but Stalin had purged almost all of them. Not Russians but Jews—Fanny Kaplan and Leonid Kanne-giesser—had shot Lenin and Uritsky. Solonevich went on deriding the arguments of the anti-Semitic ideologists, but without noticeable effect. The Jews and their crimes were an essential part of right-wing ideology, and Solonevich was accused of not being sufficiently familiar with the classic anti-Semitic literature.[36]

Extreme anti-Semitism is not universal even now among the contemporary Russian right. Whatever criticism has been voiced against Solzhenitsyn, no one in his right mind will argue that he has accepted Black Hundred doctrine. Among the writings of the leading exponents of the New Right and the new conservatives such as Prokhanov and Kurginyan, one finds

---

at one time an exceedingly rare book, as stated in the reprint; I am grateful to Dr. Hagemeister for having obtained a copy for me.

35. This was the name of a pre-1914 periodical published by Markov II, a leader of the far right who in later years became a follower of Hitler. Zemshchina renewed its publication in 1990.

36. Solonevich's essay appeared in his journal *Golos rossii* (Sofia) in six articles through 1936. He defended himself against the accusation of not having read the anti-Semitic literature by mentioning the fact that Shmakov, the leading nineteenth-century exponent of this field, was his wife's uncle.

only relatively rare references to Jews and anti-Semitism. Even Vadim Kozhinov, after three years of relentlessly publishing statistics as to how many Jews had belonged to the Central Control Commission of the Communist party in 1926 and similar such recondite historical problems, suddenly declared in an interview with the British Broadcasting Corporation in 1991 that Russian Jews were wrong to take attacks against them so seriously; the Jewish issue was not among the most urgent ones confronting Russia.

Viktor Yakushev, a former member of Pamyat and the leader of one of the most extreme fascist sects in Moscow, declared in an interview in 1991 that his political ideals were Lycurgus the Spartan, Genghis Khan, and Adolf Hitler. Yet with all this he found "nothing more lunatic and repulsive" than the anti-Masonic, anti-Semitic propaganda of the so-called patriots. The Jewish question was no longer of importance; the Jews left in Russia were mere onlookers. His group opposed anti-Semitism and favored Zionism.[37] Even in some of the publications of Pamyat and kindred groups there was a decline in interest in anti-Jewish material.

Nevertheless, up to the disintegration of the Soviet Union the Jews certainly remained Russia's main enemy, in the eyes of the right, and it is questionable whether this will radically change in the foreseeable future. Mention has been made of some obvious changes in the content of anti-Jewish propaganda after 1987. Before that date Jews ("Zionism") had been attacked because of their anticommunist, pro-imperialist activities; after 1987 it was argued that, on the contrary, communism had been a Jewish invention—that all, or nearly all, Communists had been Jews, half-Jews, or at least the spouses of Jews. Even Stalin, even Beria, became Jews or half-Jews after the fact. Stalin furthermore acquired a Jewish wife, named Rosa Kaganovich. No such person ever existed.

According to *Molodaya gvardiya*, 77 percent of all top positions in the supreme government council had been in the hands of Jews in the 1920s, plus 76 percent in the War Ministry and 81 percent in the Ministry of Foreign Affairs.[38] These and similar statistics appeared regularly in virtually all right-wing journals and brochures. One author claimed that as the result of Judeo-Bolshevik rule some 67,558,000 Russians had perished.[39] Other publications mentioned figures twice as high—including not only the gulag

37. Interview with V. Pribylovsky, *Panorama*, (July 1991). For a political profile of Yakushev, see *Rossiya*, 25 (June 1992).

38. S. Korolev, *Molodaya gvardiya*, 6, 1989, and I. Savelev, *Molodaya gvardiya*, 6 (1990). The author is a former KGB colonel, a specialist in "ethnic psychology."

39. *Spiski palachei rossii* (samizdat: Moscow, 1991).

but also the victims of the Second World War, even though, according to common belief, this war had not been conducted by the Zionists against the Russian people.

The figures purporting to show to what extent Communists had been the creatures of world Jewry were based predominantly on two books published in Nazi Germany: Hermann Fehst's *Bolshewismus und Judentum*, which appeared in 1934, and Rudolf Kommos's *Juden hinter Stalin* (1938 and 1944).[40]

The facts given in Fehst's book are on the whole correct, if often tendentiously interpreted. The Kommos book is mere propaganda; its basic thesis is untrue, for there were no "Jews Behind Stalin." The Politburo had only one Jewish member, and Kaganovich's influence steadily declined. Contemporary Russian anti-Semitic writers go even beyond these Nazi authors in their claims, inasmuch as they freely invent Jewish identities for leading Communists and noncommunists (such as Kerensky) who had no Jewish antecedents whatsoever.

There was a high proportion of Jews in the Russian revolutionary movement after the turn of the century, more among the Mensheviks and the Social Revolutionaries than among the Bolsheviks.[41] This is a well-known fact, and it is also true that for about a decade after 1917 Jews played a role in the party and state leadership far in excess of their part in the population. There were also a great many Jews in leading positions in the Red Army and the GPU-NKVD, the secret police. There were even more in the Ministry of Foreign Affairs and Foreign Trade; Jews (it was believed) were more likely than Russians to know foreign languages and to feel at ease in a foreign surrounding. Frequently Jews appeared as commissars, as representatives of Soviet power in places where few Jews had ever been seen before. Thus they were identified with the deeply unpopular policies of the new regime. Jews qua Jews had not decided to launch the Red Terror, nor to unleash the civil war, let alone the collectivization of agriculture. But they appeared frequently as the executors of these policies. It is not known that there was a specific anti-Jewish reaction in Russia after 1920. But it is equally obvious that the actions of these *déracinés,* non-Jewish Jews were bound to be remembered by the Russian victims of

40. The Kommos book was republished in Germany in 1989. There was a third book written in Russian by A. Diky and published in the United States. Some spadework in this direction had been done by (or for) Henry Ford, whose writings on international Jewry and bolshevism had also appeared in Russian (Berlin, 1925 and 1941).

41. The most reliable work so far available concerning the ethnic composition of the Bolshevik party in 1917–1921 is an enormously detailed but so far incomplete privately published study by Ya. Menaker, *Zagovorshchikii* (Jerusalem, 1990).

Communist policies. It was more difficult to blame Russian Communists, even Georgians, whereas the Jews were an obvious target. Jewish émigré authors warned at the time that there might be a day of reckoning. But their words were not heeded, and it is, of course, quite possible that the Jews would have been blamed in any case, even if they had not been overrepresented in the Communist leadership.

The reasons why there were so many militants of Jewish origin among the Soviet leaders are obvious and need not be discussed in detail. Before 1917 they were subject to oppression in most respects: They had no rights; they could not live where they wanted and could not pursue the professions they wanted; most of them could not study. This situation naturally bred young revolutionaries. If they entered positions of influence this was not, as latter-day anti-Semitic propaganda maintained, to exact revenge, but to build a new society in which (they erroneously thought) there would be freedom and equality for all; nothing was further from their minds than "Jewish domination."

Between 1930 and 1940 a new native intelligence squeezed the Jews out; those in high positions were purged by Stalin, who distrusted and hated them. Eventually no single Jew was left in the top echelons of the Soviet government, the army, the KGB, the Ministry of the Interior, the Ministry of Foreign Affairs, the party leadership. There were no Jewish ambassadors, nor were Jews party secretaries on the district or regional level (except, perhaps, in Birobidzhan). This created certain problems for the purveyors of anti-Semitic propaganda. It was easy enough to concentrate on the unspeakable crimes of a Trotsky. But he was ousted from power in 1924, deported from the Soviet Union in 1929, and killed, at Stalin's behest, in 1940.

True, there was still Lazar Kaganovich, who lingered on among the leaders until 1957 and survived for another thirty-three years, a lonely man and forgotten by all (except the anti-Semites). In the writings of the Soviet right, Kaganovich became a figure of demonic power, more powerful than Stalin himself—Stalin's evil genius. As far as the right was concerned, it had not been Stalinism that had engulfed and shaped Soviet Russia, but Kaganovichism. But this thesis could not be indefinitely maintained. Those who remembered "Iron Lazar"—as he was called when he was Moscow's mayor in the 1930s—also recalled that he had not been more unpopular than other leaders. There had been nothing specifically Jewish about him; he was just one of Stalin's faithful henchmen, like Voroshilov, Molotov, and others. Younger Russians were not interested in Kaganovich, and in any case, he had been the last leader of Jewish origin—after him there were none.

The Jew as the embodiment of evil still had his uses for the writers of historical novels, a propagandistic genre that should not be underrated. But something more tangible was needed for mass propaganda, something relevant to the bitter problems facing contemporary Russia. To attack the Jews in 1990 was in some ways like making the Tatars responsible for the Russian tragedy; it could be done, but it was not very convincing.

There was another approach open to the anti-Semites. While the Jews were no longer politically prominent, their share in the cultural life of the country was far out of proportion to their numbers. Furthermore, their cultural impact was very negative as far as the spiritual values of the Russian people were concerned. They were systematically undermining and corrupting Russia's people, as the extreme right saw it.

As far as statistics were concerned the right's claims were quite correct. The number of Jewish students was high despite all the restrictions that had been imposed on them. Jews were disproportionately represented in the Academy of Science, the universities (especially in the natural-sciences departments and in medicine), the cinema, literature, music, the law, and the media. Once it came to such specialized fields as chess or playing the violin, the incidence of Jews was positively shocking.

The extreme right demanded that the proportion of Jews in these professions should be limited to their percentage of the total population (0.69 percent, according to Pamyat publications). A Russian writer named Sorokin made it known that he did not want Georgians or Bashkirians or Jews to write poems in Russian.[42] He did not want it because he did not trust them: They could not render faithfully the melody of the native language; only a Russian could do that. A Bashkir should write for other Bashkirs, a Jew for other Jews. A well-known Russian critic stated that the writings of Isaac Babel might be an event of significance in Jewish literature; their place was not in Russian literature. And the same was true with regard to the paintings of Chagall.[43]

There have been heated debates on such lines in various countries; Heine was declared to be un-German by German professors well before Hitler, and even Mendelssohn was banned after 1933. There is no accounting for taste, and Sorokin's convictions are, no doubt, sincere and deeply held. But they are not shared by most of his fellow countrymen; Pasternak and Mandelstam, not to mention the bards Vysotsky and Galich, are more

---

42. *Nash sovremennik*, 8 (1988).

43. There was considerable resistance against commemorating Chagall in his native Vitebsk. But at least one Russian right-wing critic took Chagall's side and wrote that his paintings were more Russian (or White Russian) in character than those of the Russian constructivists.

widely read than the poems and songs of even the most famous of Sorokin's political friends. To argue from a racial point of view is not easy in a multiethnic society such as Russia, which has seen so much intermingling of races and nationalities. Studies of the Russian nobility have shown that most of even the most ancient and famous families are of mixed blood and many are of foreign blood—Tatar, Polish, German, and so on. I have picked, more or less at random, some fifty names of leading representatives of the Russian right, past and present. Not a single one appears in the standard work on Russian family names by Boris Unbegaun.[44] This work of reference is not infallible; the name Yeltsin, for instance, does not appear either. The patriotism of these men and women is beyond suspicion, but their ethnic provenance is not. "Everyone's blood is impure," as Konstantin Leontiev wrote a hundred years ago. Rigorous search for racial purity was a risky enterprise in Nazi Germany; in modern Russia it should be prohibited altogether.

Some thoughtful nationalist writers have included certain Jewish writers, composers, and artists, such as Rubinstein and Levitan, and philosophers such as Shestov and Frank, among those who have been truly able to understand and express the Russian spirit. (All of them were converted Jews.) But most Jews, these writers claim, have not been able or willing to achieve this degree of identification with the Russian spirit, because of their innate cosmopolitanism, their restlessness, their lack of roots, and their constant quest for modernism. The literary critics of *Nash sovremennik* and *Molodaya gvardiya* have argued that this is true even of those who have fought for Russia (like Boris Slutsky) or given their lives for it (like Pavel Kogan, M. Kulchitsky or Josef Utkin): There was in their work something exaggerated and fanatic, a lack of harmony, very much in contrast to truly Russian poets.

There may well be some truth in such allegations; it is difficult to imagine even the versatile Ilya Ehrenburg as a poet of the Siberian forests, the taiga or the Cossack *stanitsa*. But then each national literature consists of a multitude of themes, moods, and approaches. For the great majority of Russians the children's verses of Samuel Marshak were and are as much part of the national tradition as the popular songs of the Stalinist period composed by Isaac Dunayevsky.

Cultural anti-Semitism, in any case, is limited in its appeal to sections

44. Shmakov, Shafarevich, Glushkova, Aksiuchits, Korotsev, Barkashov, Stelmakh, Kozhinov, Zhirinovsky, Bashilov, Shundik, Kunayev, Vikulov, Krupin, Bushin, Loshchits, Prokhanov, Katasonov, Slipenchuk, Gunko, Burlaev, Erokhin, Rash, Pikul, Purishkevich, Myalo, Ostashvili, Lykoshin, Prokushev, Senin, Pridius, Nevzorov, Sartakov, Diky, Zhevakhov, Ostretsov, Lichutin, Bursov, Petelin, Isayev, Bondarenko, Doroshenko, Sbitnev, Nogtev, Sterligov, Ziuganov, Nauman, Baburin, Yemelin.

of the intelligentsia. It would be infinitely more effective if the anti-Semites could show that at times of severe shortages "the Jews are better off" than the rest of the population. But this argument has seldom been used; the number of Jews among the *nomenklatura* and the other recipients of high incomes had not been that great. True, Jews have been among those opting for private enterprise and the extreme right has directed much of its ire against the "Mafia," which, they claim, has acquired a stranglehold over the Russian economy, gaining (or stealing) billions of rubles (or dollars). But to the extent that this Mafia has been identified, the individuals concerned have been Russians (including former high party officials) and members of the "southern" clans—that is to say, Caucasians and Central Asians. Jews are no longer a prominent, obvious target.

In view of the Jewish exodus from the former Soviet Union and the steadily diminishing role of Jews in all aspects of Russian life, the objective basis of anti-Semitism—that is to say the political and social conditions that generated anti-Jewish feeling—has shrunk. True, there is no direct connection between the extent of anti-Semitism and the "objective conditions"; in Germany, in the early 1930s the Jewish issue was objectively not of paramount importance, which did not prevent the Nazi party gaining power on an ideological platform in which anti-Semitism played an important role. Anti-Semitism, very likely, will be of less use to the Russian right in future but it will certainly not disappear.

There persists in certain sections of the population a deep-seated xenophobic mood, a fear and hate of aliens, the need for an enemy. The metaphysical, abstract Jew can still be conjured up by the anti-Semites to provide an explanation for Russia's great misfortunes. The young may no longer be greatly interested, but among the generation now in their sixties the response could be greater at a time of great emotional turbulence and traumatic shocks.

The Neo-Slavophiles and the Eurasians

Two other ingredients of contemporary Russian ideology ought to be mentioned even though they are neither new nor very promising. There was a modest revival of pan-Slavism in 1990–1991; Slavonic festivals have taken place not only in Moscow but also in cities such as Ryazan and Smolensk; cultural foundations have been set up and political conferences arranged with guests from abroad.[45] However, there has been little popular

45. The activities of various new Slavic organizations were reported in *Slavyanskii vestnik* 1991/91. *Slavyanskii vestnik* 6 (1991) appeared with the headline "The Slavs Should Rule the

enthusiasm for these initiatives, because of the widespread feeling that the Slavic brethren, inside and outside the old Soviet Union, have shown no particular interest in close relations with Russia. Given this lack of response, what was the reasoning of the sponsors of the new Slavic solidarity movement? Perhaps they assumed that in the long run, certain common interests might emerge, if not with the governments of the western Slavic countries, then perhaps with groups equally opposed to capitalism, liberalism, and Western ways in general.

More intriguing from an intellectual point of view was the revival of Eurasianism. The original Eurasians were a small group of young émigré intellectuals, mainly concentrated in Prague, who published in 1922 a collection of essays entitled *Iskhod k vostoku* ("Exodus to the East"), which became their manifesto. The common denominator of this group was the assumption that while Western culture had been of great importance for Russia in the past, Russia's future was in the East.

The belief in Russia's Asian mission was not new; it had its supporters among nineteenth-century military leaders as well as philosophers and poets. Their view was that Russia was in many ways different from the West; it should not copy European institutions, but turn its energies toward the East, where it might play a positive and important role. The Eurasians adopted some of the Slavophiles' views but rejected others, precisely because they realized that there was little substance to the often-invoked Slavic solidarity. They accepted some Communist ideas (or, to be precise, were impressed by the dynamic character of the new regime) and believed that once it appeared that bolshevism had no positive ideas to offer in the long run, Eurasianism would take its place as Russia's new guiding doctrine.

Not all these thoughts were specifically Russian. The Eurasians liberally borrowed from the new science of geopolitics, and the concept of the old, exhausted West confronting the young and dynamic peoples of the East had also first emerged in Germany.

Eurasianism flourished for about a decade; by 1933 the steam had gone out of the movement, which was split down various lines. Much attention was paid to the Eurasians at the time because of the literary talents of Eurasian's leading exponents and also a certain freshness in their approach. As one of their early members, the theologian Florovsky, put it, they asked many of the right questions, but most of their answers were wrong or

---

[Far] East"—which may not be easy to coordinate with the Eurasian slogans, on which more below.

Tsar Nikolai II

Sergei Nilus, editor of the *Protocols of the Elders of Zion*

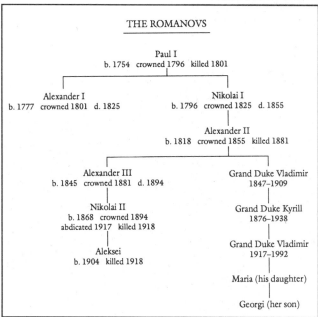

THE ROMANOVS

Paul I
b. 1754   crowned 1796   killed 1801

Alexander I
b. 1777   crowned 1801   d. 1825

Nikolai I
b. 1796   crowned 1825   d. 1855

Alexander II
b. 1818   crowned 1855   killed 1881

Alexander III
b. 1845   crowned 1881   d. 1894

Nikolai II
b. 1868   crowned 1894
abdicated 1917   killed 1918

Aleksei
b. 1904   killed 1918

Grand Duke Vladimir
1847–1909

Grand Duke Kyrill
1876–1938

Grand Duke Vladimir
1917–1992

Maria (his daughter)

Georgi (her son)

These articles in *The Times* (London) were the first to reveal that the *Protocols* was a forgery.

The Truth About "The Protocols"

A LITERARY FORGERY

From **THE TIMES** *of*
August 16, 17, and 18, 1921

LONDON:
PRINTING HOUSE SQUARE, E.C.4

ONE SHILLING NET

The first of many American editions of the *Protocols*.

"The Protocols"

WITH

PREFACE AND EXPLANATORY NOTES

EVERY PATRIOTIC AMERICAN
MUST READ THESE
PROTOCOLS

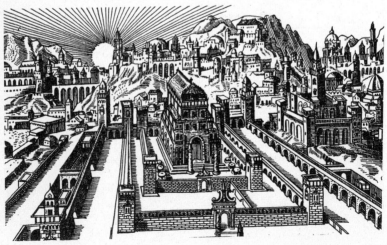

King Solomon's temple in Jerusalem—symbol of the archenemy, the Masons.

Сергѣй Нилусъ

ВЕЛИКОЕ
ВЪ МАЛОМЪ

Записки православнаго

A new edition of the *Protocols*, published in 1992.

A combined meeting of Russian nationalists and neo-Bolsheviks, Moscow, 1992.

A nationalist demonstration, Moscow, 1992. The banner reads, "Russia, get up from your knees." Cossack leader Vladimir Naumov is at the microphone.

A Cossack meeting, Moscow, 1992, with commander Alexander Martynov in the center.

Valentin Rasputin, a leading contemporary Russian writer and, in recent years, a guru of the extreme right.

Vladimir Zhirinovsky, leader of the liberal-democrat party and the most talented orator of the far right.

Alexander Prokhanov, editor of *Den* and unofficial minister of propaganda for the right.

The "black colonel," Viktor Alksnis, leader of the Soyuz faction in the Russian parliament.

Yuri Vlasov, former Olympic gold medalist in weight lifting.

Gennadi Zyuganov, former head of the Russian Communist party, now a leader of the national-Bolshevik camp.

Colonel-General Albert Makashov, who lost to Yeltsin in the election for the Russian presidency.

Professor Igor Shafarevich, mathematician and member of the Academy of Science. He popularized the term "Russophobia."

Popular television anchorman Aleksei Nevzorov, a flamboyant idol of the far right.

An up-and-coming man on the Russian right, lawyer and parliamentarian Sergei Baburin.

Nikolai Lysenko, a former Pamyat militant who is now the head of the National-Republican Party.

Viktor Aksiuchits, leader of the Christian Democrats.

Mikhail Astafiev, head of the Constitutional-Democratic Party.

Dmitri Vasiliev, leader of Pamyat.

Alexander Rutskoi, deputy president of Russia.

Professor Eduard Volodin, right-wing ideologist.

Alexander Solzhenitsyn, novelist and exile.

Igor Artemov, head of the "Moscow Russian Union."

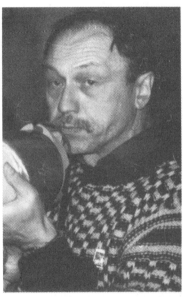

Yuri Lipatnikov, leader of the nationalist opposition in Yekaterinburg.

Nikolai Pavlov, one of the leaders of the Rossiya parliamentary faction.

РАЗДАВИМ ГАДИНУ!

ДЕЛЕЦ ПОРНОБИЗНЕСА

ПРЕЗИДЕНТ, ГОВОРЯЩИЙ НА ИДИШ

"Let us smash the reptile—the porno-merchant," a cartoon from *Narodnoya Delo*, 1991.

Two deputies celebrate the recognition of the Russian association of homosexuals in a cartoon from *Otchizna*, 1991.

A cartoon from a fascist magazine demonstrating the dangers of allowing racially impure students at universities.

An array of current publications from the extreme right.

русское

ВОСКРЕСЕНИЕ

№ 8 / 16

"Ныне я уверен, ч[то]
действую вполне [в]
духе Творца Всемог[у]-
щего: БОРЯСЬ З[А]
УНИЧТОЖЕНИЕ
ЖИДОВСТВА,
БОРЮСЬ ЗА ДЕЛ[О]
БОЖИЕ".
Adolf Hitler "Me[in]
Kampf"

ГАЗЕТА РУССКОГО НАЦИОНАЛЬНО-ОСВОБОДИТЕЛЬНОГО ДВИЖЕНИ[Я]

The masthead of *Russkoye Voskresenie*.

This 1992 cartoon from *Russkoye Voskresenie* lampoons Yeltsin and Gorbachev as the running dogs of the Jewish devil. The caption reads, "Shame on the intelligentsia, which has betrayed the people."

An anti-Semitic cartoon from *Russkoye Voskresenie*. The caption reads, "Get these reptiles out so they don't foul [our country]."

КТО В АМЕРИКУ БЕЖИТ ?-ТЕТЯ ...ИД
И ДЯДЯ ...ИД С НИМИ БЕЙТАРЁНОК-
МОЛОДОЙ ...ИДЁНОК

НЕТ РАЗЖИГАНИЮ НАЦИОНАЛЬНОЙ ВРАЖДЫ !

Another anti-Semitic diatribe from *Russkoye Voskresenie*, this one on Jewish emigration from Russia. "A no to the racial incitement," reads the caption.

A press conference held by the leaders of the united right-wing opposition. *Left to right*: Nikolai Lysenko, Viktor Aksiuchits, Nikolai Pavlov, Mikhail Astafiev, Andrei Golovin.

A group of Cossacks in their traditional uniforms, standing on guard duty at a conference of right-wing leaders, Moscow, 1992.

irrelevant.[46] They never made it clear whether they had a real, existing East or an abstraction in mind; whether they wanted a synthesis of Europe and Asia or rejected both; whether their devotion to the Orthodox church was deeper than their admiration for Islam and Buddhism. In retrospect, Eurasianism reminds one of the fashion of Third Worldism in the West in the 1950s and 1960s, which had little to do with Third World realities, but a great deal with the misplaced hopes attached in some circles to the alleged cultural, political, and economic potential of the Third World.[47]

If Eurasianism as a political and cultural alternative did not make much sense in the 1920s, and eventually died a natural death, what caused its renaissance seventy years later? It is not easy to find an answer. Partly it was the old desire to dissociate Russia from the West. But Asia in the 1990s was even less promising ground for Russian geopoliticians than it had been in the 1920s. Neither the Japanese nor the Chinese, neither the Afghans nor the Persians, certainly not the Kazakhs and the Uzbeks, wanted any part of the Russians in the role of *Kulturträger,* nor did they regard Russia as a welcome bridge to the West, a spiritual relation, or a close political ally.

It goes without saying that Russia has traditional interests in Asia and the Pacific as well as in Europe. The old Soviet Foreign Ministry tried to develop economic and cultural relations with these countries: *Yevgeni Onegin* was translated into Chinese; Asian song contests took place in Alma-Ata; Soviet ethnologists established cooperation with institutes in Hawaii, Australia, and even Tonga.[48]

But all this did not amount to a "transfiguration" or an alternative geopolitical orientation. Fantasies of this kind rest on assumptions dating back to past ages, before airplanes were invented and when "land bridges" were still a factor with a certain importance.

There was a Russian intellectual tradition somewhat similar in certain respects to geopolitics. It goes back to Dmitri Mendeleyev (1834–1907), the famous chemist who was also an amateur political philosopher. He pronounced the thesis that the future center of gravity of the Russian empire would be somewhere near the city of Omsk in Siberia. His ideas

46. *Sovremennye zapiski,* 34 (1928).

47. *Nash sovremennik* also rediscovered Eurasianism, albeit with some delay. V. Kozhinov, "Istoriosofia Euraziitsev," *Nash sovremennik,* 2 (1992), claims that while they were not always right they still were the spiritual heirs of Pushkin and Tolstoy. Essays written by the leading Eurasian authors such as G. Vernadsky, N. S. Trubetskoi, P. Savitsky, and others were republished in *Nash Sovremennik,* 2 and 3 (1992). The right-wing Russian Writers' Association also became deeply involved in the Eurasian fashion in 1992, to the detriment of its literary preoccupations: *Literaturnaya gazeta* (June 10, 1992).

48. G. Shevelyov, "Transfiguration of the Spirit," *International Affairs* (December 1991).

resurfaced many years later in the works of Alexander Prokhanov, the self-styled geopolitical novelist. Prokhanov wrote that "the enemy is preparing to strike against the fatherland simultaneously from all corners of the world," and therefore Russian defense had also to be global, thus justifying the intervention in Afghanistan.[49] Prokhanov's geopolitics attracted both supporters and critics.[50] But the whole debate was overtaken by the Soviet exodus from Afghanistan and the secession of the Central Asian republics—as a result of which the Russian center of gravity was no longer likely to be somewhere near Omsk.

Thus, Eurasian geopolitics was used by some on the right in the age of expansion; could it be of service also in an age of retrenchment and disintegration?

The resurgence of the Eurasian myth has provoked mistrust not only among Russian democrats but also among liberal nationalists. From a historical and cultural point of view Eurasianism's assumptions are untenable: It was Scandinavia and Byzantium, not the East, that played a crucial role in the emergence of a Russian state and Russian culture. No Asian influences in Russian culture can be found before the sixteenth century, and not many appear thereafter.[51] Eurasianism, as Likhachev has argued, nowadays serves to pave the way for and to justify a "policy of the strong hand." Others see in the old and new Eurasianism a specifically Russian form of isolationism—or perhaps no more than one possible scenario discussed on the right and not to be taken too seriously, in conjunction with other equally dubious and mutually exclusive scenarios such as the "Berlin-Moscow axis" and neo-pan-Slavism.

Students of Russian conservatism have noted its strongly utopian and metaphysical character; perhaps nowhere else has the right shown so much disdain for pragmatism and common sense.[52] But the greatest weakness of Russian right-wing politics and thought—now even more than in the past—has been its paranoiac style. The compulsive belief in conspiracies is not a Russian monopoly; in a famous essay, Richard Hofstadter has called it an "old and recurrent mode in our life."[53] The anti-Masonic fashion of the 1820s and 1830s was followed by a wave of anti-Catholicism, and the paranoid tradition, in one form or another, has continued to the present

49. *Literaturnaya gazeta,* 28 (August 1986).

50. On this debate, see Milan Hauner, pp. 221–25.

51. Dm. Likhachev, *Literaturnaya gazeta* (February 6, 1992).

52. Boris Slavnyi, "Grazhdanskaya obshestvo ili grazhdanakaya voina?" *Znamya* 2 (1992).

53. R. Hofstadter, *The Paranoid Style in American Politics* (Chicago, 1966), p. 6; E. Shils, *The Torment of Secrecy* (Glencoe, Ill. 1956).

day with the fantasies about President Kennedy's murder as a recent example.

The paranoiac style is part and parcel of Middle Eastern, particularly Arab, politics.[54] It can be found in France, Italy, and Japan, on the extreme right as well as on the left. An Identikit picture of a paranoiac of this kind can easily be drawn: He believes in an all-powerful enemy, with whom no compromise is possible and who has to be destroyed quickly, for time is running out and the apocalypse is at hand. The enemy controls everything in the land. To defeat the enemy, everybody has to be suspected.

The paranoiac will adduce masses of facts, especially on cruelty and sadism. Some of the facts may well be correct, but then suddenly there will be a quantum jump from one set of facts to another that is breathtaking and totally irrational. Thus, to give but one example, a paranoiac may present perfectly correct details about the youth in Germany of the writer of the present book. He will then present an accurate historical survey of the Nazi party. Then—the jump: L. lived the first seventeen years of his life in Germany; therefore he must have been a prominent Nazi leader. Or, alternatively, the Nazi leaders must have been Jewish.

But it is also true that most of the time such fantasies have been limited to sects of the extreme right and left, whereas a majority of citizens, irrespective of their political opinions, have not given credence to manifestly absurd ideas.

In Russia, large sections of the right, not only its lunatic fringe, have shown stubborn resistance against accepting the realities of politics. Instead, the search for the hidden hand of the Satanic forces has dominated their thinking, just as a similar pattern shaped the Bolshevik mentality for many decades. It is a well-known fact, in the life of individuals as of nations, that facing a clear and present danger may have a sobering effect, curing (at least temporarily) manias of this kind: A person in danger of drowning will understand, one would assume, that the real danger facing him is not being chased by lions in the desert. To what extent does the Russian crisis have a sobering effect on the thinking of the right?

The record leaves not much room for optimism. A few examples chosen more or less at random should suffice. Thus, the belief that there was a marshals' plot against Stalin in 1936–1937 has not been given up, even though there was never any reason to believe in its existence. The evidence adduced by the conspiracy theorists for their allegations is either nonexistent or preposterous. The main source is the "German historian Paul Carrell" (Schmidt), the author of several popular histories of the

54. D. Pipes, "Dealing with Middle Eastern Conspiracy Theories," *Orbis* (winter 1992).

Second World War.[55] Carrell's (Schmidt's) books were published almost thirty years ago; they contain no serious factual evidence pointing to a conspiracy by Tukhachevsky. The other source is Isaac Deutscher, who in his biography of Stalin (1949) expressed—among other strange and mistaken ideas—the view that there might have been a plot. He, too, had no evidence, and in later editions of his book he dropped his claims, albeit reluctantly. In a similar way, the Russian extreme right continues to believe in the Doctors' Plot of 1952.

Another common manifestation of persecution mania is the belief that virtually all leading members of the extreme right who die have in reality been killed by "Satanic forces." The allegations that Lermontov and Esenin were assassinated by political enemies have been mentioned. When two leading anti-Semites, Begun and Evseyev, died in 1991, and when a third, Smirnov-Ostashvili, hanged himself, it was taken as self-evident that they had been killed by the liberals. The same argument was made openly or by implication with regard to lesser figures such as Selezneyev, Tsikunov (Kuzmich), and Oleg Shestakov ("he died of a stroke or an internal bleeding or cardiac insufficiency. We all know what this means. . . ."). There were in each case loud and frequent demands to open investigations to apprehend the real murderers.[56]

On the last day of 1991 a right-wing militant named Nikolai Kislov hanged himself in St. Petersburg. The right-wing Moscow periodical *Puls tushina* (26, 1992) immediately announced that he had been murdered and demanded a special investigation. The reason given was that Kislov's glasses were not found at the place where he had committed suicide.

The right-wing bard Igor Talkov was shot in St. Petersburg on October 6, 1991. He was thirty-five years old and very popular in right-wing circles. In an interview shortly before his death he said that while he was not a member of Pamyat he felt close to its views.[57] Talkov was shot in a theater during a performance; the scene was witnessed by many people. There was a woman involved—another pop star, named Aziza—or a money dispute, or both. But the explanation given out by the right in dozens of articles, declarations, and speeches was that Talkov had been killed not because of Aziza but because he was a patriot, a monarchist, and

55. Yuri Emelyanov, "Byl li zagovor Tukhachevskovo?" *Slovo*, 12 (1991). Carrell worked for the Ministry of Propaganda; the author mixes him up with another Schmidt who was Hitler's interpreter.

56. For the Shestakov case, *Russkii vestnik*, 33 (1991). Several other figures of the extreme right who have recently died have now been added to the list of martyrs: Podkolzin, Petrov, Yumin, and Ivanov. Editorial note in *Russkii vestnik*, 14 (1992).

57. Special supplement, *Russkii vestnik*, 26 (1991).

a good Christian. "How much longer will Satanic forces enjoy open season on our best people, the flower of the nation?" There were bitter complaints that the authorities showed no interest in revealing the real murderers, but on the contrary tried their best to obliterate clues.

General Viktor Filatov and the writer Dmitri Balashov are well-known figures on the Russian right. Filatov was the editor of the *Voenno-istoriches-kii zhurnal* when it published (with the moral support of Marshal Yazov and the General Staff, according to Filatov) excerpts from *Mein Kampf*.[58] This publication was no doubt done, as Filatov has argued, out of purely academic interest and to give Russian readers a fuller opportunity better to understand the intellectual history of our time. More interesting is Filatov's claim that the U.S. Congress *(sic)*, following Zionist commands, decided to pick certain Soviet leaders—such as Gorbachev, Yakovlev, and Shevard-nadze—to carry out its orders to destroy the Soviet Union: "It was necessary to put at the head of the state a man, a whole new crew, who would destroy everything, which was successfully done." Similar allegations were made by Sergei Baburin, a lawyer and prominent member of the Russian parliament—not an extremist but a leader of the Russian People's Assembly and similar front organizations.

In his writings Balashov shows a measure of skepticism and tolerance. He concedes that the old Judeo-Masonic conspiracy theory is too simplistic to make sense in the modern world if taken literally, and that the idea of "world domination" is both crazy and impractical.[59] However, within a few lines of having made these far-reaching concessions to common sense, Balashov finds himself back in the old world of plots—the murder of Stolypin, the German-American-Jewish gold paid to Lenin, Ahad Ha'am as the secret ruler of the globe, and the *Protocols*.

A colleague of Balashov, the highly respected right-wing critic Mikhail Lobanov, has compared the democratic conspiracy to a hydra with a thousand heads, programmed to "subjugate all of us to a Satanic, Masonic world government." The equally famous poet T. Glushkova has written about the "thoroughly coordinated character of the antinational conspiracy."

Underlying such judgments is the conviction that the real truth about world events is not the one published in the mass media, talked about by political leaders in West and East, described by political scientists and academic historians. The truth is carefully hidden and is open to the

58. *Den,* 4 (1992).

59. "Yeshche raz o velikoi Rossii (5)," *Den* (January 26, 1992). On Balashov's views see also *Slavyanskii vestnik* (April 1991).

understanding of only a select few. Only they have the capacity to identify the real forces shaping historical events, the true interests and designs behind the world of make-believe that most people mistake for the real world.

To give one last example, only simpletons believe that the German economic miracle was the result of the Marshall Plan, the currency reform, the existence of a skilled, hardworking labor force, initiative, business and political leadership, cooperation between trade unions and big business. For the true explanation one has to look on a deeper level: Under Hitler trillions *(sic)* of dollars were exported abroad, mainly to Latin America. There, they were invested in narcotrafficking; from the profits of this business the German miracle was financed.[60]

In embracing conspiracy theories, sections of the Russian right have surrendered reality and reason. One cannot put the blame on the trauma of 1991, for many of these fantasies existed well before. It is difficult not to feel sympathy with Russian patriots facing a world in which there seem to be but few rays of hope. It is legitimate to ask why the Russian people should be the subject of so terrible tribulations. Like a collective Job, Russia seems to be born unto trouble as the sparks fly upwards. But no blows of fate justify subscribing to the kind of madness that has been part and parcel of far-right doctrine. Conspiracy theories are the opium of right-wing extremists; once the habit has been deeply ingrained, it seems to be exceedingly difficult and painful to shed it.[61]

60. S. Kurginyan, *Narodnaya pravda* (November 1991).

61. The idea of the official nationalist doctrine as a narcotic appeared in Pyotr Struve's writings (*Patriotica* [St. Petersburg, 1911]) and before him in Solovyov.

Part
Four

THE STRUGGLE FOR POWER, 1987–

Chapter Twelve

TSARS AND COSSACKS

The Monarchists

IN THE 1950s, during his Argentine exile and shortly before his death, Ivan Solonevich was asked how high he rated the prospects of a monarchical revival in Russia; he replied without hesitation: "About one hundred percent." Such an estimate was considered ridiculous at the time by all but a handful of staunch supporters of the Romanov dynasty, mostly in their seventies and eighties. After the demise of communism a restoration of the monarchy in Russia still appears highly unlikely, but it is no longer dismissed as wholly impossible.[1]

When Nikolai II and his family were murdered in 1918 no obvious candidates for the throne of the Romanovs were left. His brother Mikhail, whom he had chosen as his successor when he was forced to abdicate the year before, was assassinated in 1918. Nikolai's mother Maria Pavlovna, a Danish princess, returned to her native country, where her welcome was less than cordial. Generally speaking, European monarchs showed little solidarity with and willingness to help the various first and second cousins of the tsar who fled to the West.

The monarchy had few friends left at the time, either inside Russia or outside. It had been discredited by too many scandals and too much

---

1. According to a public opinion poll, 5 to 6 percent favored a monarchical system in spring 1992; the idea of a constitutional monarchy appealed to 34 percent of Russians below the age of twenty-five. *Literaturnaya gazeta* (June 3, 1992).

incompetence, too little willingness to make concessions to changing times. The anti-Bolshevik forces of the White movement did not put the restoration of the monarchy high on their banner: It was not a popular cause.

Inside the Soviet Union the Romanovs were gradually forgotten. Even in the émigré community, despite the presence of not a few monarchists, it was only in August 1924 that Grand Duke Kyrill Vladimirovich (1876–1938) announced that, being the oldest surviving member of the Romanov dynasty, he was the only legitimate heir to the Russian throne. (He was a grandson of Nikolai I and a cousin of Nikolai II.) This claim was considered doubtful by the family council of the Romanovs and by the Supreme Monarchical Council in Berlin, for Grand Dukes Dmitri Pavlovich (1891–1942) and Nikolai Nikolayevich (1856–1928) could also stake claims, and had broader backing. Kyrill's main support came from the German extreme right, including Hitler's Bavarian entourage. In Kyrill's defense it ought to be said that he probably did not even volunteer himself as tsar; his interest in politics was strictly limited, subordinate to his passion for sports cars. He was pushed by a politically ambitious wife named Victoria Fedorovna, a princess of Saxe-Coburg-Gotha. Ironically, Victoria was unacceptable to many monarchists. She was a divorcée who, having been married before to a prince of Hesse, had never converted to Orthodoxy. Worse yet, Kyrill's own mother, another Danish princess, had adopted Orthodoxy only *after* he was born, and his legitimacy as a pretender to the throne was therefore in doubt.

After 1924 the monarchists remained divided in their loyalties. Some favored Kyrill, who made his home in Coburg, Bavaria; others supported Nikolai, who lived in Paris. Then Nikolai died and Kyrill moved on to France. But at the time of Kyrill's death in 1938 only a minority of Russian monarchists backed him, and for a decade after there was no pretender at all to the Russian throne. Nikolai Nikolayevich had no children and Vladimir, Kyrill's son (born in Finland in 1917), did not stake a claim at the time.

Inside Russia, monarchism was not a political trend that could be openly advocated before *glasnost*. A few historical novels were published that took a slightly less hostile attitude toward the last Romanovs than had been the custom before; in certain right-wing circles, dissident and mainstream, it became the fashion to collect monarchist memorabilia as others collected icons. The publication of Solzhenitsyn's *The Red Wheel* rekindled interest in the monarchy.[2]

2. Manifestations of promonarchist sentiment inside the Soviet Union and in the émigré community are described in detail in John B. Dunlop, *The New Russian Nationalism* (New York, 1985), chapter 5, passim.

It was only under *glasnost* that a number of groups openly sponsoring monarchism came to the fore. Perhaps the best-known monarchist spokesman during the early days was Aleksei Brumel, the brother of a former world-record holder in the high jump. However, he represented no one but himself, nor is it certain whether he was a practical joker or regarded the whole issue as a good opportunity to promote himself. Somewhat more serious was the Pravoslav Constitutional Monarchist party, headed by Sergei Yurkov-Engelgard, which first made its existence known in November 1989. During the following year some seventy more monarchist groups came into being, not to mention the conversion to monarchism of most of the Pamyat factions. Several well-known cultural and public figures such as the writer Soloukhin, the movie producer Geli Ryabov, a television personality named Nevzorov, and the singer Andrei Baranovsky made their monarchist sympathies known. (Nevzorov's enthusiasm cooled subsequently.) Prewar monarchist ideologists, above all Il'in and Solonevich, were widely reprinted in right-wing publications—in fact, they were given more publicity than almost any other émigré thinkers and writers of the right.

Since none of the seventy-odd groups had a large membership, and since many of them were short-lived—merging, splitting again, and changing their names—a detailed description seems to be unnecessary, except of the more important among them.[3] The Christian Renaissance Union was headed by Vladimir Osipov, whose name has been mentioned earlier on in this study. He had been among the dissidents of the 1960s and was twice arrested and sentenced to lengthy terms in the gulag. Having been originally a fighter for human rights, he embraced religion and nationalism in prison; the survival of the fatherland, he thought, was more important than the rights of the individual. He had been one of the chief editors of the religious samizdat journal *Veche,* belonging to the moderate wing of Russian nationalism. Despite ideological differences he appreciated the struggle waged by Sakharov and the liberals. As *glasnost* got under way, Osipov increasingly involved himself in various initiatives in favor of the "spiritual and biological rescue of the Russian people," and eventually the establishment of a Patriotic-Christian-Monarchist movement in late spring of 1990.

The usual internal splits occurred. While Osipov was traveling abroad, Evgeni Pashnin, his deputy, tried to depose him, accusing Osipov of, among other mortal sins, pro-Zionist activities.[4] However, Osipov and his

3. For a short description and an enumeration of the sources see V. Solovei, *Vstanet tretii rim—Pravoslavnie monarkhisti sevodnya* (Moscow, 1992), pp. 3ff.

4. Osipov's views have been anything but philosemitic, but unlike other leaders of the far right he has refused to make the Jewish issue a cardinal one in his program. However, *Zemshchina,* mentioned below, is published by the extreme wing (headed by V. Demin) of Osipov's Christian Renaissance.

followers prevailed in the struggle for power and, in collaboration with other groups such as the Zemskii Sobor and the Brotherhood of the Tsar-Martyr Nikolai II, they persevered in their attempts to further the cause of monarchism in Russia.

The monarchist camp agrees on certain basic assumptions and is divided on many others. It agrees that monarchy is the most suitable political system for Russia and that the church ought to be the main pillar of tsarism. Most maintained before August 1991 that the Russian empire should be strong and indivisible. Monarchists disagree on whether the coming monarch should be absolute (as before 1905) or constitutional. They disagree on the person of the monarch—should it be a scion of the Romanovs or a person to be elected by a national assembly, and if so, who should choose the new tsar and in what way?

The most extreme monarchists belong to Zemshchina, a small group that continues the tradition of Markov II, a notorious figure during the early years of the century. It is uncompromisingly antidemocratic, opposing the right of all other parties, national minorities, and religions to exist.[5] A quantitative analysis of the material published by this group would show that it devoted considerably more space to ritual murder, the Talmud, the Hasidim, the *Protocols,* and other such topics than to the monarchist idea or to individual tsars. It has even attacked the patriarch, Alexei II, for excessive liberalism.[6] Virtually every issue of *Zemshchina,* the group's organ, includes announcements concerning the coming of the Antichrist. According to Zemshchina, the monarchy has to be absolute; "without a tsar Russia is a widow, and its people orphans."[7]

They interpret *Narodnost* (the third component of the old nineteenth-century triad, "Autocracy" and "Orthodoxy" being the others) in the old-fashioned way: They do not believe that the tsar has to consult the people; *Narodnost* means that the attitude of the people toward their ruler has to be one of humility, meekness, and unquestioning subservience.

Such a concept of the monarchy is by no means identical with the ideas of the Slavophiles on "inner freedom" or even of Solonevich and Il'in on the future of a monarchy. They put considerable emphasis on popular

5. During 1990 and 1991 some sixty issues of this two-page weekly were published. It is printed with letters of microscopic size, and to a considerable extent consists of reprints of articles published before 1917 or in émigré journals of the 1920s or 1930s. On *Zemshchina,* see the comments of a fellow right-wing journal: *Domostroi,* 16 (1991).

6. *Zemshchina,* 59 and 60 (1991). This refers to the tenor of speeches made by the patriarch during a trip to the United States in 1991, and the fact that he disavowed attacks against the Archpriest Alexander Men, the cleric of Jewish origin who was assassinated in 1990.

7. *Zemshchina,* 1 (May 1990).

initiative, popular spirit, and instinct. The Slavophiles believed that Russia created the tsars, not the tsars Russia.

The author of a recent article on the advantages of a monarchy in comparison with a democratic republic noted that a third of the countries of Europe are monarchies—including Luxembourg, Liechtenstein, and Monaco. True, all these monarchies are constitutional, that is to say imperfect. "Only Russia gave the world the most perfect state system—that of an absolute monarchy, enlightened by the Orthodox church." The author found yet another perfect example of an absolute monarchy: France at the time of the Three Musketeers.[8] (With equal justice the author could have mentioned Saudi Arabia in more recent times, though its rulers draw their inspiration from another religion. Furthermore, students of absolute monarchy are aware of the fact that it was never quite absolute; readers of *The Three Musketeers* may recall that Cardinal Richelieu's power was equal to that of the king.)

Thus, the fundamentalists view the people as subjects who have been born to obey, not as free citizens with rights and obligations. Constitutional liberties that might be appropriate for Europeans would be out of place in Russia, in view of what the monarchists see as the essentially anarchic character of the people. Constitutional liberties lead by necessity to pluralism, that is to say to internal friction and the undermining—and ultimately the downfall—of authority.

The future monarchy will be Russian in its character: neither capitalist nor socialist, neither totalitarian nor democratic but *Pravoslav*, with the patriarch acting as the tsar's right hand. Russia does not need an ideology but faith, not politics but spiritual values, not democracy but *sobornost*, not a union of republics but Great Power status. There will be a consultative body (or bodies) and a state council, but they will not have the right to pass laws.[9] By and large this is a concept of the monarchy as it existed before Peter the Great.[10]

Most monarchists agree, broadly speaking, on these guidelines; one will look in vain for innovations in their ranks. Even the Constitutional Monarchists (PRAMOS) reject a parliament; they stand for a Russian-style *Ständestaat* and suggest the reintroduction of the "table of ranks," first

8. F. Yurev, *Russkii vestnik*, 2 (1992) (supplement). A. Dumas is the most widely read author in Russia.

9. The program of the "All-Russian Party of the Monarchist Center," adopted in St. Petersburg on December 1, 1991, envisages a complicated legislative process in which the monarch participates as well as two appointed consultative bodies.

10. *Zemshchina*, 1 (1991). Solovei, *Vstanet tretii rim*, pp. 15–16.

introduced in the early eighteenth century. Outstanding personalities from among the army, the police, and the administration should be rewarded with estates in recognition of their services. Such a system would not be all that different from the (unofficial) arrangement that existed from Stalin to Brezhnev, when members of the *nomenklatura* were given dachas.

A paternalistic society of this kind is the antithesis of a civil libertarian society; there is no room for individual liberties as interpreted in the West. The central role is played by the state, not by society. It is the task of the monarch to take care that justice is done and that the laws are observed. But what if the tsar or his servants behave unjustly, rule tyrannically, violate God's laws? This question preoccupied the medieval Catholic church, which suggested remedies including even tyrannicide.

The Russian monarchist thinkers prefer not to consider this possibility. The people's will, as the monarchists see it, cannot be expressed directly or by way of a parliament but only through a strong central power based on objective values and on competence.[11]

Most questions concerning the socioeconomic character of the future monarchy are left open, but its spokesmen have expressed the firm belief that once a monarchy is installed, Russia's economic problems will be solved promptly.[12] V. Osipov has been one of the few monarchist thinkers to give some thought to these issues. He favors a market economy and the right to own property, provided it is introduced gradually and a "spiritual infrastructure" exists. He advocates a third (Christian) system as an alternative to both capitalism and socialism.[13] Classical capitalism is opposed to the spirit of the Christian religion, but "people's capitalism" is not. Such a modified capitalism provides, for instance, for workers' participation in profits. Monarchists are in favor of private initiative but also of state regulation.

Christian (like Islamic) thinkers have never had much success formulating a specific religious social and economic program for the modern world; other religions have not even tried. Thus, beyond mere generalities the Orthodox monarchists have not produced any novel ideas. They feel themselves more comfortable with agriculture than with industry and banking, let alone the postindustrial society. They want a healthy, prosperous peasantry, something akin to the American farmers, to emerge in the village.[14] The monarchists suggest a return to the pre-1917 fiscal system; they favor

11. *Russkii vestnik* (supplement), 2 (1992). (Y. Bulychev)

12. Ibid.

13. *Nash sovremennik,* 12 (1990).

14. *Domostroi,* 17 (1991).

moderate progressive taxation and demand that the value of the ruble be restored, so that it will regain the authority it had before the national catastrophe of 1917. They also advocate a return to the social legislation enacted under the last tsars: Young families should receive assistance, and everyone should have twenty-four paid holidays each year. Various ecological improvements are demanded, as well as a ban on pornography and sexual license, and a struggle against alcoholism and smoking.[15]

Monarchists agree that while there should be tolerance for the non-Russian nationalities, the position of the Russian people should be dominant. The programs of the various monarchist factions are not very specific in this respect, nor are they quite clear with regard to the relationship between state and church. While all confessions should have the right to practice their religion, the Orthodox church has to be sui generis. Antireligious propaganda is to be banned; the church should have its own media outlets, including television. The Communist commissars in the army are to be replaced by military chaplains. Education under the monarchy will be in a strong patriotic spirit.[16]

Monarchists disagree on the identity of the next tsar; their quarrels became acute when the pretender Vladimir Kyrillovich (1917–1992) and his family visited St. Petersburg and were welcomed by the mayor. When Grand Duke Kyrill died in 1938 he left three children: Maria, who married a German prince; Kyra, who married Louis Ferdinand of Prussia; and Vladimir. Vladimir lived quietly in the family mansion in western France and later in Spain; he did not claim the throne until after his marriage in Madrid in 1948 to Leonida Georgievna Bagration-Mukhransky.[17] (As Vladimir grew older, there was a striking resemblance between him and King George VI of England, just as the last tsar resembled George V.) Of the monarchists in the Russian émigré community—small groups in North America, Latin America, and Australia—probably a majority paid homage to the pretender. But others did not.

Why the reservations about Vladimir among Russian and other monarchists? The issues involved were highly complicated; they were connected with the Russian law of succession to the throne, which has been changed or modified several times over the last hundred and seventy years. Vladi-

15. Ustav rossiiskovo osvoboditelnovo soyuza (1990). Program Khristianskovo patrioticheskovo soyuza (1988); Programnie Printsipy V.P.M.Ts. (January 1992).

16. Ibid.

17. The couple had a daughter named Maria, born in 1953, who is the mother of a son named Georgi. The son, aged eleven in 1992, regards himself as a future ruler of Russia, according to his grandfather.

mir's antagonists claimed that the status of his father as the chief pretender was disputed by the rest of the Romanov family. Furthermore, they said, Kyrill disqualified himself from the ascension to the throne when he divorced his first wife and married his cousin Victoria who, among other things, was also a princess of England. According to the law of the Romanovs (and the Russian church) such marriages between cousins are recognized only if the permission of the tsar is obtained. But Kyrill, for one reason or another, did not bother to get this permission.[18] True, in 1905 the tsar forgave his cousin, but not entirely, and thus Kyrill's children were to be called only "his (or her) highness the prince" but they were not recognized as full-fledged grand dukes.

Vladimir, to make matters even worse, allegedly married his Georgian bride in a secret ceremony. According to rumors among monarchist fundamentalists, Maria's mother's maiden name was Zolotnitsky, which, they claim, is a Jewish name. Worse yet, Maria was married earlier on to an American, allegedly a Jew named Kirby, who died during the war. There are at least a dozen other complaints concerning Vladimir. His father, the fundamentalists argued, behaved none too loyally in March 1917 when Nikolai was forced to abdicate—but then no one else behaved loyally either. Vladimir reportedly visited a Russian émigré Boy Scout camp and greeted the Scouts with the familiar "Be prepared." According to the fundamentalists this is a well-known Masonic formula.[19] According to the same source (L. Bolotin) a distant aunt of Vladimir's wife was possibly married to Lavrenti Beria at one time. The genealogical inventiveness of these monarchists is admirable; one can only wish they had kept some for their political-social-economic program.

Some Russian monarchist groups, such as the Pravoslav Constitutional Monarchist party and the Dvoryankoye Sobranie, recognized the claims of Kyrill (who stood for a constitutional monarchy) but others did not.[20] However, with Kyrill's rejection more problems arose. If he was not a suitable candidate for the throne, who was? Since the older sons of Nikolai I married non-Orthodox wives, one had to look among the descendants of his younger sons.[21] But all this happened three or four generations ago, and

18. N. Talberg, "Mysli starovo monarkhista," *Zemshchina,* 28 (46) (1991). A. Shiropayev, *Russkii vestnik,* 28–29 (1991). L. Bolotin, *Tsar kolokol,* 1 (1990), and also *Tsar kolokol,* 10 (1991). A. Verkhovsky, *Volya Rossii,* 3 (1991). These articles base themselves in the main on even more detailed articles or books published in past years, specifically M. Zazykin, *Tsarskaya vlast* . . . (Sofia, 1924) and K. Weimarn, *Istinnoye vozrozhdenie i restavratsiya* (place of publication unknown, 1984).

19. *Russkii vestnik,* 28–29 (1991). Based on *Tsar kolokol.*

20. *Rossiiskii obzor,* 1 (1991).

21. Talberg in *Zemshchina,* 28 (45) (1991).

while there seem to be several possible candidates, it is more than doubtful whether any of them would survive for very long if one were to scrutinize their marital affairs, business associations, and social affiliations, not to mention membership in such associations as the Boy Scouts. Grand Duke Vladimir died in Miami in April 1992; his daughter Maria, who married a prince of Prussia in 1976, succeeded him as the head of the Russian imperial family. But, as a spokesman for the family made clear in a letter to the London *Times,* the family had not recognized the Prussian prince and did not recognize the claims of his offspring. Hence the conclusion drawn by present-day Russian monarchist groups that the new tsar should be elected and proclaimed by a *zemskii sobor,* as the first Romanov was in 1613.

A monarchist conference met in Moscow in May 1991 to prepare for the convening of a *sobor.* Some ten new regional groups joined the organization, including two each from Cheliabinsk, two from the Crimea, and two from St. Petersburg. It was decided to establish a new *oprichnina,* in the name of God, the Father, the Son, and the Holy Spirit.[22] This resolution must have come as a surprise not only to most Russians, but even to many monarchists, who might have considered it both blasphemous and ridiculous. The *oprichnina* was the Praetorian guard of Ivan IV (the Terrible). Founded in 1565, it installed a reign of terror against the aristocracy and also the church and was given land in recognition for its services. In other respects the *oprichnina* proved ineffective; it failed to prevent the invasion of the Crimean Tatars, who sacked Moscow in 1572, and it was dissolved soon after.

The historical *oprichnina* served Ivan the Terrible; it had nothing to do with the election of the tsar. What made a group of monarchists try to reestablish a terrorist elite four hundred years after the event? They stated in their manifesto that a new tsar could not possibly be democratically elected by the people: This was in contradiction to Russian tradition. He could be chosen only by the "best people in the country" (a term coined by Stalin and frequently used by him). The monarchists had in mind clergymen, military and police commanders, and other key figures in society, provided they were monarchists and in full agreement with the program of this group. They would be the new *oprichniki,* of whom the *sobor* would consist. A follow-up meeting in Moscow in October 1991 made it known that a decision on the personality of the future tsar would be taken once the *sobor* had seven thousand members.[23]

Russian monarchists sometimes point to the return of the monarchy in

22. *Zemshchina,* 17 (34) (1991).

23. *Zemshchina,* 53 (1991).

Spain after Franco as a precedent that augurs well for Russia. But there were great differences in the historical and political circumstances which make the comparison of doubtful value. There was no strong promonarchy feeling in Spain at the time, but many Spaniards gave Juan Carlos the benefit of the doubt. He was in most respects an attractive candidate; and he did not come to his high office as a leader of the extreme right promising to take the country back to the age of Philip II. On the contrary, his attachment to the constitution and democracy was genuine, and he played an important role as an integrative figure in the smooth transition to a democratic Spain.

In Russia monarchism is sponsored by the extreme right, which strictly limits its appeal from the very beginning. While antidemocratic sentiments and the longing for a strong leader may be widespread, a military dictator or similar figure would probably attract more popular support. Many, probably most, monarchists do not want a forward-looking tsar but a ruler who would take the country back to a distant and not very attractive past. The experience of other countries has shown that political success in this age for the right (and, a fortiori, for the extreme right) is impossible without the use of modern politics. Mussolini and Hitler had learned this lesson and created modern mass movements; they would never have come to power had they relied on a *sobor* and an *oprichnina*. It is most unlikely that Russia will be an exception to this rule. A system monarchist in all but name was a possibility in certain Communist countries such as Romania and North Korea; in postcommunist Russia neither the psychological nor the social conditions exist for such a choice. Russia may need a strong government; Bagehot once wrote that monarchy was a strong government because it was an intelligible government. But that was in another century and another country. In Russia, the monarchist idea is likely to remain a sectarian dream rather than a realistic alternative.

The Cossack Revival

Among the many unexpected events of the late 1980s was the reemergence of the Cossacks, previously believed to have been extinct as a group for a long time. The mythology of the Cossack had persisted, even spread. But few in Russia or outside had expected to see again the legendary horsemen—now mostly on foot, with their ataman in a green Mercedes in the streets of Rostov, Krasnodar, and Stavropol. They reappeared complete with their traditional uniforms, their *kinzhaly* (daggers), and, of course, their flailing whips, the *nagaika*.

A brief historical digression is needed at this stage to shed some light on the character of the Cossack revival, many years after the historians had announced that the "frontier knights" with their hallowed traditions had disappeared forever.[24]

The traditional romantic image of the Cossacks was one of horsemen of incredible skill and bravery riding on the steppe, proud of their freedom, defending Russia's borders against its enemies. Originally there had been many escaped serfs and even outlaws among them, but gradually they had become staunch defenders of the tsar and the Orthodox faith. Under the leadership of Ermak and the Stroganovs they had spearheaded the Russian advance to Siberia and ultimately the Pacific.

The Cossacks have been exceedingly lucky in world literature: There are few more heroic, yet popular figures than Taras Bulba, with his belief that the only good life is that of a soldier. And there are few more tragic scenes than that of Taras hiding under a load of bricks to smuggle himself into the city of Warsaw, where Ostap, his son, is about to be tortured and executed.

Tolstoy's *Cossacks* is a love story, taking place in the Caucasus in the 1850s. Olenin, a young Russian officer and nobleman, falls in love with Maryana, who eventually turns him down because she instinctively realizes that the distance—in culture, in way of life, and in background—between the two is too large and cannot be bridged. Somewhere Tolstoy wrote, albeit with a little exaggeration, that all Russian history has been made by the Cossacks.

The story of Gregori Melekhov, the hero of Sholokhov's *And Quiet Flows the Don,* is a more recent epic of war (and civil war) and love (and unrequited love). Owing to these and other famous books, the attractive image of the Cossack survived long after the warriors, with their lances and sabers, galloping over the sunlit steppe had become obsolete and vanished.

There was something quintessentially Russian in this military caste, a point frequently made by the present-day leaders of the Cossack revival. But Cossack myth and reality are by no means identical. Many, perhaps most Cossacks were not Russian but Tatar by origin or belonged to one of the many Turkic or Mongol tribes. Most of their raids were aimed at plunder and brigandage, and usually they sold their services to the highest bidder. They fought with Muscovy against the Poles, with the Poles against

---

24. The story of the Cossacks has attracted many Western historians and there are probably more excellent studies on this aspect of the history of Russia than most others. D. Longworth, *The Cossacks* (New York, 1969); R. H. McNeal, *Tsar and Cossack 1855–1914* (London, 1987); Albert Seaton, *The Horsemen of the Steppes* (London, 1985); Peter Kenez, *Civil War in South Russia* (Berkeley, Calif., 1977); G. Stökl, *Die Entstehung des Kosakentums* (Munich, 1953); R. Karmann, *Der Freiheitskampf der Kosaken* (Puchheim, 1985).

Russia, and so on. They were comparable to the *Landsknechte* in sixteenth-century Central Europe. Most of their income came from intercepting and robbing trade convoys from east to west and from north to south, and for every peaceful Cossack and fisherman there was probably a river pirate.

True, there were great differences between "registered" and "unregistered" Cossacks (those recognized by the authorities), between those making their home in the Don region and the Ukrainian Cossacks who served the Poles and Lithuanians. There was bitter enmity between the Ukrainian Cossacks and the Saporozhens (of whom the fictional Taras Bulba was a member) even though they were close neighbors. In the Russian civil war of the early seventeenth century, the *smuta,* the Cossacks played a destructive role, changing sides frequently and prolonging hostilities. As Kliuchevsky, the great Russian historian, noted, they "lacked all moral and ethical substance." Since the Cossacks had often supported Russia's enemies—up to and including Charles XII of Sweden—they were not completely trusted in Moscow, even as they came under Russia's control and were paid a subsidy.

Eventually, their original function of policing Russia's border and launching raids against Russia's enemies disappeared. In the middle of the nineteenth century they settled in various parts of the Russian empire and were given certain economic privileges. They had to spend four years on active military service in the Russian army, and eight years in the reserves.

By the early twentieth century some four million Cossacks lived in Russia. They were mainly concentrated in the Don and Kuban, and to a lesser extent in the Caucasus, the Urals, and the Far East (Ussuri, Semirechie). But nowhere, not even in the Don, did they constitute a majority. The Cossacks were divided into eleven armies *(voisko)* and when war broke out in 1914, 300,000 of them were mobilized.

However, as the Cossacks became sedentary, their military prowess decreased. Though they were individually brave, their ability to maneuver in bigger formations was less than impressive, and even as horsemen they were no longer held in high esteem by friend or foe. During the nineteenth century, with one exception in the Caucasus, they saw no active service, but were used by the government as "law-and-order forces" against national minorities such as the Poles, against working-class demonstrations, and against Jews. They became the most faithful servants of the state, closely identified with the tsar and hated by the enemies of the monarchy.

This image of the Cossacks was not however, entirely correct. Many Cossacks felt that they suffered discrimination, as their services for the state were (as they saw it) only inadequately compensated. Their leaders, appointed by the government, were non-Cossack officers and administrators.

In the first general elections after 1905 the representatives of the Cossacks in the Duma supported left-of-center rather than right-wing parties. When the tsar was forced to abdicate in 1917, this was, by and large, welcomed by the Cossacks, who shared the opinion of most Russians on the failure of the monarchy.

In the months that followed and during the civil war the Cossacks tried to regain the autonomy they had possessed, before Peter the Great's time, in the Don and Kuban regions, where about half of all Cossacks were concentrated. They even established an All-Russian Cossack Federation.

As so often in the past, the old Cossack sicknesses—unending debate, on the one hand, and the unwillingness to move away from their native settlements, on the other—reasserted themselves. They had capable military leaders such as Kornilov (who was half Mongolian by origin), Kaledin, Mamontov, and Krasnov. But these leaders did not see eye to eye. Krasnov was pro-German in orientation, Kaledin pro-French. Their cooperation with the White armies was anything but close, because the Cossacks' interests and independence rather than the "White cause" figured most strongly in their thoughts and actions.

They did not have the support of the non-Cossack population in their midst, and there was considerable internal dissent within their ranks: The soldiers returning from the front had either been infected by subversive (revolutionary) propaganda, or were war-weary, having seen enough fighting and wanting to return to their *stanitsy* at almost any price. While the advancing Bolsheviks helped to establish a "Don Soviet Republic," Krasnov, who had become ataman after Kaledin's suicide, set up a "provisional Don government," which he regarded as independent of Russia. It had considerably expanded (and quite unrealistic) boundaries. After some early victories against the Reds, the Don Cossacks were defeated, and later on in 1919 and early 1920 so were those in the Kuban. Tens of thousands of Cossacks escaped over the Turkish border. Of those in the Far East, some fled to Manchuria and settled there.

Following the Communist occupation the Cossacks were subjected to extensive persecution. True, under Krasnov some 45,000 Red Cossacks had been shot or hanged, but the Communist rulers engaged in the elimination on an even more massive scale of the Cossack elite and the rich peasants, that is to say everyone who had a cow. According to some estimates, about a million Cossacks perished. In later years this policy of "de-Cossackization" was decried even in the official Communist history books.

The Russian right was looking as usual for some Jewish culprits in this context; did Jews not persecute the Cossacks with special hatred in view of the Cossacks' role in the pogroms? It was difficult to put the blame on Trotsky, because he had not taken a special interest in this theater of war; Stalin and Voroshilov had been much nearer the scene. But a decree was found, signed by Sverdlov, which seemed to implicate this Bolshevik leader more deeply than others in the anti-Cossack policies. But Sverdlov had died in March 1919, well before the Don and the Kuban had finally been reconquered by the Reds.

In truth, the Cossacks had been quite unpopular with the democratic and radical parties, in view of the role they had played in the suppression of these movements before 1917. And so the Cossacks lost whatever autonomy they had possessed; many were killed or deported; those who remained were now part of the Rostov oblast or the Stavropol *krai*. Even the singing of Cossack songs was frowned upon, and Cossack uniforms were banned. (However, many uniforms seem to have been hidden, for there was an abundance of uniforms and regalia when the Cossacks re-emerged from the underground in 1990.)

A second blow came with the collectivization of agriculture in 1929–1930. This was not directed specifically against the Cossacks, but they suffered at least as much as their neighbors, and little remained of their way of life. It was not surprising, therefore, that the Germans found collaborators among the Cossacks after the invasion in 1941. Had they shown more enthusiasm in mobilizing the Cossacks, several Cossack volunteer divisions would have come into existence, rather than the one headed by von Pannwitz. Adolf Hitler was even appointed by the Cossacks "supreme dictator" of their nation.[25] But Hitler and Rosenberg still regarded the Cossacks as *Untermenschen*, though of slightly better stock than the Russians. They insisted that Cossack units be commanded by German officers and General Krasnov's project of a "Greater Cossackia" extending from the central Ukraine to the Volga never had full German support.

It all ended in yet another tragedy for the Cossacks. Generals Krasnov, Shkuro, and several other leaders, together with thousands of their followers, were handed over by the Allies to the Soviets; the commanders were executed in 1947. In later years this was denounced by some Western writers as a great betrayal. At the time Churchill had asked his generals: Did they fight against us? And when an affirmative answer was given, he felt no compunction.

During the war Stalin had permitted a revival of Cossack traditions within modest limits. But once the war was over, this revival ended and with it the dreams of autonomy, however modest.

25. *Nationale Kosakenbewegung, Die Kosakenfrage* (Prague, 1943), p. 11. See also Udo Gehrmann, *Das Kosakentum in Russland zu Beginn der 90er Jahre* (Cologne, 1992), p. 23.

The Cossack renaissance got under way in the spring of 1990 at a meeting in Rostov, when a lawyer named Samsonov was elected the first local ataman. Later on, in November 1990, a wider group *(krug)* met for the first conference of the Don Army (Voiska Donskovo) and elected Mikhail Mikhailovich Sholokhov as its ataman. Sholokhov Junior, a philosopher by training, was a professor at the police academy with the rank of colonel. The son of the famous writer, he enjoyed great authority and like most Cossack activists was a member of the Communist party. (It should be noted in passing that Sholokhov did not hail from a Cossack family, but was merely an honorary Cossack.)

The Cossacks' immediate demand was for their rehabilitation by the supreme Russian leadership; on December 9, 1991, Yeltsin published a decree establishing a committee that was to tackle this issue.[26]

In the meantime another reborn Leninist philosopher, Valeri Zhukov, appointed himself ataman of the Ural (Yaitski) Cossacks. But he was not recognized by the local (Communist) Cossack leadership, which had another candidate, Martynov, for ataman. Martynov went on to become head of the "Union of Atamans," and V. U. Naumov was made ataman of the Kuban Cossacks. Within a year there existed a Cossack organization stretching "from the Dniester to Sakhalin, from Dushanbe to Chukotka"—that is, from one end of Russia to the other.[27]

But this sweep was more impressive on paper than in the real world. The old curse of Cossack politics reasserted itself: constant internal bickering, endless debate, and little action. As Krasnov had warned his fellow Cossacks in 1918: "We make a great deal of noise but do little." Sholokhov's son, who had tried to follow a moderate line was deposed in the October 1991 election at Novocherkassk, one of the traditional centers of Cossack settlement. This followed the murder of a local ataman, Aleksander Podkolzin, in fighting over some lands that took place at Sunji in the Ingush region. Under a former air force general, this region had declared itself independent. Among the Chechens and Ingush there were many Cossacks; they had been comrades in arms of the Cossacks of the Don and Kuban in the fighting throughout the nineteenth century. But once separatist movements prevailed, the Ingush forgot auld acquaintance and the "foreign" Cossacks were expelled. They complained about human-rights violations and threatened countermeasures. Ataman Mesheryakov, who

26. *Kazachiya volya*, 1 (1992). The report of this committee was confirmed and made legal by Yeltsin in June 1992.

27. Martynov report, *Kazachie vedomosti*, 4 (December 1991). It is reported that Martynov, a former party member and head of a Moscow factory, became an Orthodox church member on the eve of his election. Martynov's chief deputy, Vladimir Naumov, was also a member of the political establishment and worked in a leading position for the Moscow Soviet.

had replaced Sholokhov, was the candidate of the more militant wing among the Cossacks, but he too was a former Communist party official.

After the euphoria of the early days had passed there were deserters from the ranks of the Cossacks who lost interest in the cause. In the Urals and the Far East the response had been less than overwhelming from the beginning; only a few joined the movement, perhaps three thousand of the sixty thousand Cossacks living in Uralsk, a city of almost a quarter of a million and the main Cossack concentration in the Urals. If there were not enough Indians, there were too many of those who wanted to be chiefs—especially those who had lost in the elections. Y. Galushkin, a local ataman and one of the most extreme leaders, ignored the Union of Atamans. G. V. Kokunko and A. A. Ozerov likewise took a dim view of it and declared that the old forms of Cossack organization had outlived their usefulness and new frameworks were needed. Even in the Don region there was no unity. Thus a Cossack delegation from Cherkask, together with Kokunko and a self-appointed Siberian general named Dorokhov, went to Moscow to lobby the government and the Soviet parliament without coordinating their activities with the Union, even deriding their leadership and belittling its importance. There were many other signs that the old Cossack anarchy was reasserting itself.[28]

The Cossack demand for rehabilitation was justified. But once specific demands were made, it became obvious that many of these were unrealistic or collided with the rights of other peoples. The Cossacks demanded the return of all lands that had once belonged to them, as well as forests, rivers, and natural resources; all transactions made since 1917 should be declared null and void. However, the average Cossack had possessed more land prior to 1917 than the average Russian peasant. The difficult question of what land and natural resources had belonged to the Cossacks quite apart, there had been massive transfers of population during the last seventy-five years. Whole cities, factories, airports, power plants had been built on these lands. The Cossacks' claim to rule a city such as Rostov with 1.1 million inhabitants was preposterous; there never had been a Cossack majority there, and they were a minority now. The same was true with regard to smaller cities such as Krasnodar and Stavropol. Some Cossack spokesmen

28. The main source for information on the Cossack revival is *Kazachie vedomosti,* a monthly supplement to *Russkii vestnik* and *Kazachiya volya,* published in Cherkask in the northern Caucasus. There were also some forty local Cossack news sheets, which appeared irregularly. For a fuller list of regional Cossack publications see the Bibliographical Note and Udo Gehrman, *Das Kosakentum in Russland.* Lastly there was *Kuban,* a monthly political-literary magazine that devoted its pages mainly to historical reminiscences and anti-Jewish and anti-Masonic propaganda. It did not cover current Cossack activities.

demanded the "repatriation" (that is to say deportation) of non-Russians, such as Armenians and Georgians. But the "Caucasians" were only a small fraction of those who had settled, and once the Cossacks disputed the rights of the Russians (or of some of the minor Caucasian nationalities) they were bound to run into hostility and retaliation. Outside the Don and the Kuban such demands were even more unrealistic.

The Cossack leadership sent letters with various complaints and demands to the presidents of Kirghizia, Moldavia, and Kazakhstan, but these were in no hurry to reply. The Cossacks registered their protests against a possible return of the Kurile Islands to Japan, claiming that individual Cossacks had been among the discoverers of these islands. They demanded a referendum in Birobidzhan about the future of that Jewish autonomous district in the Far East—which, they said, had been illegally established sixty years earlier on Cossack land.[29] In this demand they received the support of Zionist leaders who had never been enamored of the project. But it was more than doubtful whether the Russian majority in Birobidzhan had any intention of becoming part of a Cossack autonomous region.

Among the first decisions of the Cossack *krug* in 1991 was to establish their own bank and a stock exchange to finance their activities. But these decisions would hardly have attracted much attention, whereas the separatist slogans did. On the one hand, Cossacks swore undying allegiance to Russia and willingness to defend it against all its enemies. Yet on the other, they demanded the establishment of their own autonomous region or even republic in the Don with special reference to the law of April 26, 1991, concerning the rehabilitation of peoples that had been subject to repression. Thus the Cossacks regarded themselves as a people, distinct from the Russians; they appeared as Russian patriots and separatists at the same time.[30] They demanded stronger leadership in Moscow, yet at the same time threatened to cut off deliveries of food from the Don and the Kuban to Moscow and St. Petersburg.

To give greater emphasis to their demands, the Cossack leadership in the Don issued an appeal to register all Cossacks for some form of military service. Political enemies, such as N. Peredisty, the editor of the newspaper *Democratic Don*, were physically attacked and beaten up.[31] Next, Cossack units went to the markets and the railway stations in the guise of "people's

29. *Kazachie vedomosti*, 4 (1991). See also *Rossiskii obzor*, 1–2 (1992). According to this source some 350,000 descendants of Cossacks had joined the new organizations by 1991. The figure seems exaggerated.

30. *Komsomolskaya pravda* (October 26, 1991).

31. Ibid (January 15, 1992).

avengers" imposing law and order. Two of six who were arrested had criminal records—one for rape, the other for speculation. At the stations they inspected the passengers' luggage and took away meat, butter, and other foodstuffs. At the market they demanded that a dealer reduce the price of onions and mandarins from twenty rubles to fifteen, and when he refused, they took the fruit away and delivered it to some institutions such as orphanages and schools.[32] Before setting out on this mission they had gone to church to get the blessing of a priest, who presumably was quite unaware of their intentions. Wherever they went they shouted "Foreigners out!"

But the Robin Hood game was not always innocent; in Novocherkassk a group of Cossack youngsters beat a man to death simply because he looked like an Armenian or Georgian.

However, even if the motives of the Cossacks had been altogether pure, the attempts to establish alternative structures and to challenge the existing authorities by way of violent, even terrorist means were altogether unacceptable. They created problems even for the Russian right, which had welcomed the Cossacks as storm troops but could not afford to lose the support of those Russians exposed to exorbitant demands for restitution in Rostov as in Moscow.

The Cossack leadership tried to lobby the Ministry of Defense and the army command, again offering their services protecting the borders of Russia. They suggested the establishment of purely Cossack tank and motorized units. But the army could not be of much help; at a time when hundreds of thousands of regular officers and soldiers had to be dismissed from the army for budgetary reasons, it was not in a position to employ new auxiliaries. Some Cossack leaders threatened that unless one gave the younger Cossacks some jobs, they would become radicalized. Already there was a "White army" romanticism spreading among the younger Cossacks, and units bearing the name of Kornilov (the famous counterrevolutionary of 1917 fame) and of Shkuro had appeared in Rostov.[33]

Some of the Cossack leaders probably did not like the turn to the extreme right. This statement applies not only to the former Communists among them, for whom a name like "Kornilov" was anathema. The more knowledgeable among the Cossacks knew that the relationship between the

---

32. *Trud* (February 4, 1992); *Rabochaya tribuna* (January 23, 1992). For a defense of the Cossacks in connection with their activities in the Don region and in Moldova, *Domostroi*, 14 (1992).

33. *Syn otechestva* (February 1992). In early 1992 Cossack units appeared in Transdniestria defending the local Russians against the Moldovan authorities, thus opening yet another front. *Kazachie vedomosti*, 2 (1992).

Cossack and the White armies had never been that close. They suspected that it was politically unwise to put all their ideological eggs into one extremist basket. But the Cossack revival largely based itself on certain traditions, and these happened to be those of Cossack émigré ideologists such as Ivan Rodionov, a pro-fascist writer who had disseminated rabid Black Hundred propaganda from Berlin. This tradition was continued by the literary magazine *Kuban*, which of all the Russian political-literary magazines was the most consistently radical-right-wing in orientation. It also had one of the smallest circulations (twenty thousand in 1992). When the new leadership tried to show Cossack strength at a procession in honor of St. Serafim of Sarov in Diveyevo, fewer than two hundred appeared, most of them from the Kuban. But the extremists, as usual, made most of the noise and received most of the publicity. They shaped the image of the Cossacks as far as public awareness was concerned.

The reemergence of Cossack organizations in 1990 was in some respects only natural in view of the breakdown of a strong central power. So were the resulting conflicts between them and various nationalities in the Caucasus. The survival of a Cossack identity and traditions came as a surprise only to the extent that it showed that the impact of Soviet education and indoctrination had been much less thorough than generally believed. It had not eradicated certain old traditions.

The Cossacks' demand for their rehabilitation as a group was justified. But their demands for political autonomy were unrealistic, since they did not constitute a majority anywhere and since it was impossible to undo the economic, social, and demographic changes that had taken place over the last seventy years. Insistence on their rights, as they interpreted them, was bound to lead to political and physical conflict not only with non-Russian nationalities but also with the Russian residents. The Cossacks were right to resist pressure (to give but one example) from the Chechen, who wanted to expel them from lands they had cultivated for generations. But such conflicts could be solved only by way of negotiation. The Cossacks were entitled to press their demands for cultural autonomy—to have their own schools, a "Cossack faculty" at the Kuban university, to produce movies about the Cossacks, and even a Cossack encyclopedia.[34]

Whether these and other aspirations would best be served by support for the extreme right in Moscow was doubtful at the very least. The atamans were on the whole careful in their pronouncements, and they were

34. *Kazachie vedomosti*, 4 (1991). In their program the Cossacks defined themselves alternatively as a people and a "distinctive ethnic formation"—two entirely different concepts. *Narodnaya pravda* (January 1992).

moreover so occupied in dealing with their own internal and external conflicts that they did not become deeply involved in the anti-Masonic and anti-Jewish campaigns.[35] The enemies facing the Cossacks in Novocherkask and the northern Caucasus were neither Masons nor "Zionists." Furthermore, there were some fundamental divisive issues to be tackled: Was Cossack agriculture in the Don and the Kuban to be private or, as the former Communists wanted, collectivist? The ideological advisers of the Cossacks wanted more than a folklorist revival; they believed that Cossacks had to take a firm stand on the extreme right of the political spectrum. They tried to persuade their followers that the democrats and political reformers in Moscow, such as Yakovlev, were emissaries of the Antichrist, and that a good Cossack should read only anti-Masonic and anti-Jewish literature— as if these were the main issues facing the Cossacks in their national revival.[36] If the ideologists of *Kuban* had their way, there would be a replay of the events of 1918–1919, and the fact that these had ended in disaster before seemed not to deter them.

However, the Cossack revival has by no means been monopolized by the extreme right. If there has been no unanimity as to whether the Cossacks are a social stratum or an *ethnos* (distinct nationality) or sub-*ethnos,* the leadership continues to be even more disputed. Most of the new atamans are former Communist officials or directors of big farms (sov-khozy), donning fancy uniforms. They would like to preserve as much as possible of the social and economic conditions that prevailed under the Soviet regime. They oppose, for instance, decollectivization in agriculture; as far as they are concerned the Cossack revival should be national in its outward form and its folklore, but Soviet in its content. The Cossack revival reflects in microcosm the renaissance of National Bolshevism. But there are other forces among the Cossacks who support the Russian government rather than the "patriotic opposition," who have realized that they have a unique chance to build a new Cossack middle class and that at this time the checkbook is a more powerful weapon than the *shashkia* (saber) or even the tank.[37]

Soon after their political resurgence the Cossack camp split several ways and there were further divisions on a regional basis such as the rivalry between the *Rada* and the *Voisko* in the Kuban region. The Don Cossacks supported the (Muslim) Abkhazians in their struggle against the Georgians;

35. Martynov interview with Eduard Volodin, *Den,* 17 (1991).

36. *Molot,* quoted in *Digest moskovskikh novostei* (January 18, 1992).

37. Yu. Averyanov, "Sovremennoye rossiskoye kazachestvo; politicheskii portret," *Nezavisi-maya gazeta* (May 19, 1992).

other Cossacks were on the side of the (Christian) Georgians. Me-shcheryakov, the "red ataman," was replaced by Albert Vetrov, a leader of the "Whites." But the differences between Reds and Whites were not always visible to the naked eye: Both wanted to expel Armenians and other foreigners from the Northern Caucasus; both were against the privatization of agriculture. Both collaborated with the Russian right, some with the more moderate elements, others with the extremists.

Communism had been the enemy par excellence of the Cossacks for many decades, having brought about their ruin in the 1920s and 1930s. Yet in the post-Soviet era the Cossacks found themselves in one camp with their bitter enemies, a strange but not altogether illogical coalition. This collaboration between the right and the Bolsheviks was a general phenomenon, but it found striking expression in the specific case of the Cossacks.[38]

38. For developments among the Cossacks in 1991–92 see *Literaturnaya gazeta*, October 7, 1992; *Megapolis Express* 35, 1992; *Nezavisimaya gazeta*, October 14, 1992; *Moskovskie Novosti*, October 18, 1992, as well as the Cossack periodicals mentioned above.

Chapter Thirteen

PAMYAT

PAMYAT IS THE GENERIC NAME since the 1980s of several right-wing extremist groups in Moscow, Leningrad (St. Petersburg), and other Russian cities. An inchoate movement as far as both its doctrine and its organization are concerned, Pamyat has attracted an enormous amount of publicity ever since it became politically active during the early days of *glasnost;* it could well be that for every member of Pamyat there has been an article in the Russian and Western press.[1] In addition there have been many dozens of television programs showing Pamyat in action. If it was the main aim of Pamyat to attract maximum attention in the media, the movement has been a phenomenal success.[2]

There is no certainty with regard to Pamyat's origins. According to reliable sources various patriotic groups came into being in the late 1970s, engaging in a variety of voluntary cultural activities such as the restoration of monuments and churches in Moscow and the vicinity; there was also a "circle of book-lovers," which met with poets such as Kunayev, Chuyev, Sorokin, and Nozdreyev and prose writers such as Shevtsov, Dmitri Zhu-

1. The estimates of membership vary between a few hundred and ten million (Emelyanov). Fifteen hundred was the highest number ever present at a single meeting, the inauguration of Pamyat's journal in 1990.

2. However, the output of anti-Zionist literature has been on an even greater scale. Between 1965 and 1985 some ten million such books were published in the Soviet Union, that is to say five books for every Soviet Jew.

kov and Chivilikhin or arranged readings from the classics such as Tyutchev. There were memorial meetings in honor of the battle of Kulikovo, the battle of Borodino, the singer Shalyapin, the rocket scientist Tsiolkovsky. During the early days these groups attached themselves to existing cultural institutions at the Ministry of Civil Aviation and the Ostrovski Museum. Later on, in 1983, the Metrostroi—cultural center of the Moscow subway system—and the Gorbunov Cultural Center became Pamyat's home. Among the early members were some painters, sculptors, composers, but also manual workers; most of them apparently belonged to the Communist party. Their activities received limited publicity in local newspapers and were without exception constructive.[3] The name Pamyat was apparently adopted in 1983. It was inspired by the novel *Pamyat* by Chivilikhin, which had been published one year earlier.

Dmitri Vasiliev, a photographer who also had some training as an actor, joined Pamyat in 1984. He had been active on the fringes of patriotic circles, was a great showman and an excellent speaker in a pronounced demagogic style. Having worked for a number of years as an assistant to the famous and fashionable painter Ilya Glazunov, he had good connections on the right. Vasiliev soon emerged as the most dynamic figure within Pamyat, and under his guidance the society became thoroughly politicized. It was registered with the authorities as a historical-patriotic association. Its main propaganda theme was, at first, the battle against alcoholism, but this was soon overtaken by an anti-Jewish campaign, specifically connected with the destruction of national monuments in Moscow that were attributed to Jewish architects. The *Protocols of the Elders of Zion* became the most frequently quoted document in Pamyat propaganda. When E. Bekhtereva, one of the Pamyat leaders, was attacked and injured in the course of a robbery in a Moscow street, this was widely denounced as a Zionist attack even though the attacker, who was apprehended, was a professional criminal of purely "Aryan" stock.

With politicization Pamyat began to change its character. Some of the early members dropped out; a few died; others, while sharing Vasiliev's views by and large, found it difficult to get along with him on a personal level: He clearly wanted to be the group's undisputed leader. The disagreements were mainly about style. Pamyat had been from the beginning a movement of activist patriotic circles, and Vasiliev's radicalism did not

3. On the early history of Pamyat, see V. Pribylovsky, *Panorama* (Moscow) 8, 9, 10, 14 (1990); *Russkaya mysl* (Paris, July 30, 1987); *Sobesednik*, 49 (1990). See also V. Solovei, *Pamyat: istoriia, ideologiia, politicheskaya praktika* (Moscow, 1991). Gerd Koenen, "Pamyat," in *Osteuropa*, 3 (1990). L. Dadiani, "Die Gesellschaft pamjat," (in Yiddish, *Sovietish Heimland*, 11 (1990).

constitute a new departure. Inevitably the emphasis prior to 1985 had been on cultural activities, for the Communist party's monopoly on politics could not then be disputed. Seen in this perspective, Pamyat's politicization after 1985 seems inevitable; it would have happened even if Vasiliev had not appeared on the stage.

What bothered the founding members was his cheap, theatrical effects; he would appear at a meeting with a false beard, claiming that the disguise was necessary to escape from the Zionist gangsters who were out to get him and that in any case, his life was in mortal danger. The shrillness, the exaggerations, and the outright lies were aesthetically displeasing to some of his erstwhile colleagues. Furthermore, Vasiliev could not get along with people who had their own ideas about strategy and tactics. He was at his most effective as leader of the black-uniformed groups of young men who constituted his Praetorian guard.

But Vasiliev got results, in contrast to the impractical intellectuals who had constituted Pamyat's leadership earlier on. Up to this point the story resembles the situation in Munich among the extreme right in 1921 just after the arrival of Hitler, whose appearance transformed the scene. The message of Pamyat was spread outside Moscow by means of tapes and occasional visits; the meetings of Pamyat at which Vasiliev was present attracted many more listeners. There were street demonstrations, above all in Manezh Square in Moscow and Leningrad, and on one occasion Yeltsin, then party secretary of Moscow, received a Pamyat delegation. Pamyat organized a protest meeting against the erection of a victory memorial on Poklonnaya Hill; in Leningrad there was a demonstration against the destruction of the old and famous Angleterre hotel, where Esenin had committed suicide. On these occasions the Pamyat members were joined by individuals who did not share its political program; in Leningrad the local Spasenie group was probably stronger. But Pamyat's main stress was on political propaganda, and it was in this context that Pamyat was to receive a great deal of publicity beginning in 1987.

During the summer of that year several leading members of Pamyat were expelled from the Communist party, notably Kim Andreyev, its president—largely a ceremonial appointment. At about the same time several Soviet newspapers (but not *Pravda, Trud,* or *Krasnaya zvezda*) published long articles criticizing Pamyat activities.[4] The writers made the obvious points—that Pamyat propaganda was not anti-Zionist in inspira-

---

4. The most notable were those by E. Losoto in *Komsomolskaya pravda* (May 22, 1987); Alimov and Lynev in *Izvestiya* (June 2, 1987); P. Gutiontov in *Sovietskaya rossiya* (July 17, 1987); A. Cherkizov in *Sovietskaya kultura* (June 18, 1987), as well as articles in *Ogonyok, Moskovskaya pravda,* and elsewhere.

tion but anti-Jewish, that its arguments were not novel but in the tradition of the Black Hundred and the Nazis, that its beer-hall (kvasnoi) patriotism was suspect, and that, generally speaking, the group's fantastic allegations were causing a great deal of harm abroad and disorientation at home. These negative articles produced a flood of letters for and against Pamyat that became the subject of more articles.

The attitude of the party's central organs during this period was ambiguous. Support for Pamyat came from highly placed individuals in the Central Committee, the KGB, and the armed forces; there was more assistance on the regional level. Pamyat was regarded as an important (if somewhat misguided) counterweight to the liberals, and above all to the radical dissidents, whose activities became more bothersome at precisely this time. There was also opposition against Pamyat among circles in the party leadership, the media, and even the KGB. But Gorbachev and those close to him, including Yeltsin, preferred to ignore the subject and did not comment on it, either because they did not consider it of sufficient importance or, more likely, because they did not want to open an additional political front at a time of growing political trouble. Even when Pamyat activities became an international scandal, the party leadership continued to refrain from commenting.

A typical Pamyat meeting would open with the ringing of church bells or the playing of patriotic marches. This would be followed by recitals from the works of patriotic writers past and present; on occasion a movie would be shown, highlighting some national monument or the beauties of northern Russia or of Siberia. There would be short speeches on subjects such as the systematic destruction of national monuments, above all in Moscow; the responsibility was put on "Zionist" architects acting in close association with foreign Masonic enemies of Mother Russia. The stage was set for the appearance of Vasiliev, who would talk for one to three hours and even longer. He had a standard speech, though there would be modifications in accordance with current events.[5]

Vasiliev always stressed the terrible domestic situation, dwelling not so much on the country's economic plight but on its social and moral decline: the rise of crime, the preoccupation of youth with rock culture, the dissolution of family ties, the growth of alcoholism. At the same time he would express regret with regard to the schools' and the media's neglect of national traditions. All this was explained not as an accident, or as the fault of a Russian people neglectful of its patriotic duties, but as the consequence

---

5. The speeches were circulated in samizdat; several can be found in the Radio Liberty Samizdat archives. One was published in Kontinent, 50 (1986).

of a careful, detailed plan by international Jewry and the Masons. The *Protocols,* Vasiliev always stressed, had to be studied by every Russian patriot, for all their predictions had been borne out. Copies of the *Protocols* had been found in Lenin's personal library; if the leader of the international proletariat found the book of vital interest, every Soviet citizen had to acquaint himself with this key document to world events.

The speeches were replete with the most fantastic inventions and accusations against Jews and Freemasons.

ABOUT THE HOLOCAUST: Vasiliev said: Who was Eichmann? He was a representative of the Jewish people.

ABOUT SATANISM: If one takes a rock record intended to be played at 33 rpm, and slows it down to 7 to 14 rpm and plays it backward, one hears an oath to Satan in English. We are losing our youth which has been immersed in this American, Zionist anticulture. In Leningrad alone there are 2,500 discothèques. In a shop on Nevsky Prospect [Leningrad's most famous street] a picture by Sazhin is shown with the devil as the main hero. In the watch shop Omega, also on Nevsky Prospect, many watches with a golden star of David are displayed.

ABOUT YOGA: They want to sell us a great deal of Yoga inspiration. What has it in common with the very rich historical tradition of our people? It is just another stratagem to infiltrate surrogates of Western culture.

Vasiliev's speeches were exceedingly restrained as far as the Communist party was concerned. He identified himself as a "nonparty Bolshevik"; he had only praise for Lenin, Stalin, the Soviet armed and security forces, and the then leadership. As an example of the positive attitude of the Communist leadership toward the Russian national tradition, Vasiliev quoted Lenin's order of May 17, 1918, giving instructions to repair the Vladimir Gates in the Kremlin, and the Kremlin in general. In conversation with Lunacharsky, Lenin said that it was "absolutely vital that the basic pillars of our culture should not collapse." As for Stalin, he had called all Russians brothers and sisters in his famous radio speech of July 1941; he had invoked Alexander Nevsky, Kutuzov, Suvorov, and the other military heroes of the Russian past.[6]

Pamyat professed to assist Gorbachev and the Politburo in the struggle

6. Speech in Leningrad (1986). See Semen Reznik, *Krasnoye i korichnevoye* (Washington, D.C., 1992), pp. 199 ff.

for reform. The church was hardly mentioned except for occasional references to its patriotic role in the past, and the monarchy did not figure at
all. A change in this respect came only in 1989–1990 when Vasiliev's
Pamyat gradually dissociated itself from the Communist party and its
ideology and embraced the Orthodox church and monarchism with great
enthusiasm. Its anti-Semitism remained the keystone of its doctrine, but
since the *Protocols* were no longer Pamyat's monopoly, and since everyone
on the extreme right had read them by then, Pamyat had to look for new
ideas.

The anti-alcohol struggle, which had figured so prominently during the
early days, was virtually dropped. The party leadership had adopted the
same line, and the cause had not proved to be popular.

However, the main danger to the cohesion of Pamyat came not from
the outside but from within its own ranks. Two leading early members, the
brothers Vyacheslav and Evgeni Popov, were ousted in 1987 "because of
their activities intended to undermine Pamyat's unity." Internal dissent
came into the open with a demonstration by Pamyat members on the eve
of the anniversary of the battle of Kulikovo at Radonezh (now Gorodok)
and the attempt to put up a sculpture by a patriotic artist. Some five
hundred members took part in the demonstration, which was stopped by
strong militia forces. Vasiliev had been against this show of strength but was
apparently overruled. The Radonezh demonstration was headed by Igor
Sychev, one of Vasiliev's chief rivals. Sychev and some hundred supporters
also put a wreath at the Minin and Pozharsky statue in Moscow and staged
a demonstration at Red Square, in the course of which Sychev publicly
declared that Vasiliev was a *samosvanets*—an impostor.

Vasiliev countered with an unexpected diplomatic initiative; he suggested to the informal democratic groups of the left a common declaration
against the defamation of dissidents of the left *and* right in the Soviet and
Western media. At the same time, anti-Semitism, Zionism, and fascism
were to be denounced. But the democrats were not interested.[7]

Also at this time Vasiliev mobilized a number of leading Pamyat figures
to sign a long manifesto entitled "Purification." He began with the usual
conjuring up of dangers: International Zionist capital was trying by every
possible means to transform the Russian people into the slaves of Zionist
scoundrels and greedy speculators. Owing to the actions of Pamyat, which
had arisen from the depths of the Russian people, there was now a force
that could thwart these evil designs. But unfortunately, all kinds of villains,
having emerged within the ranks of Pamyat, were trying to split the

7. Pribylovsky, p. 7.

movement and were, consciously or unconsciously, working for Zionism.

The list of these villains was long. It included not only the brothers Popov, but also Lipatnikov in Sverdlovsk, who had established himself as the head of a Siberian movement. Particularly dangerous rivals were Riverov and Lysenko, the leaders of a Leningrad group called Pamyat-3, who had been quite successful in arranging a series of mass demonstrations in Rumyantsev Square. All Riverov really desired was to study moviemaking in Paris, and he wanted to arrive in the French capital a famous man, not a nobody. Last there was Pamyat-2, the Sychev faction. With the help of some early supporters of Pamyat, such as G. Frygin, Sychev had established a group in Moscow that was more moderate and acceptable to the authorities. Their main exploit was the attempt to persuade the son of the famous singer Fyodor Shalyapin, who had come to Moscow for a short visit, to become an honorary member of Pamyat-2.[8]

The "Purification" manifesto is of some historical interest. While Vasiliev's group continued to be quite active on various levels, the issuance of the manifesto was almost the last time that he could mobilize a number of militants and intellectuals, who soon after went their own ways. Alexander Dugin and Gaidar Jemal resurfaced as ideologues of the New Right in the weeklies *Den* and *Politika;* Barkashov left to found his own political party and publish his own writings.[9]

To retrace all the splits and mergers that occurred on the extreme right would be nearly impossible; they were as frequent as those on the left. Splits occurred for a great variety of reasons, personal and ideological, and there was no Hitler or Mussolini on the political horizon in 1988–1989 capable of uniting the various sects.

Among the leaders were some extraordinary characters, none more so than Valery Emelyanov, an Orientalist by training, whose VASAMF (the Russian abbreviation for Global Anti-Zionist and Anti-Masonic Front) predates Pamyat; it was first mentioned in a book by Emelyanov published in Paris in 1979. (The book, entitled *Dezionization,* was also brought out in a big printing in Arabic in Damascus). The novelty in Emelyanov's message was that Christianity was a Zionist sect, that Jesus Christ had been a Freemason and that Prince Vladimir (who had brought Christianity to Russia) was the son of a Jewish woman and the grandson of a rabbi.

In 1980 Emelyanov was arrested and a Moscow court found him guilty of having killed his wife, Tamara. Having cut her to pieces, he asked a friend named Bakirov to help him burn a big bag, which, he told Bakirov,

---

8. *Vechernaya Moskva* (April 9, 1988); *Moskovskaya pravda* (April 17, 1988).

9. *Russkii vestnik,* 10 (1991). He is the author of a pamphlet: "Era rossii," (samizdat, 1991).

contained Zionist literature. Disposing of the corpse was more difficult than Emelyanov had assumed; the next day the police appeared, the body was found, and Emelyanov was arrested. In September 1980 the case came to a Moscow court; Emelyanov argued throughout the trial that the Zionists had killed his wife, a story that was not accepted even by his own lawyer. Tamara's mother, a simple woman, asked, "Why kill her but not him?" The trial certainly did not shed much light on the whole affair; Bakirov, the prime witness, could not be found. Later it became known that he was an employee of the KGB.

Something had obviously gone wrong, but Emelyanov had powerful protectors. While the prosecutor had asked that Emelyanov be convicted of murder with aggravating circumstances, the court had Emelyanov committed to a mental institution, the famous Serbsky Clinic. Within a few years he was a free man again; his release came without the knowledge of either the Serbsky Clinic or the Ministry of Health.[10]

Emelyanov joined Pamyat almost immediately after his release in 1987 and was among its main speakers on various occasions. However, the old Pamyat members, including Vasiliev, rejected Emelyanov's demands for a leading role, and Emelyanov's paganist slogans collided with Pamyat's increasingly Orthodox orientation. Eventually Emelyanov proved to be too extreme even for the neopagans and he was excluded from their community in 1990.

In 1991, Emelyanov's Pamyat consisted of a few dozen followers; they established a military sports club in Moscow but were, on the whole, not much in evidence. For a number of years A. Dobrovolsky had been Emelyanov's deputy. He had begun his political career as a member of a democratic dissident group (headed by Galanskov and Ginsberg) but, as it appeared at the trial, either had been an informer all along or had decided in prison to cooperate with the KGB. His evidence helped to send his comrades to prison for long terms. After his release he turned to the extreme right and was the author of the widely circulated samizdat articles "The Victims of the Dark Forces," "The Alchemy of the Spirit" and "Aroma Yoga."[11]

Some observers of the extreme right-wing scene have argued that strictly speaking VASAMF was not a Russian movement since it fought for the liberation of all mankind from the "Jewish yoke," and its program devoted more attention to the Arabs (specifically, the PLO) than to Russian

10. S. Reznik, who was present at the trial has described the circumstances in considerable detail. *Krasnoye i korichnevoye*, pp. 47–82.

11. Pribylovsky, p. 48; Solovei, p. 24.

concerns. Foreign political initiatives and foreign money may well have been involved in the emergence and survival of this as well as some other factions.

It is exceedingly difficult to generalize about Pamyat, partly in view of the many splits, but mainly because it wanted to be a movement rather than a political party with a detailed, specific program. As Vasiliev wrote on one occasion: A popular movement should not have a political program because a spiritual renaissance is not predominantly political in character.[12] He could have added that a specific sociopolitical platform was bound to limit the mass appeal of such a movement. Its violent attacks against Jews and Freemasons were sufficient to give Pamyat its particular character and a reservoir of goodwill. To this one could add certain ecological concerns; everyone was in favor of cleaner air and water, or at least pretended to be. Furthermore, there was Pamyat's preoccupation with the traditional heroes of Russian history, from Alexander Nevsky to Stolypin, and its opposition to the "Americanization" of Russian culture and to other "alien influences." But these catchwords were common to the whole Russian right.

A specific political position was Pamyat's opposition to the war in Afghanistan, characterized as "criminal."[13] But not much daring was needed to voice such a demand in December 1987, when everyone knew that the war was deeply unpopular, that the political leadership was trying hard to extricate the country, and that the end of the war was only a matter of time.

The deliberate vagueness of Pamyat can be noted throughout its history, beginning with its friendly attitude toward the Soviet system and the Communist party. Such an attitude neutralized the authorities and made it easier to gain at least indirect support from some leading intellectuals.

When well-known writers such as Rasputin, Proskurin, and Belov were asked about their attitude toward Pamyat, they made it known that while they were not members and did not accept all its views or approve all its actions, they believed that Pamyat engaged in positive activities and should not be dismissed as a fascist, purely negative force, as the liberals claimed it was.[14]

The liberals insisted on strong action by the authorities under paragraph 74 of the Soviet Criminal Code ("incitement to racial hatred"). But

---

12. Vasiliev interview in *Znamya kommunizma* (September 9, 1988).

13. *Vozvanie patrioticheskovo obedineniya Pamyat* (samizdat, December 1987); Archiv *Samizdat,* Radio Liberty, Munich AC G138.

14. V. Kozhinov, *Nash sovremennik,* 10 (1987); Rasputin speech in Gorky, 1988.

the nearest Vasiliev's Pamyat ever got to official sanctions was a warning by the KGB on May 28, 1988, in connection with his "antisocial activities, which could provoke national strife."[15]

For some time after that date Pamyat concentrated on cultural activities in the tradition of its early work: restoration of several Moscow monasteries and cemeteries, such as the Donskoi Monastir, the Starosimonovsky, the Tolgsky, and the Holy Danilov. At about the same time several Pamyat members established an agricultural cooperative somewhere in the Yaroslavl district, raising swine and organic vegetables.[16] In later years it was argued that Pamyat's Moscow activities were financed by the Yaroslavl cooperative, but this was not widely given credence.

While foreign correspondents' interest in Pamyat did not abate, there was growing unrest in its own ranks. For the mainline Russian nationalists, Vasiliev was too extreme; for the lunatic fringe he was not radical enough. The break with the Leningrad branch was followed by further splits in Moscow. A group of Moscow militants headed by a physician named Filimonov excluded Vasiliev from their ranks in October 1989 because of "moral turpitude, financial machinations, and ideological deviations." The "ideological" charges referred to a seminar run by Dugin and Jemal ("rascals and Satanists") on nonreligious lines. Their doctrine was said to be offensive in spirit to Orthodox believers. Behind Filimonov there was apparently a somewhat mysterious personality named Viktor Antonov, an astrologer by profession, who was formerly Vasiliev's personal adviser.[17]

These were difficult days for the Vasilievites. The intellectuals left Pamyat; Jemal realized, albeit somewhat belatedly, that there was no room for a Muslim in a movement that had become increasingly Pravoslav in character. He went on to become a leading activist in the Muslim community, appearing as an apologist for Saddam Hussein. His colleague Dugin, as mentioned elsewhere, discovered the intellectual riches of the French *Nouvelle Droite*.

Vasiliev's group was reduced to a few dozen members, and the Filimonovites seemed to have carried the day. In January 1989 they published a detailed political-social-economic manifesto in samizdat, which seemed to show few differences with Pamyat-1, except that it was far more detailed than anything Vasiliev had ever written. But this manifesto became an embarrassment when two Soviet writers discovered that large sections had been lifted from the program of the German National Socialist Workers

15. *Argumenty i fakty*, 28 (1988).

16. Solovei, p. 42.

17. Solovei, p.51.

party.[18] According to some sources the author of the manifesto was young Viktor Yakushev. His name has already been mentioned in another context; later on, in the fall of 1990, he became the leader of an openly national-socialist group in Moscow, the National Socialist Union.[19]

Yet another splinter group ought to be mentioned, because though small it was to cause a major scandal that one way or another was to affect the whole Russian right. Konstantin Smirnov-Ostashvili, a Moscow factory foreman, had left Pamyat-1 in late 1987. He complained that while Vasiliev was always babbling a great deal, his group was short on action; Vasiliev advised his followers to wait and meanwhile he himself had become a millionaire.[20]

Smirnov-Ostashvili wanted action, and together with a small band of followers he founded the "Union for National Proportional Representation–Pamyat." Their program ran in brief as follows: since only 0.69 percent of Russia's population was Jewish, Jews' part in every profession should not exceed this ratio.[21] Furthermore, all half-Jews should be considered Jews.[22] The Smirnov-Ostashvili group threatened Soviet Jews with a giant pogrom, and it demanded that Jewish emigration stop immediately so that Jews could not escape just judgment. (On other occasions the group was willing to accept a Jewish exodus if world Jewry paid 100,000 rubles for each individual.) The manifesto further demanded an increase in the budget of the KGB and the rehabilitation of Emelyanov, who had unjustly been accused of killing his wife. Emelyanov was grateful for such support and remained a loyal supporter of Smirnov-Ostashvili during the latter's trial, long after other leading members of the extreme right had dropped him.

Fame came to Smirnov-Ostashvili following a raid by his followers on January 18, 1990, when they tried to break up a meeting of the liberal writers' group April in the Central Writers' Building. Some thirty or forty hooligans burst into the hall, threatened those present with dire consequences, and announced that they would be back. The glasses of an elderly writer were smashed. The police arrived—as usual in such cases—after

18. E. Proshechkin and V. Todres in *Sovetskii tsirk,* 29 (1989).

19. Solovei, p. 57.

20. From the stenograph of a press conference. Mark Deich and Leonid Zhuravlev, *Pamyat kak ona yest* (Moscow, 1991), p. 95.

21. The manifesto appeared in *Russkoye voskresenie,* 2 (1990).

22. Smirnov-Ostashvili, as the name conveys, is not of Russian stock. The same might be true with regard to Vasiliev, who always refused to give his true patronym "because his father's family underwent very cruel persecution." Interview with Surah Chavchavadze, *Kav kasioni,* 2 (1990).

considerable delay. A few of the assailants were arrested and were released
after their identity had been established.

Much publicity was given to the incident, which, it soon emerged, had
not been a spontaneous outburst but carefully planned. The writers lodged
an official complaint, but General Karabainov, a KGB spokesman, said that
he did not think that the case should be brought to court. This fueled the
anger of the liberal writers, who proceeded to attack the ideological wire-
pullers behind Smirnov-Ostashvili.

The right, on the other hand, ridiculed the whole affair: Why make a
mountain out of a molehill? After all, Smirnov-Ostashvili was a man of no
consequence. And no one had come to grief, whereas in the clashes in
Central Asia and the Caucasus dozens of people had been killed. There
were insinuations that April had somehow staged the incident. Spokesmen
for the liberals countered, arguing that it was a case of routine Russian
fascism (Starovoitova) and that unless one resisted such beginnings the
attacks would escalate. All fascist movements started in a small way, said the
liberals, not with a "march on Rome."

Smirnov-Ostashvili's own journal described the sequence of events as
follows: A hungry worker (Smirnov-Ostashvili) had strayed into the building, and became very angry on seeing plenty of delicious food not elsewhere available.[23] Later on, Smirnov-Ostashvili had yet another explanation: He was one of Moscow's leading and most effective polemicists. He
would show the liberals that even a YEvtushenko could not stand up to him
in a debate for more than three minutes.

Eventually, on July 24, the trial started, in a Moscow court. It was to
last ten weeks. Smirnov-Ostashvili emerged as a man of great self-confi-
dence and limited intelligence. He asked first that a lawyer from Germany
(*any* lawyer from Germany) should represent him; later he argued that only
Kurt Waldheim could understand him and should be invited. Then he
suddenly disappeared, to be arrested two weeks later in a barbershop. When
judgment was passed he refused to acknowledge the ruling because the
Soviet Union was an "occupied country."[24]

The trial was given wide coverage in the foreign press, because groups
of Smirnov-Ostashvili's opponents, including several writers, appeared in
the courthouse almost daily; his supporters demonstrated and distributed
their literature in front of it. It was an ideal spot to get acquainted with the
views of the extreme right. In fact, the trial brought out little that was new
to students of the fringe groups. Smirnov-Ostashvili had made his position

23. *Russkoye voskresenie,* 5 (1990).

24. Details about the trial in Deich and Zhuravlev, *Pamyat,* passim.

clear in several long interviews even before the trial had started: Vasiliev was a puppet and a crook; the time for discussions with the liberals was over. His group did not want to stage pogroms against the Jews but merely to bring them to trial for their crimes against the Russian people.[25]

The extreme right called the trial a farce but was lukewarm in its support for the defendant. Only one of the Pamyat splinter groups (headed by Alexander Kulakov and by Svezhnikov) sent uniformed squads to demonstrate. Other leading figures on the extreme right were reticent; Smirnov-Ostashvili was clearly an embarrassment. As a Moscow newspaper wrote, not only the leading patriotic spokesmen but even the rest of Pamyat distanced itself from him like the "devil whenever he smelled incense."[26] Smirnov-Ostashvili's own friends complained that only the Pamyat newspaper in Novosibirsk, *Situatsia, Vokresenie,* and the National Bolsheviks of *Molodaya gvardiya* supported him; the rest of the "patriotic" press was silent. Some newspapers, such as *Veteran* and *Moskovskii literator,* even implied that he was a provocateur, possibly of Jewish extraction.[27] (Smirnov-Ostashvili's grandmother was named Stoltenberg—a German, not a Jewish name.)

On October 12, 1990, Ostashvili was given a two-year sentence. He was sent to a labor camp and according to prevailing custom he would have been a free man within some nine or twelve months. He boasted that under his influence, the whole camp, including its administration would turn "patriotic" within six months. However, on April 26, 1991, he hanged himself in the camp. It was reported that he had committed suicide because of general dejection or because some of his fellow inmates had made jokes about his allegedly Jewish extraction. Others predictably argued that it was a clear case of "Zionist ritual murder" and that the writers of April were the assassins.[28] After all, it was no accident that he had died in the month of April. . . . Smirnov-Ostashvili's followers demanded that the legal authorities should launch an investigation. There was an investigation, but its results were not made public. Thus, the activities of Smirnov-Ostashvili, like those of the rest of Pamyat, remain shrouded in mystery. Smirnov-Ostashvili frequently boasted that he had close links with the KGB; but so did the leaders of other right-wing factions, and his may have been empty boasts.

If Smirnov-Ostashvili was indeed murdered, it is unlikely that politics

25. *Megapolis express* (July 24, 1990).

26. *Vechernaya Moskva* (October 12, 1990).

27. *Veteran,* 38 (1990); *Istoki,* 4 (July 1991).

28. *Istoki,* 4 (July 1991).

was involved, for this unhinged man had clearly done more harm than good to his cause. He had not been an asset but an embarrassment to the far right.

Last, yet another Pamyat faction ought to be mentioned. In 1987, when Smirnov-Ostashvili left Vasiliev's group in disgust, the artist Igor Sychev also seceded with several of his followers. Sychev's group constituted perhaps the most serious competition to Vasiliev's. While the other factions concentrated on composing leaflets—or, in Vasiliev's case, on giving interviews to the press—Sychev's group frequently appeared in the streets of Moscow between 1988 and 1990. They put wreaths on the grave of General Brusilov, of First World War fame. They volunteered to do restoration work on various cemeteries. They broke up the election meeting of Vitaly Korotich, the editor of *Ogonyok*, and on several occasions they demonstrated in Ostankino, in front of the Soviet television studios, which they had named "Tel Avidenie" a pun on *televidenie*, "television."[29] Altogether they engaged in some ninety actions, including memorial meetings for the family of the last tsar and protest meetings against the growing anti-Russian sentiment in the Baltic countries.

The ideology of the Sychevites was, to put it mildly, eclectic. They demonstrated in favor of the last tsar but also in favor of Stalin. They concentrated their attacks against "red Zionism" (i.e., Marxism) rather than against Judeo-Masonic plotters.[30] Gradually Sychev (like Vasiliev) moved from National Bolshevism to the concept of a "people's monarchy." Certain party circles clearly preferred the Sychevites to all other Pamyat factions, and articles to that effect appeared in the media.[31]

In the autumn of 1990 Sychev suddenly appeared at a reception arranged by the Moscow Jewish community and declared that his group was neither fascist nor anti-Semitic and had nothing whatsoever against Jews.[32] In an interview with the widely read magazine *Kommersant* he said that "we now begin to understand that Zionism aims above all at establishing a Jewish state in Israel"—and that his group had nothing whatsoever against this endeavor. Furthermore, it was wrong to think that the Jews were guilty of all crimes, such as the murder of the tsar's family and the genocide of the Russian people. After all, there were many Jews and

29. Solovei, p. 72; S. Reznik, *Krasnoye*, pp. 152–89. Interview in *Nedelya*, 12 (1990).

30. Various samizdat leaflets and *Osnovnye polozhenya* of the RNDF (Russkii Narodni Demokraticheskii Front—Dvizhenie Pamyat: the official name of the Sychevites).

31. This distinction was not accepted by the liberals. *Stolitsa*, 38 (1991).

32. D. Radyshevsky, *Moskovskie novosti*, 42 (1990)

Zionists in the White movement.[33] But this sudden and astonishing turn did not last long; in the following year there were again anti-Jewish demonstrations. What did not change was the enmity between Sychev and Vasiliev. Vasiliev not only imputed to his rival Jewish grandfathers and grandmothers, he also maintained that Sychev was a relation of Trotsky. For Sychev, Vasiliev was an agent provocateur, not a bona fide patriotic militant.

After the crisis of 1989, when the Vasiliev group was near extinction, Pamyat-1 recovered surprisingly quickly, whereas some of its rivals disappeared from the scene. The Smirnov-Ostashvili group vanished after the death of its leader; Alexander Kulakov, who had staunchly supported Smirnov-Ostashvili, first decided to drop the name "Pamyat" and then, at least temporarily, embraced Buddhism. Filimonov first retired to work in a monastery and graveyards and then decided to found yet another short-lived right-wing journal called *Polozhenie del.*

This left the field open for Vasiliev and to a lesser degree for Sychev, both of whom moved toward the monarchist idea and the church. It is difficult to judge whether their conversion to monarchism was genuine; it is virtually certain that the rapprochements with the church were tactical maneuvers, since neither of the two leaders was a pious Christian. The Vasilievites assumed that in the church they would at least find some protectors and, more important, a promising recruiting ground. Even those church leaders who had their doubts about Pamyat or even rejected it would find it difficult openly to condemn these neophytes, second to none in their Orthodox zeal, always willing to provide black-uniformed youngsters for guard duty at church processions and other such occasions. Black, Vasiliev said, was the color of mourning in Russia; it had, apparently, nothing to do with the Italian blackshirts, the German SS, or Mosley's British fascists. However, the Vasilievites also adorned themselves with all kinds of belts, insignia, and jackboots that had nothing to do with mourning.

The new Pamyat journal, also named *Pamyat,* which began to appear in 1990, reflected the new doctrine both in its outward form and in its contents.[34] The outward form was extraordinary, because this was the only journal in Russia using the old, pre-1917 orthography. As *Pamyat* explained, according to the teachings of the Orthodox church only the old orthography was the right one. But since official church publications used the "new" orthography and showed no intention even under *glasnost* of

---

33. *Kommersant,* 18 (1991).

34. Four issues of samizdat *Pamyat* were published in 1990, later on two of a more substantial, officially registered journal. The circulation was allegedly 100,000 in 1991, but there is reason to believe that many, probably most, copies were given away.

returning to the pre-1917 style, the explanation was not quite convincing.[35]

New-*Pamyat* doctrine combined many references to church holidays, saints, and general religious affairs. The name of Nikolai II, the Martyr Tsar, was frequently mentioned, and *Pamyat*'s attachment to the concept of a monarchy was stressed. A new Russian monarch was to be named by a general assembly, a *sobor,* similar to the assembly of boyars that had elected Mikhail Romanov in 1613. Since Pamyat was in principle opposed to democracy, *Pamyat* avoided the term "elected" whenever possible. *Pamyat* did not clarify the identity of the new monarch it wanted, except that it opposed the pretender Vladimir Kyrillovich Romanov. The tsar was to be someone worthy of the position—probably someone like Dmitri Vasiliev.

At the same time, the attacks against the world Jewish and Masonic conspiracy continued, but they took second place to the new, "positive" content of Pamyat doctrine.[36] Furthermore, new enemies appeared, such as the separatists in Georgia and elsewhere, who had to be singled out and unmasked.[37]

Altogether, the new *Pamyat* made a very old-fashioned impression both outwardly and as far as substance was concerned. The impression was created that the editors had not enough material to fill the sixteen pages at their disposal; they featured old speeches and articles that had appeared many years ago and all kind of symbolic drawings to cover the empty spaces.

By 1991 Pamyat had not only an official organ but even a small radio station, which started one-hour evening broadcasts on September 30, 1991. How were these activities financed and to what extent did they enlarge Pamyat's appeal? The answer to the first question is not known. According to the official version, the Pamyat "kibbutz" near Yaroslavl had contributed half a million rubles annually to the group's budget, but even if that was true, this sum was hardly sufficient to keep a radio station on the air and to cover the losses involved. Pamyat's attitude toward the army and the KGB was positive: "We must not destroy them." It seems more than likely that at least some assistance had come from these quarters on past occasions.[38]

35. "K voprosu o staroi i novoi orfografii," *Pamyat,* 1 (1991).

36. For examples of anti-Semitic attacks, see "Obrashenie" (samizdat, June 1990); excerpts from the *Protocols* and anti-Semitic cartoons in *Pamyat,* 2 (1991).

37. *Pamyat,* 1 (1991), p. 13.

38. Interview in TV documentary *Passport* (Averbukh, April 1992). According to the KGB colonel in charge of "Zionist" affairs, most Pamyat leaders had been recruited by his organization.

Despite the growth of the Pamyat publicity machine, the group's impact did not become substantially larger. In 1987–1988 it had had a near monopoly on the extreme right; its demonstrations were considered daring by some, shocking and scandalous by others. By 1991 there was enormous competition on the extreme right, and the old magic of the name "Pamyat" ceased to function; the media's interest also declined. But Vasiliev did not give up. When the "Congress of Civic and Patriotic Organizations" was convened in Moscow in February 1992, he gate-crashed it with his followers (he had not been invited), and compelled the organizers to let him speak.[39] But Vasiliev's message was not in any significant way different from the other speakers': The situation was bad and getting worse; a strong hand was needed to lead the country out of its crisis. When subsequently it came to clashes between Pamyat and the followers of some Pamyat renegades also present at the congress, the Cossacks acting as guardians of the peace had to intervene, separating the warring factions with their whips.

Pamyat had not only lost its monopoly, it had been outflanked. Vasiliev's old rival Emelyanov had appointed himself head of a "global Russian government" on December 21, 1991, expressing his willingness to collaborate with the Russian president and his government "while not shying away" from a confrontation with them.[40] Emelyanov, needless to say, was not a serious competitor, but the many other new patriotic organizations had overtaken Pamyat as far as the favors and the interest of the right-wing public were concerned. However, Emelyanov was not the only one to establish himself as an alternative ruler. The "Russian party" went him one better and announced the formation of a new Russian government including General Filatov and Fomichev, the editor of *Puls tushina*.[41] The Pamyat faithful rightly felt aggrieved that their historical merits were not appreciated. But there is little gratitude in politics, and instead of finding some honorary place for Vasiliev and his group, the new wave of "patriotic" organizations regarded Pamyat as a political embarrassment; the very name "Pamyat" was to be eschewed because it had negative connotations.

39. *Novoye russkoye slovo* (February 14, 1992). Rutskoi, the Russian vice president, appeared on this occasion and received a strong ovation. The meeting had reportedly been financed by the Russian commodities and raw-material stock exchange. See also T. Yakhiakova in *Moskovskie novosti*, 5 (1992).

40. *Nezavisimaya gazeta* (February 1, 1992). Perhaps to outflank his old rival, Vasiliev countered by calling for violent action against the government. *Vechernaya Moskva* (March 20, 1992). On other occasions (*Den* 11 [1992]) the intention was to create the impression that Pamyat consisted of moderate monarchists and pious churchgoers and that all other assertions were groundless and "illiterate."

41. *Russkie vedomosti*, 5 (1992).

They would still defend Pamyat against liberal detractors, following the guiding principle "No enemies on the right." But they would keep it at arm's length.

Seen in historical perspective the role of Pamyat was that of a precursor; it was the first in a field that later on became crowded. There was a reservoir of goodwill and support for a movement of this kind, but Pamyat could not make the most of it.[42] The very antics that had helped Vasiliev to attract attention in the early days later made him merely notorious, as he did not succeed in transforming himself into a serious leader and his followers into an acceptable political movement. That was beyond his abilities and vision. Pamyat drew heavily on the Black Hundred tradition, which had been of some use in a country largely politically illiterate, and it did not necessarily need an approach that was more sophisticated; the Zhirinovsky phenomenon showed that primitive clowning and the appeal to base instincts could be quite effective politically. The failure of Pamyat demonstrated that postcommunist groups of the extreme right needed something new in style and content to advance their cause.[43] A rehash of the Black Hundred and the *Protocols* was bound to have only a limited appeal just as Hitler and Mussolini could not act as mentors in a situation that was different in so many respects. The general situation in postcommunist Russia favored the emergence of a strong populist movement gravitating to the far right. But Pamyat was not sufficiently creative to ride the crest of this wave.

42. The candidates supported by Pamyat in the 1989–1990 elections all failed. They could have still comforted themselves with the thought that the tide might turn at some future date.

43. The "respectable right" carefully kept Pamyat out of its major political initiatives such as the "Word to the People," the coup in 1991, and the "National Salvation Front" in 1992. Pamyat reacted by provoking some minor scandals such as the invasion of the offices of the *Moskovski Komsomolets* newspaper. They also set up their own front organization in October 1992, which included a few monarchist sectarians and Averyanov, a priest belonging to the Orthodox Church Abroad. It carried no political weight.

Chapter Fourteen

THE REVIVAL OF THE ORTHODOX CHURCH

ACCORDING TO A PUBLIC-OPINION POLL CARRIED OUT in the Soviet Union in June 1991, 63 percent of those asked expressed their trust in the Russian Orthodox church, as compared with only 18 percent who trusted the Communist party. A few months later the results would have been even more in favor of the church. There was, however, a second question: Are you a believer? Only 8 to 12 percent gave an affirmative answer.[1]

These two sets of figures express in a nutshell the dilemma facing religion in Russia. On the one hand, there is a strong conviction that following the bankruptcy of Communist ideology an alternative source of beliefs and moral values is needed to fill the spiritual void and preserve the fabric of society. But a great majority of Russians still finds it difficult to believe in the Orthodox church in its present form. Most citizens are aware of the danger of a moral void; they know from the history of their country that the church has stood for unity in time of feudal division and has called for resistance against foreign invaders. But it was a different church and a different people in a different age. Much has been written and said about the deep religiosity of the Russian people, and by no one more strongly and frequently than Dostoyevsky: The moral idea was in Christ—specifically, in Orthodox Christianity, because in the West Christ had been distorted and

1. A. Hampel, "Nach dem Martyrium der Lüge," *Frankfurter Allgemeine Zeitung* (December 21, 1991).

diminished. According to Dostoyevsky the profound error of the Russian intelligentsia was not to acknowledge the church in the Russian people.[2] But no one wrote more emphatically about the difficulty of believing—and Dostoyevsky also noted that there was a strong tendency in Russia to reject God with religious intensity.

When the era of reform dawned it was widely believed that the Russian Orthodox church would fill the vacuum created by the demise of communism. But these expectations failed to take into account the enormous cultural and social changes that had taken place under communism. Nor was the church ready for the opportunities that suddenly opened. Great respect was paid to it: The patriarch officiated at the funeral of the victims of the coup of August 1991, and again at the inauguration ceremony when Boris Yeltsin became president of Russia. There was great intellectual curiosity, and hundreds of thousands of copies of the Bible, prayer books, and other religious literature were printed in 1990–1991. Two thousand new churches were opened (or reopened) in 1989 and 1990, but there were not enough priests to officiate. There were doubts—not to put it more strongly—with regard to the competence, the faith, and the general character of some of the priests, high and low, who had graduated from the seminaries under communism.

There were various reasons for the church's failure to attract the masses and become a decisive factor in Russian life. One was the rigidity of the church, its insistence that even the smallest points of ritual were of crucial significance. This had antagonized would-be believers well before the Revolution. Liturgy was more important than mystery, and there was not enough for the heart, for those looking for solace and spiritual comfort. True, there were some laymen in the early years of the century who stood for new directions, such as the pursuit of *sophia*—divine wisdom—and of mysticism.

But the church looked with misgivings on the ideas of these nonconformists. Berdyaev was saved by the Revolution of 1917 from being excommunicated by the church although Bulgakov was by the Karlovats synod in the 1920s. Some have argued that only thanks to its rigidity and opposition to modernistic influences that the church survived under communism; there may be some truth in this contention. But it is also true an approach that had its merits at a time of persecution was of no use after persecution ceased. Yet those who had opposed modernism all along found it difficult, or even impossible, to adapt to new conditions.

There were other factors impeding Orthodoxy in the new era: More

2. K. M. Mochulsky, *Dostoyevsky* (Princeton, N.J., 1971), p. 429.

than seventy years of Soviet rule had enormously weakened the church. Less than 10 percent of the churches that had once existed were still in use, only a handful of monasteries had survived, and the number of priests had been kept to a minimum by the Communist rulers. Great care had been taken that there should be no outstanding, charismatic figures among them. The church had survived, but an enormous price had been paid by way of concessions to the authorities, in sycophancy, in political collaboration and betrayal of what should have been most holy to the church.

It could be argued that there was no other way to survive; and it ill behooves observers in free societies to criticize those acting under constant, relentless, and hostile pressure. But we are concerned not so much with motives and extenuating circumstances, of which there were many, but with consequences. And there can be no doubt that the Orthodox church was deeply compromised.

Some of the main stages in the recent history of the church should be recalled. Patriarch Tikhon was arrested in 1922, thousands of priests were killed or exiled, churches and monasteries destroyed or closed, church property seized. After Tikhon's death Metropolitan Sergei, who eventually became his successor, tried to "normalize" church-state relations. He promised civic loyalty to the Soviets and recognition of the Soviet Union as the "civic motherland": "her happiness, and successes, being our happiness, her misfortunes—our misfortunes."[3] Another church faction, the Living Church, went even further in looking for an accommodation with the Communists. Julius Hecker wrote: "If there exists a possibility of religious revival among the intellectuals of Soviet Russia, it will be inspired by prophets who will arise from the Soviet ranks with a message which will reflect the needs of Soviet culture.[4] The renovationists failed to attract a significant number of believers. Some of them eventually became atheist agitators; others, including Hecker, perished in the purges. One of their spiritual leaders, Metropolitan Nikolai Platonov, had begun his career as a Black Hundred militant, later joined the Living Church, then became an atheist, but on his deathbed apparently returned to the Orthodox church.

Sergei's historical compromise, the "Declaration of Loyalty," was a disaster from the church's point of view. But it was not the failure of one individual church leader. Sergei acted, after all, in good faith, but there is reason to believe that even as far back as the 1920s, some of the clerics around him were secret-police agents. Antireligious persecutions continued

3. D. Pospelovsky, *The Russian Church Under the Soviet Regime, 1917–1982* (Gestwood, 1984), vol. 1, p. 105. Jane Ellis, *The Russian Orthodox Church* (Bloomington, Ind., 1986).

4. J. Hecker, *Religion and Communism* (London, 1933), p. 154.

throughout the 1930s with even greater vigor, and it took the military defeats of 1941 and 1942 to induce Stalin to make some concessions to the church. Sergei became patriarch—the office had been vacant for more than a decade—some churches were reopened, and the patriarchate was even permitted to publish a bulletin. Sergei and a few metropolitans were invited to meet Stalin and Molotov in person. The Soviet leaders were no doubt concerned by information they had received about a religious revival in the occupied areas under Nazi auspices.

What of the Orthodox church abroad? An émigré bishops' synod headed by Metropolitan Antony (Khrapovitsky) in Sremski Karlovski in Yugoslavia had established itself as the supreme authority. It remained there up to the end of the Second World War. It pursued an extreme right-wing line; it excommunicated Sergei Bulgakov, the head of the Paris Theological Seminary (where most of the new theological thinking was taking place) for alleged liberal heresies. Thus, a split occurred with the Russian church in Western Europe which recognized the authority of Metropolitan Evlogi Georgievsky rather than that of Serafim Lukyanov.[5]

The Karlovats policy after the rise of Nazism was predictable—the synod issued calls for full support for Hitler in his endeavor to destroy the Judeo-Masonic regime in the Soviet Union. On occasion they showed zeal beyond the call of perceived duty: World Jewry, they announced at their second *sobor* in 1938, was engaged in subverting the Christian world by organizing the narcotics trade. The synod accused the Catholic church of rapprochement with Judaism, and the German Catholic church (!) of defending the Jews from Hitler and for protesting against anti-Semitism.[6]

After the war, most of them escaped to Western Europe and the United States, where the Karlovats tradition was continued. Some of the most emphatic collaborationists, such as Metropolitan Serafim of Paris, made their peace with Moscow, were forgiven, and returned to the Soviet Union. When it was politically expedient, the Soviets showed a truly astonishing measure of forgiveness.

After the end of the war the church in the Soviet Union came under new pressure despite all manifestations of abject subservience, despite the "Te Deum" services on the anniversary of the October Revolution and on Stalin's birthday. Patriarch Aleksei Simansky advised his priests to keep a very low profile, so as not to provoke new attacks. However, by the early

5. Marc Raeff, *Russia Abroad* (New York, 1990), pp. 123ff.

6. Pospelovsky, *The Russian Church,* vol. 2, p. 266. For the history of the Russian church abroad, Gernot Seide, *Geschichte der Russischen Orthodoxen Kirche im Ausland* (Wiesbaden, 1983), which tends to gloss over the dark pages in the history of the church abroad.

1960s, under Khrushchev, a major new antichurch campaign got under way. Many churches were closed; priests and believers were arrested or beaten up by the police; the new crackdown extended even to a ban on the sale of candles in church. If it had not been for the Politburo's wish to use the church in frequent world peace conferences, even harsher restrictions might have been imposed.

After Khrushchev had been deposed, persecutions eased, but church leaders did not attempt to make use of the slightly greater freedom of action—as other churches, such as the Georgian and the Armenian, did.

When Patriarch Aleksei died in 1970, aged ninety-two, the management of church affairs seems to have been largely in the hands of Daniel Ostapov, his valet. The new patriarch was Pimen (Izvekov); he had been in prison but had also served as a major in the Red Army and was said to have had an (illegitimate) family. He was the least controversial candidate at the time, but he suffered, even according to his supporters and well-wishers, from an excessive fear of the Soviet authorities.[7] Otherwise, it would be difficult to explain the fulsome praise of "Brezhnev, the beloved peacemaker"—after the invasion of Afghanistan. (It ought to be mentioned that individual bishops occasionally took a more independent and courageous line without suffering any significant harm.) After an interregnum following Pimen's death, Aleksei II was elected in 1990.

The Communist leadership undoubtedly wanted the Orthodox church to disappear in the same way as it expected the liquidation of all religious communities. However, it was in no hurry: The church constituted no danger whatsoever to the party's hold over society. The number of churches and priests steadily declined; among the churchgoers there were more old people than young, more women than men, and the marginal sections of Soviet society were more strongly represented than the core. Had the government adopted more stringent measures, it would have driven the church underground and made it more difficult to control. The church was also of some, albeit limited, use as an instrument of Soviet foreign policy: It was needed as a showpiece to demonstrate that the Soviet Union was a democratic state, and that freedom of religion was practiced as promised in the constitution (paragraph 52 of the Constitution of 1977).

Our concern in the present context is not with the fate of the Orthodox church as such under communism, but its role as a national, integrative force and its relationship with the patriotic movement. Prior to *perestroika* Russian nationalists, by and large, showed only limited interest in religion. True, there were Christian believers among the dissenters of the right, and

7. Pospelovsky, *The Russian Church,* vol 2, p. 391.

also among those in the political mainstream. Even the nonbelievers among the nationalists did not denigrate or deny the role of the Orthodox church in Russian history. But if they protested, to give an example, against the destruction of a church, their concern was with the building qua historical monument rather than qua house of God. Most nationalists writing in *Nash sovremennik* tended toward National Bolshevism rather than the spiritual message of Orthodoxy. Perhaps they thought that an excess of patriotism might be treated with greater leniency by the authorities than a religious-nationalist deviation. With some notable exceptions, such as Solzhenitsyn, Shafarevich, Soloukhin, and Osipov, the nationalist camp rediscovered the church as an ally only after 1987.

The Orthodox church, on the other hand, was strictly limited by the authorities to a small part of its original ministry. Just as it was not permitted to engage in missionary or evangelical activity or to care for the needy, it was not allowed to take a political stand even if this coincided wholly or in part with Communist policy. Orthodox priests felt, no doubt, some degree of sympathy with the nationalists and conservatives, and they may have secretly hoped for a national revival, which would give them greater freedom one day. But they were not permitted to take any such initiative.

This, in very broad outline, was the situation of the church on the eve of the reform era, which opened entirely new prospects to it but also confronted it with unforeseen dangers.

Schism?

Like all other religions the Russian Orthodox church has been subject to schisms, and it came as no surprise that under *glasnost* more splits were to occur. The Ukrainian Orthodox church asserted its autonomy in 1989, the year after the first community affiliated with the Russian Church Abroad established itself in Suzdal. Following the emergence of more such communities in other cities in European and Asian Russia, an umbrella organization named the Free Orthodox church emerged. These developments created much concern among the leadership of the Russian Orthodox church and also among prominent laymen. Aleksei II, the patriarch, said in an interview that the schism was the most serious problem facing his church.[8] Several leading writers, including Belov, Rasputin, and Shafarevich, published a manifesto in which they said that while it was not up to

8. Interview, *Russkii vestnik,* 31 (1991).

them to interfere in church affairs, neither could they keep silent in view of events that were tragic and possibly irreversible. The differences between the churches were not insurmountable: The liturgy was the same; so were the body and blood of Christ and the unavoidable day of judgment. But if the Church Abroad persevered in its negative attitude toward the Moscow patriarchate, forbidding Moscow's parishioners to receive the Eucharist, the conflict would lead to mutual accusations and excommunications.[9]

Archpriest Lebedev, a spokesman for the Free Orthodox church, replied that unity could not be forced at the cost of the betrayal of truth. The critics had shown insensitivity to divine truth; they should not have protested against the Free Orthodox church but should have demanded that the whole Moscow episcopate go into retirement.[10]

Despite the appeals for reconciliation the splits continued and became even more acute. The rivals seized each other's churches and properties; they interrupted church services; in some cases the dispute led to physical violence, in others courts had to decide between rival claims.[11] The priest Gleb Yakunin was denounced as an accursed "Judeo-Mason" (the weekly *Den* even called him a crypto-Hasid) and it was suggested that as an agent of the CIA he should transfer his activities to Israel. Other Orthodox priests, on the other hand, were denounced as veteran servants of the KGB.

The first known clash occurred in Kashira, a regional center near Moscow, where the local authorities, following the intervention of Metropolitan Juvenal, a key figure in the Russian Orthodox church, decided against the claims of the schismatics. At Suzdal the Free Orthodox church community was more successful and kept its church despite its secession from the Moscow patriarchate.[12] By the end of 1991 there were some forty Free Orthodox communities from St. Petersburg in the West to Barnaul in the East. Several dissident priests were elected to the Soviet parliament.

What were the bones of contention between the two churches? Some were of no great consequence. In 1981 the Russian Church Abroad had canonized Tsar Nikolai II and his family. This was, of course, unacceptable in Russia under communism. Ten years later the Russian Orthodox church was perfectly willing to follow suit, even though from a canonical point of view such a step was highly doubtful: Nikolai II had not died a martyr for the faith, nor had he produced any miracles. In any case, at its convention

9. "Ne dopustit raskola," *Moskva*, 3 (1991).

10. "Pisately, chto vy pishete?" *Pravoslavnaya Rus*, 14 (1991).

11. N. Babasyan, *Novoye russkoye slovo* (January 2, 1992).

12. About Kashira, *Moskovskie novosti*, 50 (1990); about Suzdal, *Moskovskie novosti*, 22 (1991); see also *Pravoslavnaya Rus*, in 1991, passim.

in April 1992 the Orthodox church decided to initiate the steps that would lead to the canonization of the tsar and his family.

Some of the Free Orthodox Church's accusations against the Russian Orthodox church were demagogic and untrue. The latter was allegedly collaborating with the World Council of Churches in an endeavor to "unite all heresies and religions," thus surrendering its own major tenets.[13]

"Ecumenism" is one of the cardinal heresies as far as Orthodox fundamentalists are concerned, and insufficient anti-Catholic and anti-Protestant zeal has always been a major sin in their eyes. With other charges against the Moscow patriarchate they were on safer ground. They cited "Sergeianism," the Russian church's policy, dating from 1927, of collaborating with the Communist leadership and praying for it. The Russian Orthodox church argued that Sergei, acting under duress, only followed the example of the Apostles, rendering unto Caesar the things that were Caesar's and unto God the things that were God's (Matthew 22:21 and Mark 12:17). They argued furthermore that out of 150 bishops who resided in Russia at the time, only thirty-five disagreed with Sergei (Stragorodsky), metropolitan of Nizhni Novgorod, who was at the time acting patriarch.

They argued furthermore that other Orthodox churches behaved exactly the same way, for instance under Nazi rule. But it was precisely in this context that the Russian church's arguments were most vulnerable. For the "things that were Caesar's" were, of course, infinitely more far-reaching in a totalitarian regime than in any other.

If the Free Orthodox Church gained some sympathy in view of its struggle against the Russian church, which was reluctant to dismiss even the most blatant collaborators from its ranks, its position was damaged as the result of the activities of the most senior cleric in its ranks. Archbishop Lazar had been the priest Konstantin Vasiliev until he appointed himself head of a "truly Russian church"—the "Catacomb church"—and archbishop of Moscow and Kashira. Lazar paid an "official visit" to the right-wing weekly *Den* in early 1992, in the course of which the usual invocations of the *Protocols*, the Masons, and the Satanists were made. He went on saying that though he came from a (nonbelieving) family of the intelligentsia and had graduated from a university, he was not an alcoholic, whereas the great majority of the priests of the Moscow patriarchate were

---

13. *Nash sovremennik*, 12 (1990); it later appeared in the *Journal of the Moscow Patriarchate*, 2 (1991). It is surprising that this important message of the ROC appeared in a lay journal before it was published by the official organ of the Moscow patriarchate. This message was a reply to an epistle by the Orthodox Church Abroad which had been signed by Metropolitan Vitaly of New York as well as the archbishops of Los Angeles and San Francisco and the bishop of Berlin and Germany.

heavy drinkers.[14] They also were corrupt, so was the Russian intelligentsia and society in general.

While Lazar invoked the authority of Christ, on several occasions he also based himself on the teachings of Hinduism concerning karma. His appearance left the impression of a man whose mental balance was less than complete. This was pointed out in an open letter by a group of prominent Orthodox laymen, again including Rasputin and the inevitable Shafarevich. They were bothered, it appeared, less by the archbishop's Black Hundred views than by his unbridled attacks against the Orthodox church.[15] They pointed out that it was by no means clear by what right Lazar spoke on behalf of the Catacomb (True) Church.[16] Before 1986 there had been a handful of "passportless Christians," some inside the gulag, a few outside. But there was no reason to assume that "Archbishop" Lazar had been among them—unlike, for instance, the priests Dudko and Yakunin, who had spent many years in a camp. Some thought Lazar intentionally fraudulent, but it was also possible that he was manipulated by (to use Russian right-wing language) "sinister forces."[17]

Next Archbishop Lazar made a dramatic appearance in Moscow at the founding meeting of Otchizna, one of the National Bolshevik and military groups that mushroomed at the time. "There are so many clever people here," he declared. "Why don't we simply seize power?" There was stormy applause; the priest then went on, attacking *Krasnaya zvezda,* the Russian army's daily newspaper, which had not been known before for excessive philosemitism. Was it not an outrage that the Red Star publishing house also printed (among many other periodicals) the *Yevreiskaya gazeta,* the organ of the Moscow Jewish community?[18]

The "Archbishop," in brief, called for a coup and civil war, which irritated the meeting's organizers, who thought it—at the very least—untimely, and emphasized all along their attachment to the constitution. They dissociated themselves from the emotional "catacomb priest." However, various right-wing spokesmen have shown a preference for the

14. *Den,* 5, 1992. In his pastoral message for 1992, Lazar came out squarely on the side of the fighters against Judeo-Masonic conspiracy. *Russkii stag,* 1 (1992).

15. *Den,* 8 (1992).

16. It has been suggested that the KGB in 1989–1991 supported the Free Church in order to bring about a schism. D. Pospelovsky, in *Vestnik R. Kh. DD.,* 159 (1990).

17. The Catacomb (True) Church is not identical with the Orthodox church. It was expected at one time that a merger, or at least a united front, would come into being. But the Orthodox Church Abroad refused to recognize the orders of many True Orthodox bishops, which, as the case of Lazar shows, may have gone to individuals of doubtful provenance, character, and views.

18. *Krasnaya zvezda* (February 25, 1992); *Nezavisimaya gazeta* (February 25, 1992).

Church Abroad over the Moscow patriarchate, in view of the fundamentalism and the more outspoken nationalist sentiments of the former.[19]

Collaboration

The saddest chapter in the history of the Russian Orthodox church is the close cooperation between the dignitaries of the church and the Communist party leadership and the KGB. Such collaboration, needless to say, was not limited to the church; it is doubtful whether any religious community, except perhaps the very smallest, was not infiltrated and manipulated by the KGB. Nor is collaboration a specifically Russian phenomenon; it also existed in Nazi Germany and fascist Italy, except that Hitler and Mussolini were ideologically less hostile toward the Catholic and Protestant churches. As long as the churches were loyal to the state they could more or less freely manage their own affairs. In the Communist regimes of Eastern Europe supervision and infiltration were infinitely more thorough. If in Poland the strength of the church gave it a certain freedom to maneuver, the record of the DDR shows that the Protestant church was under close control until almost the very end. To a lesser degree, this also applies to the much smaller Catholic church, which was of less interest to the state authorities.

Following the revelations of 1991 and 1992 it appeared that it was virtually impossible in Russia to define with any certainty the borderline between church and KGB; the "difference was simply that some people wore cassocks and others uniforms and shoulder straps."[20] Patriarch Aleksei II conceded that no church appointment above a certain level could be made without the permission of the party and the KGB ("I don't know what induced the KGB to make me archbishop of Vilnius. . . ."). In this respect there was no difference between appointments in the church and in the government or the army. The same point had been made earlier on by K. Chartchev, the former head of the state committee dealing with church affairs.

Should these revelations have come as a surprise? Probably not, for the close cooperation between church dignitaries and the party had never been a secret. Previous patriarchs, such as Sergei (Stragorodsky) and Aleksei I

19. *Russkii vestnik*, 10 (1992), p. 12. Pamyat seems to have been among them, but it was disavowed by Mark, archbishop of Berlin and Germany. *Nezavisimaya gazeta* (April 8, 1992).

20. *"Chekisti v ryazakh"* (interview with the Rev. G. Edelstein), *Argumenty i fakty*, 36 (1991). Exactly the same words (about KGB infiltration from top to bottom) were used by the priest Andrei Rybin, who had worked for six years in the external department of the Moscow Patriarchate. *Russkaya mysl* (February 28, 1992).

(Simansky), had hailed Stalin in the most fulsome terms as "chosen by God," "savior of the fatherland and the church," "wise builder of the happiness of the people"; there is no reason to believe that they were lying—they had genuinely believed in him, who had made them patriarchs.[21] Furthermore, unlike the party, the church had never even expressed regret with regard to its Stalin cult. When in the 1960s and 1970s a few daring clerics had criticized the church's collaboration with the enemies of religion, the church had attacked the dissenters, had deprived them of their appointments, and had not lifted a finger to protect them unless they recanted. Loyalty to the Communist party leadership had always been the supreme consideration, and the church dignitaries had supported every single Communist and Soviet initiative in domestic and foreign policy.

A case could still be made in favor of collaborationism: In every country the church had to show loyalty to the secular authorities and even to pray for the leaders' health and success. True, Soviet power was different in view of its unreservedly negative attitude toward religion and its wish to see religion disappear. But the prime concern of the church was not politics but the spiritual sphere and the preservation of the faith. For this reason it had to think in terms of centuries rather than in a short-term perspective. If painful concessions had to be made by the church, there was always the chance that the political masters would change their views one day—or be replaced by others less inimical to religion—as indeed happened in the Soviet Union. What would have been gained if the Orthodox church had chosen the road of martyrdom, and if, as a result, even more churches had been closed, and even harsher limitations imposed?

The case for accommodation would have been stronger if the government had rewarded the church for its loyalty. Instead, two-thirds of the 22,000 churches that were still open at the time of Stalin's death were closed subsequently, so that by 1975 at most 7,500 were still in use. Furthermore, according to new regulations introduced under Khrushchev, priests lost virtually all control over their communities; they were no longer permitted to visit even sick or dying parishioners at home. They could not perform the last rites; they were not permitted to allow children to enter a church.

A few lowly clerics protested, but the leaders of the church remained silent. However, pragmatic considerations apart, it is doubtful whether a church preaching obedience to God and the supremacy of Christ (He is before all things, and by him all things consist": Colossians 1:17) was entitled to make concessions that deprived it of its moral authority. The

21. Zoya Krakhmalnikova, *Russkaya mysl* (December 20, 1991).

New Testament says, "The Church is subject unto Christ" (Ephesians 5:24). This and many other sayings could not possibly be squared with the church's practice of abject subservience.

It had been assumed for a long time that the KGB had its agents in the church leadership. But there was a great deal of difference between suspicion and certain knowledge, nor was it known how close the relationship had been. The first to shed some light on the collaboration were former leading officials of the Council on Religious Affairs and Cults, the institution that had been for many years the supreme authority for the church.

When the secret archives of the KGB became available, files were discovered concerning the activities of various members of the Holy Synod, the supreme body of the Russian Orthodox church. Thirteen princes of the church had been given nicknames, such as "Abbat," "Kuznetsov," "Aptekar."[22] Most of the reports were signed by Timoshevsky, the then head of the fourth department, fifth main directorate of the KGB, dealing with religious affairs. While precautions had been taken to obfuscate the identity of the agents, progress reports had been regularly submitted and from these it proved to be not too difficult to identify the individuals concerned. Thus it was reported, for instance, that agents "Antonov," "Ostrovsky," and "Adamant" had taken part in church meetings in Budapest and Geneva, and had traveled in 1989 to talk to the pope in Rome. The Orthodox delegations were small in each case and their membership could be verified from the *Journal of the Moscow Patriarchate* and from the *Information Bulletin* of the same institution. A few hours' work showed that agent "Antonov" was no other than Metropolitan Filaret of Ukraine and Galicia.[23] The priest Gleb Yakunin, who was a member of the parliamentary investigation commission dealing with the KGB archives, said in 1992 that the use of agents had continued until very recently, and probably still went on.[24] Accusations of various kind were leveled against Metropolitans Pitirim, Juvenal, and Kyrill—and even the patriarch himself. Juvenal's nickname was "Adamant," according to the discoveries in the files, but he, like other church leaders, found his defenders. Andrei Kurayev reminded the

22. *Argumenty i fakty,* 1 (1992). A leading agent among the Buddhists was given the nickname "Sayana." The victims were also given nicknames. Thus Father Alexander Men was "Missioner," Sakharov was "Asket," his wife, Elena Bonner, was "Lisa." Solzhenitsyn was "Pauk" ("The Spider").

23. A. Nezhnyi, *Ogonyok,* 4 (1992). Filaret was deposed in June 1992, but not because of having worked for the state security services.

24. See the articles by M. Pozdnayev in *Stolitsa,* 26 (1991), by the same author in *Nezavisimaya gazeta* (September 17, 1991), by S. Lezov in *Strana i mir,* 6 (1990), various articles by the priest Mark Smirnov in *Stolitsa,* 43 (1991) and *Rossiya* (March 22, 1991). Replies on behalf of the church appeared sporadically in *Moskovskii tserkovnyi vestnik,* for instance in January 1992, but the patriarchate lacked effective publicists.

public that the priest Alexander Men, one of the few great liberal theologians of recent decades, had served in Juvenal's diocese; the metropolitan had obviously protected the priest, who was not among the KGB's favorite clergymen and who had been widely published abroad.[25]

There were, of course, differences in the agents' roles: Some were "KGB men in cassocks"; others had a less elevated status. If the KGB reported, for instance, that in 1982 1,809 meetings with churchmen had taken place (a count that excluded reports in writing) there is no reason to assume that every one of those contacted was a full-time agent; some may not even have known that they were passing on information to the secret police. One priest's story of the ways and means used by the secret police to recruit agents seems to have been fairly typical. Within two days of having submitted his application to the theological seminary, he received a visit from a KGB captain, who warned him in a fatherly way to choose another career: Young men were seduced and raped by the local archimandrite.[26] When he persisted, he received another visit: Someone opposed his application. But the KGB was willing to open the necessary doors if he would prove that he was an honest man and not anti-Soviet. All the KGB captain wanted was that the young man call him back in a few days—which he did. The telephone conversation was banal: How did the would-be priest feel? Did he get enough to eat? And that was all—for the moment. The KGB would contact the new recruit as needed.

According to this source, prior to 1985 virtually everyone who wanted to enter the theological seminary was contacted in a similar way by the secret police. Later on, the KGB limited recruitment to the more promising candidates, usually those with higher education, likely to rise high in the church hierarchy:

> In our year we did not hide these contacts from each other. On the contrary, we warned each other: "I have been called to a certain place. If something happens, you know where I have been detained." Returning from such a meeting we informed each other about what had been discussed, what questions had been asked, and warned those who seemed to be in danger.[27]

The first approaches made by the KGB were, as a rule, seemingly innocent: They wanted to know about suspicious foreigners, and what decent citizen could refuse a patriotic duty of this kind? The questions about inner church affairs, about coworkers and parishioners, would come later. However, this particular approach could be used in Moscow, not in

25. *Moskovskie novosti* 10 (1992).

26. *Sobesednik,* 8 (1992).

27. Ibid. These events took place in 1987–1988.

the many places outside the capital in which no foreigners had been seen in living memory, or which were out of bounds to them.

When the priest approached by the KGB captain proved to be renitent, he was sent to the infidels—Ceauşescu's Romania. The last time an attempt was made to approach him was ten days before the coup that failed in August 1991. According to his impressions, almost every second Russian Orthodox priest cooperated with the KGB. Yakunin gave a considerable lower figure—some 15 to 20 percent—but that apparently referred to agents rather than to occasional contacts. Bakatin, who was head of the KGB for a few months after the August coup and thus had a unique opportunity to familiarize himself with the secret files, made it known that only a few of those contacted by the KGB categorically refused to co-operate.

One group of people was not shocked by the accusations of coopera-tion with the KGB, and that was the extreme right. On the contrary, those to be denounced were the Edelsteins with their charges about "KGB officers in cassocks." Before the Revolution the "Edelsteins" had been kept at arm's length by the church. The KGB, after all, had been purged of all Jews owing to Stalin and General Ryumin, to whom great honor was due in retrospect. (Ryumin had been the main organizer of the Doctors' Plot; he was executed after Stalin's death.) Attacks against agents and collabora-tors were "total anti-Christian propaganda."[28]

But the democrats too did not see eye to eye with regard to their attitude vis-à-vis the collaborationists and agents. Some, like the reformist priest V. Polosin (who had been elected to Parliament), expressed the view that to have acted as a government informant was not per se a violation of canon law.[29] The liberal Shusharin wrote that the system of planting agents in the church was both odious and pointless, a thesis that was bitterly attacked by Z. Krakhmalnikova for belittling the "industry of treason," for "evil communications corrupt good manners." (1 Cor. 15:33.)[30] While the patriarch had said that it was a sin to accuse the innocent, a samizdat journal alleged that the patriarch's KGB nickname was Drozdov.[31] The KGB infiltration may well have been senseless, but as in East Germany and

28. *Russkoye voskresenie* 4 (12) (1941). Among the dissident priests of the post-1953 period one finds a considerable number of non-Russian names. Most of them, such as Eshlimann, were not of Jewish origin, and the name of the new patriarch was Ridiger; another metropolitan is named Wendland. For another defense of church–KGB collaboration, see the editorial in *Russkii vestnik,* 9 and 10 (1992).

29. *Megapolis-express* (January 3, 1992).

30. D. Shushanin, *Nezavisimaya gazeta* (January 31, 1992). Z. Krakhmalnikova, *Novoye rus-skoye slovo* (March 3, 1992).

31. *Pryamoi put,* quoted in Krakhmalnikova.

elsewhere it certainly undermined morale and created mutual suspicion long after the system had ceased to function.

True, the tyranny of the secret police was mitigated by corruption. If the KGB had deeply infiltrated the church, church dignitaries had also learned the art of gaining the goodwill of their KGB contacts with small—and not so small—presents, drinking bouts, and so on.[32]

High church dignitaries who were not collaborators still volunteered to help, and behaved exactly according to the expectation of party and government. They did not have to be given instructions; they knew by experience and instinct what was expected from them. Less than a year before the August coup, Patriarch Aleksei said in an interview with *Pravda* that he was praying that the differences of opinion in the party not become worse and precipitate disaster—a prayer that was obviously ignored by God. In 1989 Metropolitan Pitirim appeared at the Supreme Party School; when asked by an interviewer how he felt in that strange place he replied, "Natural and easy."[33] Both church and party, the metropolitan opined, faced the same problems—world peace, culture, and the moral level of society—so there was much room for cooperation.

At about the same time, a propaganda brochure by Pitirim was put out by the Progress publishing house. According to the Orthodox "foreign minister," relations between state and church were excellent, and had always been good. If individual priests had been punished by Soviet power, that was only because they had been politically hostile to the regime. But the clergy had gradually realized that they would lose their flock if they persisted in opposition to the government, which had the support of the majority of people. At present there were no dissidents in the church. Yakunin, for instance, had been suspended from the priesthood in 1966, and the courts had sentenced him not because he was a Christian activist but because of black-marketeering—that is to say, selling icons. The support misguided Western clerics gave such wicked elements was very regrettable.

Such pronouncements were the rule, not the exception; church publications were full of them. The very least that can be said about such declarations of loyalty is that they were exaggerated, and, in any case, went on for too long; it seems they had become second nature.

Aleksei II, Metropolitan of Leningrad, Tallinn, and Novgorod, was

32. G. Edelstein described how the permit for a new monk to reside in the Holy Spirit Monastery in Vilnius would be obtained. The police would not normally give such a permit, the KGB would—provided the presents were right. *Argumenty i fakty,* 36 (1991).

33. *Moskovskie novosti* 11 (1989).

elected the fifteenth patriarch of the church in June 1990, and the question was widely asked at the time whether he would be the fifth Soviet or the fifteenth Russian patriarch. His political pronouncements after his election were conciliatory and showed a new sense of independence. He found good words for Tikhon, the patriarch who had opposed Soviet power in the early 1920s. He gradually dissociated himself from Sergeianism, the policy of submission to the party. He later said that it was Sergei's tragedy that he tried to reach an honest bargain with criminals who had usurped power.[34] When asked whether he did not feel aggrieved by the Communist party's persecution of the church, the patriarch replied with a quotation from the poet Maksimilian Voloshin: "Under torture we learned to pray for the hangmen."[35]

While the liberals detected a tendency on the part of the patriarchate to find a new political base in a fundamentalist-patriotic-Communist alliance, Aleksei II did little to encourage such speculation. He said he had no political program other than the Evangelium. When Blokhin, a prominent right-wing member of parliament, claimed he tried to enlist his support for the establishment of a regime on the lines of Franco's Spain, he published a statement that he had never discussed any such topic.[36] When the right suggested that he should (again) deprive Yakunin of his clerical appointment because his parliamentary activity was "anti-Christian," the patriarch answered that it was not customary in the Russian Orthodox church to take such steps for political reasons.[37] When *Literaturnaya Rossiya* published an appeal signed by national Communist writers and public figures, the signature of the patriarch was among them, but was promptly disavowed.

The patriarch never pretended to infallibility but on a variety of occasions asked his flock to forgive him and to pray for him.[38] The most outspoken and moving testimony of personal atonement was his interview with *Izvestiya*. He talked about the silences, the enforced passivity, the expressions of loyalty by himself and other church leaders, which had caused pain to God and men; he asked for forgiveness, understanding, and prayers.[39]

34. *Izvestiya* (August 7, 1991).

35. *Literaturnaya gazeta* (November 28, 1990).

36. *Izvestiya* (April 26, 1991).

37. "Patriarkh i Politika," *Moskovskii tserkovnyi vestnik* (June 1991). This long article was written by Deacon Andrei Kurayev, a young priest and leading adviser to the patriarch.

38. *Rossiiskaya gazeta* (Feb. 19, 1991).

39. *Izvestiya* (June 7, 1991).

The patriarch was not fully believed by the intelligentsia: At the time of the August 1991 coup he had been slow to make a stand against the rebels; true, they were anathematized, but only belatedly. The priests who had appeared in Yeltsin's White House had been dissidents like Yakunin.

The behavior of the church during the critical days became the subject of minutest investigation, which is not, however, of immediate relevance in the present context; suffice it to say that the patriarchate had clearly been in no hurry to take sides.

Another accusation brought against the patriarch was that there was a "cult" of Aleksei II, whose entourage praised him as the "instrument of the Holy Spirit." Such a cult, the critics maintained, was in the old Soviet tradition, not that of the Orthodox church; it was "ideological and propagandistic."[40] Others, such as Sergei Averintsev, whose liberal credentials were above suspicion, defended him: The patriarch had, after all, denounced the bloodshed in Vilna. One Orthodox intellectual claimed that the alleged love affair between the patriarch and the "patriotic forces" was one-sided, and that the intelligentsia, hypercritical of the church, was repeating its traditional mistake, continuing the wholesale condemnation of the church and religion that had been so typical of the pre-1917 era, and that the authors of *Vekhi* had decried.[41]

However, even the patriarch's well-wishers in the democratic camp noted that he was the only hierarch of the church who "publicly and unequivocally" repented his former compromises with party ideology. It was hinted that at the time of the coup there had been a split, that the patriarch had wanted to come out in favor of the democrats but the twelve members of the Holy Synod had not agreed.[42] (In the Holy Synod the patriarch has two votes; six members are permanent, six alternate.) Some compared the position of Aleksei II in the synod with that of Gorbachev in the Politburo in the beginning of *perestroika*, when the new general secretary had no majority for his policy.[43]

The composition of the Holy Synod, originally established by Peter I to replace the patriarchate, came under close scrutiny. The presence of the metropolitan of Kiev, who had acted as a KGB agent, was noted. So was the presence of Juvenal, who should not have been a member: Church law

40. Z. Krakhmalnikova, *Russkaya mysl.*

41. For further attacks see, for instance *Demokraticheskaya Rossiya* (March 22, 1991) and the reply "Patriarkh i politika."

42. Ya. Krotov, *Kuranty* (August 27, 1991). It is widely believed that one of the strongest supporters of the Russian right in the church leadership is Metropolitan Kyrill of Smolensk and Kaliningrad, who is the influential head of the foreign-affairs department of the Moscow patriarchate.

43. M. Frankov, "Mysteries of the Holy Synod," *Moscow News,* 6 (1992).

barred vicars—bishops who had no diocese of their own but were merely assistants of the patriarch—from membership. Another person who attracted much attention was Kyrill, head of the "department of external relations," a star pupil of Metropolitan Nikodim, one of the theorists of "Communist godblessedness." From the files of the KGB it appeared that Aleksei had supported Nikodim in 1970, when a new patriarch was elected. (Pimen was eventually elected.) But given the Byzantine relationship between the church and the KGB, it could have been that Aleksei assumed at the time that a good reference on his part would make the candidate undesirable to the secret police.[44]

Other anomalies were noted. How was one to explain that the foreign-affairs department of the patriarchate employed a hundred officials, largely KGB agents, whereas other departments, including the patriarch's personal staff, consisted of only ten people? The patriarch's main speechwriter, Kurayev, argued in a long article that Orthodoxy and liberalism were incompatible and said that he was not a democrat.[45] These and other contradictory statements tended to show that the Orthodox leadership was split on many issues, and that the power of the patriarch was severely limited.

Like the Slavophiles, Aleksei II believed that Russia had its own destiny, different from that of other peoples. He favored a renaissance of Holy Russia, involving a revival of the best features of Russian tradition. But at the same time he said that it would be utopian to dream of restoring the conditions that prevailed seventy or three hundred year ago. Russian Orthodoxy was not just a national ideology; it was the search for life in God, and from that perspective all political and national aspects were secondary.[46]

If the extreme right liked the patriarch's insistence on Russia's traditional spiritual uniqueness, they disliked his thesis that Orthodoxy was never chauvinistic and never took an anti-Semitic position.[47]

With regard to the monarchy, the patriarch was noncommittal. Grand Duke Vladimir Kyrillovich visited him in his residence and told him that he

44. Ibid. On Nikodim see also Dyakon Andrei Rybin, *Stolitsa,* 10 (1992).

45. *Nezavisimaya gazeta* (March 5, 1992).

46. *Komsomolskaya pravda* (April 16, 1991); "Patriarkh i politika."

47. Interview with BBC, reprinted in *Panorama* (December 1990). These declarations were attacked not just by the extreme right but also by fundamentalists inside the church, such as the Soyuz pravoslavnikh bratstv ("Union of Orthodox Brotherhoods) and in their in-house journal, *Vestnik.* These circles claimed that even the war between Serbs and Croats had been unleashed by a hidden "Talmudic leadership." In their public utterances they were somewhat more cautious, arguing that they had nothing against Jews as a nationality, only against the "Talmudists" among them. Interview with Natalya Babasyan in *Nezavisimaya gazeta* (May 21, 1992).

was willing to serve Russia in any capacity. But the question of the restoration of a monarchy in Russia, the patriarch said, was difficult.[48]

While Aleksei II thus clarified his position on various issues, individual clerics actively participated in politics in their private capacity. Clerics attended "patriotic assemblies"—except, of course, those sponsored by anti-Christian groups. Some refused to accept the words of the patriarch about the nonchauvinistic, and non-anti-Semitic character of the ROC, and in their writings continued the Black Hundred tradition with much vigor.[49] Others advocated a more liberal line.

The Russian Orthodox church showed no eagerness to become involved in politics, certainly not on a day-to-day level, an attitude quite intelligible in the light of its bitter experiences in recent times. Orthodox laymen had fewer doubts and scruples. Thus, at an April 1990 conference in Moscow, the Russian Christian Democratic Movement (RCDM) was born. Its aim, according to its first program, was to pass from a policy of destruction and hate to the ideals of creation and solidarity. The party wanted to create a society in which the ideals of spiritual freedom, mercy, and *sobornost* were anchored and that rejected the application of violence in domestic and foreign policy.

This program placed the party squarely in the democratic camp; it was to be a Christian Democratic movement on the West European model, and it supported *glasnost* and *perestroika*.[50] Its spiritual father was the priest Dmitri Dudko, its copresidents were Viktor Aksiuchits and Gleb Anishchenko, its membership (according to its own figures) fifteen thousand. It belonged to the Democratic Russia alliance, the forces supporting Yeltsin, and during the August 1991 coup Aksiuchits was among the defenders of the White House. The new party had close relations with the NTS in Germany, from which it allegedly received technical help to set up its offices in Moscow.

However, within a few months of its founding the RCDM began to move to the right. It still regarded National Bolshevism as the main danger but more and more frequently it turned against the "cosmopolitanism" of the Christian left, which, it claimed, argued that a Christian had no right to be a patriot.[51]

48. Press conference in Moscow, reported in *Novoye russkoye slovo* (November 17, 1991).

49. For an illustration, Georgi Fedotov of the Pskov-Pechorskii monastery, *Molodaya gvardiya* 8 (1991).

50. *Nasha strana,* 4 (1990). The party published two journals, *Put* and *Vybor*. In 1991 the party also had five regional periodicals. *Vybor* was at the time the most serious and interesting journal of the Christian intelligentsia.

51. S. Lezov, "Natsionalnaya idea i Khristianstvo," *Oktyabr,* 10 (1990). See the reply by M. Antonov, the spokesman of the far right, *Den,* 21 (1991).

This was not quite what the Christian left did argue. But it *had* maintained that as Christian politicians put more emphasis on national concerns, the interest in spiritual values that had figured so prominently in the beginning would decline and perhaps vanish.

These predictions came true sooner than had been expected. The general outlook of the RCDM before the coup of 1991 was not different from that of other moderate parties, and its view on the future of the Soviet Union resembled Solzhenitsyn's. The RCDM did not favor the secession of republics from the Union, nor would they put obstacles in the republics' way.[52] However the question of Russian statehood preoccupied them more and more, because Russia was clearly not identical with the old Russian Federation (RSFSR), an artificial creation with many millions of Russians living outside it.

Was there a real need for a Christian party in Russia? There had been, after all, no such party before 1917. According to the leaders of the RCDM the absence of such a party had been one of the reasons for the disaster of 1917. For only Christianity could provide a counterweight against atheistic communism befuddling the minds of the people. And in the present situation it could do more than any other force to bring about a moral and spiritual revival. The philosophical heritage of the religious thinkers of the beginning of the century was the RCDM's ideological basis.[53]

After the August coup and following the disintegration of the Union, the Russian Christian Democratic Movement shifted sharply to the right. It was among the sponsors of the Congress of Civic and Patriotic Organizations that took place in Moscow in February 1992. Aksiuchits, who acted as chairman, was forced to listen to a speech by Vasiliev, the Pamyat leader. (In June 1992 Aksiuchits was replaced as a leader of the "Russian Assembly" by Ilya Konstantinov.) The congress was dominated by chauvinist forces, and the organizers found themselves in the role of the sorcerer's apprentice, having let the genie out of the bottle. When Anishchenko declared that National Bolshevism was still an enemy, and that it was wrong to look for culprits only among "sinister forces" (Jews and Masons) he was shouted down: "Judas" and "Hang yourself" were among the more restrained interjections heard, as the *Protocols* were sold in the foyer and delegates boasted of "military actions" that were soon to take place.[54]

The leaders of the RCDM had looked for a rapprochement with the

52. Interview with Anishchenko, *Stolitsa,* 13 (1991).

53. V. Aksiuchits, *Moskovskii tserkovnyi vestnik* (January 1991). Much information about the state of affairs inside the church and the orthodox parties is contained in a roundtable discussion "Religiya i politika" *Voprosy Filosofii,* 7 (1992).

54. M. Perevozkina, *Russkaya mysl* (February 14, 1992).

"patriotic" forces out of genuine concern for the fate of Russia and also out of the fear that it was dangerous to leave patriotism in the hands of extremists with fascist inclinations. They had underrated the danger—that in a competition with the Black Hundred and those who shouted loudest, moderate groups would be pushed aside. The spiritual values of Christianity, as Lezov had predicted, would be dismissed as an alien, half-Jewish element by the "patriots," whose image of Christianity was that of the Black Hundred, not of Berdyaev and Bulgakov, of Likhachev and Averintsev.

Traditionally, the Russian Orthodox church has considered Roman Catholicism a dangerous rival and enemy. In this respect little changed in the reform era and on this front the Orthodox church and the "patriotic forces" have found much common ground. For the Russian right, Catholicism has always been a hostile force, almost as dangerous as the Masons and "Zionists."[55] The reasons for this enmity are in part historical; they go back to the days of the ecclesiastic schism, of Byzantium, and of the Polish invasion of Russia in the seventeenth century. In the mind of Russian nationalists, Catholicism has been synonymous with the infiltration of Western ideas. While some Russians have converted to Catholicism, there have been hardly any cases of Roman Catholics embracing the Orthodox church. The Uniate (Catholic) church in the western Ukraine has been another bone of contention, and the rival claims for churches and church property became more acute in the age of reform. The fact that the Vatican, unfurling the banner of ecumenism, has actively worked in recent years for closer collaboration between the confessions has caused even greater suspicion in the Russian Orthodox church. The appointment of two Catholic bishops (in Moscow and Novosibirsk) has been interpreted as yet another sign of Roman Catholic aggression: Not a single church should be given to the agents of the Vatican, nor should the Catholics be permitted to open a theological seminary.

The Roman Catholics have been exceedingly cautious in their activities inside Russia. Thus, they have suggested the establishment in Moscow of a Christian university in collaboration with the Orthodox church,[56] but the idea was not acceptable as far as the Russian church was concerned.

How is one to explain this almost pathological fear of Catholic activities? To some extent, it is rooted in a feeling of inferiority. The Russian Orthodox church believes that its priests are not equal to those of the

55. For an illustration, see Diakon German Ivanov-Trinatsatyi, "Ostorozhno—Vatikan," *Moskva*, 6 (1991).

56. Igor Shevelev, *Novoye russkoye slovo* (February 6, 1992).

Catholics, who have enjoyed a far longer and better theological training. Furthermore, vastly superior financial resources are at the disposal of the Vatican. Patriarch Aleksei II has been more conciliatory than other Russian church leaders; in early 1992 he invited Archbishop Kondrucevich, the Vatican representative in Moscow, for a long conversation about possible future cooperation. But a deep suspicion remains among Orthodox fundamentalists (as among Roman Catholic conservatives), and relations between the two confessions are likely to remain distant even though in reality neither has much to fear from the other.

The Orthodox Church in a New Age

The reasons for the less than total success of the Russian Orthodox church in the new conditions have been discussed in some detail. What are its future prospects, and what are the chances of a common religious-nationalist front? Most clergymen feel more at home with the nationalists than with the liberals. The nationalists will not constantly remind them of their past collaboration with the Communist regime and demand purges in their leadership. While there is much interest in religion among the liberal intelligentsia, the church leaders assume, probably correctly, that they will not be able to keep these unquiet spirits in the fold: They will not subject themselves to church rules and discipline, but at best will advocate all kinds of doubtful modernist changes from inside the church. Most right-wingers rediscovered religion, as has been noted, late in the day, and their true belief in certain basic aspects of Christian doctrine remains suspect. Like the "German Christians" in Nazi Germany, they have no use for the Old Testament because it is too "Jewish." They have no use for "theologians" such as Berdyaev or Bulgakov, or even Pavel Florensky, who perished in a Soviet camp. In the last analysis the interests of state and nation will always matter more to the right than spiritual redemption does. But unlike the democrats, the right will cherish and honor the church, at least outwardly; they will not insist on innovations and cause other such trouble.

The former Communists, too, have courted the Orthodox church, promising it in future the status of a state religion.[57] The temptation to cooperate actively with the right may be great, perhaps overwhelming, for church leaders. Most of them belong to the prereform era and have no sympathy with democratic ideas. Others may recall the message of Paul's

---

57. A speech on these lines was made by Ivan Polozkov in February 1991 at a patriotic meeting, Mark Smirnov, *Rossiya*, March 15, 1991.

letter to the Corinthians: that there should be no intercourse between righteousness and lawlessness, as there is nothing in common between light and darkness, and between a holy shrine and false idols.

Purely religious considerations quite apart, leading churchmen may be guided by common sense. The Russian Orthodox church suffered grievously as the result of its close collaboration first with tsarism and later with communism. Elementary prudence suggests that it should keep out of active politics, at least until conditions in Russia are more stable. But this may not be the case for a long time to come. Quietism is not a heroic posture, and some may charge the church with lack of patriotism. But quietism is the one course of action most likely to help the church in its recovery and survival. During the twentieth century the Russian Orthodox church has lost the Georgian church, the Russian churches in the Baltic countries, and most recently the Ukrainian church, which also became autocephalous. Any further secessions would reduce the Russian Orthodox church from the status of a world religion to that of a provincial creed. While a church does not, or at least should not, have great power aspirations, any further decline in the Russian church's influence would certainly affect its standing and ability to fulfill its mission.

However, if religion has a long-term future in Russia, it is not through the power and glory of secular politics. There is, again, the temptation to gain a position of power and influence through integration with the state on both the ideological and political level. This is what leaders of the Russian right have demanded with their appeals to the church to take a leading part in a patriotic revival. There has been such a tradition in Russian history, but it led eventually to the disaster of 1917. There has been another tradition, aiming at a different goal: that of Christian love, of a Christian community delivered from hate and fear—the "nonpossessor" heritage, in theological terms. It is between these two traditions that the Orthodox church will ultimately have to decide. It cannot, and should not divorce itself entirely from public affairs, but it is not a political party and it has above all to preserve its religious destiny. It is a dilemma common to all religions, but it is nowhere more acute than in the case of the Orthodox church.

Chapter Fifteen

THE NEW NATIONALIST ESTABLISHMENT: LITERARY MANIFESTOS AND POLITICAL INITIATIVES

As POLITICAL CONTROLS WERE LOOSENED under *glasnost,* many organizations of a nationalist orientation came into being; they were mainly of a professional or a regional character. All of them were small and hardly any lasted for longer than a year or two in their original form. They received their impetus from the general political ferment and the growing influence of the liberal-democratic forces, whose activities they strongly resented. Among the first to sound the tocsin to rally the right-wing camp were well-known authors such as Yuri Bondarev and Vasili Belov, the village writer; their leading organs were the daily newspaper *Sovetskaya Rossiya* and *Literaturnaya Rossiya,* the weekly organ of the Writers' Union of the Russian Republic. In a passionate speech in 1988, Bondarev compared the domestic situation with the state of affairs in 1941, when Nazi armies had invaded the Soviet Union and threatened Russia and its people with extinction. Who were the new barbarians? Those who wished to paralyze the resistance of the Russian people to their enemies, who wished to deprive them of their spiritual values, morally to disarm them. An effort comparable to Stalingrad was needed to draw Russia back from the brink of the abyss.

Among the earliest "patriotic" organizations was the Brotherhood of Russian Artists (Tovarishchestvo Russkikh Khudozhnikov), founded in November 1988). The "Russian Center" in the U.S.S.R. Writers Union, as well as various historical and ecological associations, should also be mentioned. The Fund for Slavonic Literature and Culture and the "Union for the Spiritual Renaissance of the Fatherland (SDVO) were founded in March 1989. In May 1989, under the auspices of the Moscow town soviet, the society Otechestvo (Fatherland) was established; its proclaimed aim was the promotion of Russian culture. Its chairman was Apollon Kuzmin, about whom more below; his deputy, Colonel Rutskoi, was an Afghan veteran who later became Russia's vice president.[1] Various groups also appeared whose names included the terms *"Sobor"* or *"Sobornost"* and *"Rossiya,"* as well as *"Yedinenie"* or *"Yedinstvo"* ("union" or "unification"). There was also a "Fund for the Rebuilding of the Cathedral of Christ the Savior."

There was much overlap in both the leadership and the composition of these groups; they signed each other's appeals and tried to coordinate their antiliberal propaganda in their periodicals and publishing houses. Yet they were not very effective, and it was often difficult to discover what elements distinguished the many groups. There was, on the one hand, the intense feeling that "something ought to be done," but there was no group that could impose its authority. The ambitions of the patriots' leaders usually collided; the intelligentsia, by and large, was not attracted by the extremist spokesmen's slogans, which were often shrill, even hysterical, and which lacked positive, constructive content. Nor was there much collaboration between organizations in Moscow, Leningrad, and other parts of the country. Complaints about the evident lack of coordination came from all sides of the patriotic camp.

During the last few months of 1989 several appeals were published in *Sovetskaya Rossiya* which found, however, only a small echo. Far greater publicity attracted the manifestos by the Russian writers that appeared in *Literaturnaya Rossiya* in February and March 1990, in particular the "Letter of the Seventy-four."[2] These manifestos were directly addressed to the Supreme Soviet and the Central Committee of the Communist party, obviously in the expectation of political action in response to their call to combat the mortal danger facing the fatherland.

The clear and present danger was identified. Above all, it was the spreading of the myth about a Russian fascism that allegedly sabotaged reform. The aim of this mendacious propaganda by the enemies of Russia was to destroy the patriotic forces, to destabilize society, and eventually to seize power. True, fascism was imported into Russia, but the culprits were the Jewish fascists, the Zionists, systematically spreading the lie that pogroms had taken place in prerevolutionary Russia. In truth, the Jewish

1. For a full survey of the nationalist groups see V. Pribylovsky, and V. Solovei, *Russkii natsionalisticheskii establishment,* unpublished research paper (Moscow, 1992).

2. *Literaturnaya Rossiya* (February 2 and March 2, 1990).

Nazis were responsible for the Holocaust: They had organized Auschwitz and Dachau, the ghettoes of Lvov and Vilnius, to "cut off the dry branches of the Jewish people." Through their outlets in the media the Russophobes were inciting enmity between various nations, undermining the defense readiness of the country.[3] Furthermore, the Zionist Nazis were organizing "storm troops" called *Betar* inside Russia.

The signatories of the "Letter of the Seventy-four" were convinced that their manifesto had a tremendous impact; as one of them put it, their ideological foes were stunned and speechless, they had not a single argument to answer the patriots' accusations.[4] In fact the letter was a succès de scandale, but had not much political impact. Valentin Rasputin, who had signed it was appointed by Gorbachev to the president's new Advisory Council; but the council was of no consequence and soon ceased to function. Rasputin resigned from it even before that. The letter was of interest as reflecting a certain mindset.

What had induced a sizeable group of writers, among them some of undoubted talent, to sign a document according to which a handful of Jewish youngsters with no interest in Russian politics constituted a mortal threat to the survival of their country? According to one witness, the manifesto reflected the feeling that deep discrimination had been exercised against the Russian people for seventy-two years. "Moral terror, racist in character" had been directed against Russian patriots.[5] The patriots had also been angered by insinuations in the liberal press that they had somehow been behind the Smirnov-Ostashvili demonstration against the April group of writers that had taken place in January 1990. It seems more than likely that Smirnov-Ostashvili had not received his marching orders from the nationalist establishment. But this does not explain a reaction on the part of the "patriots" that was perfectly irrational—to put it in the mildest possible way—was of no interest to the broad public, and was ignored by the political leadership.

The next attempt on the part of patriotic intellectuals to influence Soviet politics was a document entitled "Action Program 90." Its author was Valeri Skurlatov, who had been among the nationalist militants in the Brezhnev era, and who has figured earlier on in our history of the Russian right as the main popularizer of the *Book of Vlas*.[6] "Action Program 90,"

3. According to the manifesto the patriotic press reached a mere 1.5 million readers, the "Russophobes" sixty million.

4. Tatyana Glushkova, *Moskovskii literator*, 17–18 (1990).

5. Ibid.

6. For his biography, see *Rossiskoye vozrozhdenie*, 1 (1990). After a career in the Komsomol, he was head of a department in the Diplomatic Academy of the Foreign Ministry. During the

also called the "manifesto of White Bolshevism" was a nine days' wonder, bitterly attacked by the liberal media as a blueprint for a right-wing coup. The agitation ceased when it turned out that the "Action Program" had been composed by only one man, and that the impression created that it was supported by a broad section of the party leadership and the public was quite wrong.[7]

Of considerably greater importance was the "Message to the People" of July 1991, which came to be regarded by many observers as the ideological preparation for the August coup. There were twelve signatories, the writers Bondarev, Prokhanov, and Rasputin; the publicist Eduard Volodin; the sculptor Vyacheslav Klykov, the singer Lyudmilla Zykina; the generals Boris Gromov and Valentin Varennikov; and Yuri Blokhin, the head of the mainstream conservative Soyuz parliamentary faction; Gennadi Zyuganov, the general secretary of the Russian Communist party; and Starodubtsev and Tizyakov, two major economic managers.[8] This claimed that power in the Soviet Union had been taken over by "pompous and crafty money-grabbers," by enemies of Russia, traitors, slavishly bowing to their transatlantic well-wishers. A popular patriotic movement had to be created; all divisive factors had to be put aside so as to prevent a civil war and the ruin of the state. As the manifesto proclaimed, there were capable, patriotic leaders who could replace the traitors at present in power.

Three of the signatories to the "Message to the People" took an active part in the August coup; nevertheless, it is not certain whether the publication played a crucial role in the preparation of the coup. The antireform forces had discussed a takeover for a long time; Shevardnadze had uttered a warning in December 1990, as had some others. The leading members of the junta showed singular ineptness in organizing the coup; they did not even try to mobilize wider popular forces. They did not inform their potential right-wing allies; the decision to act was probably made on short notice, without careful preparation, because Gorbachev was about to return from his holiday in the Crimea.

The nationalist establishment seems to have been surprised by the coup. The National Bolsheviks of Edinenie welcomed it and promised its full support. Alexander Prokhanov, appearing on Moscow television,

---

reform era he reemerged as the founder and cofounder of various political parties such as the Russian National Front (RNF).

7. *Rabochaya tribuna* (October 3, 1990); *Pravda* (October 15, 1990).

8. *Moskovskaya pravda* (July 23, 1991); Gromov, deputy minister of the interior, subsequently withdrew his signature, and Zykina declared that the full text had not been shown to her.

called it "a blessing for Russia."[9] (True, later on Prokhanov hinted that the coup might have been a provocation of sorts.[10]) Since the coup was over so soon, many leading figures of the right had no chance to comment on it—which in retrospect was probably all to the good, from their point of view.

Soyuz

We ought to turn now from the literary manifestos aiming at the coordination and unification of the patriotic camp to the political initiatives that took place in the Soviet Union in 1988–1992. The most important of the new groups to emerge in the Soviet parliament was Soyuz. It came into being as the antiseparatist spearhead of the Russian minorities in the Baltic republics and Moldova, and was headed by leaders from these parts such as Colonel Viktor Alksnis from Latvia, Evgeni Kogan from Estonia, and Yuri Blokhin from Moldova. Soyuz constituted itself as a parliamentary faction in February 1990; its official foundation meeting took place in December 1990. With more than five hundred deputies, it was at the time the single strongest force in the Supreme Soviet.[11]

The leaders of Soyuz tried, no doubt deliberately, to attract as many supporters as possible from both the nationalist and the Communist camps. In its program, dated April 1991, it tried to accommodate both Communists and anticommunists, relegating quarrels about the "socialist choice" (whether to opt for a socialist system or not) to a secondary place. Soyuz supported a "third way" between capitalism and communism that should "absorb everything valuable from the experience of world civilization and international social democracy."[12] This third way was not to be mere eclecticism but a search for "new approaches to the solution of political and national conflicts," excluding extremisms and integrating everything positive and rational that had been borne out by global practice and common sense. Soyuz leaders did not want to intensify their quarrels with the party leadership—Gorbachev—but, on the other hand, they did want to keep their distance from the leadership. Soyuz was in favor of a transition to the market, but a transition that

9. *Sovetskaya Rossiya*, (August 20, 1991); *Rossiiskaya gazeta* (September 4, 1991).

10. *Komsomolskaya gazeta* (September 3, 1991).

11. Sergei Mitrokhin, *Panorama* (September 1991).

12. *Politika*, 5 (May 1991).

would benefit the majority of the population and not just the black-marketeers.[13]

However, their enthusiasm for a real market economy seems to have been limited. In their program documents, they did not discuss the privatization of major factories, banks, and other enterprises. Alksnis and his colleague Nikolai Petrushenko, also a colonel, frequently spoke of the necessity for strong government, referring to Chile under Pinochet as an example. But on other occasions they affirmed their devotion to constitutional and civil rights and demanded that the political struggle should be carried out peacefully and in a civilized way. With such a broad, catch-all program Soyuz hoped to attract Communists of the old conservative school, including Ligachev, as well as noncommunists, stressing all along its attachment to patriotic ideals and a strong central power. Soyuz had the support of the powerful military-industrial complex and of part of the officer corps as well as of *nashe*—"our people"—the Russians who were oppressed in the non-Russian republics and had fled to Russia or were about to escape.[14]

After the collapse of the Soviet Union, Soyuz members could plausibly argue that their worst fears had come true: The Union had ceased to exist; *perestroika* had proved to be a failure. But the group did not derive much tangible benefit from these disasters. Soyuz had been the strongest opposition group in Parliament, yet it had not gained much credibility as a true alternative to the Gorbachev and Yeltsin administrations.

During the summer of 1991 Soyuz tried to transform itself from a parliamentary faction into a countrywide movement, but it showed little determination and political know-how in the process. The previous careers of Soyuz's leaders had not been in politics. Alksnis, to be sure, came from a family of Old Bolsheviks; his grandfather had been a prominent victim of the 1937 purges. But his own career had been in military engineering. While the leadership of Soyuz passed resolutions staking its claim to become the chief conservative opposition party, it lacked true grass roots. It organized few meetings and demonstrations, and the circulation of its journal was tiny, 25,000.

Soyuz was short on new ideas—there were few ideologues among its leaders—and for this reason New Right thinkers such as Dugin were given a free run in the group's publications. Anti-Masonic attacks were published

13. Ibid. The Soyuz journal changed its name to *Obozrenie* in 1992.

14. According to Alksnis the generals, exactly like the more junior officers, were convinced that the present political setup could not last. But they tended toward caution and did not want to endanger their position by premature action. *Literaturnaya Rossiya*, 7 (1992). For a critical appraisal of the political forces supporting Soyuz, see A. Khiva, *Izvestiya* (May 11, 1991).

and there were occasional favorable references to the positive (but not leading role) of the church in the new Russia. Much of the time the group steered clear of the grosser forms of anti-Semitism typical of most groups of the extreme right. Soyuz was an inchoate movement, inasmuch as many of its members belonged at the same time to one or more other patriotic groups.

Soyuz's leaders were much in demand by the media.[15] But they were not asked to participate in the coup of August 1991, whether because they were considered rivals by the conspirators or because their political role was belittled. Alksnis and Petrushenko had not Zhirinovsky's talent as a demagogic spellbinder—nor could they deliver equally shocking, irresponsible statements. But nor were they moderates; after all, they accused the political leadership of selling out the country and demanded that Bakatin (who, Alksnis claimed, had ruined both the Ministry of the Interior and the KGB) and Gorbachev should not escape just punishment for their crimes.[16]

The weakness of the Soyuz position was that with all their stress on nationalism, they were identified in the public mind with the old Communist party and the various new Communist groups, such as the United Front of the Toilers (OFT), the Marxist Workers Party, the Communist Party of the RSFSR, and the many others that competed at this time for the public's support.[17]

Nina Andreyeva

At a time of trouble hitherto unknown political leaders tend to come to the fore. There has been a term for this kind of figure in Russian history: *samozvanets,* a false pretender, literally "one who called himself." But not all were political impostors; political geniuses happen to be rare at the best of times, and when a breakdown occurs in the political system, all kinds of marginal people who normally would not stand a chance are swept to the

15. The statement of the Soyuz leadership appeared in *Politika* during the 1991s. Alksnis, Blokhin, Petrushenko, and others also gave countless interviews to the press and television. A few examples should suffice: Alksnis in *Den,* 5 (1991); *Sovetskaya Rossiya* (January 24, 1991, and November 21, 1990); Petrushenko in *Avrora,* 12 (1991).

16. *Literaturnaya Rossiya,* 7 (1992).

17. There were some ninety such organizations in 1991, including "Women for a Socialist Future for Our Children," the "Russian Academy," the "Russian University," and the "Association for the Composite Study of the Russian Nation." For a comprehensive, annotated enumeration see I. I. Antonovich, in *Izvestiya Ts. K. KPSS* (July 1991), as well as the reference work edited by Pribylovsky, mentioned above.

surface. Some may be demagogues or charlatans, others people of strong, single-minded convictions who think they are called to save the country and who, by accident, find themselves in a position to gain national attention. Some of these political comets last for a very short time only; others show greater staying power.

The first of this new league of contenders was Nina Andreyeva, based in Leningrad, who tried to rally the diehard Old Bolsheviks on a national Communist platform. "I Cannot Sacrifice Principles," published in *Sovetskaya Rossiya* in March 1988, was an instant sensation. For three weeks this manifesto of the counterreform forces was believed to be the new party line. But then Gorbachev returned from his annual leave, *Pravda* published a detailed rebuttal, the other newspapers followed suit, and poor Mrs. Andreyeva had to leave her apartment temporarily in view of the unwelcome publicity. But she decided to stay in politics and in May 1989 a new national Communist organization called Edinstvo (Unity) was founded under her leadership.

Andreyeva was born in Leningrad; her family had moved there from the neighborhood of Tver (Kalinin). They had been peasants (and religious believers). Her father worked as a stevedore in the port of Leningrad, her mother as a fitter in the Kirov works. Her father was killed during the siege of Leningrad; so was her older sister, and one brother who fought in the army. She graduated from school with distinction, studied chemistry, and married a fellow teacher, a professor of Marxism-Leninsm. She joined the Communist party in 1966.[18] While she was in the party there were allegations that she had received an official rebuke for behavior unbecoming a party member. Andreyeva was a Stalinist fundamentalist who thought that the "reformist" leadership under Gorbachev had betrayed the cause of communism. But there was also a nationalist twist in her manifesto, and in subsequent speeches, which constituted a deviation from Marxism-Leninism. It is for this reason that her place is in a review of right-wing forces in contemporary Russia. She picked up from Engels the concept of "reactionary nations" and stood it on its head. Whereas for Marx and Engels most Slavic peoples, and above all the Russians, had been reactionary, for Nina Andreyeva all enemies of Russia and all Russophobes belonged to this

---

18. The main sources for Nina Andreyeva's life and thought are her many interviews. Among the more interesting are the following *Sobesednik* (June 1990); *Soyuz* (July 1990); *Argumenty i fakty*, 22 (1990); *Megapolis express* (October 17, 1991); *Znamya yunosti* (Minsk) (February 1991), and *Chas pik* (July 26, 1991) (a conversation with Josef Ben Dor, an Israeli diplomat). Nina Andreyeva was also interviewed by many foreign journalists. Her speeches and articles were published in *Interdvizhenie* (December 1990); *Voenno-istoricheskii zhurnal*, 6 (1990), and elsewhere.

category—that is, most Western nations, all the separatists inside the Soviet Union, and, needless to say, the Jews.

The Gorbachev leadership was revisionist, capitulation- and restoration-oriented. It was no longer Bolshevik but had gone over to the Menshevik camp. The decision to introduce a market economy was a disaster; in five years of *perestroika* the Soviet Union had suffered greater losses than in the Second World War. It was transforming the country into a semicolony supplying raw materials to the imperialist plunderers. Soviet foreign policy was also a catastrophe; the swallowing up of the DDR by the Federal Republic marked the beginning of the countdown to preparations for a new war in Europe. Andreyeva was not, in principle, against a multiparty system in Russia, provided all the parties were socialist in orientation.

Nina Andreyeva did not relish being branded a neo-Stalinist, but she defended Stalin against his detractors. He was a wise statesman, an extraordinary personality who operated under extremely complicated historical conditions. He had created a superpower out of a backward country. As for the Jews, she was aware of the fact that not all of them were Zionists; the man who had vouched for her when she joined the party had been a Jew; he had served in the war and also in the KGB. ("He was like a father to me.") However, the Zionists were Russophobes, spreading calumnies about Russia and calling on Russian Jews to leave their country.

Nina Andreyeva, in brief, wanted the Soviet Union to remain undivided, a superpower, and Communist in character. She supported the initiatives aimed at establishing a Russian Communist party under Ivan Polozkov and Boris Gidaspov. But these initiatives did not go far enough for her taste, nor did the Russian Communists want to have Nina Andreyeva.

Thus Edinstvo was founded; according to her claims it had some sixty branches outside Leningrad. Andreyeva was a welcome guest at national-Communist gatherings in Minsk and elsewhere. She attacked Gorbachev, Yakovlev, and Shevardnadze for restoring capitalism and giving independence to the Baltic republics. Later she attacked Yeltsin even more harshly; she called him a "political impostor," quoting Gus Hall, the secretary-general of the American Communist party. She expressed regret that Leninism was no longer taught in the schools.

Nina Andreyeva had some enthusiastic followers, but their number was not great. Unreconstructed Leninism and Stalinism were no longer in fashiom, and as for her nationalist arguments and slogans, she had to cope with much competition. Nina Andreyeva had neither journals to broadcast her message, nor an organizational genius at her side, and for these and other reasons her group did not become a factor of major political importance. By 1992 she was, in fact, more than half forgotten.

Zhirinovsky

A far more colorful figure than Nina, the Russian Iron Lady, was the Muscovite Vladimir Volfovich Zhirinovsky, who like her suddenly appeared on the Russian political scene. He was also more successful, being almost as much in the limelight as Gorbachev and Yeltsin. After his astonishing performance in the elections for the Russian presidency, when he attracted almost six million votes ("as many as all the people in Switzerland," in his own words), no day passed without at least one long Zhirinovsky interview in the media.

Zhirinovsky, one of six children, was born in Alma Ata in 1946; his mother was White Russian, his father apparently a Jew by origin. The family had lived in Lvov before the war. Young Zhirinovsky attended the Afro-Asian Institute of Moscow University and also studied law for a while. He served as an officer in the Soviet army in the Caucasus. His political career began relatively late; in 1987 he was a member of Fakel, one of the many Moscow "informal groups." Later he joined the Democratic Union, from which he seceded in December 1989 with several other members to establish the new Liberal Democratic party. His political idols, as he said on one occasion, were Bismarck, de Gaulle, Pinochet, and Stolypin.[19] From 1983 to 1990 he headed the legal department of the Mir publishing house.

A man in his forties should have had friends (or enemies), colleagues who had known him in earlier stages of his career. Yet surprisingly little was learned of Zhirinovsky's earlier life. According to his own account he was "young, energetic, and well educated." When someone compared him with Hitler, he replied that in contrast to him Hitler had been a stupid man, a mere noncommissioned officer, in short an inferior person. According to some accounts he had at one time been active in VAAD, the central Russian Jewish organization; according to another source he had been to Turkey on business trips and had run into difficulties there.[20]

19. *Yuridicheskaya gazeta,* 9 and 15 (1991).

20. For Zhirinovsky's early life see S. Mitrokhin in *Svobodnoye slovo,* 16 (1991) and N. Aleksandrov in *Zhizn,* 7 (1992). For his later life V. Batshev and M. Gorbanevsky, "Komitetch-iki." Part 1 appeared in *Posev,* 1 (1991); part 2 in samizdat. (*Radio Liberty* AC 6580, June 28, 1991). For his finances see *Kuranty* (April 16, 1991) and *Ogonyok* 2 (1992). Also the interview with Zhirinovsky's erstwhile aide Leonid Alimov, *Stolitsa,* 27 (1991) and *Novyi Vzglyad,* 38 (1992). For his business deals with Turkey, A. Tarasov in *Izvestiya* (February 12, 1992).

Zhirinovsky founded the Liberal Democratic party (LDPSS) in March 1990 together with Vladimir Voronin, another unknown political figure. The party was originally presented as a circle of the friends and admirers of Andrei Sakharov, who had died a short time before. However, neither Sakharov's widow nor those close to him had ever heard of Zhirinovsky, and his appearance caused disbelief and suspicion. The program of the party was "liberal-centrist" (in Zhirinovsky's own words); it stood for the rule of law, the rights of man, a multiparty system, de-ideologization, and a strong presidency.

By the time its second party congress took place, in October 1990, the LDPSS had moved to the right; human rights were dropped from its agenda, as was the multiparty system, and the emphasis was now on law and order. In April 1991 the party was officially registered; according to Soviet law all parties had to provide the names of at least five hundred members in eight republics. Zhirinovsky had considerable difficulty in complying with this provision; in the end he submitted a list of 108 signatures from Moscow district and 1,120 from Abkhazia. The lists did not give the signatories' first names and their addresses, but the authorities accepted them anyway. After he had polled six million votes, no one bothered to raise these small legal details again.

Zhirinovsky soon quarreled with his lieutenants Voronin, Krivonosov, and Bogachev. The liberal media treated him like a clown, but all this did not prevent his seemingly unstoppable rise in the political firmament. There were other pretenders to leadership on the right, such as Skurlatov. But only Zhirinovsky succeeded in attracting millions of voters. How did he achieve that? He seems to have realized early on that even negative publicity was better than no publicity. Hence the outrageous, nonsensical statements at the impromptu press conferences, hence the clowning, the grandiose promises, and the blood-curdling threats. Everyone knew that he was at most half serious, but he would always provide a good story for the media. Some of Zhirinovsky's former associates, such as Bogachev, accused him of being a KGB agent; others, for instance Alimov, argued that he was temperamentally unsuited to be a full-time employee of the Committee for State Security, which is probably correct. He was merely playing a political game, showing the KGB that he was not against them and that he was expecting their help.[21] Yet others compared him to the priest Gapon who had played an important role in the Revolution of 1905—a creature of the tsarist Okhrana, who had however pursued at the same time a policy of his own, so that in the end no one (including himself) knew for certain for

21. A. Meshkov in *Stolitsa,* 27 (1992).

whose benefit he was working. Yet others compared him with Zubatov, a secret-police colonel who at the time of the 1905 revolution had established unions that were half independent, half state controlled.

Zhirinovsky's language certainly was not that of the intellectual establishment. The Lenin period had been a rape, Stalin's was the era of homosexuality, Khrushchev's that of masturbation, Brezhnev's that of group sex, and Gorbachev's the age of political and economic impotence."[22] He promised his listeners vodka at a much cheaper price—seven rubles—thus violating one of the taboos of the right. But then anti-alcohol stands had never been popular among the masses. Zhirinovsky advocated economic liberalism coupled with political centralization. All political parties, including his own, had to be dissolved, and an iron fist was needed for at least two years so that Russia would survive.

His most provocative statements concerned Russia's borders and the fate of the non-Russian nationalities: Russia should return to the borders of September 1917; Lithuania, Latvia, and Estonia should be made administrative districts under Colonel Alksnis. In an interview with a Lithuanian newspaper Zhirinovsky said he would bury atomic waste along the border with the Baltic countries so that the Balts would die of radiation sickness and starvation. Nuclear testing would be transferred from Semipalatinsk to the Baltic countries. In a conversation with a Finnish newspaper Zhirinovsky considered the possibility of reincorporating Finland into the Russian empire.[23] Strikers would be arrested when he came to power, and profiteers exiled.

On other occasions he declared that his party stood for strict observation of the law and that it did not want to come to power over corpses. He attacked Jewish journalists who were constantly attacking him, yet told an Arab journalist that the problem of the Palestinians had to be solved in Jordan (which he called an "artificial state")—a solution previously proposed by General Ariel Sharon. He welcomed the "Message to the People" of July 1991, in which the right demanded a (military) dictatorship to save the nation. After the August coup he declared that the plotters had failed because they had not included him in their ranks.

Before the elections for the Russian presidency, Zhirinovsky predicted that he would narrowly beat Yeltsin. After the results became known he said that time was working for him and that in the coming elections he would

---

22. *Liberal,* 1 (1990).

23. For some typical Zhirinovsky interviews and articles: *Sovetskaya Rossiya* (July 30, 1991); *Golos armenii* (October 25, 1991); *Dialog,* 10 (1991); *Nezavisimaya gazeta* (July 25, 1991); *Selskaya zhizn* (June 4, 1991); *Vremya* (TV, April 14, 1991); *Delovaya zhizn,* 24 (1991); *Chas pik* (May 27, 1991).

be victorious. All this time he kept up close relations with the Communist party—even though he attacked its ideology. His party's publications were printed by Communist publishing houses. His electoral campaign was financed by Andrei Zavidia, a self-styled entrepreneur, previously a major figure in Soviet management, who was also his running mate for president. Later on, in September 1991, Zavidia bought *Sovetskaya Rossiya*, the daily newspaper that served as the main mouthpiece of the right.[24] Where had Zavidia's millions originated? After the coup, a document was found in the archives of the Communist party Central Committee according to which a loan of three million rubles had been given to Zavidia.[25] Since the Central Committee was not normally in the banking business, political considerations seem to have been involved.

The attitude of the right and the extreme right toward Zhirinovsky was ambivalent. The extreme right either tried to ignore him or attacked him as a half Jew.[26] The more moderate, "respectable" right attempted to keep him at arm's length; on occasion *Den, Literaturnaya Rossiya* or *Politika* would interview him, but he was frequently not invited to their congresses and demonstrations, largely because they feared that he would steal the show with his unbridled demagogy. On the other hand, they could not entirely ignore him, because he was the most gifted rabble-rouser on the right. The great weakness of the Zhirinovsky party was that everything seemed to depend on the personality of the leader.

The Social Base of the Russian Right

What was the social basis of the Zhirinovsky phenomenon? In most respects his supporters were no different from those of other groups on the Russian right. There were not many intellectuals or "class-conscious" workers among them, but members of the lower echelons of the party and state administration and of the police, people who had a position, however modest, in the old system which they had either lost or feared to lose.

Zhirinovsky's party came into being as a radical group of the center

24. Interview with Zavidia, *Komsomolskaya pravda* (September 28, 1991). Zavidia also owned *Literaturnaya Rossiya* and other right-wing publications.

25. *Ogonyok*, 2 (1992).

26. *Russkoye Delo* (Petrograd) 1 (1992). On one occasion in 1992, speaking to students of history, Zhirinovsky was pressed with regard to the nationality of his grandparents. He said that they had died before he had been born, that to the best of his knowledge they had been Russians. But if it turned out that he also had non-Russian blood, he would be glad, because it was only proper that those ruling a multicultural state such as Russia be of mixed parentage.

rather than of the right. The turn toward nationalism came only in 1991; previously the demand for the abolition of all nationality-based discrimination had been high on his list of priorities. When someone called his party bourgeois, Zhirinovsky answered that he wished that this were true, but that given Soviet conditions it could not be.

With the worsening of the economic situation in 1992 many Russians faced a substantial drop in their income and standard of living, not to mention the fear they felt of unemployment. As the danger of war receded, the armed forces were cut, military production was reduced or discontinued, and part of the internal security forces was made redundant. The number of people affected, together with their dependents, amounted to tens of millions. The old Marxist concept of the lumpen or lumpenization resurfaced in this connection; with equal justice one could have referred to the *spostati* of all classes, those who had been rejected and had lost their place in society. According to public-opinion polls carried out in early 1992, some 60 to 80 percent of Moscow citizens were unhappy with their lot; some 73 percent suffered from acute stress and 53 percent from what they defined as "uncertainty."[27] It can be taken for granted that a substantial number of people suffer at any time, in every society, from these afflictions of modern life (and the human condition). It is equally certain that the number of sufferers was higher in Russia during this period of ferment than earlier on. Given the political, social, and economic discontent, the prospects for radical parties improved. And since the left wing was discredited, a swing to the right seemed almost a foregone conclusion.[28]

It would be wrong, however, to underestimate psychopolitical factors. The participants in the antidemocratic protest meetings were by no means only those who had most suffered materially as the result of the reforms. There seems to have been among the discontented a well-above-average percentage of "Gray Panthers": aggressive elderly men, fanatical grandmothers, having to make ends meet on wholly insufficient old-age pensions. But the mental outlook of these people of middle and old age was equally important; it had been formed in the late Stalinist period or under Stalin's heirs. While they were not ardent believers in Leninist ideology, they tended to prefer the certainties of a bygone period to the uncertainties of the Gorbachev and Yeltsin era. For many of them freedom of expression

27. *Izvestiya* (January 27, 1992 and February 27, 1992).

28. There have been few attempts so far to investigate the social roots of Russian politics in the age of reform. One of the rare exceptions is A. S. Arestova, "Sotsialnaya basa sovremennogo politicheskogo dvizheniya v SSSR," *Mnogopartiinost i obshestvennoye dvizheniya* (Moscow, 1992). On *lumpenization* see, in particular, M. N. Rutkevich, "Sotsialnaya Polarisatsiya" *Sotsiologicheskie Issledovaniya*, 9, 1992.

and the emergence of a multiparty system had little to recommend them. Under Stalin, Khrushchev, and Brezhnev Russia had been a superpower, respected—or at least feared—all over the world. A breakdown of law and order had been as unthinkable as ethnic conflict. No wonder that support for movements advocating a "strong hand" was massive.

It could well be that the ideal of a strong hand held more attractions than did nationalism per se, though these two frequently go together. Public-opinion polls in parts of Russia have shown a spectacular increase in the number of the *gosudarstvenniki,* those advocating strong central power, during 1991 and 1992.[29] On the other hand, similar polls have shown a surprisingly lukewarm attitude with regard to national pride.[30] It would be mistaken to read sweeping conclusions into surveys that may not be representative; as various Russian authors have stressed, ethnic solidarity in Russia is probably as strong as elsewhere.[31]

After the Coup

The Russian right survived the August 1991 coup without major injury. True, the signatories of the "Message to the People," which had been published a month earlier, came under fire in the liberal press; Zhirinovsky was jostled and spat upon in a Moscow street, and some right-wing newspapers could not appear for a week or two. But by early September it was business as usual as far as the Russian right was concerned. No one was arrested; no one was even interrogated. Rasputin and Bondarev announced that their "Message" merely expressed their pain about the unprecedented tragedy of Russia, and that no one had been involved in a coup; Prokhanov made it known that he would be only too willing to sign the manifesto all over again.[32]

After the Second World War, distinguished intellectual collaborators with the Nazis, from Charles Maurras to Knut Hamsun, had been arrested, some had even been executed. How to explain the total lack of retaliation in a country such as Russia where repression in such cases had been the rule

29. V. Solovei, *Fenomen zhirinovskogo* (unpublished manuscript; Moscow, 1992); see also L. Byzov and N. Lvov in *Vek 20 i mir,* 3 (1989).

30. S. Vasiltsov, *Rodina,* 5 (1989). According to this investigation a mere 3.6 percent expressed great pride in Russian cultural achievements.

31. L. M. Drobisheva, "Etnicheskoye samopoznanie russkikh . . ." *Sovetskaya etnografiya,* 1 (1991); V. Solovei, *Fenomen.*

32. Bondarev in *Literaturnaya Rossiya* 35 (1991); Rasputin in *Russkii vestnik* (December 25, 1991); Prokhanov in *Literaturnaya Rossiya,* 40 (1991).

in the past? Partly it was because the coup was over so soon and many right-wingers did not even have the chance to express their support. Or was it magnanimity in victory? Perhaps Yeltsin and his team wanted to show that the days of violent repression were over. Perhaps they did not take their intellectual adversaries very seriously. Only time would tell whether such tolerance vis-à-vis those who had done the intellectual spadework for the coup was in the best interests of Russian democracy.

The nationalists went, no doubt, through some anxious moments during August 1991, expecting a backlash that never came. For a few days they kept very quiet, but once the immediate danger seemed to be over, some of them founded a committee to collect evidence on the basis of which Gorbachev was to be put on trial for high treason.

Their attitude toward Yeltsin was more complicated. While they instinctively knew that he was not one of them, some nationalists played with the idea of giving Yeltsin "critical support" during the fall of 1991. Perhaps he could be trusted, after all, more than other politicians to pursue a patriotic "Russian policy." But such sympathies never went very deep, did not last long, and were soon transferred to Yeltsin's deputy Colonel Rutskoi, who had openly quarreled with his boss.

The breakup of the Soviet Union following the coup was an enormous shock for the Russian right and indeed for all Russian patriots, a time of despair and mourning. But at the same time the spokesmen of the right claimed that never in the postrevolutionary period had the situation been as auspicious for "patriots" as after the failure of the coup.[33]

There was the widespread feeling, most forcefully expressed earlier on by Solzhenitsyn, that most of the republics had been millstones on the neck of Russia, and that the homeland would have been better off financially, politically, and even spiritually, without this burden. But against this there was the grief of believers in *derzhava*, state power: A little, truncated Russia could not possibly be the standardbearer of the historical Russian idea, as they interpreted it.

How can one explain this paradoxical reaction? The politicians and thinkers of the far right drew some of their optimism from the fact that the Communist party (including the National Bolshevik Russian Communist party) had ceased to exist. As a result, there was no longer any room for illusions such as had prevailed among sections of the right before the coup. The political scenery had become much more simple; the democrats and liberals now faced only one serious other contender in the struggle for power: the right-wing, "patriotic" camp. And since the democrats were in

33. M. Antonov, *Literaturnaya Rossiya,* 40 (1991).

power and their chances of success were virtually nonexistent, time was working for the right.[34] True, some nationalist leaders conceded that their camp had not so far succeeded in working out a serious socioeconomic program that would constitute an alternative to the policy pursued by the democrats. But since, as they saw it, the economic reforms carried out by Gaidar's team had such traumatic "antipopular" consequences, perhaps the call for a new leadership would gather strength and become an irresistible force even if no one knew exactly what the right stood for. Thus a three-pronged right-wing offensive got under way during the winter of 1991–1992, attacking the leadership for its impotence in dealing with separatist trends (as, for example, in the case of the Tatars); for insufficient support given to the Russians in the former republics (as in Moldova); and last, for incompetence in economic policy.

During that winter the different components of the right wing showed readiness to work closer together. Not all the new initiatives were well thought out and not all attracted a wider public. Thus the anti-Yeltsin demonstrations on Red Square in March 1992 were largely attended by elderly people; and the attempt at Voronovo, near Moscow, to convene the old Supreme Soviet, which had been dissolved, made a farcical impression. An evening of readings devoted to the poems of Anatoli Lukyanov (the former head of the Soviet parliament, and a writer of sorts) was also not likely to mobilize the masses.[35] Lukyanov had been a close friend of Gorbachev, but had double-crossed him and joined the "putschists."

Of greater political interest were the foundation meetings of various new political bodies. First in line was the Russian Liberation Union (ROS) which met on December 21, 1991, in the Trade Unions Hall, where facilities were provided free of charge. The main speakers were of the right-wing establishment (Alksnis, Volodin, Shafarevich) and the slogans voiced contained no surprises. The ROS opposed giving the Kurile Islands back to Japan, favored the organization of resistance against the Mafia, favored deals with the former republics that had split away only on the basis of world market prices. There was one original suggestion—to establish a "shadow cabinet" (both on a regional basis and in Moscow), which could take over the government of the country at any given time.

Despite Shafarevich's appeal to drop all sectarian interests, recriminations continued between the various extremist and conservative groups.

---

34. Views similar to Antonov's were expressed by Prokhanov in *Den*, 21 (1991); E. Volodin in *Sovetskaya Rossiya*, 28 (September 1992), and I. Shafarevich, *Pravda* (November 1, 1991).

35. The recital took place in the *Gorizont* movie house on March 26, 1992. Several stars of the right declared that they were willing to be locked up in Lukyanov's cell if he were permitted to read his own poems. The idea was, however, rejected by the authorities.

Sergei Baburin, a young official hailing from Siberia, was elected president of the new organization. A lawyer by training, Baburin had made a name for himself in Parliament during the Gorbachev years. Having been elected on a democratic ticket, he later veered more and more to the right and was frequently mentioned as a future leader of the right.

In January 1992 the third congress of the "Slavic Assembly" took place. It was attended mainly by extremists like "Archbishop Lazar"; Alexander Barkashov, the leader of the Russian National Movement (RND), a leading anti-Semite and organizer of karate squads; and Alexander Sterligov, a former KGB general who had opted first for service in the Yeltsin administration and later for a business career and involvement in right-wing politics.[36] The meeting was attended by several right-wing eccentrics from Poland and Bulgaria. One of them, a Bulgarian philosopher, asked: "How can you tolerate a government whose members cannot pronounce the letter (R) properly?" This question was widely reported in the Moscow press.

The most serious and ambitious attempt to consolidate the forces of the right was the "Congress of Civic and Patriotic Organizations," which opened in February 1992. It took place in a Moscow movie house, and was attended by some 2,500 delegates; the initiative came from groups of former centrists who had moved to the right—the Christian Democrats, led by Aksiuchits, and the Kadets, headed by Nikolai Travkin and Mikhail Astafiev. The meeting was addressed by Alexander Rutskoi, the Russian vice president, who was seen by the moderate right as a desirable replacement for Yeltsin.[37] But the assembly also listened to Vasiliev, the head of Pamyat, who had not been invited, but gatecrashed the meeting and forced the chairman and the audience to listen to his harangue while Cossacks with their traditional uniforms and whips kept order.

The purpose of the "Patriotic Organizations' " meeting was, in the words of Aksiuchits, to rally millions of people who had "lost their way," and to save the Russian state. Sizeable delegations from various parts of the former Union attended, as did representatives of eight "Cossack armies," all right-wing parliamentary factions, and scores of other organizations, including the "Christian Entrepreneurs," the "Merchant Guild," the "Nobility's Assembly," various officers' groups, two monarchist organizations, and so forth.

---

36. This group was largely identical with the Russian National Sobor, founded in Nizhni Novgorod and headed by Rasputin, Sterligov, and V. P. Feodorov (the governor of Sakhalin).

37. On the proceedings, *Pravda* (February 10, 1992), *Sovetskaya Rossiya* (February 11, 1992), and *Nezavisimaya gazeta* of the same period. The resolutions were published in a special thirty-two-page supplement to *Obozrevatel* (February 1992).

The meeting was financed by one of the new stock exchanges. Rutskoi's speech was listened to attentively but not always with enthusiasm; he mentioned, inter alia, the undesirable black uniforms of Pamyat. Nor were Aksiuchits and the other former centrists received with general applause. In their speeches there was too much stress on "democracy," "rule of law," and a patriotism that was "no one's enemy." One nationalist leader (Evgeni Kogan) referred to the ex-centrists as yesterday's establishment figures; *Sovetskaya Rossiya* found that the tenor of the meeting was too anticommunist, and for the vocal extremists of the right the whole affair was too tame and respectable. They did not like the democratic formulations and they missed the invocation of their traditional enemies. Eventually, on February 9, 1992, the congress voted (by no means unanimously) for the establishment of a Russian People's Assembly (*Sobranie*-RNS), which was essentially based on an alliance of three groups—the Christian Democrats, the Kadets, and Baburin's Russian National Union.

The main points in the Assembly's program were to prevent the disintegration of the historical Russian state, to stop political and economic chaos, and to lower the crime rate. For these purposes the RSFSR should be recognized as the successor of the Russian empire and the U.S.S.R. All agreements and treaties that caused the country's disintegration should be regarded as anticonstitutional (this referred, for instance, to the transfer of the Crimea to the Ukraine in 1954, and the reacquisition of South Ossetia). The armed forces should remain unified under RSFSR jurisdiction, and protection should be given to Russians living in other republics. The ideological and political course of action of the Russian (Yeltsin) government was considered by the Assembly as directed against Russia's interest and the will of the nation. Hence the need to replace Yeltsin's with a truly patriotic government.[38] But there were some references to democracy and human rights in the manifesto, which the extreme nationalists opposed. They disliked the new venture because it was no more than "extending support to Yeltsin from the right."

On March 11, 1992, following these meetings, the leaders of some twenty right-wing patriotic groups signed a declaration about the creation of a "united opposition." The short manifesto stressed the unity and intactness of Russia, the affirmation of spiritual traditions in all stages of Russian history on the basis of tolerance so as to prevent another collision between "White" and "Red." It bitterly attacked the economic reforms

---

38. *Postfactum* (February 9, 1992). The ouster of Gaidar in December 1992 was regarded by the right as a half-victory and the prospect of a center-right government (Volsky-Travkin) did not generate much enthusiasm in their ranks.

and the "betrayal of Russia's national interests at the behest of the international reactionary forces," which had been the main instigator of the downfall of the U.S.S.R. At the same time the "united opposition" stressed its attachment to constitutional political struggle and the concept of a civil society. Among the signatories were the Russian Assembly, four Russian Communist parties, and the Russian Party of National Renaissance. The various Pamyat factions and Zhirinovsky's movement were kept out.[39]

The consolidation of the forces of the right continued throughout 1992. At a convention of the Assembly in June 1992, 1,100 delegates took part. The meetings were held in the most prestigious conference halls of the capital, the extreme sectarians were kept out of the limelight, and the composition of the right-wing alliance appeared more clearly than before: The center-right forces were well represented, as were the former Communist party and the old trade unions. The new capitalists took part; they were headed by the president of the Nizhni Novgorod stock exchange and some public figures hitherto considered independent, such as Yuri Vlasov (an Olympic gold medalist in weight-lifting) and the well known movie director Stanislav Govorukhin, who had just produced a powerful and depressing documentary, *The Russia We Lost,* glorifying the late tsarist period. The meeting elected a new shadow government; there was, in the words of one observer, less emotion and better organization than in previous meetings.[40]

Certain broad trends have emerged concerning the Russian right ever since freedom of political organization returned to Russia. The early years of *glasnost* belonged to the sectarians and extremists. They were the first to appear on the political scene; they were certainly the shrillest and loudest. But their ideas were usually too bizarre, their activities too outlandish to be taken seriously. True, they continued to be active and their publications multiplied, but in view of their internal divisions, their inability to cooperate, and the absence of a leader of stature and mass appeal they did not become serious contenders in the struggle for power. Thus the political initiative passed to the "respectable" right, a coalition of "yesterday's men" from among the Communist party, the economic planning bureaus, and the security forces—and new groups and personalities who had appeared in the Gorbachev-Yeltsin years.

39. *Sovetskaya Rossiya* (March 10, 1992). One of the slogans in a leaflet distributed by the Russian Assembly in early April 1992 proclaimed: "Without Marxism-Leninism, without nationalist extremism."

40. *Nezavisimaya gazeta* (June 16, 1992). But the emotion was by no means entirely missing. *Den* habitually referred to the government as "traitors" and "occupiers." The democrats were characterized as people preaching American chauvinism, cultural racism, and the inhuman doctrine of the market (*Den,* 22 [1992]).

This did not mean that the extremists could be written off. Their hour of opportunity could still come at a time of political and economic breakdown. They were a factor of some importance as the storm troops of the right and, on the other hand, as the purveyors of some of their ideas. And lastly, the dividing line between the extremists and the "respectable right" was by no means hard and fast—it was more a matter of degree and emphasis than of fundamental principle and belief. When Sterligov, the KGB general reborn as a leader of the right, invoked "brutal and severe measures," he probably had in mind the same measures espoused by the extreme right.[41] Whereas the sectarian literature of 1989–1991 was written for a barely literate public, the weekly *Den,* which came into being in 1991 as the flagship of the "spiritual opposition," clearly had middlebrow (if not highbrow) political and literary ambitions in the beginning. But not many months passed before it began to lower its sights, what with the publication of excerpts from Adolf Hitler, the *Protocols,* and "conspiratology" of the most ludicrous kind. The articles were written in better Russian than that of the sectarian sheets, but there was no less abstruseness or madness.

What can be said in favor of those trying to streamline and modernize Russian nationalism? Kurginyan, who had the benefit of a scientific education, realized the importance of technology in the future development of Russia; he tried to combine "state democracy" (that is to say, something akin to Gaullism plus) with a civilized, pragmatic patriotism and "White Communism" (that is, the seemingly acceptable part of the achievements of the Soviet heritage).[42] But not only did these attempts lack consistency, there was something synthetic in the desperate attempt to find a new neoconservative doctrine, Russian style. Kurginyan realized that a new overarching "message" was needed, something akin to a new religion. But religions, even secular ones, even metareligions, are subject to organic growth; they cannot be manufactured in think tanks. With his extravagant charges—that the Russian democrats (the "Mafia") worked for the fascistization of Russia as the prelude to the fascistization of the world—Kurginyan was inviting ridicule; after all, his intellectual record was not that of one of the world's leading antifascists. And the extreme right distrusted him because of his close involvement with leaders of the Communist party during the last year of its existence, because of his ethnic origin, and

41. *Nezavisimaya gazeta* (June 16, 1992).

42. Kurginyan was greatly assisted in his writings and in the activities of the post-*perestroika* club by two aides: the economist Gennady Avrekh (b. 1941) and Vladimir Ovchinsky (b. 1955), an expert on law and the shadow economy (the "Mafia"). Among Kurginyan's other writings *Rossiya i mir* and *Metafizika gosudarstvennosti,* both Moscow 1992, should be mentioned.

because they did not like a Russian nationalism oriented to the future rather than the past.[43]

With Dugin we move from the realm of a quasi-rational approach to the depths of irrationality. True, Dugin too has progressed beyond the old-fashioned Russian extreme right. He realizes that not the Masons but the para-Masons are the enemy, and not the Jews per se, not even those living in Israel, but on the contrary the diaspora Jews. He dismisses socialism as part of mondialism, which is the enemy par excellence, and this has brought him into conflict with the National Bolsheviks, while others on the extreme right suspect him because of his lack of enthusiasm for the Russian Orthodox church. For Dugin, the inventor of "conspiratology," world history has to be rewritten. The eternal conflict between Atlanticists and Eurasians begins in ancient Egypt and it leads to the struggle between the good (Eurasian) and bad (Atlanticists).[44] Among the Nazis, the Eurasians were represented by Martin Bormann and Haushofer; in current Russian politics, by Nikolai Lukyanov, former chairman of the Supreme Soviet. In any case, Dugin's new doctrine seems to lead well beyond traditional Russian nationalism (though he would be most reluctant to admit it) to some European ultraconservatism.

From the breakup of the Soviet Union on, the "patriotic" camp began to win over new followers from the democrats. The Democratic Russia Alliance, which had originally been Yeltsin's power base, split, with the Christian Democrats and others moving to the right. But this was not the end of the process, merely the beginning. As one deputy, a former Yeltsin democrat, put it succinctly: "I am a Russian to my bones. For this reason a united Russia is more important for me than a democratic Russia."[45] Nor does Yeltsin believe that Russia was ever an empire in the usual sense, for Russians built up their enormous eastern territories peacefully. They were the donors with respect to all their neighbors.[46]

If some of the democrats moved toward patriotism, some of the

43. In addition to his regular contributions to *Den* in 1991 and 1992, see also *Yuridicheskaya gazeta,* 14–15 (1991) and 1 (1992), as well as *Glasnost* 50 (1991).

44. *Den,* 7 (1992). His "Introduction to Conspiratology" appeared in *Den,* 14–18 (1991), his "Anatomy of Mondialism" in *Politika* (November 1991). For a detailed survey of the doctrines of Kurginyan and Dugin see V. Solovei, "Russkii natsionalisticheskii establishment—novaya volya" (unpublished; Moscow, 1992). In September 1992 the first issue of a new periodical *(Elementy)* appeared. Edited by Dugin it contained various geopolitical articles but also pictures of Hitler, Himmler, Goebbels et al. (*Éléments* was the title of the mouthpiece of the French New Right).

45. Anatoly Medvedyev, in *Novoye vremya,* 17 (1992).

46. *Literaturnaya gazeta* (April 22, 1992); *Russkaya mysl* (April 10, 1992).

nationalists groped their way back toward national socialism, or even bol-shevism, where their ideological journey had started. An interesting exam-ple was Mikhail Antonov, the leading nationalist publicist, whose name has been mentioned more than once in our review of the New Right. Looking back in 1992 on the "patriots' " lack of success even in the face of horrendous mistakes by the liberals, Antonov tended to put the blame on right-wing ideological delusions. As he saw it, the right had gone too far in its anticommunism; it was simply not true that, as Shafarevich and others argued, socialism was nothing but a death wish on the part of millions of people. Could it be seriously denied that precisely under the Stalinist regime after the Second World War the Soviet Union had been at the zenith of its power, having created the world's best system of public health and education?[47] With their anticommunist attacks against this system, with their constant harping on the "genocide" of the Russian people and the leading part of aliens in establishing and maintaining the system, the furious national patriots were the right flank of the "destroyers of Russia." Hence Antonov's conclusion: To preserve Russia's independence from Western encroachments and from attempts to turn Russia into a cheap source of raw material for the exploiters, the country had to become a great power again. But this was impossible without a great messianic idea embracing the whole of Russian history—that is to say, including bolshevism and Stalinism. And since a return to the world before the Revolution was impossible, this meant, by process of elimination, a return to the system that, with all its imperfections, had made Russia a strong power for seventy years.[48]

Mention has been made of the main voices of the right who had been heard first in the 1960s and 1970s, such as Igor Shafarevich, Valeri Skur-latov, and Mikhail Antonov and the gurus of *Nash Sovremennik*. These were followed by the "black colonels," such as Alksnis and Petrushenko, who made their appearance in the Supreme Soviet under Gorbachev. Andreyeva and Zhirinovsky seemed at one time among the most promising contenders for power, but after them came yet another generation of ideologists such as Prokhanov and Dugin, as well as "organization men" who may now be only at the beginning of their political career. Perhaps the most renowned of them was Sergei Baburin, whose name has figured earlier

47. M. Antonov, "Na uzkoi doroge sektantstva," *Literaturnaya Rossiya* (May 15, 1992).

48. Ibid. But this appeal seems to have fallen on deaf ears as far as many prominent figures on the extreme right are concerned. The poet Tatyana Glushkova, to give but one example, engaged in a crescendo of condemnation of the international criminals, the leaders of the Bolshevik party, who had engaged in a "holocaust without precedent of the Slavic people." *Molodaya gvardiya*, 5–6 (1992). This was exactly the shrill rhetoric that Antonov and his friends decried because they thought it would lead to the defeat of the patriotic forces.

in the story of the Russian right. But Baburin's field of action, in the final analysis, was the parliament; as a popular—let alone national—leader, he had not yet earned his spurs.

There are other less well known figures such as Ilya Konstantinov, a native of Leningrad who made his debut in the Russian Christian movement and was instrumental in drawing some of the striking workers in the Siberian coal mines to the cause of the right.[49] Mikhail Astafiev, Nikolai Travkin, and Nikolai Pavlov made their name as leaders of various centrist groups that gradually veered to the right. Like Baburin, most had been members of the Communist party before 1985; Travkin had been a "Hero of Soviet Labor" and one of the showpieces of the Brezhnev era.

Closer to the old Communist party were Viktor Anpilov, a native of the Kuban and head of the Russian Communist Workers party, who declared that much in Pamyat appealed to him. Anpilov had represented the Soviet media in Nicaragua, whereas Nikolai Lysenko, leader of the National Republican Party of Russia, had been an active member of Pamyat. But he realized early on that this was not an ideal springboard for an ambitious young politician. Born in Irkutsk district, he is still in his early thirties, like Baburin and Anpilov. According to the constitution they are too young to be elected president of Russia. On the extreme right Alexander Barkashov made a name for himself. Also a graduate of Pamyat, he established the "Russian National Unity Group," was active in the convening of various Slavic congresses, and became equally famous as a karate instructor and an author of old-style polemics against Jews and Freemasons.[50] More statesmanlike was V. Feodorov, a somewhat older man who had become governor of Sakhalin under Gorbachev but later joined the right wing.

Few of these new figures were great orators exuding the charisma of a true political leader. On the other hand, eccentrics were not lacking. One such was Aleksei Nevzorov, a very talented television producer. Nevzorov was almost constantly involved in amazing adventures—someone had tried

49. For a profile of and interview with Ilya Konstantinov, see *Moskovskii literator* (May 1992).

50. Almost all leaders of the New Right belong to the same age cohort; they were all born in the 1940s and 50s, with Baburin and Konstantinov among the youngest. Most have some academic degrees—Nikolai Pavlov in the life sciences, Anishenko (of the Christian party) in Russian literature. Aksiuchits did not win his degree in philosophy, but studied it for five years. The same is true with regard to the central Cossack leadership; Martinov (b. 1942) has a degree in economics; his deputy Vladimir Naumov (b. Moscow, 1951) studied languages at the academy of the Ministry of Defense. Ataman Pyotr Feodorov is a geophysicist by training. The one exception is Barkashov (b. Moscow 1953), who comes from an impeccable working-class background and left school at seventeen. In 1992 the Palea publishing house put out a series of biographical booklets on leaders of the Russian right including Baburin, Sterligov, Limonov, Prokhanov, and others called *Zhizn zamechatelnykh Rossiyan* (Moscow, 1992).

to kill him; a Scottish duchess had fallen in love with him. It usually turned out after a little while that the reports were greatly exaggerated.

Of all the new-style Russian nationalists Nevzorov is undoubtedly the best-known, the most popular, and at the same time the most despised. His St. Petersburg television show, *600 Seconds,* is watched by seventy million viewers. It was initially a local chronicle, mainly of crime, in which Nevzorov figured as a courageous, unpolitical, anti-establishment figure, voicing the concerns of the man in the street, attacking the Communist bureaucrats and the "Mafia" (that is to say, merchants and dealers demanding exorbitant prices). However, within a year the program became highly politicized—favoring a strong, united Russia, defending the interests of Russians outside Russia. Nevzorov dropped his erstwhile monarchism and rabid anticommunism and moved closer to a National Bolshevik stance. Yet, paradoxically, his extreme attacks against his perceived enemies often had an effect the opposite of what he intended. He probably saved Sobchak, the Leningrad mayor, by his unbridled attacks. At a time when the human-rights records of the Baltic countries became suspect, he generated support for their governments among the Russian intelligentsia—again as a result of clearly distorted reports from Riga. He helped to discredit Kriuchkov, the last head of the KGB, by leaking his secret report to the Soviet parliament. Nevzorov had wanted to help Kriuchkov, but the report in question (about CIA-American intrigues) strained credulity to such an extent that it had the opposite effect. In these cases many Russians seem to have reached the conclusion that any individual denigrated to such an extent by the famous television reporter-producer could not be all bad. But Nevzorov did remain an important influence, not through any new and original ideas, but by helping to set the political agenda.

Another such eccentric was Karem Rash, a Kurd by nationality and a teacher by profession, who was very popular among the armed forces. He made it known in many articles that the Soviet army was not only brave and professionally competent but also the embodiment of all moral and cultural values.

The world of right-wing politics was very much a man's world but there were a few exceptions such as Nina Andreyeva, some female poets and essayists, and above all the striking-looking Sashi Umalatova, who acquired admirers in view of her unbridled attacks in Parliament against Gorbachev and later Yeltsin.

What action has been taken by the authorities against leading members of the para-fascist groups? According to the Russian constitution and the criminal code, incitement to racial hatred is a punishable offense, so, of course, are the illegal carrying of arms and violent physical attacks. But the legal authorities and the police were reluctant to take strict measures. There were virtually no precedents; charges because of racial incitement had practically never been made in Soviet history.

It was only in the summer of 1992 that Aleksei Batogov, editor of a *Stürmer*-like journal named *Russkoye voskressenie,* was arrested. But his friends and colleagues jumped to his defense: It was unjust to arrest him because he was an invalid; it was unwarranted to accuse him of racism because he had worked for the South African service of Moscow Radio. And it was out of place to call him a fascist because his mother had worked for Russian military intelligence in World War Two. Batogov was released after a few days and his journal continued to appear.[51]

In St. Petersburg Aleksei Andreyev, the head of squads of Nazi-like storm troopers, was arrested in September 1992, but only following some violent attacks as the result of which an Azerbaidjani merchant had been killed. St. Petersburg was one of the main fortresses of the extreme right which had the support of sections of the local militia. In fact, its leader was a police captain named Yuri Belayev. His superiors explained that it was none of their business what a police officer did in his spare time. Russia had become a very free country indeed or, in other words, chaos prevailed.[52]

Why has the Russian right not been more successful given the auspicious political conditions? To some extent the question seems premature, because its future prospects are far from negligible in view of the critical political and economic situation likely to prevail in Russia for a long time to come. Two circumstances come to mind that seem to have played a role in the early phase of the emergence of the nationalist movement after 1987. One is the absence of leaders of genius or at least of great talent, capable of mobilizing the masses such as Hitler or Mussolini did. More important yet, the differences of opinion among the patriots have been enormous as noted more than once. This concerns the political future as well as the economic system, the preservation of parts of the Bolshevik ideology and practice, the question of the borders of the new Russia, and many other issues. What holds the new Right together is its total rejection of the reform regime. There is no unanimity on what Russia should be like in the postreform age.

All this made lasting collaboration between the various components of the Russian right unlikely. But it does not rule out the establishment of a common front for a limited period of time. The presence of a common enemy and the desire to overthrow the reform government make for

51. *Literaturnaya rossiya,* September 18, 1992.

52. *Izvestiya,* September 18, 1992.

strange bedfellows as the establishment of the National Salvation Front has demonstrated. Founded in September 1992, it had its first convention the month after.[53]

This and similar initiatives made it appear that the announcement of the final and irrevocable demise of communism is somewhat premature, in Russia as in other successor states of the Soviet Union. National Bolshevism has a long and intricate history, but almost always it has been of greater intellectual than of political significance. Politically, in other words, it had been ineffectual as in Weimar Germany. If it should be more effective in Russia than elsewhere, it will be because of the presence of a third force, the *gosudarstvenniki*, those believing in the necessity of strong central state power. They are not necessarily believers in extreme ideologies nor do they reject altogether economic and social reform provided it does not proceed too fast and too far.

The support of the *gosudarstvenniki* could provide financial and organizational support to the Nationalist-Communist coalition and even a certain measure of respectability. But at the same time it imposes a discipline that cannot be to the extremists' liking. The *gosudarstvenniki* want above all order at home and normal relations with the major powers. They want an authoritarian regime but no excesses, which leaves not much scope for the National Bolshevik utopia. Its followers are bound to feel betrayed. Was it for business as usual that they went to fight for the glorious counterrevolution?

53. On the first convention of the National Salvation Front, *Russkaya mysl,* October 30, 1992, some two dozen patriotic groups of right- and left-wing persuasion were represented. Only the Slavic Assembly of KGB general Sterligov and Anpilov's Communist faction boycotted the meeting. Zhirinovsky and *Pamyat* were not invited.

Chapter Sixteen

CONCLUSION: RUSSIAN NATIONALISM TODAY AND TOMORROW

I

NO ONE HAS WRITTEN MORE ELOQUENTLY about the existence of different natural and national qualities, without which the world would be a boring and gray place, than Academician Dmitri Likhachev, the grand old man of Russian historiography and letters. He has argued with great force that true patriotism spiritually enriches individuals and nations and that it is the noblest of feelings: "It is not even a feeling, it is the most important aspect of both a personal and social culture, of the spirit in which a person and a whole nation can somehow rise above themselves and set goals that are beyond personal aims."[1] Likhachev draws a sharp dividing line between patriotism and nationalism, "the greatest of human misfortunes": "It lives in the shadows and only pretends to be based on love for one's country. But in fact it is spawned by malice and hatred for other nations and for those people in one's own nation who do not share these nationalistic views."

As Likhachev sees it, nationalism as a sentiment stems from a lack of confidence and from inadequacy. It is the manifestation of a nation's weakness, not of its strength. Usually only weak nations are infected by nationalism; they try to maintain themselves with the help of nationalist passion and ideology.

1. D . Likhachev, "O Russkom," here quoted from *Reflections on Russia* (Boulder, Col., 1991), pp. 55–59; see also *Zametki i nabliudeniya* (Moscow, 1991).

For most of their history, Likhachev says, Russians have lived in peace with their neighbors; he cites the great historian Sergei Solovyov (the father of Vladimir Solovyov) to the effect that Russians cannot be enticed by unpleasant boasting about their nationality, and he also adduces Dostoyevsky, who wrote that "narrow nationalism is not in the Russian spirit."[2] Hence Likhachev's conclusion that "a conscious love for one's nation cannot be combined with hatred for others': If a person loves his own people and his own family he will more likely love other nations and other families. Each person has a general inclination toward hatred or love. . . . Therefore hatred of other people sooner or later is passed on to some people in one's own nation. . . ." In its most highly realized forms, patriotism is always peace-loving, actively peace-loving, and not simply indifferent to other nationalities.

Likhachev is for some Russians the conscience of the nation, its supreme moral authority. But are his views historical fact or categorical imperative? Some of his observations have certainly been borne out by historical experience. Those who represent themselves today as the most pious of the Orthodox, praying louder than the rest of the congregation, beating their breasts harder and bowing lower during religious services, often show greater enthusiasm for the fight against what they perceive as evil than they do for the practice of Christian love. Not for them the preoccupation with salvation and love for one's neighbors; not for them the story of the Good Samaritan or the Sermon on the Mount. Their main preoccupation is with the devil rather than with God. Satan fascinates them more than Christ does, and the struggle against the devil and his servants takes precedence over all other commandments. There is a striking absence of love—perhaps an inability to love—among the zealots.

A critic has noted the absence—with a few exceptions—in the literature of the far right of the lyrical element and of love poetry.[3] Women, and in particular younger women (who are considered ideologically unreliable), are more often than not depicted in a negative light. The only romantic love that does appear in this literature is that of the nationalist eros—the knight in shining armor defending the fatherland (*rodina*), a "female."

How much support is there for Likhachev's views? He is not a politi-

2. Dostoyevsky continues: "Our people display their deficiency with relentless force and are ready to talk about their defects before the whole world and to complain endlessly about themselves. . . ." It is only fair to add that on other occasions Dostoyevsky wrote about Russian nationalism in a different vein.

3. Natalya Ivanova, "Russkii Vopros," *Znamya* 1 (1992), p. 200. There has been, however, a traditional misogynistic note also among the Communists; Trotsky's "Literature and Revolution" (1923) is a prime example, Stalin's and Zhdanov's comments on Anna Akhmatova another.

cian, not the head of a party. But there is a considerable section of the educated Russian public who constitute the moderate nationalist camp and who are in broad sympathy with at least some of his views. They have in common an emphasis on patriotism; in many (but not all) cases they share a religious faith. They want to live in a free Russia (not necessarily on the pattern of Western democracy) and they were deeply saddened by the loss of large territories populated predominantly by Russians. Among them are, to give but a few names, Sergei Averintsev, a distinguished historian of medieval culture and theology; Alexander Tsypko, one of the political scientists who acquired fame in the *glasnost* era; and some of the editors of the literary magazine *Novy mir,* as well as literary critics such as Igor Vinogradov and Alla Latynina. Above all, there were Solzhenitsyn and his circle.[4] Finally there are political leaders from Yeltsin to Sobchak who, following the downfall of the Soviet Union, have insisted with increasing frequency and intensity on Russian concerns and interests. It is probably easiest to define the views of the national liberals if we compare them with the radical democrats, who are, by and large, in the Sakharov tradition.

For the radicals the creation of democratic institutions is the paramount task; the absence of such institutions was the main cause of Russia's misfortunes in the past, and they fear that freedom in their country will not be secure until such institutions are firmly entrenched. They have no wish to imitate the West slavishly, but nor do they feel an inner urge to follow a specifically Russian social and economic policy. They see no specific Russian tradition that could serve now as a guide for the perplexed.

Most of the radical democrats are not religious believers. They regard the loss of traditionally Russian territories as a misfortune, but do not see a possible way to undo it, at least not in the foreseeable future. They have no agreed program concerning Russia's economic system. Some support a classical liberal approach on the lines of Friedrich von Hayek and Milton Friedman; others prefer a mixed economy. They strongly insist on a multi-party system and regard the extreme right as the main threat, which, if in power, would lead Russia back into tyranny, war, and total disaster. They love the culture of their native land; in fact, they are often more Russian— in the tradition of the nineteenth-century intelligentsia—than they know. But they are pitiless in their criticism of the dark sides of Russia's past. They are open to Western influences and their feeling of nostalgia for the old Russia is not as intense as that of the national liberals. They tend to agree

4. There has been, not surprisingly, constant ideological fluidity. While Solzhenitsyn has been defended against the democrats by a liberal such as G. Pomerants, some of the erstwhile Christian Democrats (A. Gulyga, Y. Kublanovsky, Aksiuchits) have moved toward the national-ist camp.

with what Ernest Renan wrote in a famous essay more than a hundred years ago: "Nations are based on consent; the existence of a nation is a daily plebiscite. Nations are not eternal; they had a beginning; they will have an end."[5]

In broad terms these are "liberal democrats" in the European sense, whereas the moderate nationalists are conservatives who are not in principle averse to political democracy in Russia. But given Russia's past and the enormous difficulties lying ahead, the nationalists think that an (enlightened) authoritarian regime is more or less foreordained. They hope that religion will play a crucial role in the future. They tend to idealize pre-1917 Russia, and envisage a political and social regime not altogether unlike the one prevailing then—cleansed, of course, of its negative features but in line with old Russian traditions. Most of them believe that the price that had to be paid for freedom was probably too high. What future is there for a Russia deprived of the Ukraine, White Russia, the Crimea, and predominantly Russian northern Kazakhstan?

This is the strongest point in the moderate nationalists' thinking and it is shared to some extent by liberals and radical democrats. The balkanization of the former Soviet Union is a tragedy; it will certainly make democratization infinitely more difficult. It is paradoxical that at a time when borders are going down in Western and Central Europe, the trend in the East is toward secession and separatism. While theoretically every nationality, even the smallest, has the right of sovereignty, objective factors—not least the intermingling of races and peoples in the modern world—often make this impossible. There is no moral commandment that nationalities should exert their abstract right. Scotland has been part of the United Kingdom for about the same period the Ukraine has been part of Russia. There is resentment in Scotland (against being ruled by London) similar to that prevailing in the Ukraine. But most Scots have understood that no one would gain if Scotland were a fully independent sovereign state. It was the mistake of many Russians to show insufficient sensitivity vis-à-vis the minority nationalities such as the persistence of the belief that the Ukrainians had no more in common than a language, or perhaps only a dialect.[6]

5. A lecture at the Sorbonne, "Qu'est-ce qu'une nation?" (Paris, March 11, 1882). Renan added: "The European federation will probably replace them. But this is not the law of the century in which we live." In later years he considered this speech his credo and hoped that it would be remembered in a future in which modern civilization would be engulfed in the deadly uncertainties of nationalism and race.

6. The printing of books in Ukrainian—with some exceptions—was forbidden from 1863 to 1905. Until recently the trend among the cultural elite in the Ukraine was toward bilingualism. Shevchenko, the national poet, wrote more in Russian than in Ukrainian. Gogol and Korolenko wrote only in Russian. Russian historians have bitterly reproached their Ukrainian colleagues

Soviet rule was in some (cultural) respects less repressive toward the nationalities than tsarist rule had been, but the Soviet experiment in coalescence *(slyanie)* was unsuccessful since it was imposed from above. Resentment of Moscow continued to grow, and once political controls were removed there was no keeping the nations and nationalities from seceding, whatever the cost. In the Soviet Union, and previously in tsarist Russia, membership in a multinational state had certain advantages, like being a member of a prestigious club. But once the reputation of the club declined sharply, this particular motive disappeared. If Russia had tried to accommodate Ukrainian nationalism, the split would probably not have occurred. But a serious attempt, on the basis of a true federation involving home rule, was never made and once the majority of Ukrainians had voted for full independence, there was little the new Russian leadership could do to maintain the Union. A closer relationship may emerge in the more distant future, once the dreams attached to sovereignty fade. But in the meantime, Russian patriots will only feel impotent frustration at existing without Kiev, the cradle of Russian culture and statehood. The only alternative, from a patriotic Russian point of view, is to invade the Ukraine, hardly a practical proposition. Some Republicans in America believe to this day that Roosevelt and Truman "lost China" in 1938–1948; Russian nationalists now blame Gorbachev and Yeltsin for the loss of the Ukraine, rather than those who preceded them during the last two hundred years.

II

The breakup of the Soviet Union is the central event bound to shape the course of Russian nationalism and of Russian politics, as far ahead as one can see. It could be compared with the impact of the Treaty of Versailles (1919) on postwar Germany and with the loss of North Africa for French politics in the 1950s and 1960s. Versailles—the feeling of national humiliation—was one of the main factors in the rise of national socialism; the retreat from North Africa brought France to the brink of civil war. Seen in retrospect, the losses suffered by Germany and France were far from fatal. Germany lost its unimportant colonies and a few provinces such as Alsace-Lorraine, Poznań, and parts of Upper Silesia inhabited largely by reluctant

---

from Hrushevski to Doroshenko and our days for making excessive claims for the roots and the extent of an independent Ukrainian consciousness, statehood, culture, and, of course, Ukrainian borders. These criticisms have not always been wrong, but it was a case of the pot calling the kettle black.

Germans. The loss of the Maghreb resulted in the exodus of several hundreds of thousands of Frenchmen. The new Russia, on the other hand, has no more than half the population of the old Soviet Union, and many millions of ethnic Russians now live outside Russia; they have become ethnic minorities at the mercy of new, not-too-tolerant masters.

Ten years after the loss of the Maghreb, France was better off and at greater peace with itself than ever before. Seventy years after Versailles, forty-five and more years after another lost war, Germany is the strongest country in Europe.

The Russian shock was more severe. True, the loss of empire did not come as the result of a military defeat. True, some Russian nationalists had argued for a long time that their country would be better off without the Central Asian republics and perhaps also the Caucasus. Russia, they claimed, had been exploited and in some ways subverted by the non-Russian republics; a few nationalist spokesmen, such as Valentin Rasputin, had suggested well before August 1991 that Russia should take the initiative and leave the Union. But imperial ambitions and the feeling of historical mission were still very much present—and, in any case, no one had assumed that the Slavic republics, too, would secede.

The full extent of the trauma was realized only as time went by. As in Germany after 1918, there was much readiness to accept all kinds of "stab in the back" theories: The disaster had been caused by Russia's sworn enemies abroad and at home. There was growing resentment, particularly of the ingrates in the Baltic countries, the Ukraine, and Moldova, but also of the Caucasus, which had, after all, benefited to no small extent from Russian help and protection. There was growing anger about the treatment of the Russians outside Russia, and demands were made that the Crimea and the major Russian enclaves in the Ukraine, Kazakhstan, and elsewhere should become part of the Russian Republic. Was it not the duty of the Russian government to protect Russian interests outside the borders of the old RSFSR; had not all self-respecting countries throughout history been ready to protect the lives and interests of fellow citizens if these had been in jeopardy?

This mood was widespread and it would have been suicidal for the Russian democrats to leave patriotism and the defense of national interests to the right. As in Germany after Versailles, it would have been tantamount to surrendering the country to the extremists. The assertion of Russian power and the defense of Russian interests were not only justified but politically vital. The great danger was that the republics that had seceded would prove increasingly recalcitrant in their nationalist intoxication, un-willing to accommodate legitimate Russian interests. This in turn, would make the Russians even more resentful and hostile, and the result would be conflicts even less amenable to solution. Appeals to reason in such circumstances are bound to fall on deaf ears, and the stage is set for an outburst of the worst instincts. This was the lesson of the new order established after Versailles. The lesson of France was that a right-wing, patriotic leadership was needed to make the country accept the retreat, adjust itself to a new status, and step back from the brink. Are these lessons applicable to Russia? Each historical situation is unique, but these are the closest parallels one can think of in recent history.

III

Russia, it is sometimes said, has been condemned by history and geography to be a great power. But what if the forces of cohesion should be weaker than generally believed? What if the disintegration of the Soviet Union should be followed by the disintegration of Russia and the emergence of several independent or semi-independent smaller units, such as Tataristan, Siberia, Yakutia, and others? This possibility was discussed even before the Soviet Union ceased to exist, and it certainly cannot be ruled out at the present time.[7] The argument runs approximately as follows: It is easy to imagine Russia as a great power or as a multitude of small units. Anything in between is unstable and unlikely to last. True, there are forces opposing further disintegration, but how strong are they? These forces are the Russian nationalists and the old Communists on the one hand, and the West on the other. The West wants a "new world order" in which peace and quiet prevail, so that it can cultivate its own garden. A united Russia (provided it is not *too* strong) would serve Western interests better than a chaotic state of affairs, which would create new political and economic problems, possibly a stream of refugees, and, generally speaking, a big zone of insecurity extending from St. Petersburg to Vladivostok.

Sooner or later (the argument continues) empires tend to reappear in a diminished form, as the old Roman empire has been reincarnated as modern Italy. The readjustment might be painful—Britain and France did not easily find a new role in the world—but eventually normalization takes place, the old imperial dreams and manifest destinies are forgotten, and a new routine sets in.

How likely is normalization on these lines? No one knows with any

---

7. Denis Dragunov has been among the most persuasive proponents of this thesis in a series of articles in *Vek dvatsatiy i mir,* in *Druzhba narodov,* and in *Stolitsa,* 19 (1992).

certainty how strong the nationalist forces are and how they are likely to fare in future.[8] However, there is reason to assume that if a *smuta*, a time of troubles and disorder, should take place, it will not last long and will eventually lead to a new order of sorts. The comparison with France after the loss of the Maghreb is immaterial, for the loss of territories in Russia's case is infinitely greater; so is the number of Russians living outside the Russian Republic. If France had fallen apart and split into a dozen provinces in the 1960s there would have been a precedent. But France did not disintegrate. While small might be beautiful in other respects, human coexistence on the territory of the former Russian Republic would not necessarily be more peaceful or in other respects more beneficial if instead of one entity there were ten or a hundred. On the contrary, centrifugal trends on the territory of the Russian Republic are likely to strengthen Russian nationalism rather than weaken it. They could provide a new impetus for reunification—by necessity, imposed from above—an impetus that has been absent in the recent past.

The assumption that political conditions in Russia will become normal as the result of successful economic reform cannot be taken for granted. A quick improvement in the economic situation is unlikely and, in any case, man does not live by bread alone. He (or she) needs spiritual beliefs, myths, and symbols—and some countries, such as Russia, need them more than others. Human existence is not a financial balance sheet, a series of profits, losses, allocations, and budgets. In this respect postcommunist Russia is a desert. Both communism and nationalism are adrift; this is why they may find it easy to get together on the basis of some common denominator; the churches seem to have neither the message nor the apostles that could generate the energies, the enthusiasm, the willingness to sacrifice that will be needed in the years to come. Such a vacuum opens the door to all kinds of madnesses. After the Second World War, Germany and Japan succeeded in building prosperous and civilized societies without the benefit of a specifically German or Japanese idea or faith. True, their defeat had been total, which made it easier to make a new start and shed outdated beliefs. It would have been suicidal for Germans, Italians, or Japanese to refuse to accept their fate; they had to accept it to survive. The Russians, on the other hand, were not defeated in war; on the contrary, successive generations have been educated to believe in their country's invincibility, military and

8. The Russian public seems to be evenly divided on this issue. According to a public-opinion poll in early 1992, 44 percent of those asked thought that there was a high probability that the nationalist patriots would grow stronger and eventually take over, whereas 46 percent thought such a probability was low. V. A. Grushin in *Moskovskaya pravda* (March 5, 1992).

otherwise. In these circumstances a truly new beginning is psychologically much more difficult.

IV

At a time of deep crisis, the negative and ugly aspects of Russia's past—tyranny, darkness, and servitude—tend to obtrude, rather than the beautiful and harmonious features. But there always was a Russia that was a source of pride to its sons and daughters, a Russian people showing "great cheerfulness in the midst of desperation, very tolerably agreeable, and gay."[9] Foreign visitors who wrote scathingly about the psychological effects of despotism also noted the hospitality and kindness toward perfect strangers, the charity shown to cripples and blind men, and the *shirokaya natura*. They had much to say about the decency of common people, about Russia's many great talents and cultural achievements, about a literature that went further back in time than English, French, and German, a literature that "enlightened and transformed all of the human world" (as Solovyov put it), a folklore as rich as the Russian language, and folk songs, sentimental, sad, and gay, as moving and beautiful as any in the world. They also noted Russia's openness to new influences, an openness greater, perhaps, than any other country's.

Nature played a crucial role in the development of the particular character of the Russian people—the infinite wide-open spaces, the forests, the majestic rivers. No people have been closer to nature than the Russians, and no authors have more lovingly written about it. Likhachev has called the Orthodox church "happiest Christianity, a faith of great sensuous beauty": "Note that even Catholic churches are barren in their grandiosity. But see how a Russian church, thanks to its light, brightly shining iconostasis, thanks to the humanistic organization of space, its cosmic nature, and golden flames, is simply beautiful, and it shines."

And Orthodoxy was not all empty pomp and ritual: Helmuth von Moltke, the great strategist of the last century, was not a man easily swayed by impressions or given to exaggeration, nor did he belong to the Orthodox church. Yet attending the coronation of Alexander II in the Kremlin, he was most deeply moved by the solemn, splendid procession, the wonderful church melodies, and the magnificence of the occasion. Russians have loved their country with a love "like a Russian, strong, fierce, and gentle" (Lermontov); they have fought and defeated foreign invaders even when resistance seemed hopeless.

9. J. G. Kohl, *Russia* (London, 1842), p. 66.

It is not at all difficult to compose a long ode to the beauties of Russia, the sterling character and the great achievements of many of its sons and daughters. What other people would have survived the ordeals that have been Russia's part throughout history? True, much of this belongs to a rural Russia that has gone forever. The nostalgia of the Russian right is pure Rousseau, though the rightists have never read the sage of Geneva. Rousseau wrote that a rural community could be the only guarantee of freedom and happiness; from the capital, "permanent pestilence is exuded, which undermines and eventually destroys the whole nation." One could not think of a more fitting envoi to Vasili Belov's 1986 *Vse vperedi* ("Everything Is Still Ahead"). But neither the golden nor the silver age of Russian culture emanated from rural communities; and if, as Likhachev and others believe, there will be yet another cultural renaissance in the years to come, it will again come from the cities.[10]

The greatness of Russia has never been in dispute, and the greater the achievements, the greater the pain felt at the end of seventy years of ruin and destruction. Where the moderate nationalists (and a fortiori the extreme nationalists) have gone wrong is in the belief that only they have been feeling the pain, whereas the radical democrats are "cultural nihilists," ignoring or despising everything Russian. This is not even correct with regard to the Soviet regime; if under Lenin, Stalin, and their successors irreplaceable monuments were destroyed and other horrible damage was done, it is also true that many more copies of the Russian classics were printed (and more plays were performed and more art was exhibited) than in the seventy years before the Revolution. Under Soviet rule, a wholly negative attitude toward traditional Russian culture prevailed for only a few years and only in a few disciplines.

The accusations that the liberals have a "nihilistic" attitude toward Russian history and culture are untrue—unless, of course, one implies that a true patriot had to admire and cherish everything that happened or was produced before 1917, however evil, ugly, or stupid: "Our country, right or wrong."

The charges of "cultural nihilism" and "cosmopolitanism" on the part of the Russian right against the democrats are red herrings, with one exception: the role of the Orthodox church in future Russian society. Not all those on the right are religious believers, and not everyone on the left is an atheist. But it is true that the democrats, by and large, stand for a secular society, whereas the rightists, including the moderate Russophiles, are willing to give the Orthodox church a central role in the political life of their country. In recent years the Russophiles have rediscovered Russian

10. Likhachev was among those believing in a revival. See *Moskovskie novosti* (March 22, 1992).

religious thought of the first half of the twentieth century, and they have been influenced by the more conservative among these thinkers.[11] All of them believed that Christianity had a contribution to make to the political reconstruction of Russia, but their views diverged widely. Georgi Fedotov was a democrat, whereas Ivan Il'in (whose role was discussed earlier in our study) rejected a multiparty system and advocated a mixture of dictatorship and theocracy. Anton Kartashev proposed a middle way: a Christian state that was not a full-fledged theocracy.[12]

The extreme right opted wholeheartedly for Il'in, frequently reprinting his political essays—but seldom, if ever, his theological writings. "Love thy neighbor," as far as they are concerned, applies only to fellow Orthodox Christians. The moderate Russophiles, including Solzhenitsyn, were more attracted by Kartashev. The democrats, while paying due respect to the church, are tied to the idea of a modern, secular state and to the separation of church and state. Thus the true ideological dividing line between democrats and moderate Russophiles is not their degree of attachment to Russia's past and culture but their conception of the absolute, eternal value of the nation and the political role of the church in a future Russia. Even this dividing line is somewhat artificial, because many conservatives are not religious believers, and because the church is reluctant to assume too active a part in the conduct of political affairs. In the last analysis, the true differences between the democrats and the moderate nationalists seem to be not intellectual, but rooted in emotion and instinct—which makes them more rather than less real.

V

How valid is Likhachev's distinction between patriotism and nationalism? It certainly has supporters all over the world. What do we understand by patriotism? asks a French thinker, Claude Casanova. The term obviously comes from the Latin; *"patria"* means "the country of the fathers"; one does not choose it, it comes to us by an accident of birth. But in European consciousness since ancient times, the fatherland is not just the country in which one lives but also the country one loves, with which one is connected

---

11. *Novy mir,* to give but one example, devoted more space to religious than to political-social discussion in 1990–1992.

12. For the writings of Fedotov, Berdyaev, and Il'in, see the bibliographical note below. Kartashev's important contribution in this connection is *Vozsozdanie svyatoi rusi* (Paris, 1956). For a short discussion of the issues involved, see N. N. Petro in *Christianity and Russian Culture in Soviet Society* (Boulder, Colo., 1990).

through many ties of tradition and culture, which one adopts and by which one is adopted. The nationalist, on the other hand, makes his fatherland a fetish, the subject of an exclusive cult. His love for the fatherland is superior to all others'; his fatherland is essentially different from all others and preferable to them. One's national duties are more important than all others: "Nationalists are excessive and exclusive patriots, their patriotism limits their humanity."[13]

But Russian nationalists of the far right take violent exception to such differentiations. At their most primitive they claim that patriotism, nationalism, and chauvinism are synonyms, just as they maintain that until the Bolshevik revolution "Black Hundred" meant the same as "patriot."[14]

On a more sophisticated level, they shy away from such outrageous statements; even Pamyat, to say nothing of the less extreme groups, prefers the term "patriotic" to "chauvinist." While they justify the Black Hundred post factum, the term is shunned by all but a few sectarians on the right because its meaning has become too derogatory. But in their hearts and in their political practice extreme rightists make little distinction between patriotism and nationalism. As they see it, nationalism is the most sacred inspiration in life; only through belonging to a nation (or a folk) does the life of the individual gain spiritual meaning; the differences between nations are fundamental; and the commitment to one's nation transcends all other obligations. These, broadly speaking, are also the views of most Russian nationalists. Whether they regard their own nation as superior to others is not material in this connection; some do, others don't.

Who belongs to the nation? Only ethnic Russians who also belong to the Orthodox church. Catholics, Muslims, Protestants, and Jews can be Russian subjects; they can be tolerated and given freedom of religious practice; they can even be given certain civil rights. But since "Holy Russia" is meaningless for them, they cannot be true Russians.[15] Some enlightened spirits on the right are willing to make concessions; certain individuals of non-Russian blood can become true Russian patriots and identify themselves thoroughly with Russia through a great effort and their willingness to sacrifice for their fatherland. But these will always be a very few. Others, more extreme, will not make any exceptions whatsoever: "A Jew baptized is a thief pardoned," as a Russian proverb says.

13. J. C. Casanova in *Commentaire*, 1 (1992), p. 5.

14. "Spravochnik patriota chernosotentsa," in *Russkii traktir*, 1 (1992).

15. This has been the prevailing view since the later Slavophiles. We have quoted from Ivan Aksakov, "Myslima li Russkaya narodnost vne Pravoslaviya?," an article originally published in *Den* (August 1, 1864); republished in *Russkii rubezh*, 4 (1992).

This kind of argument involves the Russian right in many problems and inconsistencies for which there may be no answer. The religious test for membership in the Russian nation is senseless in the postcommunist era— for, as has been mentioned, even according to the most favorable polls, less than half of the Russian population are religious believers let alone practicing members of the Orthodox church.[16] To replace the religious with a racial test for belonging is not feasible, partly because as a result of Nazism this kind of doctrine has become impossible for all but a few sectarians to accept. Even if the situation were different, racial doctrine would not be applicable in a country that has experienced so much intermingling of peoples and races. It would be interesting to have genetic tests in Russia one day; the results would probably surprise and shock Russian nationalists. To paraphrase the Code Napoléon, they will reach the conclusion that "la recherche de l'origine est interdite."

Nevertheless, the distinction between (good) patriotism and (bad) nationalism is open to question for a variety of reasons, some of them historical. Patriotism was not always held in such high esteem as today. It was not only Dr. Johnson who said that patriotism was the last refuge of a scoundrel, and Dryden was not alone in his "never was patriot yet, but was a fool." Lessing wrote a friend that he had no understanding of what love of the fatherland meant; at best it was a "heroic weakness," which he was glad to miss. Schiller, who was admired and quoted at least as much in Russia as in his native land, wrote Körner in the year of the French Revolution that "Patriotic interests are important only for "immature nations" and that it was a poor and trifling ideal to write only for one nation. Goethe's thoughts were on the same lines up to the end of his life, and Pushkin lamented the misfortune of having been born in Russia. Shafarevich, the most relentless hunter of Russophobes, singled out Heine for his lack of respect for national ideals. Heine, a Jew, was an easy target, but those familiar with the history of European culture know that indifference to patriotism was the prevailing view of the Enlightenment and the generation after. They were cosmopolitan believers in *humanitas* and the progress of all mankind; neither patriotism nor nationalism figured high on their list of values.

While some of its roots go back to the late eighteenth century, only with the Napoleonic wars was nationalism invented in Europe (to use E. Kedourie's phrase) and began its victorious progress through the world.

16. According to a Vox Populi poll of September 1991, 51 percent of women asked and 27 percent of men consider themselves religious believers—not necessarily believers in the Orthodox church.

Ever since, there have been debates about nationalism as a force for good and evil. It is also true that liberals (and Marxists) have, to their cost, traditionally underrated the political impact of nationalism. It cannot seriously be doubted that in nineteenth-century Europe nationalism often (not always) was a positive, integrative force (as the family and the clan—or the empire—had been in earlier historical periods) and an ally of democracy, whereas in the twentieth century it has more often than not been an ally (or a tool) of aggressive, tyrannical regimes and its consequences have been permanent conflict, intolerance, repression, disunity. Against this it has been argued that nationalism by itself is neither good nor evil, but a natural force, and that there were destructive wars well before there was nationalism. But since the means of destruction have become so much more deadly, war has become even less affordable than before, and its mainsprings, such as nationalism, even more dangerous. There is no common denominator between the ideas of Herder or the democratic nationalism of Mazzini and Garibaldi and the tribalist wars in Eastern Europe in our time. Nationalism's inspiration has been far from purely idealistic; Lewis Namier once wrote that when the societies of Central and Eastern Europe reached the stage at which access to state employment became an object of ambition, the question of language became one of paramount importance, and out of disputes over languages came nationalism.

This observation referred to the nineteenth century. But it is also true with regard to contemporary Eastern Europe and, a fortiori, most of the successor states of the Soviet Union. There never was a Byelorussian nation nor is there an "objective need" for one now. Xenophobia has become the main integrative force, and its ideological claims in history and culture are often mendacious: Among its historical "heroes" there tend to be as many villains as saints. In the hands of demagogues this kind of aggressive nationalism, with its innate need for outside threats, becomes a tool to manipulate the masses, to deflect their attention from the truly important issues (political, economic, and ecological) facing their societies. In brief, this kind of nationalism is a prescription for disaster.

The early ideologues of nationalism, of whom Herder was the most important, were humanists. They were preoccupied with belonging and group culture, and they believed that all cultures (like all nations) were equidistant to God. They were in the tradition of the Enlightenment. Here we touch the basic difference between contemporary right-wing nationalism in Russia (and elsewhere) and its original inspiration: the issue of "anti-Enlightenment." To the right-wing nationalists the philosophy of the Enlightenment is the work of Satan. The idea of being a cosmopolitan citizen of the world and the concept of pan-human values are despicable, the exact antithesis of the values and ideals of a true patriot.

It was not always like this. When, in his famous speech about Pushkin, Dostoyevsky claimed that Russia's destiny was incontestably all-European (Western, one would now say) and universal, when he talked about the all-humanitarianism of Pushkin's genius, and when he argued that to become a genuine and all-around Russian meant to become a brother to all men, *a universal man* (italics in original), he may have been exalted and somewhat woolly, but he was undoubtedly sincere. It is impossible to imagine a contemporary spokesman of the Russian right speaking in the same vein. A break has occurred; there is a revolt against reason, and the ideas of freedom and of common human values have been rejected.

More than two hundred years after the event one is only too aware of the naïveté of the Enlightenment, of its unduly optimistic assumptions about individuals and about mankind in general. Writing fifty years after the demise of fascism, one is even more palpably aware of the alternative. The Enlightenment has reappeared as the champion of liberty and justice against the forces of darkness and barbarism. These are the battle lines in contemporary Russia.

At this stage of the debate, Russian "liberal conservatives"[17] tend to quote Ecclesiastes to the effect that there is to everything a season and a time to every purpose under heaven, a time to cast away stones, and a time to gather stones together. After so much fighting has the time not come for all men and women of goodwill to remove the barricades and to join forces in reconstruction and healing?[18] Peaceful cooperation has much to recommend it in a country that has seen so much strife. But there can be collaboration only if there is common ground. With its crucial emphasis on Russian exclusivity, on Russophobia, with its deep enmity against cosmopolitans and "cultural nihilists," with its psychological need for enemies, can the Russian right envisage the removal of barricades, which it may need as much as Honecker needed the Berlin Wall?

Is the difference between (benign) patriotism and (malign) nationalism, as Likhachev sees it, merely a question of degree? Everyone loves, or should love, his fatherland; but those who love it at the expense of all other human ties, values, and obligations are a menace.

Or are patriotism and nationalism two different sides of a coin, or perhaps more accurately, two different pages in an atlas? The basic differences between liberal Western and authoritarian Eastern nationalism have

17. The term was apparently coined by S. Frank.

18. Alla Latynina and Yuliya Latynina, "Vremya razbyrat barrikady," *Novy mir,* 1 (1992).

often been noted.[19] Nationalism in the West emerged in countries that were ethnically more or less homogenous or at least had well-defined borders; they were economically and culturally highly developed. Nationalism in Eastern Europe (and in the Third World) arose—or was invented—in conditions that were altogether different; hence its antiliberalism, its suppression of minorities, its frequent conflicts and wars with neighbors, and generally speaking its destructive character. True, not all Western nationalism always behaved according to high standards. But since the bitter lessons of two world wars, Western nationalism has, by and large, lost its aggressive character.

In recent years nationalist politicians and groups have mushroomed all over Eastern Europe and the successor states of the Soviet Union. Since their trend is predominantly toward separatism or aggrandizement (or both), their potential for conflict and destabilization is immense. The prospect that moderate nationalism will prevail over its nastier alternative is uncertain. It is quite immaterial whether people become nationalists because they are fanatics or villains or romantics or neurotics or because it has to do with modernization or because of genuine, objective, practical necessity.[20] Even if it is based only on an imagined bond, nationalism seems to be an essential part of the human condition at the present stage of historical development.

VI

What is Solzhenitsyn's contribution to the worldview of moderate Russian nationalists? In many respects he has been its central inspiration. The fact is that many of his predictions (about the weakness of the West, about the Chinese danger, and so on) were proved wrong. In the 1970s he reached the pessimistic conclusion that 50 percent of mankind was slithering down the same slope and a further 15 percent was teetering on the brink. ("Our Pluralists"). Throughout the 1970s and 1980s he complained about the constant Western retreat before an aggressive Soviet Union. But about the

19. John Plamenatz, "Two Types of Nationalism," in E. Kamenka, *Nationalism, the Nature and Evolution of an Idea* (London, 1973). The author, a student of Marxism and nationalism, was a native of Montenegro.

20. All these interpretations have had their proponents in the debates on the origins of nations and the theories of nationalism of recent decades. See, for instance, E. Gellner, *Nations and Nationalism* (Oxford, England, 1983); Anthony D. Smith, *The Ethnic Origins of Nations* (Oxford, England, 1986) and *Theories of Nationalism* (London, 1983); Benedict Anderson, *Imagined Communities* (London, 1983); and many other studies. On recent East European nationalism, Misha Glenny, *The Rebirth of History* (London, 1990), is of interest.

state of Russia he has been more right than wrong. Unlike the extreme right, he does not believe that only aliens are responsible for all of Russia's misfortunes; the need for atonement and a moral regeneration is central to his thought. Unlike the extreme right he does not oppose a democratic system in principle. But he does believe that for a long time to come Russia will not be ready for such a system. Authoritarian rule with a human face seems to him the system most fitting Russia's needs. Fundamental issues divide him from the liberals. For Solzhenitsyn, as for the Slavophiles, the concept of inner freedom is central; Western pluralism, capitalism, and political democracy have given rise (as he sees it) to a materialistic society, devoid of spiritual values. He sees a different future for Russia: His religious belief is deep and the emphasis on humanism and pan-human values is largely meaningless for him. His views about the degree of perfectibility of human nature are those of a conservative. His doctrine has been called neo-neo-Slavophile, but "Russophile" would be a more appropriate label. He is neither a Russian imperialist nor a *gosudarstvennik*, a believer in state power as the supreme value—though of course he feels great sadness about the loss of many old Russian territories. Last, unlike the democrats, he considers the pre-1917 tsarist system, while not faultless, the least evil that Russia has had in its history. For this reason the February Revolution of 1917 was an act of monumental folly that by necessity brought about the victory of Bolshevism. The many volumes of *The Red Wheel*, which kept him occupied for more than two decades, are an attempt to prove this thesis in the form of a documentary novel.[21]

Solzhenitsyn's authority is high on the right and among the nationalists, except among some extremist sectarians who accuse him of treason, of having informed on fellow prisoners, and similar crimes. Even his critics on the left admire his courageous stand before and after the publication of *Ivan Denisovich*, and it is generally admitted that *The Gulag Archipelago* had a liberating influence of historical proportions.

Western critics have on the whole taken a negative view of Solzhenitsyn, the post-1970 ideologue and writer, in contrast to the early Solzhenitsyn. Not that his critique of the West was all wrong, though he never really understood, or made a serious attempt to understand, the mainsprings of Western thought and society. His political philosophy is that of a self-made man; it is not original but a rediscovery of ideas that have been known,

---

21. Solzhenitsyn's political philosophy has been commented on by a supporter in great, probably excessive detail. Dora Shturman, *Gorudu i mirm*. A well-reasoned critique is Vyacheslav Vozdvizhensky, "Solzhenitsyn—kotoryi?" in *Ogonyok* 47 and 48 (1991). Another recent exchange was between Alexander Ageyev and Andrei Nemzer in *Nezavisimaya gazeta* (June 4, 1992).

discussed, and accepted or rejected for a long time. Whether someone opts in the end for humanism, a liberal democracy, and internationalism or for religion, conservatism, and a "Russia first" doctrine, is a matter of individual preference; such a decision can be neither approved or disapproved, justified or refuted. The divide between Solzhenitsyn and Sakharov is to a large extent that between conservative and liberal utopianism.

Many Westerners have been annoyed by Solzhenitsyn's sweeping claim of having pioneered anticommunism. He seems genuinely to believe that until he appeared virtually no one knew about the gulag. While his book is probably the longest, whole libraries, which reached a wide public, had been written on the subject. In an even more extreme form these claims recur in the case of Igor Shafarevich, Solzhenitsyn's Sancho Panza. Shafarevich maintains that the Western liberal establishment justified and protected Stalinism from beginning to end.[22] In fact, Western liberal anti-Stalinism was the most informed and most powerful opposition to Stalinism well before Solzhenitsyn and Shafarevich ever appeared on the scene. It was also unconditional in its rejection.

It is Solzhenitsyn's merit to have realized (unlike the extreme right) that the old "Russian idea" with its stress on an imperial mission is out of place in contemporary Russia. The present assignment facing Russian patriots is to rebuild their society and country, not to rule other peoples. The Russian idea as the Slavophiles interpreted it had strong messianic elements; it implied that eventually Russia's mission was to bring spiritual salvation also to the West. Belief in the moral degeneracy and base materialism of the West is deeply entrenched in Russian nationalist thought, as it was in German. The many imperfections of Western societies are beyond dispute. But it does by no means follow that in the foreseeable future Russia will be in a position to provide a cure for Western maladies. The country's motto ought to be "Messiah, heal thyself"—or something on those lines. Perhaps some universal message will emerge at the end of the present purgatory. But this should not be taken for granted—and in any case is a long way ahead.

VII

French right-wing nationalism in the twentieth century extended from de Gaulle to the Action Française and beyond to the French fascist parties. In Britain it ranged from Churchill to Oswald Mosley. The gamut on the

22. "Dve dorogi k odnomu obryvu," *Novy mir,* 7 (1989).

Russian right is equally wide. The basic difference between de Gaulle and Churchill, and the fascists of their countries, was not just that they refused to live with an invasion by a foreign aggressor who wished to occupy and dominate their countries. They had accepted the democratic rules of the game; later on, with all their faith in the extraordinary virtues of their own countries, they were willing to accept decolonization and to cooperate with their neighbors in establishing a new democratic order in Europe. They were tolerant of their enemies at home; when it was suggested to de Gaulle at the time of the war in Algeria that he order the arrest of Sartre (for calling on French soldiers to desert), he rejected the suggestion out of hand, for "Sartre too, is part of France." In the century before, Bismarck, a diehard autocrat, had accepted parliamentarian procedures, albeit with great inner resistance.

Is there a similar mental readiness among the Russian right? There are, needless to say, some who call for repentance and tolerance and have nothing to learn from Western democrats. The present book predominantly deals with those who have not reached this stage and perhaps never will.

There was a time when the European right rejected freedom; their conversion to modern democracy came only gradually. The German Deutsch-Nationalen and the Action Française were bitter opponents of democracy. There was an antiliberal intellectual backlash in Western Europe in the 1890s. Its main enemies were capitalism, parliamentary democracy, and the liberal bourgeois society and culture to which these had given rise. This was the revolt against the world of reason and positivism; it was the embrace of irrationalism and violence, blood and soil, racism and various *völkisch* doctrines. It helped to prepare Europe for two world wars.

Russia did not experience this intellectual fashion, only *Vekhi* which were antimaterialistic but not antidemocratic. But Russian society had never embraced liberalism; the Russian response to radicalism was the Black Hundred, triggered off by the revolutionary movement of 1905; it was equally antiliberal and anticapitalist. Like the Action Française the Black Hundred were a halfway house on the road to fascism, with their strong populist, anticapitalist elements, their xenophobia, their aggressive nationalism, and their as yet inchoate (that is to say "unscientific") racism.[23] The Black Hundred were still tied to the pillars of the ancien régime, the monarchy and the church. They were not modern; they did not know how

---

23. It is hardly necessary to point to the differences between these two movements—the one with its predominantly middle-class appeal and strong emphasis on respectability, the other with its appeal to the lumpen.

to adjust their policy to a changing world. They were unable to produce a leader and a strongly organized, centralized party. Their propaganda failed to reach most sections of the population.

There were other such "halfway houses" elsewhere in Europe: the Belgian Rex and the Romanian Iron Guard, with their strong religious elements.[24] In each case there were specific reasons for the emergence of these hybrid movements.

In the ninety years since it first appeared the Russian right has not made any significant progress. It has neither advanced toward the acceptance of democracy nor made the transition to full-fledged fascism. There have been certain changes: Nineteenth-century pan-Slavism no longer makes sense in the contemporary world and it has been replaced by Russophilia. Some Moscow intellectuals have been borrowing heavily from the postfascist *Nouvelle Droite*. But it is most unlikely that the rehash of geopolitics and Eurasianism, of Judeo-Masonic conspiracy theories recycled as "mondialism," and of German metaphysical philosophy with an admixture of neopaganism will ever amount to more than the parlor games of a handful of intellectuals. Thus, there has been no significant progress beyond the Black Hundred—and there are historical reasons for that. While communism was in power and the Soviet Union existed, racism could not be openly preached. It was incompatible with Marxism-Leninism even in the Stalinist phase. It would have been suicidal from an anticommunist point of view, for the Whites stood, after all, for one Russia, united and indivisible.

It is true that as communism is bankrupt and the Soviet Union has fallen apart, a political vacuum has come into being. But it seems to me unlikely that it will be filled by a native Russian fascist movement. Soviet leaders, on the whole, shielded their people from a surfeit of information about Nazism and Italian fascism; for over half a century only a handful of books was published about this subject, none of them very illuminating, and many aspects of fascism were altogether taboo. But even the least informed Russian knows that Hitler was not a good man, that the Nazis treated the Russians (not just the communists) as subhuman beings, killed millions of them, and caused immense destruction. All this is too deep in popular memory to permit a revival of Nazism at the present time. The most that can be attempted (and it is attempted) is to introduce national socialism through the back door, without any reference to Hitler, Mussolini, and historical fascism.

There may be yet another factor that makes it difficult to preach

24. The Iron Guard's patron saint, the Archangel Mikhail, was also the patron of the Black Hundred.

unalloyed fascism in present-day Russia, and this is, paradoxically, fascism's resemblance to Stalinism. The Russian ultra-right stands for authoritarian government. But the "cult of the individual," as it existed under Hitler and Stalin, cannot be propagated in Russia now except perhaps among the most backward section of society. The same, mutatis mutandis, applies with regard to the central role of the state party, an essential fixture of fascism. Russians have been immunized at least for some time to come against the leading role of a party of this kind under whatever guise.

A pre-fascist political group such as the Black Hundred has certain features in common with similar such movements elsewhere. Mention has been made of antiliberalism and anticapitalism as well as militarism and the belief in the central role of the armed forces in domestic as well as foreign affairs. Other typical features are the myth of decadence and national rebirth and the belief in an organic and hierarchic state and in a historical *Sonderweg* (a special development and mission). All this can be found in the history of the extreme right in other countries.

But there are certain features specific to the Russian right at least with regard to emphasis. This refers above all to Satanism, the Judeo-Masonic plot, and Russophobia. As has been shown, all fascist, para-fascist, and pre-fascist movements believed to some extent in conspiracies; none liked Jews, Freemasons, or detractors of their respective history and culture. But in no other country have the ultra-right-wing patriots been hypnotized to the same degree by the intrigues and other hostile actions of enemies who were almost entirely imaginary—and in any case were of no great consequence. What could have been the reason—atavistic fear, a feeling of inadequacy and inferiority vis-à-vis the diabolical enemy, or perhaps a peculiarly Russian fanaticism? But if such fanaticism had existed, it would have shown itself in other ways, which it did not. There have been other cases of cultural ultra-nationalism comparable to present-day Russia.[25] But nowhere has the belief in conspiracies been so pronounced.

In both Britain and France the dramatic events of 1789–1793 induced some contemporaries to see the key in a giant plot hatched by *philosophes, Illuminati,* Freemasons, Jesuits, and various cosmopolitans. In Germany this phenomenon even appeared several decades earlier and played an important role in the genesis of German conservatism.[26] But by the middle of the nineteenth century, at the very latest, Western conservatism had

25. For instance, the prophets of *Kulturpessimismus* in Germany around 1890; and Papini and his friends in Italy during the decade prior to World War I.

26. The key work is Ernst von Goedthausen's *Enthüllung des Systems der Weltbürger Republik* (Leipzig, 1786). For a discussion of these views, Klaus Epstein, *The Genesis of German Conservatism* (Princeton, N.J., 1966), passim.

outgrown such fantasies. They tended to recur, but never for very long, and they survive only on the margins of political life. Fascism was afflicted by many myths, but the paranoid fear of plots was never very central in its doctrine. It was (and is) only in Russia that this issue has been of paramount importance.

Perhaps it is unfair to charge the Russian ultra-nationalists with a lack of originality. For the number of doctrinal varieties is as limited on the right as it is on the left. In one form or another all the ingredients of a movement of the extreme right, conservative or fascist or para-fascist, have been used somewhere in the past. As far as fascism is concerned there is truly nothing new under the sun; except perhaps the fact that in Russia it is postcommunist in character. Only the future will show what this could mean in practice; perhaps only that with all its opposition to communism it is bound to inherit certain essential features of communism.

VIII

Much thought has been given by students of twentieth-century history to the determinants of the growth and success of fascism. It is by now common knowledge that, as in the case of communism, "objective conditions" are not sufficient by way of explanation. Objective conditions— economic crisis, breakdown or absence of democratic institutions—have frequently existed. But unless there was a *Führer*, a *duce*, who together with like-minded followers created a dynamic mass movement, such opportunities have passed unused. Experience does not bear out the assumption that once the objective conditions exist, the leader is bound to appear anyhow sooner or later. His presence is a historical accident, and for this reason predictions about the likelihood that a fascist movement will seize power are risky. While it is not impossible in the case of contemporary Russia, it still seems unlikely, be it only because of the fissiparous character of the Russian far right—which is not accidental (as Marx would have said) but a result of the wide variety of interests and inspirations represented in these circles.

It is easy to think of reasons that seem to favor the growth of some extreme nationalist movement—the feeling of national humiliation following the breakup of the Soviet Union; the need to pursue an assertive policy vis-à-vis the former republics in view of Russian interests and the presence of many millions of Russians abroad; the bad economic situation and the need to engage in unpopular reforms; the frequent impotence of the authorities in the face of a breakdown of law and order; the fact that democratic institutions are not deeply rooted in Russia; the traditional psychological need for a strong hand; the old Weimar dilemma of how to run a democracy in the absence of a sufficient number of democrats; the deep divisions on the left. All these and other circumstances seem to bear out those on the Russian right who have claimed all along that time works for them. Indeed, some observers have argued that the prospects of Nazism were less good in 1932 than they are in Russia at the present time, if only because when the German crisis came, democratic forces had been in power for more than a decade.[27] And is it not also true that postcommunist Russia is repeating the mistake committed by Weimar—giving absolute freedom to the enemies of democracy?

But for a variety of reasons, adduced more than once in the course of this study, a full-fledged fascism still seems unlikely in Russia—if only because in contrast to widespread belief history never repeats itself.

An authoritarian system based on some nationalist populism appears more probable. The blueprints for a national socialism have existed for some considerable time—the Russian national idea (as interpreted by the far right) based on a "union between labor and capital," a broad political movement, and on the security forces assuming the necessary functions of control in society.[28]

Such national socialism derives a substantial part of its inspiration from the ideology of a bygone era. It is Communism purged of its Marxist-internationalist elements, anti-Western, anti-democratic, with a firm belief in specific Russian spiritual values and a political culture. The presence of so many leading former party officials, army and KGB generals among the leaders of the right is as striking as the survival of so many of the old ideas. If Henri IV reached the conclusion that Paris was well worth a mass, some of these tend to believe that Moscow is well worth some genuflections in an Orthodox cathedral; in other cases the conversion to the "Russian Idea" (as they interpret it) may be genuine. What was there in common among the thirty-nine public figures who signed the manifesto of the "National Salvation Front" in September 1992?[29] At first look precious little, for they included unreconstructed Marxists (such as R. Kosolapov), national social-

27. L. Gintsberg, "Grozit li fashism?" *Nezavisimaya gazeta* (April 28, 1992). Dr. Gintsberg, a historian, is the author of three books on Nazi Germany.

28. Vladimir Yadov, "Rossiiskii natsional sotsializm obyavlyaet manifest," *Izvestiya* (April 9, 1992). This refers to a paper by the academician G. Osipov, *Den* (March 29, 1992).

29. The manifesto was published in full in *Sovetskaya rossiya*, September 22, 1992; Konstantinov's comment in *Megapolis Express*, October 14, 1992.

ists (such as Lysenko), as well as monarchists and inveterate opponents of any kind of socialism such as Shafarevich. But when Ilya Konstantinov, the chief organizer of the Front, argued that the differences between the "left" and the "right" of the national opposition were really quite superficial, he was in some respects not very far from the truth. They were united by hatred of a common enemy and also by certain common beliefs in their vision of a future Russia.

Thus, ironically, with all the disdain expressed for bolshevism for so long among the Russian right, with all the curses uttered against godless bolshevism, all the maledictions against the cosmopolitan and anti-patriotic Marxists, all the imprecations hurled against the "grave diggers of Russia," the nationalists of the extreme right found themselves in a common front with yesteryear's party and state *nomenklatura*. And no one could say with any certainty how firm this coalition was and how long it would last.

IX

To be a good Russian, it is said, one has to cast one's eyes back to the glorious deeds of virtuous ancestors. This is how patriotic inspiration has been provided everywhere, especially at a time of spiritual as well as political crisis. Totalitarian revolution and liberal reform have failed. Neither the international proletariat, nor fellow Slavs, nor the other nations of the former Soviet Union have shown enthusiasm for linking their fate with the Russians'. In the circumstances a retreat to the nation seems the logical and the only possible response. Other nations have reacted in a similar way at a time of crisis. The slogan *"Nashe"* ("Ours") is an equivalent of "Sinn Fein," which means "We Alone"; no phrase has been dearer to the heart of French nationalists than "La France seule." In comparison with the chauvinistic rhetoric in the successor states of the Soviet Union and other East European countries, Russian nationalism, except in its most extreme manifestations, seems almost moderate.

The glorious deeds of virtuous ancestors, the golden age, the paradise lost and to be regained are, of course, mere myths for there was no golden age. But myths still have their uses, and if all other bonds have broken down, why disparage the appeal to nationalism used to mobilize a people to undertake the enormous efforts that will be needed to extract it from the morass and build a new base for its existence? The nationalist temptation is great, but the doubts whether such an appeal will achieve its aim are even greater. Nietzsche once wrote that to be a good German means to de-

Germanize oneself.[30] The same may well apply to Russia in its present predicament. What Nietzsche had in mind was, of course, not to accept slavishly some foreign model, not to shed old traditions just for the sake of making a break with the past; this has been tried from Peter the Great onward and it did not work too well. What Nietzsche did have in mind was that "if a nation advances and grows, it has to burst the girdle given to it by its nationalist outlook." What Russia now needs, the glorious past and the virtuous ancestors cannot provide—namely, to build a new economy and a new society. Nationalism's great use is to mobilize the resources of a people against foreign enemies. But the threat facing Russia now does not come from outside. To the rebuilding of the country nationalism per se cannot make a decisive contribution. It can appeal to the historical and cultural cohesion of the people, to their common values, to idealism. But it has no specific ideas to offer derived from Russia's past.[31]

All this refers to moderate nationalism; the ideas of the extreme right are not only mad but evil. By creating foes where none exist, they deflect the energies of the nation from coping with the real dangers, from where they are most needed: the immense work of reconstruction. If the ultra-right's views were to prevail, it could well achieve what neither Hitler nor Stalin and his successors did: the total ruin of the country. At present this seems to be a farfetched proposition, for the Russian people is no longer an ignorant herd.

Who, then, will help Russia in its present predicament? The reply, paradoxically, is contained in Eugène Pottier's song that was for decades the official anthem of the Soviet Union: Help will not come from outside; neither God nor a master (Ni dieu, ni maître) will bring salvation. It can come only through the Russian people's own efforts, their good sense, and their fortitude in adversity.

---

30. *Menschliches-Allzumenschliches, Gesammelte Werke,* vol. 4, p. 159.

31. Nor are there straightforward prescriptions to be obtained from the history of Western nations, because the Russian situation is so different. The only lessons that can be learned are negative in character—what ideas and approaches do not work. The Russian right has been hard at work to discover hitherto untapped sources of inspiration abroad. They have only just reached the most promising, but still inapplicable doctrines: those having their heyday in pre-Nazi Germany—the *Tat* circle, the corporatist schools, Carl Schmitt's theories about authoritarian democracy and the state of emergency, the varieties of National Bolshevism. However, in Germany in 1930–1933 very few people expected that salvation would come from the church.

BIBLIOGRAPHICAL NOTE

THERE IS NO COMPREHENSIVE HISTORY of Russian nationalism and the "Russian idea." The topic is inchoate and difficult to define. Hans Rogger's pioneering *National Consciousness in Eighteenth-Century Russia* (Cambridge, Mass., 1960) deals with the Romantic age; in his later essay, *Jewish Policies and Rightwing Politics in Imperial Russia* (Basingstoke, 1986), he deals with nationalism during the early years of the twentieth century. For the very early period, see D. S. Likhachev, *Natsionalnoye samopoznanie drevnei Rusi* (Moscow, 1945). The earlier literature on the concept of the "third Rome" is mentioned in Léon Poliakov, *Moscou Troisième Rome* (Paris, 1989).

Excellent books have been written on the Slavophiles. This refers to the studies by A. Walicki (*The Slavophile Controversy* [Oxford, 1975]), N. Riasanovsky (1952), and others that have been mentioned in the text. Two general intellectual histories should also be mentioned; they are still of significance though they were written a long time ago: Ovsyanniko-Kulikovsky, *Istoriya russkoi intelligentsii* (Moscow, 1911), V. Ivanov Razumnik, *Istoriya russkoi obshchestvennoi mysli* (Moscow 1907). Dostoyevsky's writings, especially *The Diary of a Writer,* are of paramount importance in the present context; so are the essential books on Dostoyevsky, especially J. Frank's monumental biography (1976–) and Wayne Dowler on Dostoyevsky and the *pochvenniki.*

Another interesting figure is Lev Tikhomirov, the terrorist turned conservative and monarchist. Some of his writings are available in English: *Russia, Political and Social* (London, 1892).

Whether Pobedonostsev, the archconservative, should be counted among the nationalists is a moot point; he has found a biographer (Robert Byrnes). So have Cha'adayev (Gershenzon), the Aksakovs (P. Christoff), Khomayakov (A. Gratieux), Kireyevsky (A. Gleason), and even Danilevsky (Robert E. MacMaster). Some of the texts that were banned after 1917 have been republished in Moscow in the reform era; this applies to Cha'adayev's writings as well as to Danilevsky.

Much less research has been done on the right, and especially the extreme right, in the late tsarist period. There is a short Stolypin biography written by the late A. Ya. Avrekh (Moscow, 1990). Several collections of documents about the Black Hundred were published in the 1920s; in later years this became a taboo subject. Some of these sources are listed in my *Russia and Germany*. H. D. Löwe, *Antisemitismus und reaktionäre Utopie* (Hamburg, 1978) is so far the only academic study of the Black Hundred. Those interested will find further references—especially with regard to the relationship between the Black Hundred and the church—in John S. Curtiss, *Church and State in Russia* (New York, 1940).

The publication of V. Osetrov's book on the Black Hundred, written from a sympathizer's point of view, has been held up by a Moscow court order, but a million copies of an abridged version *(Chernaya Sotnya)* were printed by the Soviet army publishing house (Voennoye Izdatelstvo) in 1991. *Vekhi* ("Landmarks," 1909), available in English translation (New York, 1977), is essential reading with regard to the attitude of one section of the Russian intelligentsia. So is the collection of essays *Iz glubiny* (Moscow, 1918). They were republished in the Soviet Union under *glasnost,* as were essays by right-wing publicists of the early twentieth century (especially Menshikov and Sergei Sharapov) and, of course, various editions of *The Protocols of the Elders of Zion.* The edition now most frequently reprinted appeared at Sergiev Posad in 1917. To the standard works on the *Protocols* mentioned in the text the following should now be added: P. A. Taguieff, *Les Protocoles des Sages de Zion,* 2 vols. (Paris, 1992).

Several monographs on the Russian emigration ought to be mentioned:

Robert H. Johnston, *New Mecca, New Babylon* (Kingston and Montreal, 1988)
Marc Raeff, *Russia Abroad* (New York, 1990)
B. Prianishnikoff, *Novopokolentsy* (Silver Spring, Md., 1986)
John Stephan, *The Russian Fascists* (New York, 1978)
Gleb Struve, *Russkaya literatura v izgnanii* (Paris, 1984)

Robert C. Williams, *Culture in Exile—Russian Emigrés in Berlin* (Ithaca, N.Y., 1972)

Johnston's book is of importance with regard to the Russian right in France and includes further references. Stephan covers the Russian fascists in Manchuria, and Prianishnikoff is essential for the early history of the NTS.

Grand Duke Kyrill published an autobiography in English (*My Life in Russia's Service* [London, 1939]) which leads, however, only up to 1917; it contains a postscript by his son Vladimir, the pretender who died in April 1992. Of the many autobiographies written by Russian émigrés two ought to be singled out as they are of particular significance in the present context:

Roman Gul, *Ya unes Rossiyu,* 2 vols. (New York, 1984)
V. A. Varshavsky, *Nezamechennoye pokoleniye* (New York, 1956)

The number of books on nationalist thought in the emigration is legion. The following are among the most important:

N. Berdyaev, *Novoye srednevekoye* (Berlin, 1924)
N. Berdyaev, *Istoki i smysl russkovo kommunizma* (Paris, 1951)
N. Berdyaev, *The Russian Idea* (various editions)

G. P. Fedotov's essays have been collected in several volumes: *Litso Rossii* (Paris, 1988); *Zashchita Rossii* (Paris, 1988); *Rossiya, Yevropa i my* (Paris, 1973); *Tyazhba o Rossii* (Paris, 1982).

Ivan Il'in's writings on nationalism and the monarchy (see also below) have been republished in recent years in Moscow in right-wing magazines and also in hardcover. There is an intellectual biography by D. Poltoratsky.

Ivan Solonevich's *Narodnaya monarkhia* (San Francisco, 1978) has also been reprinted in Moscow. In addition, a great many books and even more articles on the subject—by authors ranging from weighty figures of the right such as Peter Struve to fanatical conspiracy theorists such as F. Vinberg (*Krestnyi put* [Munich, 1921])—have appeared. I have discussed some of these in my *Russia and Germany.* Some are critically reviewed in a more recent study by Jane Burbank, *Intelligentsia and Revolution* (Oxford, England, 1986). The literature on the Russian church inside the homeland and abroad is vast. Of general works the following should be mentioned:

M. Bourdeaux, *Patriarch and Prophets* (New York, 1970)
Jane Ellis, *The Orthodox Church* (Bloomington, Ind., 1986)

A. Kartashev, *Ocherki po istorii russkoi tserkvi*, 2 vols. (Paris, 1959; Moscow, 1992)

Ioann Kronshtatskii, *Khristianskaya filosofiya* (Moscow, 1992); (reprint of the 1902 edition)

Dm. Pospelovsky, *The Russian Church Under the Soviet Regime*, 2 vols. (Gestwood, 1984)

Gernot Seide, *Geschichte der russischen orthodoxen Kirche im Ausland* (Wiesbaden, 1983)

N. D. Talberg, *Istoriya khristianskoi tserkvi* (Jordansville, N.Y., 1964)

Émigré publications on Satanism and the apocalypse include the following:

B. Molchanov, *Antichrist* (Jordansville, N.Y., 1987)

Ratibor-Jurvenich, *The Contemporary Faces of Satan*, (place of publication unknown, 1985)

Seraphim (Rose), *The Future of Russia and the End of the World*, (Jordansville, N.Y., n.d.)

Seraphim, *Orthodoxy and the Religion of the Future* (place of publication unknown, 1983)

Current events in the Russian Orthodox church in Russia and abroad have been reviewed in *Pravoslavnaya Rus* and *Pravoslavnaya zhizn* (both Jordansville, N.Y.) and *Veche* (Munich).

The leading academic work on the role of the devil in religious thought is Jeffrey Burton Russell's four-volume study, *The Devil, Satan, Lucifer, and Mephistopheles* (Ithaca, N.Y., 1977–1986).

The official organ of the Russian Orthodox church in Russia is the *Zhurnal moskovskovo patriarkhata*, which also publishes a newsletter. More recently, *Moskovskii tserkovnyi vestnik* has published articles of interest.

Among specifically anti-Jewish publications are reprints of the classic pre-1917 Russian anti-Semitic literature such as the *Protocols*, books by Liutostansky, and Shmakov, *Mezhdunarodnoye tainoye pravitelstvo*. Also Y. Brafman, *Kniga kagala*, first published in Vilno in 1869. In addition there are reprints of Russian books published in Riga and other émigré centers of the 1930s, such as Gladkoy, *Zhidy*, and Zhevakhov, *Evreiskii terror v Rossii*. In the United States after 1945: Gregori Klimov, *Tainy Sovetskykh mudretsov* and Al. Diky, *Evrei v Rossii i v SSSR* and *Russko-Evreiskii Dialog* (New York, 1970). (Diky belonged to the early émigrés; Klimov, a former Soviet intelligence officer, defected in Berlin in 1948.) Among the pamphlets, V. Ushkuinik, *Pamyatka russkomu cheloveku* (New York, 1982) should be mentioned. There have been anonymous booklets such as *Zak-*

rytaya tema (on the representation of Jews in the Soviet leadership). Another popular translation has been Douglas Reed *Spor o Zione* (Johannesburg, 1986; Krasnodar, 1992).

The samizdat publications of various Christian groups are reviewed in John B. Dunlop, *The Faces of Contemporary Russian Nationalism* (Princeton, N.J., 1983), and his other writings. Most of *Veche* can be found in Arkhiv Samizdata, Radio Liberty and the *Vestnik,* published by the Paris YMCA Press. Some notable essays written by Christian dissidents have appeared in English.

The literature on monarchism is much more sparse and is limited to journals with a very small circulation such as *Nasha strana* (Argentina) and *Tsar kolokol* (Moscow; samizdat).

Studies of Russian nationalism after the Second World War include John Dunlop, *The New Russian Revolutionaries* (1976) and *The New Russian Nationalism* (1985) in addition to those mentioned earlier on. Also Alexander Yanov, *The Russian New Right* (Berkeley, Calif., 1978), and *The Russian Challenge and the Year 2000* (Oxford, England, 1986). Dunlop's attitude is on the whole sympathetic to the moderate right, whereas Yanov considers the right a threat to its own country and the West. Mikhail Agursky's *The Third Rome: National Bolshevism in the USSR* (Boulder, Colo., 1987) should also be mentioned in this context although he is preoccupied with National Bolshevism in the interwar period.

Inside the Soviet Union the (more or less) official organs of Russian nationalism were the monthlies *Nash sovremennik* and *Molodaya gvardiya,* as well as *Sever,* which, published in Petrozavodsk, had a more limited readership. Similar material also appeared in *Kuban* and *Don. Molodaya gvardiya* tended toward National Bolshevism, whereas *Nash sovremennik* has been called the "human face of chauvinism." Ironically, *Nash sovremennik* was founded (as a yearly almanac) by Maxim Gorky, the bête noire of the Russian right, whereas *Molodaya gvardiya* was established in 1922 by the Komsomol, the Communist youth organization. Its early editors were writers of Jewish extraction, such as Alexander Izbakh, A. Bezymensky and Mikhail Svetlov. To the same camp also belongs *Moskva,* founded in 1957, though it pursued a more restrained line. Its editor was M. Alekseyev from 1968 to 1992. *Slovo,* published in cooperation with the Moscow patriarchate, is the most recent addition; like *Moskva,* it has been somewhat more moderate than the journals mentioned earlier. The circulation of all these journals has considerably declined in recent years. *Molodaya gvardiya* printed 725,000 copies in 1990; in 1992 it was down to a little over 30,000 and published an appeal to its readers (and "all true patriots") to provide financial help so as to enable it to survive. The figures for *Nash sovremennik* are 465,000 in 1990 and 164,000 in 1992. (The circulation of most Russian periodicals sharply decreased in 1991–1992.)

Among the weeklies of the right, *Den* should be mentioned, as should *Literaturnaya Rossiya* (the organ of the Writers' Union of the Russian Federation) and some local papers, such as *Literaturnyi Irkutsk* as well as *Moskovskii literator,* published at irregular intervals by the Moscow Writers' Union. *Tyumen literaturnaya* attacked even Solzhenitsyn for his contacts with "world Jewry" (2, 1991). There is some literature on Pamyat in addition to the studies of Pribylovsky, Mark Deich, and Semyon Reznik mentioned above. I. A. Yerunov and V. D. Solovei, *Russkoye delo sevodnya,* vol. 1: *Pamyat* (Moscow, 1991) includes an excellent analysis as well as essential documents.

The Eurasians published a great deal of literature in the 1920s and 1930s, and after the Second World War some scholarly studies were published about their teachings. The most important such works are Otto Böss, *Die Lehre der Eurasier* (Munich, 1961), and Nicholas Riasanovsky, "The Emergence of Eurasianism," *California Slavic Studies,* 4 (1967).

The most widely discussed novels by right-wing writers published during the early reform era are V. Astafiev, *Pechalnyi detektiv,* (Moscow, 1986); V. Belov, *Vse vperedi* (Moscow, 1986); and V. Rasputin, *Pozhar* (Moscow, 1985–1986). Also important are essays by Leonid Borodin, Vladimir Krupin, A. Prokhanov, V. Soloukhin, and others. Most widely read were the patriotic-historical novels of Valentin Pikul.

Traditional Nazi literature has been reprinted or copied in Russia in recent years. Among it: Hitler, *Mein Kampf (Moya borba),* both in full translation and in an abridged version originally published in Shanghai. Also Josef Goebbels, *Teoriya i Praktika Bolshevizma* (originally published in 1936), and Alfred Rosenberg, *Razoblachennyi Bolshevizm* (n.d); Hermann Fehst, *Bolshevizm i Evreistvo* (first published in 1934).

Among more recent anti-Jewish publications the following should be mentioned:

V. Emelyanov, *Detsionisatsiya* (Paris, 1977)
V. Emelyanov, *Yevreiskii natsizm i asiatskoye sposobstvo proizvodstva* (n.p., n.d.)
A. Romanenko, *Genotsid* (Leningrad [*sic*], 1991)

Among the publications specifically dealing with alleged Masonic plots, the following polemical works, apart from the more academic studies mentioned in the text, ought to be noted:

G. Bostunich, *Masonstvo* (Berlin, 1927)

V. Ivanov, *Pravoslavnyi mir i masonstvo* (Harbin, 1935)

N. Markov, *Voina temnykh sil,* 2 vols. (Paris, 1928)

A. Selyaninov, *Tainaya sila masonstva* (St. Petersburg, 1911)[1]

Among the journals of the contemporary right, the weekly *Den* (circulation 90,000) should be mentioned. It began to appear in 1991; edited by Alexander Prokhanov, it is the rightwing answer to *Literaturnaya gazeta.* *Russkii vestnik*—even more extreme—is edited by A. Senin. Its circulation is given as 100,000.[2] It is also a weekly and seems not to be tied to any particular group but provides an outlet for several of them. It also features frequent supplements on such subjects as monarchism, the Cossacks, and similar topics.

The most important sources for contemporary Russian nationalism are at present the periodicals sponsored by the various groups. They include the following:

Ekho (published by the Vologda Writers' Association)

Elementy (edited by A. Dugin)

Glashatai (circulation 60,000)

Giperborea (published in Vilnius; an extremist theoretical journal in Russian)

Golos Rossii (Petrograd; circulation 40,000)

Gradu i Miru (Irkutsk)

Istoki (circulation 15,000). Changed its title in 1992 to *Nezavisimaya voennaya gazeta*

Liberal (organ of the Zhirinovsky party)

Miryanin (Moscow)

Monarkhist (St. Petersburg)

Moskovityanin

Moskovskii traktir (superseded *Russkoye voskresenie* in 1992)

Nakanune (Zlatoust; circulation 5,000)

Narodnie novosty ("For God, the nation, and work")

Narodnoye delo (organ of the "Popular Socialist party")

Nasha Rossiya

Nashe (published by *Molodaya gvardiya*)

Nashe vremya (organ of the "National Republican Party of Russia"; circulation 40,000)

Otchizna (St. Petersburg)

Otechestvo (St. Petersburg; circulation 25,000)

---

1. Most of the reprints provide neither place nor year of publication.

2. These circulation figures provided by the journals are in all probability grossly exaggerated. They refer in any case to the print run, not to copies sold. There was for a variety of reasons a palpable decline in all Russian newspapers and periodicals in 1992.

Pamyat (Moscow)

Pamyat (Novosibirsk)

Politika (originally the weekly organ of the Soyuz parliamentary faction, it became *Obozrenie,* the organ of the right center coalition; circulation 25,000)

Polozhenie del (published by one of Pamyat's offshoots)

Puls tushina (named after a Moscow quarter; slogan, "Russia awakes from her slumber"; circulation 10,000)

Rodniye prostory (St. Petersburg)

Rossiskoye vozrozhdenie (organ of Skurlatov's "Russian National Front")

Russkii Puls ("Our position—opposition"; circulation 20,000)

Russkii put (published since January 1992 by the "Union for the Spiritual Renaissance of the Fatherland")

Russkie vedomosti (under the auspices of the "Russian party"; circulation 10,000)

Russkii stag (published by A. Barkashov, a former member of Pamyat, who is also the author of the pamphlet *"Era rossii"*)

Russkoye voskresenie (slogan: "Patriots unite"; circulation 40,000)

Russkoye delo (organ of the "National Democratic party")

Russkoye tovarishchestvo (organ of the "Social Organizations of Russia"; circulation 40,000)

Russkoye znamya (Saratov; circulation 8,000)

Sergiev Posad

Slavyanskie vedomosti (Minsk; circulation 50,000)

Slavyanskii vestnik (published by the Foundation for Slavonic Literature and Culture; circulation 50,000)

Soglasie

Sokol (Zhirinovsky)

Stroitelnaya gazeta (became *Domostroi;* circulation 100,000)

Tretii rim (organ of the "Russian Patriotic Movement")

Veche (published by the Novgorod Writers' Union; circulation 12,000; not to be confused with the Munich-based, right-wing *Veche*)

V bloknot patriota (St. Petersburg)

Velikoros

Volya Rossii (Yekaterinburg)

Voskresenie (pro–Smirnov-Ostashvili, pro-Iraq, pro-astrology)

Vozrozhdenie Rossii

Zemshchina (continues the tradition of a Black Hundred news sheet published by Markov II before 1914)

Some of these periodicals have published only a few issues. Some have disappeared without a trace; others have changed their names. Several are distributed free rather than sold. The figures concerning their circulation should be accepted with caution. Yet in a category apart: *Situatsia,* which is right-wing, sponsored by the Ministry of the Interior, and edited by V. Filatov, the former editor of *Voenno-istoricheskii zhurnal.* Under Filatov's editorship this was a flagship of extreme right-wing propaganda, publishing excerpts from Hitler's *Mein Kampf* and the like. Last, a number of books which do not fit into any of the categories mentioned before but have, nevertheless, a direct bearing on the subject:

I. Bickerman, ed., *Rossiya i Evrei* (reprint: Paris, 1978)
Peter Duncan, "Russian Messianism" (Ph.D. thesis, University of Glasgow, 1990)
Vasili Grossman, *Life and Fate* (London, 1988)
Ivan Il'in, *Osnovy borby za nationalnuyu Rossiyu* (Berlin, 1938)
Alexander Kappeler, ed., *Die Russen: Ihr Nationalbewusstsein in Geschichte und Gegenwart* (Köln, 1990)
Vladimir Krasnov, *Russia beyond Communism* (Boulder, Colo., 1991)
Dmitry Likhachev, *Reflections on Russia* (Boulder, Colo., 1991)
Nicolai Petro, ed., *Christanity in Soviet Society* (Boulder, Colo., 1990)
Michael Scammel, *Solzhenitsyn* (New York, 1984)
I. Shafarevich, *Russofobia* (Munich, 1989)
Alexander Solzhenitsyn et al., *From Under the Rubble* (Boston, 1975)
Alexander Solzhenitsyn, *Rebuilding Russia* (New York, 1991)
Peter B. Struve, *Patriotica* (St. Petersburg, 1911)
Y. Troitsky, *Vozrozhdeniye russkoi idei* (Moscow, 1991)

Among the basic conservative histories of Russia in the twentieth century which have been reprinted in recent years the following ought to be mentioned:

E. E. Alferyev, *Imperator Nikolai II* (Jordansville, N.Y., 1983)
S. S. Oldenburg, *Tsarstvovanie Imperatora Nikolaya II,* most recent edition (U.S.A., 1981).
N. Sokolov, *Ubiistvo tsarskoi semi* (Buenos Aires, 1978).

Arkhiv russkoi revoliutsii, edited by E. Gessen, is an invaluable multivolume work published in Berlin in the 1920s; it was reissued in Moscow in 1991–1992. The same is true with regard to the memoirs of the leading figures of the civil war (such as General Denikin) and also the studies of the early years of the terror (such as Melgunov).

In addition to the literature on the Cossack revival the following regional publications should be mentioned:

Donskoye slovo (Rostov)
Kazachya volya (Cherkesk)[3]
Kazak (Konstantinovsk)

3. A publication with the same title has appeared in Omsk.

Donskoi Kazak
Ussuriskii kazachi vestnik
Golos dona (Rostov)
Kazachi vedomosti (Moscow)
Kazachi vestnik
Jaitskaya volya
Donskiya voiskoviya vedomosti
Kavkazkii krai
Orenburgskii kazachi vestnik

The intellectual circles of the Russian New Right, small in number but vociferous and prolific, have derived their ideas from certain West European thinkers specializing in pan-Europeanism and the revolt against modernism. They have discovered the writings of Julius Evola, above all *La rivolta contro il mondo moderno,* 5th ed. (Rome, 1976).

For a good survey of Evola's philosophy of history, see T. Sheehan "Myth and Violence: The Fascism of Julius Evola and Alain de Benoist," *Social Research,* 1 (1981).

De Benoist's best-known work is *Vue de Droite* (Paris, 1977), for which he received the literature prize of the Academie Française. However, the doctrine of the European far right, envisaging something akin to Eurofascism, collides with the anti-Westernism of most on the Russian extreme right. It is more than doubtful that a lasting ideological synthesis is possible.

INDEX

ABOUT THE AUTHOR

Walter Laqueur is a leading authority on Russia and fascism. His *Russia and Germany,* first published in 1963, is a pioneering study of the relationship between the Russian extreme right and early Nazism and a crucial examination of The Protocols of the Elders of Zion. He was director of the London Institute of Contemporary History and Wiener Library from 1964 to 1992, and is now chairman of the international research council of the Center for Strategic and International Studies in Washington, D.C. He is editor of the *Journal of Contemporary History;* his works have appeared in all major languages.